TURKEY AND THE EU

Dedicated to the memory of my father, Ömer Arikan

Turkey and the EU

An awkward candidate for EU membership?

HARUN ARIKAN
Kahramanmaraş Sütçü Imam University

ASHGATE

Published by
Ashgate Publishing Limited
Gower House
Croft Road
Aldershot
Hants GU11 3HR
England

Ashgate Publishing Company
Suite 420
101 Cherry Street
Burlington, VT 05401-4405
USA

Ashgate website: http://www.ashgate.com

British Library Cataloguing in Publication Data
Arikan, Harun
    Turkey and the EU : an awkward candidate for EU membership?
    1. European Union - Turkey 2. Turkey - Foreign relations -
    European Union countries 3. European Union countries -
    Foreign relations - Turkey 4. Turkey - Foreign relations -
    1980 -
    I. Title
    327.5'6104

Library of Congress Cataloging-in-Publication Data
Arikan, Harun, 1969-
    Turkey and the EU : an awkward candidate for EU membership? / Harun Arikan.
        p. cm.
    Includes bibliographical references and index.
    ISBN 0-7546-3433-7
    1. European Union--Turkey. 2. Turkey--Foreign economic relations--European Union countries. 3. European Union countries--Foreign economic relations--Turkey. 4. European Union countries--Economic policy. I. Title.

HC240.25.T8 A74 2003
341.242'2'09561--dc21   2002190871

ISBN 0 7546 3433 7

Printed in Great Britain by, Antony Rowe Ltd, Chippenham, Wiltshire

Contents

List of Tables

Preface

This book presents an analysis of the development of the EU's policy towards Turkey and compares the EU's approach to the issues in the EU-Turkey relationship with that adopted in relation to the other applicant countries. Given that there is a standard framework within which EU-Turkey relations and, specifically, the issues identified as obstacles to Turkey's prospects for accession, have been addressed in the existing literature, the primary objective of this study is to contribute to this existing literature on EU-Turkey relations by using a different approach to analyze EU-Turkey relations in general and the EU's enlargement in particular. It seeks to construct a more comprehensive framework by examining the Turkish case not merely on an individual costs/benefits basis in isolation from the other factors but on the basis of a comparison with other applicant countries, in order to assess whether Turkey has been treated differently.

This book examines the main policy issues between the EU and Turkey and analyzes the ways in which the parties have approached these issues. Human rights and Greco-Turkish disputes and the security factor were chosen as specific policy issues for detailed analysis in EU-Turkish relationship. The reasons for choosing the first two were: firstly, the EU has cited them as reasons why Turkey is different and problematic and by implication a more difficult case than other applicants; and secondly, given that most applicant countries have similar problems (i.e. an inadequate human rights system, lack of protection for minorities and border issues between them and other applicant countries), these two issues are useful for a comparison with the EU's approach to similar policy issues in the other applicant countries. The security factor also features in both EU-Turkey and EU-CEECs relationships and provides another appropriate case study by allowing the EU's policy towards the CEECs in this area to be contrasted with its policy of 'containment' towards Turkey. This book proposes that the EU has developed an alternative approach towards Turkey, which can best be described as a containment strategy, designed to delay indefinitely the prospect of membership, while keeping Turkey within the economic, security and political sphere of influence of the EU. This is because the EU has always considered Turkey to be an awkward candidate for EU membership. However, the book argues that the EU's policy instruments and its containment strategy for Turkey have not been compatible with its overall enlargement objectives and with the way in which the EU's enlargement policy has been operationalized for other applicant states. Therefore, it argues the extent to which the EU's 'containment' policy towards Turkey has been less effective in influencing the developments of Turkey's political and economic system than it might have been and, indeed, has been in other applicant countries in a similar situation.

Acknowledgments

This book is based on a revised version of the thesis submitted for the degree of Doctor of Philosophy (Ph.D.) at the university of Birmingham (UK). In developing the arguments of the book I have received valuable advice and constructive criticism from Professor John Redmond. Therefore, I would like to express my particular sincere thanks to him. My thanks also go to Professor Andy Mullineux, Dr Daniel Wincott and Dr Paul Furlong from whose academic support and encouragement I have benefited.

There are many officials to whom I owe appreciation for providing me with an opportunity to conduct interviews in Brussels and Ankara. They include, Richard Balfe (a member of the European Parliament), Nihat Akyol (the Turkish Ambassador to the EU), Korkmaz Haktanir (the Turkish Ambassador to the UK and the former Under-Secretary of the Foreign Ministry), Haluk Illicak (senior diplomat at the Foreign Ministry of Turkey) and Van Der Meer (Deputy Head of the Turkish Unit in the European Commission).

I am also very grateful to all my family members for their full support and encouragement, in particular I owe gratitude to Ömer, Havva, Yusuf, Bengul, Ismet, Gönül, Ismail Emine and Aydin Arikan, who helped me to overcome all challenges and provided me with a source of inspiration. I would also like to acknowledge many friends. I appreciated their friendship and enjoyed their company during my study in the United Kingdom and Turkey.

Others have made more technical and administrative, but no less valuable, contributions. Therefore, I extend my thanks to Elizabeth Bradley, the Graduate Secretary of the Political Sciences and International Relations of Birmingham University, and to the staff of libraries at the European Commission, Birmingham University, the London School of Economics, Manchester University and Cambridge University from where I obtained the most important sources of information. Last but not least, I would like to thank the Turkish Government for granting me a scholarship, without their financial support this study could not have been completed.

List of Abbreviations

AA	Association Agreement
AC	Association Council
ANAP	Anavatan Partisi (Motherland Party)
AP	Additional Protocol
CAP	Common Agricultural Policy
CFSP	Common Foreign and Security Policy
CHP	Cumhuriyetci Halk Partisi (Republican People's Party)
CoE	Council of Europe
COREPER	Committee of Permanent Representatives
CSDP	Common Security and Defence Policy
CU	Customs Union
DEP	Democratic Party (Demokrasi Partisi)
DGM	Devlet Guvenlik Mahkemesi (State Security Courts)
DPT	Devlet Planlama Teskilati (State Planning Organization)
DSP	Demokratik Sol Parti (Democratic Left Party)
DYP	Dogru Yol Partisi (True Path Party)
EBRD	European Bank for Reconstruction and Development
EC	European Community
ECHR	European Court of Human Rights
ECU	European Currency Unit
EEA	European Economic Area
EFTA	European Free Trade Agreement
EMU	European Monetary Union
EP	European Parliament
ESC	European Social Charter
EU	European Union
FP	Fazilet Partisi (Virtue Party)
HADEP	Halkin Demokrasi Partisi (People's Democracy Party)
ICCPR	International Covenant on Civil and Political Rights
ICESCR	International Covenant on Economic, Social and Cultural Rights
IHD	Insan Haklari Dernegi (Human Rights Association)
JHA	Justice and Home Affairs
JPC	Joint Parliamentary Committee
MEP	Member of European Parliament
MGK	National Security Council, Milli Guvenlik Kurulu
MHP	Milliyetci Hareket Partisi (Nationalist Movement Party)
NATO	North Atlantic Treaty Organization
NGO	Non-Governmental Organization
OHAL	Olaganustu Hal (Emergency Rule Law)
OSCE	Organization for Security and Cooperation in Europe
PHARE	Poland and Hungary: Aid for Restructuring of Economies

RTUK	Radyo ve Televizyon Ust Kurulu (Supreme Board of Radio and Television Law)
SEA	Single European Act
TBMM	Turkiye Büyük Millet Meclisi (Turkish Grand National Assembly)
TCK	Turk Ceza Kanunu (Turkish Penal Code)
TEU	Treaty on European Union
TMK	Terörle Mücadele Kanunu (The act against Terrorism)
UN	United Nations
USA	United States of America
USIAD	Türk Sanayicileri ve İşadamları Dernegi (Turkish Industrialist and Businessmen's Association)
WEU	Western European Union

Chapter 1

Introduction: An Alternative Approach to Traditional Perspectives of EU-Turkish Relations

From the very beginnings of the creation of the European Union,[1] Turkey has shown a keen interest in the integration process in Europe and, indeed, has considered becoming a member of the EU to be a logical consequence of its modernization and Westernization policies. Consequently, it came as no surprise when Turkey applied for associate membership in 1959 and went on to sign the Ankara Agreement with the EU in 1963, an agreement which not only recognized Turkey's eligibility to participate in European integration but explicitly envisaged Turkey's eventual full membership of the EU.

EU-Turkey relations have, however, experienced serious difficulties resulting from the essential incompatibility of both parties' policies with the declared objectives of their Association Agreement. In particular, it seems unlikely that the ultimate objective of the Association Agreement – Turkish accession to the EU – will be achieved in the foreseeable future. On the one hand, this is because the EU has always considered Turkey to be an awkward candidate for EU membership: Turkey is different, problematic and thus, by implication, a more difficult case than any of the other applicants. The EU's skepticism towards the prospect of Turkish membership can be seen in its policies, which have basically sought to maintain and strengthen the existing Association Agreement. However, this has been inadequate to prepare Turkey for EU membership. In fact, the EU has developed an alternative approach towards Turkey, which can best be described as a containment strategy, designed to delay indefinitely the prospect of membership while keeping Turkey within the economic, security and political sphere of influence of the EU.

On the other hand, Turkey's failure to undertake the necessary policy reforms to meet requirements for EU membership has, to some extent, enabled the EU to legitimize its hard policy stance towards Turkey's membership. The lack of progress in improving its human rights regime, its rigid and uncompromising policy stance towards Greece over the bilateral issues and its inadequacy in aligning its economic system with the EU have not only increased the EU's concern about the maturity of Turkey as a candidate state, but also have undermined Turkey's own efforts to maintain and strengthen its own motivation and commitment to achieving EU membership.

The objective of this book is to analyze the development of the EU's policy towards Turkey against the backdrop of this long-standing and problematic relationship and with particular reference to the next enlargement of the EU. The following chapters examine the main policy issues between the EU and Turkey and analyze the ways in which the parties have approached these issues. In order to avoid mere assertion, the study analyzes the EU's policy towards Turkey from a comparative perspective and compares the EU's approach to the issues in the EU-Turkey relationship with that adopted with regard to the other applicant countries. From this perspective, the book investigates the extent to which the EU's policy instruments and its containment strategy for Turkey have been compatible with its overall enlargement objectives and with how the EU's enlargement policy has been operationalized for other applicant states.

The objectives of the EU's enlargement policy are to support the democratization process and to facilitate economic and institutional reforms in applicant countries, which are all necessary for the stability of Europe. Therefore, the EU has guided, catalyzed, and even directed the process of political, economic, legal and social reform in the applicant countries in Central and Eastern Europe (the CEECs) by offering them a clear prospect of membership and an accession strategy. Indeed, by offering economic and political benefits through pre-accession strategies and by stipulating membership requirements, the EU has greatly influenced the domestic policy choices in these applicant states; this has allowed it to affect even permanent institution building, and to encourage specific political and legal reforms in these countries. However, the EU has been reluctant to apply the same enlargement policy instruments and accession commitment to Turkey. Although Turkey's failure to undertake the necessary policy reforms to meet requirements for EU membership has provided some grounds for the latter's hesitation towards Turkey's membership, it cannot provide sufficient reasons why Turkey has been treated differently from the other applicant countries as they have similar problems.

Therefore, this study argues that Turkey has been treated differently, compared to other applicant countries for EU membership. Furthermore, the EU's containment policy towards Turkey has lacked the clarity and certainty that would have best encouraged and facilitated Turkey's efforts to adjust its policies to make them compatible with EU membership. As a result, the EU's role in hastening Turkey's attempts to align her political, economic and social system with EU norms has been less effective than it might have been and, indeed, has been in other applicant countries in a similar situation.

Critical Review of the Existing Literature on EU-Turkey Relations

The existing literature on EU-Turkey relations suggests that there are problems for both Western and Turkish studies in explaining the problematic nature of EU-Turkey relations. In other words, there is a standard framework within which EU-Turkey relations and especially the Turkish case for accession to the EU has been addressed by both Turkish and Western studies. The literature on the subject is excessively rigid, antiquated and opinionated, thereby reflecting only the stylized version of both Turkey and the EU's official approaches to issues between Turkey and the EU. That is, the Turkish literature and Western literature on EU-Turkey relations present the Turkish 'standard view' and the EU's 'standard view' respectively. The Western studies, in which Turkish sources were rarely used, have relied heavily on the official documents of the EU and, as a result, they cannot avoid reflecting the official position of the EU. This has clearly been the case with Turkey's accession to the EU: in particular, they suggest that economic, political and cultural issues work against Turkey, though security issues work in her favour. Therefore, on balance, Turkey cannot join the EU, but the EU still needs to keep Turkey onside within a containment policy.

As regards standard Turkish views, they have tended to reflect the Turkish government's position with regard to policy issues in EU-Turkey relations, while differing in the details. They basically criticize the EU on the grounds that the EU's policy towards Turkey has been not compatible with the declared ultimate objectives of the EU-Turkey Association Agreement. However, in their analysis, a critical approach to Turkey's slow progress in aligning its political and economic system with EU norms can rarely be seen.

Another weakness of the existing literature on EU-Turkey relations is that both Turkish and Western analyses seem to have been descriptive in character, identifying the policy issues in turn without providing a detailed analysis of the nature of the problems. To be precise, they have provided a general overview of EU-Turkey relations, and have failed to provide a convincing argument based on evidence as to why the EU has been reluctant to offer the prospect of accession to Turkey. Although both Turkish and Western analyses have offered economic, political security and the cultural framework to explain the EU's reluctant policy approach towards Turkey's membership, they seem to have lacked any analytical basis for their arguments.

Having underlined the shortcomings of the existing literature, this book, as an alternative approach, seeks to analyze EU-Turkey relations within a broader framework. This is done in two stages:

- First, a norm for the EU's enlargement policy is developed which looks at motives and criteria for accession, thus providing an analytical framework for examining EU-Turkey relations.
- Second a comparison is made of the EU's policy towards Turkey with that towards the other applicant countries by examining the EU's approaches to similar policy issues which arise in the context of enlargement. Comparing the EU's policy approaches in these different cases provides evidence as to whether or not Turkish application to join the EU has been treated differently.

Methodology

Given that there is a standard framework within which EU-Turkey relations and, specifically, the issues identified as obstacles to Turkey's prospects for accession, have been addressed in the existing literature, the primary objective of this book is to contribute to this existing literature on EU-Turkey relations by using a different approach to analyze EU-Turkey relations in general and EU enlargement in particular. It seeks to construct a more comprehensive framework by examining the Turkish case not merely on an individual costs/benefits basis in isolation from the other factors but the basis of a comparison with other applicant countries, in order to assess whether Turkey has been treated differently. As a first step in this procedure, the study identifies the EU's motivation and interests in continuing to enlarge, as well as its policy instruments in order to 'characterize' the EU's enlargement policy process. This provides an analytical framework in which to set the EU's approach to the policy issues it has identified in the Turkish case and to compare this with its approach to similar issues in other applicant countries. It also provides a more appropriate setting in which to assess not only whether the EU's policy towards Turkey has been compatible with its enlargement objectives in general, but also whether it has allowed the EU to exert influence on the development of Turkey's internal policy effectively, and to promote and accelerate Greco-Turkish rapprochement.

It is perhaps helpful to begin by clarifying difference between the concept of inclusion in 'the EU's enlargement policy process' and the concept of inclusion in 'the accession process of negotiations'. This clarification of difference between the two processes appears to be important for the purpose of this study, as the scope of this book is limited to analyzing EU-Turkish relations in EU's enlargement policy process and thus, an analysis as regards the prospect of Turkey's inclusion in the accession negotiation process is beyond the objective of this study. The inclusion in the enlargement process refers to a strategy which might lead to the stage of the accession negotiations process through meeting the criteria for accession. More specifically, the EU's enlargement policy process is a strategy designed to prepare the applicants for a later accession negotiations process through an appropriate strategy with accession credibility, providing a considerable degree of influence and financial and institutional support during the transformation process in the applicant countries. However, an inclusion in the enlargement policy process does not necessarily mean that the included applicant will automatically proceed to the stage of the accession negotiation process. The inclusion of candidate countries in the accession negotiation process depends upon a number of variables, including the process of the applicant towards meeting the accession criteria and capacity of the EU to enlarge.

To test the arguments of the study further, the security factor, human rights and Greco-Turkish disputes were chosen as specific policy issues in the EU-Turkish relationship for detailed analysis. The reasons for choosing the last two of these were: firstly, the EU has cited them as reasons why Turkey is different and problematic and by implication a more difficult case than other applicants; and secondly, given that most applicant countries have similar problems (i.e., an inadequate human rights system, lack of protection for minorities and border issues between them and other applicant countries), these two issues are useful for a comparison with the EU's approach to similar policy issues in the other applicant countries. The security factor also features in both EU-Turkey and EU-the CEECs relations and provides another appropriate case study by allowing the EU's policy towards the CEECs in this area to be contrasted with its policy of 'containment' towards Turkey.

In order to support the arguments with the evidence and avoid simply making assertions, primary source material was used in this study as much as possible. Specifically, the official documents of the EU, namely, the Commission's reports, a number of EP resolutions and declarations of the Council of Ministers, as well as official documents and official statements issued by a number of political actors in Turkey were used to support the arguments of the book. The interpretations of the primary (and the supporting secondary) source materials were backed up by a series of interviews conducted with officials of the EU and of Turkey.[2]

The Organization of the Book

The central focus of the book is the development of the EU's policy towards Turkey, with particular reference to enlargement. It examines the major policy issues and differences between the EU and Turkey and analyzes how both sides have approached these issues. Thus, chapter 2 of the book seeks to conceptualize the EU's enlargement policy, which involves considering the EU's motivation, interests and subsequent choice of policy instruments for dealing with the complexity of the next enlargement in order to develop a general model of how the EU approaches enlargement. This conceptualization is useful because it provides:

- A general framework for looking at the enlargement.
- A framework for looking at the specific example of Turkey.
- A framework for comparison between the EU's policy *vis-à-vis* Turkey and its policy towards other applicant countries.

Chapter 3 assesses the objectives and instruments of the EU-Turkey Association and investigates the reasons why the Association Agreement of Ankara has not achieved its political and economic objectives. It also makes reference to the EU's new association policy towards the CEECs and compares the instruments of the Europe Agreements and Ankara Agreement in the context of enlargement policy. On the basis of this, chapter 3 explores two main questions: whether the instruments of the EU-Turkey Association have been inadequate to serve as a useful preparatory phase for Turkey's accession to the EU and whether the EU's association policy towards Turkey has been different from its association policy towards the CEECs?

Chapter 4 examines economic instruments of the EU's policy for Turkey in a comparative perspective with the CEECs. It considers whether the instruments of EU's pre-accession instruments, including, the customs union, European Strategy for Turkey and Accession Partnership Document, have been appropriate for Turkey to prepare her for accession. Considering that the customs union constituted the central part of the EU's containment policy for Turkey, this chapter evaluates both the EU's and Turkey's motivations and interests in completing the customs union and tries to answer the question whether the customs union is best considered as part of Turkey's new strategy for membership in the long term, or whether it is part of the EU's differentiation policy *vis-à-vis* Turkey in the context of enlargement (or possibly both)? The contents and characteristics of the EU's policy instruments are closely examined, and their contribution to the readiness of Turkey to participate in EU policies is compared to the EU's policy towards the CEECs to prepare them for coping with the EU's single market and other aspects of EU membership. To summarize, the basic purpose of this chapter is to try and assess whether the EU's overall policy stance and use of policy instruments towards Turkey (since she declared her wish to became a full member of the EU) has been comprehensive enough to support the process of Turkish integration into the Union.

Chapters 5 and 6 are devoted to analyzing two of the main policy issues between Turkey and the EU in the enlargement context, namely Turkey's human rights regime and the Greco-Turkish disputes. As already indicated, these two issues were chosen because the EU has identified them as reasons for excluding Turkey from the enlargement process and treating it differently from the other applicant countries. Thus, chapter 5 is primarily concerned with the effects of Turkey's inadequate human rights and political systems on its relations with the EU and the evaluation of the EU's human rights policy *vis-à-vis* Turkey. In this respect, it firstly assesses the EU's human rights policy towards Turkey before Turkey's application for EU membership, and then focuses on the EU's human rights policy since 1987 when Turkey officially declared its wish to be a member of the EU. The division of the EU's policy into these two sub-periods is intended to reveal the evidence to support the argument that the EU's human rights policy towards Turkey has not been consistent and that it has, to a large extent, been determined by the EU's policy preference of maintaining closer relations with Turkey but delaying Turkey's membership for the foreseeable future. Finally, chapter 5 analyzes the EU's human rights policy towards Turkey in the light of the EU's enlargement policy, comparing the EU's policy towards the CEECs and Turkey with regard to the perceived effect of the enlargement process on the further democratization processes in the applicant countries. Once again, this comparative analysis is intended to shed light on the question whether Turkey has been treated in a different way to the other applicant countries.

Chapter 6 presents an analysis of the way in which Greco-Turkish disputes have become a source of conflict between Turkey and the EU. It analyzes the effects of the Greek factor in EU-Turkey relations and addresses the question as to what extent Greek objections to Turkish membership have provided a legitimate ground for the EU to delay the membership prospects of Turkey for the foreseeable future. It also evaluates how far the EU's policy objective of delaying the membership prospects of Turkey by using the Greek factor has been compatible with the security objective of the EU's enlargement policy.

Following the examination of policy issues between Turkey and the EU and their effects on Turkey's membership bid, chapter 7 analyzes the main factors behind the EU's efforts to strengthen EU-Turkey relations: is this really an EU containment strategy for Turkey, designed to keep Turkey within the economic and political sphere of influence of the EU – a means of strengthening the existing association framework without implying any commitment to accession in the foreseeable future? With this in mind, chapter 7 evaluates Turkey's 'security assets' and their impact on EU-Turkey relations within the framework of the new European security structure. The purpose of this chapter is to address the way in which the EU has re-evaluated Turkey's role in the context of the new European security arena and defence structure, and how this has affected the EU's strategy towards the challenge of Turkey's membership. This question will be analyzed in the light of security aspects of the EU's enlargement policy in general in order to compare the EU's policy towards the CEECs and towards Turkey; this comparative analysis should provide some evidence as to whether or not Turkey has been treated in a different way from others.

Finally, the conclusion, chapter 8, summarizes the findings of the study and assesses the EU's overall policy towards Turkey. In particular, it focuses on the two main questions addressed by the book: whether the EU's policy *vis-à-vis* Turkey has been compatible with its wider enlargement strategy and whether Turkey has been treated differently from the other applicant countries. In addition, it also summarizes the study's findings with regard to two subsidiary (but nevertheless important) questions: to what extent the EU's 'containment' policy towards Turkey has been effective in influencing the development of Turkey's internal policy and in hastening the settlement of the various disagreements between Greece and Turkey.

Notes

1   In line with common academic usage, the term 'European Union' and the abbreviation 'EU' is used throughout the book, also referring to the term 'European Economic Community' (EEC) and the term 'European Community' (EC).

2   Richard Balfe (a member of the European Parliament and of the EU-Turkey Joint Parliamentary Committee); Nihat Akyol (The Turkish Ambassador to the EU); Korkmaz Haktanır (the Turkish Ambassador to the UK and the former Under-Secretary of the Foreign Ministry during the period 1997–1999); Haluk Ilıcak (senior diplomat at the Foreign Ministry of Turkey, responsible for EU Affairs); Van Der Meer (Deputy Head of the Turkish Unit in the European Commission).

Chapter 2

Conceptualizing the EU's Enlargement Policy: Motivations, Conditions and Instruments for the EU's Enlargement Policy

Introduction

For the purpose of this study, clarifying the difference between the term of inclusion in 'the EU's enlargement policy process' and the term of inclusion in 'the process of accession negotiations' is important. The inclusion in the enlargement process refers to a strategy which might lead to the stage of the accession negotiations process through meeting the criteria for accession. The term of the EU's enlargement policy process refers to a strategy, designed to prepare the applicants for a later accession negotiations process through an appropriate strategy with accession credibility, providing a considerable degree of influence and financial and institutional support during the transformation process in the applicant countries. However, inclusion in the enlargement policy process does not necessarily mean that the included applicant will automatically proceed to the stage of the accession negotiation process. The inclusion of candidate countries in the accession negotiation process depends upon a number of variables, including the process of the applicant towards meeting the accession criteria and capacity of the EU to enlarge. This implies that an inclusion in the enlargement process does not involve the same considerable costs/ risks for the EU in respect of the included candidate as the accession process does.

The Turkish case provides a particularly unusual case in the sense it has not been fully included yet in the enlargement process of the EU, and indeed appears to have been treated differently. The EU has pursued a strategy of applying a containment policy to Turkey, even though it revised its previous containment policy after the Helsinki Summit in 1999. However, this revised policy is still rather vague. Thus, the question remains to be addressed as to why the EU has chosen to apply a different policy for Turkey. From this perspective, the size of Turkey appears to be one of the reasons that the EU might have chosen to treat Turkey differently because of its potentially adverse impact on the cost and risk to the EU of Turkish membership. Although size matters, it is not reason enough to explain why Turkey has been treated differently, since the inclusion in the enlargement policy process does not necessarily imply the inclusion of Turkey in the process of accession negotiation. In fact, Turkey, like other applicants, must fulfil various criteria for accession before it can embark upon the stage of negotiation process whose costs and risks the EU like to see as low as possible. That is, costs and risks of Turkish accession to the EU depend heavily on Turkey's fulfilment of the accession criteria. Besides, the concerns for the EU of Turkey's membership will depend on a number of factors, i.e. the reform of EU policies and the timing of Turkey's accession to the EU, which will certainly be later (in the long run).

Thus, this study takes a different approach to analyzing EU-Turkey relations; not on a costs/benefits basis in isolation from the other factors, but on the basis of a comparison with other applicant countries. This approach appears to be more appropriate than the standard analysis of the costs/benefits basis because, first, Turkey has not even been included in the real enlargement policy, which makes the costs/risks factors of secondary importance. Second, the EU has not openly defended its containment policy towards Turkey in the enlargement process on the grounds of Turkey's size and its relevance to the costs and risks. In fact, the EU's policy towards Turkey has been mainly driven by political conditionality – human rights and disputes with Greece – rather than any possible costs/risks concerns for itself.

Therefore, as an alternative approach for the purpose of this study, we need to establish what are the norms for the enlargement of the EU, as an analytical instrument not only in order to assess whether Turkey has been treated differently, but also to establish whether the EU's policy towards Turkey has been compatible with these norms. In fact, setting up norms for the EU's enlargement policy provides us with:

- A general framework for looking at enlargement.
- A framework for looking at the specific example of the Turkish case.
- A framework for comparing the EU's approaches towards Turkey with those towards other applicant countries.

This chapter, firstly, analyzes the costs/risks factors in the next enlargement of the EU with a reference to Turkey and the selected applicants in the Central/Eastern Europe. Then, it moves on to identify the main characteristics of the EU's enlargement norms. In this context, it considers the EU's motivation and interests in setting up its enlargement policy, as well as the factors behind the rush to apply for EU membership. Then, it examines the way in which the EU has dealt with the enlargement issue and explores the contents and characteristics of the EU's enlargement instruments by looking at:

- The requirements for EU membership and the concept of the EU's enlargement capacity.
- The instruments of the EU's pre-accession strategy for applicant countries.

Basically, this chapter seeks to analyze the following questions: to what extent, and in what ways, have the instruments of the EU's accession strategy helped the applicant countries to meet the conditions for EU membership? And to what extent has the EU effectively reduced the perceived risks of policy reversals in the applicant countries by locking them into the pre-accession strategy? Finally, the chapter draws some preliminary conclusions and observations about the EU's enlargement policy and summarizes the main characteristics of the EU's enlargement norms.

Costs/Risks Concerns in the Next Enlargement of the EU: Turkey and Selected Applicants in Central-Eastern Europe

It is perhaps helpful to begin by looking briefly at the costs/risks concerns associated with the next enlargement of the EU, and specifically with the costs/risks for the EU of Turkey's membership, compared to that of the selected CEECs. The costs/risks concerns of the next enlargement involve the financial implications of the admitted new members on the EU common policies and implications of an enlarged Union for the deepening process of the EU.

Potential Costs

As the previous enlargements of the EU suggest, the EU budget had offered the poorer acceding members a considerable amount to help them adopt the existing common policies of the EU and to create social cohesion among the member states through the Structural and Cohesion Funds and the Common Agricultural Policy (the CAP). Considering the applicant countries' levels of economic development and their relatively large agricultural sectors with a low level of GDP per capita, the estimated financial costs associated with the next enlargement of the EU appear to be very high under the existing structure of the EU, although the costs of enlargement cannot be estimated accurately, as it will depend on many factors, including which countries accede, the stage of development which they have reached upon accession, the length of any transitional periods accorded to the applicant countries and more importantly the extent and the nature of reforms in EU policies.[1] The financial implication of the enlargement concerns the two main components of the EU budget: namely the Structural and Cohesion Funds and the CAP, which together account for around 80 per cent of total EU budget expenditure (Croft and Redmond, 1999, p. 9).

The Structural and Cohesion Funds were designed to help poorer member states and regions to create social cohesion between member states. In this respect, the applicant countries' GDP per capita are much lower than the EU average; hence they would qualify for assistance from a number of EU Structural Funds, including the European Regional Development Fund and the European Social Fund. Therefore, the relatively low income in the applicant countries, combined with the number of poorer regions would considerably deplete the EU's budget.

As regards the new members' participation in the CAP, all the applicant countries have a disproportionately large agricultural sector in which a large number of its workers are employed. Consequently, the cost to the EU of their participation in the Common Agricultural Policy of the EU would be very high. From this perspective, Turkey's accession to the EU appears to be an issue. Given that Turkey's level of economic development, the size of the country's agricultural sector, average size of level of income, the level of Turkey's unemployment and the poverty of some regions in the country would be important criteria for determining the budgetary cost of Turkey's accession to the EU. Thus, Turkish accession to the EU would create a tremendous burden on the EU's Structural Funds and the budgetary resources of the CAP. It appears that the cost of Turkey's participation in the CAP would be higher than that of any country in the CEE because it is so large (see Table 2.1).

Table 2.1   A comparison of the size of Turkey with applicants of CEE

Year (1999)	Total Area (km)	Population	Unemployment (as %)
Turkey	775 381	63 451 980	6.4
Bulgaria	111 300	8 230 700	16.0
Czech Rep.	79 800	10 290 780	9.9
Hungary	93 270	10 920 087	7.8
Poland	313 879	3 866 7980	10.7
Romania	238 689	2 589 7780	6.3

Source: Eurostat, 'Statistics in Focus: Key data on Candidate countries', Eurostat Press Office, Luxembourg, November 2000.

However, most of the CEE countries would pose similar challenges to the Common Agricultural Policy of the Union, because the agriculture sector plays an important role in their economies with similar structural problems. As shown in (Table 2.2), the agricultural sector in Turkey, Poland, Romania and Bulgaria is characterized by the high percentage of the labour force. Although Turkey would be the most problematic case for being integrated in the CAP of all the applicants, it does not provide sufficient grounds for the EU's different treatment of Turkey from the other applicants, because the aim of the pre-accession strategy is to prepare the applicant countries by taking into account the specific needs of each country and by creating incentives in policy reforms in the applicant countries, including the CAP. In addition, applicants need the length of any transitional periods to be adjusted according to their readiness as regards policy issues. By implication, Turkey's agricultural sector would be prepared for EU membership in the long run, with the appropriate support from the EU through a pre-accession strategy.

Table 2.2   The agricultural sector in Turkey and selected applicants of CEE

Year (1999)	The share of agriculture in GDP (as %)	The share of agriculture in the labour force (as%)
Turkey	14.3	41
Poland	4.8	18
Romania	16.1	41.7
Bulgaria	17.3	29.5

Source: Eurostat, 'Statistics in Focus: Key data on Candidate countries', Eurostat Press Office, Luxembourg, November 2000.

As far as financial assistance from the Structural Funds of the EU is concerned, the most important aspect of these funds is their close link with per capita income. Regarding Turkey, it has a GDP per capita of less than 75 per cent of the community average, which means that virtually the whole of Turkey would qualify for assistance from the European Regional Development Fund. Furthermore, Turkey's relatively high levels of unemployment and low levels of worker skills would require financial assistance from the European Social Fund. In addition, the skill level Turkish agricultural sector would also generate large claims on the guidance fund. All things considered, Turkey would be a major beneficiary of various EU funds. However, as indicated in the analysis below, it is difficult to assess the cost of Turkey's accession to the EU, because of what the reformed structure of the CAP and Structural Funds will be at the time of Turkish accession.

Similar characteristics can be seen in the applicants of Central and Eastern European Countries (the CEECs): there are only two regions (the Czech region of Praha and the Slovak region of Bratislavsky) in 52 regions of the CEECs which are above the 75 per cent of the EU average (Eurostat, 2000). This implies that almost all the regions in the CEECs would qualify for financial assistance from the EU. The recent analysis of Eurostat suggests that in terms of the development of per-capita GDP in relation to the EU average over the years between 1995–1998 the economic growth within the CEECs at the regional level is lagging behind the EU average (see Table 2.3).

Table 2.3   GDP per head in Turkey and selected applicants of CEE

1999	GDP per capita in EU (as %)	GDP per head in PPC in ECU
EU 15	100	20 200
Turkey	29	5 900
Bulgaria	22	5 000
Romania	27	5 700
Poland	37	7 800
Hungary	50	10 700
Czech Republic	59	12 500

Source: Eurostat, 'Statistics in Focus: the GDP of the Candidate Countries' (Theme 2–40/ 2000), Eurostat Press Office, Luxembourg, November 2000.

As the above analysis suggests, it is inevitable that the CAP and Structural and Cohesion Funds need to be re-structured before the EU is enlarged. This has already been indicated in Agenda 2000 of the Commission, which states that extension of the CAP and the Structural and Cohesion Funds in their present form to the acceding states would create difficulties. Therefore, the cost of extending CAP to the acceding states will depend on two main factors: the character of the reforms and what form of the CAP is extended to the new members (Croft and Redmond, 1999).

In this regard, the EU seems to have pursued a two-track policy. On the one hand, it has pursued a policy of the continuation of the 1992 reforms of the CAP through further shifts from price support to direct payments.[2] On the other hand, the EU would make a long transition arrangement for new members' full participation in the CAP, depending on the situation of each applicant. It is likely that a long-term transition period would be endorsed by the EU member states during the accession negotiations with the applicant countries. Nevertheless, lengthy transition phases would not be attractive for the acceding states in the next enlargement; they would create long term discrimination between existing and new member states, thus making acceding countries seem like second class members of the EU (Croft and Redmond, 1999, p. 74).

As for the Structural and Cohesion Funds, the Commission proposed some reforms in these funds with a focus on a smaller proportion of the EU's population and on a smaller number of objectives (European Commission, 1997b). This was accepted by the EU Council at the Berlin Summit of 1999. The Structural and Cohesion Funds has now aimed to move from a per-capita comparison between the countries towards introducing an overall ceiling of 4 per cent of GNP on the structural funds to be received, which would reduce the cost of extending the Structural Funds to the acceding states. Nevertheless, considering that the greatest need of the new member states for funding is in the early years, the proposed reforms of the Commission has been less concerned to promote convergence and catch-up in levels of economic development in the enlarged Union (Grabbe and Hughes, 1998, p. 103). In other words, reforming the Structural Funds of the EU would make it difficult for the new members to catch up with the old ones, thereby undermining the homogeneity of the EU.

As the above analysis suggests, economic features of the CEEC and Turkey and their contrast with those of the EU constitute the economic aspect of the uniqueness of this new enlargement policy of the EU (see Table 2.4). It is more than simply another accession process, involving not only reforms of the EU institutions and its policies so that EU budget constraints are not breached, but more generally involves an adaptive enlargement policy to prepare the applicants for membership.

Table 2.4   GDP growth rates in Turkey and selected applicants of CEE

Countries	1996 (as %)	1997	1998	1999
EU-15	1.6	2.5	2.8	2.5
Turkey	7.0	7.5	3.1	-4.7
Bulgaria	-10.1	-7.0	3.5	2.4
Czech Rep.	4.8	-1.0	-2.2	-0.8
Hungary	1.3	4.6	4.9	4.5
Poland	6.0	6.8	4.8	4.0
Romania	3.9	-6.1	-5.4	-3.2

Source: Eurostat, 'Statistics in Focus: Key data on Candidate Countries', Eurostat Press Office, Luxembourg, November 2000.

Potential Risks

Apart from the financial implications, the next enlargement would raise a number of issues which relate not only to implementing existing common policies of the EU, but also to achieving the *finalite politique* of the EU. To illustrate, the next enlargement to include a number of applicants with a heterogeneous character might undermine the EU's effort to create the Common European Security and Defence Policy (the CESDP). Turkey appears to be less problematic in this respect, as she has integrated much more with the CESDP than any other candidate. Although participation in the CESDP seems to have been attractive to all the prospective members, the enlarged EU with 27 or more members would increase political and ideological diversity and make it more difficult to reach a common position on a number of policy issues relating to the CESD.

A similar concern might also apply to the economic aspect of European integration. In particular, given that post-Maastricht Europe has opened a completely new qualitative dimension of integration in the economic sphere through establishment of the European Monetary Union (the EMU), the conceivable difficulties for new members in complying with the economic *acquis* of the EU would cause a great deal of concern as regards the deepening economic process. In other words, the increasing economic diversities in an enlarged Union would undermine economic and social cohesion throughout the EU, which has always been fundamental to the economic integration of the EU.

In particular, Turkey's accession to the EU would raise considerable concern in this respect. Considering that the Maastricht 'convergence criteria' for EMU membership requires a low level of inflation, a low level of budget deficit and manageable national debt, Turkey with its high rate of inflation, a huge budget deficit, high rate of interest and great price instability would clearly have great difficulties in participating in the process of European Monetary integration. This was confirmed in a recent report of the Commission, which suggested that macro-economic stability in Turkey is not yet achieved, and thus, the prospect of Turkey's participation in the EMU appears to be distant. As the Report stated: 'although some parts of Turkey's legislation are in line with the EMU *acquis*, further progress is necessary with respect to all other elements of the EMU *acquis*'. In this respect, the report underlined that 'Turkey will need to implement the necessary changes to its institutional and legal framework by the date of accession' (European Commission, 2000, p. 48). These include the continuation of Turkey to focus on bringing down her inflationary pressures and public deficits and maintaining the pursuit of structural and market reforms.

In December 1999, the Turkish Government introduced a comprehensive 3-year macroeconomics disinflation and fiscal stabilization programme, supported by a 3-year stand-by agreement concluded with the IMF and the economic and financial sector reform programme agreed with the World Bank. One of the main aims of this comprehensive programme is to fulfil Turkey's potential as a developing economy to meet the EU's criteria for membership through bringing down her chronically high inflation and interest rate and consolidating public finance.[3] Although the Commission's report on Turkey's progress towards accession recognized that Turkey has made considerable progress in addressing the most urgent imbalances in the economy, developing a sustainable macro-economic stability in Turkey seems to remain doubtful in the short term. By implication, Turkey's accession to the EU would inevitably have implications for the economic integration of the EU. Therefore, the EU is likely to continue the policy of delaying the accession process of Turkey as long as possible on economic grounds, if no other.

Similar difficulties can be seen for the CEECs in their efforts to comply with the EMU *acquis*. The Commission has already underlined a number of issues as regards the prospects for each applicant of CEE to participate in the EMU. For example, having a detailed assessment of Romania's economic policy in its various aspects, the Commission concluded that Romania would have a number of difficulties in participating in the EMU resulting from macroeconomics instability and the inadequacy of the institutional and legal framework together with its high inflation rate of 45.8 per cent (European Commission, 2000b, p. 55). Thus, the Report suggested that Romania should undertake some policy reforms, which included improving macro-economic stability, preventing direct public sector financing by the Central Bank, liberalizing capital movement, and complying with the EMU *acquis* in price stability and central bank statutes (European Commission, 2000b, p. 56). Similar concerns and suggestions can be found in the Commission's Progress Report on Poland and Bulgaria. In fact, Bulgaria has been facing tremendous macroeconomics problems in coping with the economic *acquis* with a lack of transparency in implementing the market economy, due to heavy state intervention in the economic sphere (European Commission, 2000c). Its GDP per capita is the lowest of all candidate countries, followed by Romania's.

Basically, the next enlargement will inevitably have implications for the economic and political integration of the EU. More specifically, the next enlargement of the EU will involve not only the financial costs associated with integrating less developed applicants with a relatively large agricultural sector and low level of GDP per capita in the EU, but will also involve risks associated with the deepening process of the EU towards the declared objective of economic and political union. In other words, the next enlargement of the EU has brought the 'widening' *versus* 'deepening' dilemma on to the agenda of European integration. As indicated above, the next enlargement of the EU will increase the economic, political and ideological diversity in the EU that might create a less cohesive structure and admit a variety of conflicts in relation to the future development of EU institutions and a common policy.

In fact, an enlarged Union with such diversity and heterogeneous membership would bring together a new set of national interests which might weaken the implementation of policy on a common and uniform basis (Miles and Redmond, 1996). The reconciliation of diversities and balancing of conflicting interest among the member states would become more difficult and thus might pose additional challenges for the future development of common policies in the EU and the integrity of the *acquis communautaire* (Taylor, 1995, p. 105). This implies that the continuation of 'a single speed Europe' seems to be difficult and 'differentiated integration' and 'variable geometry' have been widely discussed concepts for resolving the dilemma between widening and deepening in the enlarged Union.[4]

However, it should be noted that although the next enlargement will have implications for the deepening process of the EU, the perceived effects of such enlargement on the deepening process appear to be manageable. The EU has developed 'adaptive' enlargement policy, providing appropriate accession instruments for applicants, with a view to reducing the perceived effects of such an enlargement on the deepening process. Further, the EU has firmly linked the enlargement of the EU not only with candidates' progress towards meeting the accession criteria, but also with its own readiness for accepting a new member(s): the criterion of the capacity of the EU to include a new member state(s) provides a safeguard for the deepening process of the EU. Moreover, the process of institutional reforms has appeared to be oriented in such a way that enlarged Union would not seriously undermine the process of achieving the *finalite politique* of the EU.

In conclusion, the analysis of this section indicates that the size of Turkey might be an issue as far as its membership is concerned, because of its relevance to costs and risks: its relatively big size would not only undermine the deepening process of the EU, but would also qualify for considerable financial resources from the EU under the EU's existing structure. Therefore, the 'too big' and 'too underdeveloped' arguments against Turkish membership presents the problematic character of the Turkish membership issue, because of the relevance of size to the costs/risks associated with Turkey's accession to the EU.

However, there seem to be some shortcomings in this approach. Firstly, the 'too big argument' considers the costs/risks concerns of Turkish membership for the EU within the framework of the present structure of EU policies, without taking into account the convergence progress that Turkey might take in the long run before it reaches the accession negotiation process. Thus, it cannot provide a good enough account of some decisive variables as regards the cost/risk factors of Turkey's accession to the EU. More specifically, there are a number of variables determining the costs/risks for the EU of Turkey's membership in the long run:

- The timing of Turkey's accession to the EU (it is almost certain that the prospect for Turkish accession to the EU is a long-term one).
- The nature of reforms in EU policies, including the CAP, Regional Policy and Structural Funds before Turkey joins.
- The stage of Turkey's progress towards meeting the economic criteria before the accession, considering that Turkey has to comply with the economic *acquis* before the accession is conceivable.
- The nature of the EU structure at the time of Turkey's accession, as it is possible, even likely, that the EU will have adopted the concept of flexible arrangements to enable it to move at different speeds in some policy areas.
- The length of transitional periods given to Turkey particularly in some key policy areas, such as the GAP and European Regional and Structural Policy.

Thus, considering the purposes of this study which is to analyze whether Turkey has been treated differently from the other applicants and the extent to which the EU's policy has been compatible with its enlargement policy objectives, a more comprehensive framework is needed to examine the Turkish case not merely on an individual costs/benefits basis in isolation from the other factors but on the basis of a comparison with other applicant countries. In addition, given that the EU's policy towards Turkey has been mainly driven by political conditionality – human rights and disputes with Greece – rather than costs/risks concerns for the EU of Turkey's membership, such an analytical framework for comparison is more appropriate for examining the EU's approach to the identified policy issues in the Turkish case and to compare this with its approach to similar issues in other applicant countries. From this perspective, identifying the norms for the EU's conduct of policy through characterization of its enlargement policy provides a more appropriate setting in which to assess not only whether the EU's policy towards Turkey has been compatible with its enlargement objectives in general, but also whether it has allowed the EU to exert effective influence on the development of Turkey's policy in key areas.

The Norms for the EU's Enlargement Policy: Motivations and Interests

Four main areas of motivation and interest have driven the next enlargement policy of the EU:

- Security motivation and considerations.
- The perceived democratization effect of enlargement in the applicant countries.
- The creation of political identity and history.
- Economic motivation and interests.

Security Motivation and Considerations in the EU's Next Enlargement Policy

The post-Cold War security challenges for the EU have played an important part in the EU's enlargement policy. The revolutionary events in Eastern Europe, which led to the demise of the Soviet Union and the break-up of the Communist bloc, have fundamentally changed the patterns of security challenges to the EU. In other words, the Soviet military and ideological challenges to Europe have been replaced by other new and potential political, societal, environmental and security problems. These parameters and characteristics of the new security challenges to the EU seem to have increased the security interdependence between the core and periphery of Europe. In fact, the resurgence of new national identities among the newly independent states, which have embarked on a nation-state building process, has resulted in many domestic conflicts. These include minority questions to do with ethnic, religious, social and cultural origins and constitutional issues against a background of the relative weakness of pluralist democratic constitutional traditions. The nation-state building process in the CEECs has fostered regional conflicts, thereby constituting a serious threat to the stability of Europe, as was seen in the civil wars in Yugoslavia. Similar to the CEECs and countries in the Balkans, Turkey has also been facing the emergence of new sources of instability: Kurdish nationalism, the spread of religious extremism, notably Islamic fundamentalism, political turmoil and economic hardship have caused much political instability in Turkey.

As a result, the EU came to the reluctant conclusion that the integration of these transitional countries into a European structure would lessen the cost of new security challenges for the EU. Indeed, considering the degree of risks and costs associated with the political and economic instability on the periphery of the EU, it has realized that European security, as a whole, cannot be guaranteed without sustained economic development and the maturing of the democratic institutions in the countries of Eastern Europe, the Balkans and the Mediterranean. The EU has assumed that enlargement would provide the necessary assets to consolidate democracy and enhance stability and security in Central and Eastern Europe. As the Report of the European Commission states:

> Enlargement is a challenge which the Community cannot refuse. The other countries of Europe are looking to us for guarantees of stability, peace and prosperity, and for the opportunity to play their part with us in the integration of Europe. For the new democracies, Europe remains a powerful idea, signifying fundamental values and aspirations, which their peoples kept alive during the long years of oppression. To consolidate their new-found liberty, and stabilize their development, is not only in their interests, but ours (European Commission, 1992, p. 5).

The Commission recommendation has been taken seriously by the EU member states: they considered the stabilization of Europe as the main objective of current enlargement policy, believing that enlargement would provide a solution for ethnic and nationalistic conflict and would effectively neutralize the dangers of authoritarian tendencies among the new democracies of Eastern Europe. For example, the Copenhagen Summit in 1993 set up an enlargement strategy in such a way as to achieve stability and security in Europe through the construction of common European institutions (European Council, 1993). Faced with this prospect, the EU increasingly perceived the next enlargement towards the CEECs as essential for the lasting stabilization of the new democracies and securing the political stability of the whole European Continent. In fact, the instruments of the EU's next enlargement strategy for the CEECs have, to some extent, sought to accommodate the political and economic needs of these countries through the EU's comprehensive pre-accession strategy (European Council, 1994). This pre-accession strategy has been strengthened by the new instruments of the accession partnership and the reinforcement of pre-accession aid. These have all been, to some extent, related to the EU's effort to neutralize the new security threats from the CEECs as a means of reinforcing peace, stability and democracy in these countries.

This security motivation of the EU's enlargement policy has not been an element in the EU's policy towards Turkey. This is because Turkey was excluded from this pre-accession strategy of the EU on the grounds that Turkey was far away from satisfying the EU's political criteria. However, given that Turkey has also been facing similar security challenges that pose security threats to the EU, the EU's policy towards Turkey seems to have been incompatible with the declared security motivation of the EU's enlargement. In fact, the instruments of the EU's containment strategy have not been sufficient to hasten Turkey's efforts to undertake the necessary policy reforms to stabilize its domestic politics.

To promote regional cooperation and good neighbourliness among the applicant countries is an important aspect of the EU's attempts to minimize the new security threats from these countries. The prospect of EU membership has clearly been an important element in encouraging better relationships among the applicant countries and the EU members. In fact, establishing good neighbourliness and friendly cooperation between the applicant countries has been one of the main conditions for

EU membership. In this context, the goal of membership for the applicant countries has been an effective tool for promoting the regional cooperation and has thereby contributed to the finding of resolutions for many bilateral issues between them. This is because they hoped that regional cooperation and establishing good relations between themselves would facilitate their objective of achieving EU membership. For example, expectation of membership was obviously the primary impulse behind the dramatic and historic friendship treaties between Hungary and Romania in 1995 (Ram, 1999).

Overall, it is clear that the EU has pushed the applicant countries into seeking ways to settle their disputes with other applicant countries and with members of the EU. From this perspective, the Greco-Turkish disputes are particular cases, not only showing whether the EU's policy approach towards these issues has been able to influence the progress toward settling of the disagreements between both parties, but also whether the instruments of the EU's containment strategy for Turkey have been compatible with the security objectives of its enlargement policy. In fact, the EU's skepticism towards the prospect of Turkish membership and the rigid linking of Greek politics to the Turkish membership with the settlement of these disputes seems to have undermined the EU's influence on Turkey. The inadequacy of the EU's policy instruments towards Turkey with regard to EU membership offers a possible explanation why the EU has been less effective in influencing Turkey's policy development than it has with other applicant countries.

For the applicant countries, membership of the EU is considered a vital instrument for their security needs. This is related to the perceived effect of membership on further stability in their domestic politics, because EU membership has been viewed by the CEECs as a political anchor to stabilize their newly established democracies and political systems. The political and security considerations of the CEECs have also been related to the fact that EU membership provides a useful mechanism for pursuing their foreign security and defence policy. Indeed, after the end of the Cold War, the CEECs have been searching for anchors for their foreign security and defence policies; in this respect, joining the EU has been regarded as an essential mechanism for their foreign security and defence policy objectives (Croft and Redmond, 1999, p. 98). Moreover, noting that post-Maastricht European integration has extended to the areas of politics, security and defence with the aim of asserting a European identity, 'the cost of exclusion from the European political integration has became almost prohibitively high' (Croft and Redmond, 1999, p. 63).

Indeed, the political and security attraction of the EU to the candidate countries has increased since the EU started to make a serious effort to create European Security and Defence Identity (ESDI) after the end of the Cold War and the demise of Communism in Eastern Europe. For instance, the Common Foreign and Security Policy (the CFSP), which was incorporated into the Maastricht Treaty as the second pillar of the EU, has became an essential part of European integration. The Amsterdam Treaty broadened the scope of the CFSP to include 'all questions related to security of the Union, including the eventual framing of a common defence policy, which might lead to a common defence'. The Helsinki Summit went further in underlining the creation of an effectively functioning CFSP as an essential element in European security and defence identity with a view to enhancing the political profile of the EU. In this regard, the role of the Western European Union (the WEU) in the process of the evolving European Foreign Security and Defence Identity has became an important issue: whether it should preserve its independent existence or it should integrate with EU as the defence component of the CFSP. Apparently, the Maastricht and Amsterdam Treaties foresee that the WEU should be developed as the defence component of the EU as the means to strengthen the European pillar of the Atlantic Alliance.[5]

As can be seen from the above analysis, since the Maastricht Treaty, European integration has become directed towards creating a political European identity. This is one of the main reasons why EU membership is considered an attractive foreign policy objective for the applicant countries. In fact, the next enlargement of the EU is usually associated with the new construction of a European political identity within the post-Cold War structure. Therefore, EU membership is a desirable objective for all candidates.[6]

With regard to Turkey, exactly the same security motivations and interests underlined above have also been of concern to Turkey. Hence, security considerations constitute one of the main motivations of Turkey's eagerness for EU membership. Turkey has viewed the EU as a political union; thus, exclusion from such political integration is hardly compatible with Turkey's security interests and its security needs. To conclude, reducing the degree of security challenges for Europe by providing necessary instruments for the applicant countries to enhance their stability and security constitutes one of the main objectives of the EU's enlargement policy. In fact, the EU has offered some policy instruments through the Europe Agreements and an accession strategy to minimize the degree of risks and cost associated with the political, social and economic instability of the CEECs. These policy instruments cannot, however, be seen in the EU's policy towards Turkey, despite the fact that Turkey has been facing similar security challenges and thus posing security threats to the EU.

Democracy and Democratization Processes in the Applicant Countries

The perceived effect of EU membership on further democratization processes in the applicant countries seems to have been another important political motivation for the EU's enlargement policy. As the previous enlargements of the EU suggest, the EU played a crucial role in the democratization process in some acceding countries. The Mediterranean enlargements of the EU to include Greece, Spain and Portugal were peculiar cases for the EU which had to support and aid them in consolidating their newly established democracies. Greece, Portugal and Spain applied for EU membership shortly after the collapse of their respective authoritarian regimes; therefore, their applications were driven by the fact that membership would promote their domestic political stability and the process of democratization. As Preston puts it:

> Successive Mediterranean enlargements became a critical test of the capability of the EU model to act as a stabilizing influence in the region and to establish a framework for the development of pluralist political and economic structures and processes (Preston, 1997, p. 63).

In this respect, the EU drew these countries into the integration of Europe as a promotion of democracy on the part of the EU. Despite the inadequacy of their political systems for EU membership, the EU considered them eligible to join without obliging them to meet firm political conditions in advance. Indeed, Greece was admitted only seven years after she adopted a democratic constitution; similarly, Spain and Portugal entered the EU a little more than a decade after the collapse of long lasting authoritarian regimes (Rose and Haerpfer, 1995). This political consideration of the EU prevailed over the negative economic consequences of those countries' accession to the EU, at least in the short term. The EU in deciding to accept them as full members overlooked their structural economic and political weaknesses (Croft and Redmond, 1999, p. 58). This was the case for Greece in particular: although the Commission had suggested that Greece was not economically ready for full membership, the European Council decided to start accession negotiations with Greece. In fact, given the structural weakness of the Greek economy, including the size of the agricultural sector in the economy and its weak industrial base, it was estimated by the Commission that Greek accession to the EC would have a negative impact on the Community budget (European Commission, 1976). Despite the Commission's negative opinion on the early Greek accession, however, the member states were concerned that rejection of Greek membership might further isolate Greece from the Western European security arrangements, as she had already left NATO.

As regards the next enlargement of the EU, one of the main objectives of the EU's enlargement policy towards the CEECs has been to promote the development in democratization and human rights in these countries. The importance of the next enlargement for these developments seems to have been a common reference point for all the EU institutions and the EU member states. For example, the Commission's Report in 1992 reflected the long-term vision of European democracy in an enlarged Europe as a means of integrating these new democracies into the European Union. Indeed, the Commission has made several references to the importance of enlargement as a political means of consolidating and embedding principles of liberty, democracy, respect for human rights and the rule of law in candidate countries, which can be seen in its Agenda 2000 (European Commission, 1997b).

The same consideration can also be seen in the European Parliament's position on the next enlargement. The EP has considered the next enlargement as an historic opportunity to ensure democracy, respect for human rights and the strengthening of common European values in Europe. As the opinion of the Committee on Civil Liberties and Internal Affairs stated:

> It is the historic task of our generation to make Europe whole, to remove the vestiges of 50 years of ideological dictatorship and repression in the Central and Eastern European Countries; hence, it is the biggest democracy project ever and if it is successful, then the Union will be the guarantor of democracy (The European Parliament, 1996a, p. 4).

In this respect, the EP has made several references to the need for democratic inputs in the enlargement process and has requested greater involvement of the European Parliament in the various stages of negotiation. Indeed, it has been involved in the enlargement process by identifying the political problems related to democratic reforms, human rights and institutional developments.

As far as the EU member states are concerned, the concern for developments in democratization and respect for human rights in the CEECs has constituted one of the main political motives in their decision to start the next enlargement process. For this reason, the EU member states have always believed that the next enlargement would anchor the CEECs in a democratic Europe and that this would reinforce the principles of democracy and human rights in these countries. The member states' desire to support and facilitate the CEECs in consolidating their newly established democracies through the enlargement process has been reflected in successive Presidency Conclusions of the EU Council Summits. For example, the Copenhagen political conditions for EU membership, including stability of institutions, guaranteeing of democracy and respect for human rights, have reflected the concerns of the EU member states about the importance of the effects of democratization resulting from the EU's enlargement strategy in the applicant countries.

As far as the applicant countries are concerned, accession into the EU seems to have been regarded as a political shelter that would protect democracies from totalitarian regimes, and provide a useful channel for carrying out necessary reforms in their political systems and legislations on human rights. In fact, one of the political motivations of the CEECs for joining the EU has been related to their desire to return to a European model of democracy. For example, the Polish Prime Minister, Tadeusz Mazowiecki, was the first leader who articulated the concept of a 'return home' in his speech at the Council of Europe in July 1990; he underlined 'the magnetic attraction of the West European societal and political model of liberal democratic government for Poland' (cited in Ram, 1999, p. 63). For this reason, by drawing an analogy from the previous Mediterranean enlargements of the EU in which the EU's decisions to admit Greece, Spain and Portugal were based mainly on the desire to consolidate their democratization processes and political development, the present applicant countries have been expecting similar treatment from the EU. Indeed, the example of the Mediterranean enlargements of the EU to facilitate democratization process in Greece, Spain and Portugal has constituted an important point of reference in their effort to gain political support from the EU in their membership application (Grabbe and Hughes, 1998, p. 6). For example, the Hungarian Foreign Minister, Kodolanyi, demanded the same treatment from the EU in 1990, as he argued; 'the Iberian enlargement had been the result of political settlement despite the insufficiencies of their economies, and the Community would do the right thing now to take a similar decision' (cited in Ham P. Van, 1993, p. 196).

However, the part played by the EU in promoting democratization and political transformation in the new democracies of Central and Eastern Europe and other applicants, including Turkey, seems to have been different from its previous Mediterranean enlargements in many aspects. This change of the EU's enlargement policy has, to a large extent, been due to the complexity of the next enlargement: there are many more applicant members with more heterogeneous political features and developments than before; the EU is now more integrated and politically advanced. Therefore, the EU has forced the applicant countries to undertake the necessary reforms to their political and human rights systems outside the EU, rather than allowing them to develop their democracies within the EU mechanism, as was the case for Spain, Greece and Portugal. In other words, the EU's new enlargement strategy seems to imply that all the applicant countries must make sufficient progress to move their political and human rights systems in the direction of the EU system before they join the EU. This is to ensure that their internal political conditions do not pose any serious problems, not only for the existing political system of the EU, but also for its future objective of creating a common European system of political values.

In this regard, the EU's enlargement strategy for the CEECs was designed to not only minimize the political costs associated with the complexity of the next enlargement, but also to support the democratization process in the applicant countries. In fact, the EU has created a very favourable environment for applicant countries to consolidate and reinforce democracy through its new enlargement strategy with pre-accession instruments outside the EU mechanism. In this new strategy, the EU, firstly, introduced very strict and firm political criteria, the so-called Copenhagen criteria, for membership, which have to be satisfied by the candidate countries to qualify for accession negotiations with the EU. Secondly, as a part of this new strategy, the EU has offered some instruments for developing and reinforcing democracy in the applicant countries. For example, a considerable amount of money has been allocated to the democratization process in the applicant countries through the pre-accession strategy and the PHARE programme. In addition, the EU has encouraged political developments in these countries by not only offering them clear prospects for EU membership, but also working closely with them to help them to improve their human rights regimes and their parliamentary democracy.

In conclusion, the EU has guided and even directed and catalyzed the reform process in the CEECs through its pre-accession strategy and through its extensive membership requirement regarding the stability of institutions, guaranteeing of democracy and respect for human rights. In fact, by offering them membership of the EU upon their fulfilling certain requirements and helping them to meet these requirements, the EU has affected direction, policy choices and the political outcome of reforms in these countries. However, Turkey is an interesting case in showing the extent to which the EU has taken a different approach from the approach taken elsewhere. Although the EU has approached the same political issues in the CEECs positively with appropriate support through the pre-accession strategy, the EU's containment strategy for Turkey has lacked the necessary instruments to help and force Turkey to speed up policy reforms in domestic politics. In fact, the inadequacy of the instruments of the EU's policy towards Turkey can offer one possible explanation why the EU has been less effective in influencing developments in the Turkish political system than it has in other applicant countries. From this perspective, given the degree of political instability and its cost, associated with the lack of democratic institutions, and breaches of human rights in the country, Turkey needs a more effective strategy than that of the EU's containment policy.

Identity Politics, History and the Next Enlargement of the European Union

Apart from the security and democratization concerns of the EU, the next enlargement seems to have been regarded as a historical and moral challenge for the

EU, presenting an opportunity to rebuild the future of Europe and create a new European unity with a new European identity. The Cold War caused unnatural division of Europe into two hostile blocs and thus the CEECs became Soviet satellites after World War II. Therefore, history is surely an important factor that has influenced prioritization of the CEECs in the enlargement process of the EU as a means of ending unnatural division of Europe. The notions of 'return to Europe' and a 'common European home' have been the concepts which indicate the identity and history factors in the politics of the EU for the next enlargement. In fact, the prospects of strengthening European unity by integrating all the 'historically' and 'culturally' close European states in the EU has been one of the important motivating factors in the background to the enlargement politics of the European Union. In this respect, a sense of moral responsibility for the CEECs seems to have been an important factor representing the cultural and historical dimension of the next enlargement of the EU.

The Cold War divided Europe; the countries in the West enjoyed prosperity and democracy, while the countries in the East experienced neither democracy nor the support of a liberal political system. The CEECs were left to come under the Soviet sphere of influence. Considering the ideological war between the East and the West, the CEECs had become a victim of the Cold War politics. Therefore, the EU has felt itself responsible for ensuring that those countries, which were victims of the Cold War, should not be sacrificed in the post-Cold War complacency. Even one year after the revolution in the CEECs, the EU Council in Dublin 1990 declared its desire to repair the division of Europe whose people share a common heritage and culture, as a means of restoring the unity of the continent through enlargement in the future (European Council, 1990). In addition, the Commissioner, Franz Andriessen, stated that 'the CEECs' history, culture and traditions are part of the common European heritage' (*Agence Europe*, 3 March 1990, No. 5206). More recently, the Christian Democrat Parties in the EU describe one of the objectives of enlargement objective as the creation of a European identity based on the shared experience of proximity, ideas, values and historical interaction (*Financial Times*, 14 December 1997). Thus, historical responsibility of reuniting two halves of Europe has constituted one of the main motivations of the EU's enlargement policy. Moreover, in the construction of post-Cold War Europe, the EU has produced a great realization that preserving the peace and security in the continent and avoiding any possible wars can only be achieved through integration. By drawing analogy from the past experiences, including the CEECs in the enlargement process can be viewed as the EU's desire to avoid any perceivable risks which might cause European wars.

For the CEECs, the 'return to Europe', which would represent the strongest confirmation of their identity, seems to have constituted a solid basis for their membership bid. They have brought history and the European identity into play to legitimize their desire to become members of the EU. Indeed, they consistently put forward the argument that they have traditionally shared the values and the norms of European or Western culture and civilization; hence, they had always aspired to belong to the West during the artificial division of the Communist regimes. Therefore, the prospect for EU membership is associated with catching up 'European values' for the CEECs. For example, the Foreign Minister of Hungary, Jeszenczky, legitimized his country's official request for EU membership by stating that 'this is Hungary's official declaration to return to Europe to which it has always belonged' (*Agence Europe*, 6 April 1994, No. 6204). Similarly, during the negotiations of the association agreement with the EU, the Head of the Polish delegation, Olechowski, asserted that 'the technocratic approach is not enough in these negotiations, which have a historical goal: give Europe back to Poland and Poland back to Europe' (*Agence Europe*, 21 March 1991). In the Czech case, the EU membership is seen as a label for confirming their identity. As the Czech Prime Minister, Vaclev Klaus, expressed it in December 1993: 'the question of our position in Europe today and in the future is in fact the question of our national and state identity' (cited in Bugge, 2000, p. 16).

As far as the Turkish case is concerned, if the European identity constructs in accordance with historical and cultural line, Turkey's 'Europeanness' becomes controversial (Aybek and Muftuler-Bac, 2000, p. 568). In fact, it appears to be a wide skepticism about its European identity.[7] However, on Turkey's part, EU membership represents the strongest confirmation of Turkey's European identity and the success of her modernization and Westernization policies. In this respect, the EU's approach to Turkey has important implications for Turkey's Westernization objective, which has gained a particular importance in recent years, because Turkish policy-makers have had difficulty in defending their Westernization policy against anti-Western forces in domestic politics. Yet, the EU's treatment of Turkey appears not only to be incompatible with its objective of creating European unity, but also insufficient to encourage the Europeanization process in Turkey. The implication of this is that the EU's different policy treatment for Turkey from the other applicants seems to have been less effective in supporting a pro-Western force in the country than it has been in the CEECs.

Economic Motivations and Interest behind the Next Enlargement of the EU

The next enlargement of the EU involves both costs and benefits for the EU: while it will have major budgetary and financial costs for the EU for a short time, it provides considerable economic gains for the EU in the long term. These economic gains from the next enlargement would come from the expansion of the EU's single market. The new members are expected to participate fully in the process of European economic integration. Hence, as part of the EU's *acquis*, they will have to adopt the entire single market legislation and competition regime. Furthermore, they will need to progress sufficiently in making their economic structure converge with the EU. These will increase the effects that the enlargement will have on the creation of trade, providing more trading opportunities for the EU members (European Commission, 1997b). In fact, trade between the EU and the applicants, including Turkey, has been growing fast. The EU had a surplus of ECU 33 billion with the candidate countries in 1999 (see Table 2.5).

Table 2.5 The EU's trade with Turkey and selected candidates of CEE

Countries (1999)	Export (ECU billion)	Import (ECU billion)	Total trade	Trade Surplus
Turkey	22.46	15.1	36.7	7.3
Czech Rep.	18.4	16.8	35.2	1.6
Hungary	18.9	17. 6	36.5	1.3
Poland	29.0	17. 6	46.6	11.4

Source: Eurostat, 'Statistics in Focus: EU External Trade', No: 27/2000 (Theme 613–2000), Eurostat Press Office, Luxembourg, November 2000.

In addition, a relatively cheap and competitive skilled labour force and a supply of cheaper natural resources with economies of scale will reduce costs and strengthen Europe, and thus enhance the EU's long-term global competitiveness *vis-à-vis* the USA and Japan. Furthermore, a larger internal market in an enlarged Union, combined with relatively high growth on the part of the applicant countries, would attract non-EU foreign investment. Last but not least, the CEECs' history of closer economic links with Russia and Turkey's role in the Caucasus, the Middle East and in the Black Sea region could strengthen the EU's economic ties in these regions.

As regards the external implications, enlargement would increase the EU's weight and its influence on the international economic system and international institutions as regards multilateral economic and financial matters. In fact, enlargement would enhance the influence and negotiating power of the Union in international institutions, such as the World Trade Organization, GATT and the World Bank. In other words, enlargement would strengthen the EU's role as an international actor which would, in turn, tend to make its trade partners scrutinize its actions carefully. This increase of the EU's weight and role in the world is important, as it would contribute effectively to the maintenance of the open world economy and mobilize resources for increased globalization, which is necessary for the EU's trade.

As far as the economic motivation of the applicants for EU membership is concerned, it is the large single European market that has attracted the applicant countries. Indeed, they realized that the 'cost of exclusion', if they did not share the benefits of being part of the EU's single market, would be very high, as their economy would be transformed through access to such a large market (Croft and Redmond, 1999, p. 63). Indeed, all applicant countries have regarded the EU as a crucial integrative mechanism for accelerating their economic development through obtaining access to the large market of the EU, huge sources of supply, as well as sources of direct and portfolio investment, technology and know-how.

In addition, the need for European economic aid and cooperation and the direct capital investment that they hoped to receive from EU members and outside the EU seem to have been the driving force behind their applications. Furthermore, joining a powerful trade bloc is beneficial in itself for the applicant countries; in fact, being a part of the EU, as one of the main players in world economic affairs, would provide better opportunities for their economic interests. Hence, the applicant countries perceived EU membership as essential.

The above economic motives and interests can, of course, be seen in Turkey's desire for membership; her economy would share benefits of being part of EU's single market. However, although the customs union has provided a degree of economic integration, it is a limited step and thus considered not to be desirable on its own. The economic instruments of EU's policy towards Turkey, including the customs union and Accession Partnership, have been found inadequate for the purpose of preparing Turkey for accession by bringing it closer to the European Union in all spheres of the EU's economic integration in the context of post-Maastrich Europe. This explains Turkey's fear about not participating in European integration in line with the CEECs, because its relevance to the cost of exclusion from the benefits of being part of the EU's single market.

In conclusion, as the overall analysis of this section has indicated, the perceived political, security and economic benefits associated with the next enlargement of the EU, provided it is well prepared, seem to be vital for both the EU and the applicant countries. Indeed, it seems that successful enlargement would integrate the applicant countries into the EU's economic and political structure and thus support the democratization process and enhance security and stability throughout the European continent. In addition, it would stimulate economic growth in Europe by further opening up markets between the existing EU member states and acceding member states, which would strengthen the EU's role as an international actor. Last but not least, the potential political and economic gains do not provide sufficient rationale for the EU's decision; in fact, the current enlargement policy of the EU has been also driven by the need to create political and European identities. The perceived benefits in this respect are naturally difficult to assess, as it involves all history, culture and solidarity, not to mention responsibility.

Therefore, the EU was bound to offer an enlargement strategy for the applicant countries, designed not only to minimize the costs and risks associated with taking in poorer countries, but also to support their efforts to institute political and economic and social reforms. However, the EU has treated Turkey unequally in this respect. Although the EU has offered a clear strategy with the necessary instruments for accession on the grounds that the political, economic and social reforms in the CEECs must be supported, the EU's treatment of Turkey has lacked these accession instruments, and thus has been inadequate to influence a similar process in Turkey. The following section will examine the instruments of the EU's enlargement strategy.

Adoptive Instruments of the EU's Enlargement Policy: Their Objectives and Influences in the Applicant Countries

Since the EU started to deepen its current phase of progress towards economic, monetary and political union at the beginning of the 1990s, it seems to have shown some anxiety about the prospect of Eastern and Mediterranean enlargement. For example, in response to the Turkish request for EU membership, the Commission's opinion was that it could not recommend starting accession negotiations with any country before 1993 at the earliest, as any enlargement would run the risk of limiting the EU's capacity to further pursue its deepening process (European Commission, 1989a). This is to a large extent related to the widening *versus* deepening dilemma in European integration. It appears that the next enlargement of the EU, to include a number of countries, would increase the economic, political and ideological diversity of the EU, thereby generating a more heterogeneous and less cohesive structure, which might cause a variety of conflicts in the development of the EU politics and also its institutions. In this respect, the costs associated with the next enlargement of the EU to include economically underdeveloped and politically backward countries seem to have been an important concern of the EU. Therefore, it was reluctant to approach the enlargement issue in the first place.

However, as indicated above, the risks and challenges for the EU associated with the political and economic instability of the periphery of Europe are very substantial. Thus, the EU had introduced a hierarchical and gradual integration strategy for the aspirant countries: first, it offered financial assistance and trade and economic cooperation for the CEECs and then signed association agreements with all of them (Michalski and Wallace, 1992, p. 113). Although the association agreements created a formal legal basis for closer relations between the EU and those countries, which opened the door for political dialogue and gave an institutionalized framework for closer cooperation, the political and economic instruments of the Europe Agreements were inadequate and protective in character, as all the association agreements had been constrained by the safeguarding measures and restrictions on sensitive goods, such as steel, agriculture and textiles (Pinder, 1991). In addition, the Europe Agreements did not explicitly make any reference to the future accession of CEECs to the EU. However, the EU realized that it could not insulate itself from the situation on its eastern borders by retreating behind trade barriers and border controls in the face of the challenges posed by the economic and political instability of these countries. Indeed, the EU concluded that the best way to stabilize these emerging democracies in the long term for the sake of the political stability of the whole European continent was to integrate these countries into the EU by creating economic wealth and thus securing political stability and regional peace. Consequently, the Copenhagen European Council in 1993 accepted the principles of enlargement and made it clear that associate countries such as the CEECs would became a member of the EU, as long as they fulfilled the conditions for EU membership.

However, in this enlargement, unlike previous ones, the EU has introduced a gradual and an 'adaptive' enlargement strategy, based on two instruments: firstly, it has set up strict and comprehensive conditions for EU membership and, secondly, it has offered a pre-accession strategy for candidate countries, designed to help and guide them in satisfying the stated conditions for EU membership before the accession negotiations start. As regards the first instrument, the EU set conditions for EU membership in the next enlargement, which are much more comprehensive and detailed than it set for any previous applicant. These strict and comprehensive political and economic conditions have been designed to minimize the costs and risks associated with the new entrants' relatively underdeveloped economic and political structure. Indeed, the strict and evolving conditions set up for EU membership seem to have been designed to force the applicant countries to undertake necessary economic and political reforms before they join the EU, so that the cost of accepting them within the EU will be reduced. In this regard, the EU's enlargement strategy seems to be new and different from any former case, with the exception of the 1995 enlargement,[8] because previous enlargements allowed the new entrants to develop their economies and political systems within the EU through a long-term transition period, as was the case for Spain, Greece and Portugal.

As for the second instrument of the EU's next enlargement policy, namely the Pre-Accession Strategy involving the Europe Agreement, White Paper, the Structured Relationship and Political Dialogue, the PHARE and Accession Partnership, it has played a twofold role: on the one hand, it has guided the candidate countries to make their economic and political systems converge towards the EU norms, with considerable financial aid, and, on the other hand, it has provided leverage for the EU to influence political and economic developments in the candidate countries. This is because all the applicant countries are eager to join the EU and hence, the EU has been in a position to judge the progress that the candidate countries have made towards the fulfilment of the conditions for EU membership.

However, Turkey seems to have attracted an entirely different response from the EU in the shape of a containment strategy that has lacked the necessary accession instrument and accession commitment from the EU to prepare Turkey for EU membership. In addition, the criteria for EU membership seem to have been applied more strictly and rigidly to Turkey than to the others. In other words, although the EU's policy post-Helsinki has melted the rigidity of its conditionality, it has firmly linked Turkey's inclusion in the enlargement process on the latter's progress towards fulfilling those criteria, which appears to be incoherent with the declared objective of EU's enlargement policy. By implication, the EU's treatment of Turkey seems to have constrained itself in influencing Turkey's political, economic and social systems.

The following sections, then, will evaluate these two instruments of EU's enlargement policy. Firstly the requirements for EU membership will be described and characterized and then the EU's pre-accession strategy for the candidate countries will be considered.

Characterization of Conditions for Entry into the European Union

The conditions of EU membership for the new applicants have been much more comprehensive than were set for any previous applicant, partly as a result of the deepening process of the EU. Indeed, since the late 1980s, the EU has gradually been evolving with the aim of establishing an economic, monetary and political union as well as asserting a European identity. Post-Mastricht Europe seems to have moved in the direction of further economic and political integration, including the achievement of creating the EMU with the establishment of a single European Central Bank and bringing the fields of CFSP and JHA into the competence of the Union's integrated legal structure. As a result, the scale of the *acquis communautaire* has became more comprehensive and more complicated than before, concentrating more on the common values and political objectives of the

EU. In other words, the context of criteria for admission to the EU has not only changed, but also has developed across an extremely wide area.

The only written condition for EU membership laid down by Article O of the TEU is that the applicant country must be a 'European State'. There is no unequivocal interpretation of that criterion. In fact, one might interpret it in geographical, cultural or political terms. The Treaty of Amsterdam makes it clearer, stating that 'the Union is founded on the principle of liberty, democracy, respect for human rights, and fundamental freedoms and the rule of law, principles which are common to the member states' (Article 6(1)). Hence the concept of a European state might imply 'those whose governments have declared their commitment to build the EU, resting upon a common sense of European identity and a shared European idea' (Wallace, 1990, p. 8). Indeed, political values and commitments, rather than religious and cultural ones, seem to have been the main features which define the concept of 'European'; as the Commission stated:

> The shared experience of proximity ideas, values and historical interaction cannot be condensed into a simple formula, and it is subject to review by each succeeding generation. The Commission believes that it is neither possible nor opportune to establish now the frontiers of the EU, whose contours will be shaped over many years to come (The European Commission, 1992, p. 5).

Apart from the written condition of being European, there are a number of conditions for EU membership. The European Council in Copenhagen in 1993 laid down a set of requirements for EU membership underpinned by their focus upon the need to narrow the discrepancies between the economic and political levels of the applicant members and the member states of the EU. However, the accession criteria identified by the Copenhagen Summit seem to have been broad and vague. Indeed, all the conditions for EU membership are considerably open to interpretation. The Copenhagen conditions for EU membership are as follows:

- Stability of institutions guaranteeing democracy, the rule of law, human rights and respect for and protection of minorities.
- The existence of a functioning market economy and capacity to cope with competitive pressures and market forces within the Union.
- The ability to take on the obligations of full membership-the so-called *acquis communautaire*; that is the new members must accept the objectives of European Union, including adherence to the aims of political, economic and monetary union.
- The capacity of the EU to absorb new member states, while maintaining the momentum of European integration, which indicates the fact that membership and incorporation must proceed only in line with the EU's ability to incorporate new member states.

The above criteria have given a clear focus and direction to the current enlargement of the EU, but has effectively slowed down the enlargement process, because it introduced very broad and stretchable economic and political conditions which needs to be satisfied by the applicant countries before accession starts. The first three conditions indicate that applicant countries must be economically and politically developed before their accession so that any costs of their accession to the EU resulting from their relatively underdeveloped economic and political system would be manageable. In fact, the Copenhagen conditions imply that new entrants should not bring unmanageable economic, political and security problems into the EU. This seems to have been particularly the case with the EU's political criteria. The EU has particularly stressed the importance of minority rights, the principles of democracy and the resolution of bilateral issues involving border and minority questions between the acceding members, as the EU seems to have been concerned that unresolved political issues between acceding states, as well as between the acceding states and existing member states, would impair the Union's cohesion and its efforts to create the CFSP. In fact, the Copenhagen political criteria for EU membership imply that the countries applying for membership of the EU must first prove that they would not import any political and security problems into the EU in which it might became embroiled.

However, the political criteria for EU membership seem to require a clearer definition of what constitutes stability of institutions, guaranteeing democracy and respect for and protection of minorities, which are highly debatable and vague concepts. The EU has never provided an explicit definition of these concepts, although the Commission has made practical assumptions about what they entail, in its opinions on applicants' readiness for membership. Therefore, the applicant's readiness for membership depends heavily upon the Commission's view. It attempts to determine whether the applicant country presents the characteristics of democracy by looking at its election system and institutional framework, together with its legal and constitutional system for protection of human rights and minority rights. In its *avis*, the Commission stresses the following basic requirements that every candidate has to meet:

- A democratic constitutional and legal system, designed to guarantee funda-mental rights and democratic pluralism without any restriction, thereby protecting the right to physical integrity, freedom of expression and the press, freedom of association, freedom of assembly, freedom of religion, and freedom of political participation.
- A representative and participatory democracy based on universal suffrage and free multi-party election, separation of power, right to law, acceptance of pluralism and respect of human rights. That is, the participatory democracy should allow the civil societal elements and interest groups to participate in the political process without restrictions.
- A democratic form of government which requires the *de facto* of separation of executive, legislative and judiciary powers of the state and fully independent of the judiciary system with adequacy in relation to number judge, their status, training and financial situation.
- An effective administrative and institutional system governed by rule of law with a transparency rather than controlled by political authorities.

Apart from these, human rights and minority rights constitute an important part of its assessment about the applicant's readiness for membership. In fact, in its *avis* the Commission evaluates the human rights and protection of minorities under a different section in which reference is given to the evaluation of civil and political rights and protection for minorities. The Commission specifies the number of existing minorities in applicant countries, their status under the constitution, their rights with regard to education and languages, and their equal treatment by the public authorities. In this regard, the Commission has made it clear that candidate countries must provide sufficient legal base for the minority rights and the protection of minorities. In addition, it underlines that special rights and preferential treatment are necessary to protect minorities, which should provide appropriate safeguards to preserve their own characteristics and tradition in such a way so as to use and teach their own languages and the survival of their customs and traditions. Furthermore, the Commission has attached a value to the extent of implementation of the International and European Conventions of Human rights, including the UN Charter, the International Covenant for Civil and Political Rights, the European Convention for the Protection of Human Right, the UN Convention against Torture and the European Convention for the Prevention of Torture and other Inhuman or Degrading Treatment or Punishment.

However, political criteria for EU membership seem to be very broad, and cannot be defined in a clear manner. In other words, an analysis of the maturity of democracy and respect for human and minority rights in candidate countries seems to be very difficult. This is partly because it is not clear the extent to which the applicant countries have to make progress in the areas of democracy, the rule of law, human rights, respect for and protection of minorities before the admission. It is also partly because there are no sufficient and useful tools for assessing the progress the applicant countries have made. From this perspective, the Commission's judgement of the extent to which each applicant has progressed rests heavily upon a general judgement about the basic quality of political life in the applicant countries, rather than a detailed examination of their political structure. Indeed, the Commission's judgements of the political maturity of applicant countries are not explicit, and the comments within each opinion are vague (Grabbe and Hughes, 1998, p. 45). In addition, the Commission assessments of each applicant's compliance with the political conditions for EU membership, have relied heavily on the answers given in the extensive questionnaire sent to all applicant countries, and reports obtained from the member states, European Parliament, the Council of Europe and from candidate countries including from NGOs in the applicant countries. These sources are, to some extent, partial and biased, as they are always open to political influence from the outside while they are being prepared. This undermines the Commission's judgement about the applicants' readiness for membership and thereby creates some doubts about the objectiveness of its assessment. To conclude, it is not clear how the Commission has assessed compliance with these political criteria on the part of the applicant countries. Indeed, although some differences were noted with regard to minorities, the Commission used virtually identical language to describe the political institutions and functions of democracy in the applicant countries. Such uniformity of language as has been used in its opinion on each applicant country's compliance with the political criteria seems to reflect certain vagueness in its assessment.

The same vagueness applies to the economic criteria for EU membership. Indeed, a 'market economy' and 'capacity to cope with competitive pressure and market forces' are broad concepts that need to be defined more explicitly. The Commission has sought to determine what constitutes having a market economy, as it has stated that an existing market economy requires a stable macroeconomic framework, equilibrium between supply and demand and is established by the free interplay of market forces with an appropriate legal system, including the regulation of property rights (European Commission, 1997c). To determine whether such conditions exist, the Commission identified some indicators, which include liberalized trade and price systems, macroeconomic stability, a broad consensus on economic policy and a well-established financial sector. With regard to the 'capacity to cope with competitive pressure and market forces', the Commission has underlined the requirement of a framework in which economic decisions can be taken by individual agents with a reasonable degree of predictability. In this regard, the Commission has made further pronouncements about the extent of state involvement in the economy, including the level of state subsidies, privatization, social security, the government's role in competition and trade policy and the administration of state aids and subsidies. However, it seems that the Commission's indicators are open to interpretation and there seems to be some room for different assessments of an applicant country's progress towards compliance with the economic conditions for EU membership. Moreover, the problem with the economic criteria is that it seems difficult to find an appropriate methodology to measure applicants' capacity to cope with competitive pressure and market forces within the Union.

The third condition is also open to interpretation. The criterion with regard to the ability to take on the obligations of full membership refers to the candidate states' administrative, judicial and legislative capacities to implement the *acquis communautaire* of the EU. The concept of *acquis communautaire* had been used in previous accessions to refer to the entire body of EU rules, political objectives and judicial decisions which member states must adhere to when they became full members of the EU. Similarly, the *acquis* has been defined for this enlargement as all the real and potential rights and obligations of the EU system and its institutional framework. However, the vagueness of this criterion lies in the fact that the *acquis* cannot be defined in a specific manner, as it is of an evolving character that implies an evolving set of demands made to the applicant countries. Indeed the *acquis* is a dynamic concept, as the EU's legislation and objectives grow through Treaty changes and EU agreements with third parties, with increases of the EU's competence and increases in legal precedents in the European Court of Justice. Therefore, the vagueness and the exclusiveness of the *acquis* has left some scope for different interpretations of many conditions for EU membership which in turn affect the demands made on the applicants.

The previous enlargements of the EU suggest that no country that joined the EU has complied fully with the *acquis* at the time of its entry. Indeed, the EU has offered them a transition period for compliance with the *acquis*, setting the length of the adoption period in accordance with the acceding members' readiness, and hence allowing longer for the less developed new members, namely, Greece, Spain and Portugal. In other words, the EU had shown a flexible approach to any acceding states in their compliance with the EU's *acquis communautaire*; hence, if they did not comply with *acquis communautaire* in full before the accession, they fulfilled the necessary conditions within the EU during the transitional period which provided target dates for the reciprocal reduction and removal of tariffs and quotas and for legal harmonization and policy alignment. For example, Spain and Portugal achieved the abolition of import tariffs in seven years and they were granted six years for their customs union within the EU with benefits of voting power and substantial financial assistance from the structural funds.

As for the next enlargement, the Copenhagen criteria in contrast underlined the fact that applicant countries needed to complete the *acquis communautaire* in full prior to accession, including accepting unconditionally the future process of integration, such as the EMU and the CFSP and intensified integration and co-operation in the areas of JHA. However, given that even some existing member states seem so far to have been unable to meet the *acquis communautaire* in full, the EU's condition that the applicant states must comply with the *acquis communautaire* before joining seems to be treating them unfairly.

With regard to the last criterion for the EU's next enlargement policy, namely the capacity of the EU to absorb new member states, this seems to provide a safeguard for the deepening process of the EU. In fact, this criterion has established the question of the EU's capacity, as regards admissions, which implies that accepting new members to the EU would depend partly upon the state of the EU's preparedness for such an enlargement. What this means for any applicant country is that the timing of its accession would not only depend on its compliance with the Copenhagen criteria, but might also depend on the Union's capacity at the time to assimilate new members within the EU system. In this respect, it provides a safeguard for the EU, allowing it to delay the enlargement process until necessary institutional and policy reforms have been undertaken. Indeed, given that the next enlargement of the EU will involve considerable institutional, political, economic and policy changes in the EU which will affect the deepening process of European integration, the criterion of EU's enlargement capacity brings out the EU's concern over the implications of taking in the new members for the EU's institutions, its common policies and its deepening process.

Furthermore, the criterion of the EU's capacity to absorb new members has acted as a safeguard for the EU, allowing it to delay the accession of any problematic state to the EU. Indeed, it could imply that some applicants might be treated unfavourably on the grounds that their accession would impede the EU's deepening process and impair its system. In other words, the weakness in the criterion of the EU's capacity to absorb new members seems to be that it could be manipulated, or to be applied more strictly to some countries than to others so as to delay or reject some applicants simply on the grounds that the EU is not prepared for their membership. Indeed, the prospect of some candidates' becoming members of the EU could not be rejected outright, but their accession might be put back or even delayed indefinitely on the grounds of the EU's 'enlargement capacity'. For example, in the case of Turkey, it might be argued that Turkey's accession would place an additional constraint on the deepening process of the EU. In the light of her relatively large size and population, Turkey's accession would raise a number of institutional, financial and policy-based issues for the EU. These include absorbing the increased number of Turkey's representatives in the EU institutions, Turkey's participation in the EU's common policies and the effects of Turkish membership on the deepening process of the EU. In short, Turkey might arguably damage the momentum of the deepening process in the EU more by joining than the other applicant countries would.

In conclusion, the detailed and comprehensive conditions imposed on the candidate countries for EU membership is consistent with the EU's gradual and 'adaptive' enlargement policy objectives, which is to minimize the costs associated with the applicants' relatively underdeveloped economic and political structure. By setting such broad and evolving conditions, the EU has forced the applicant countries to undertake the necessary economic, political and institutional reforms to increase their ability to fulfil the obligations of membership before the accession negotiations start, so that the costs to the EU of their accession will be lessened. Another feature of the EU's conditions for membership is that most of the criteria cannot be defined in a clear manner and thus might be interpreted in different ways. The criteria for EU membership represent general principles rather than well-established uniformity applied norms. As Redmond suggests:

> There is scope for different interpretations of many of these conditions, and it is not possible to give a clear definition of an acceptable applicant country. It may also be the case that the Community's criteria may be interpreted more generously for some applicants than others, with consequent political implications (Redmond, 1993, p. 210).

Indeed, the vagueness of some criteria might be used as a pretext to effectively delay or reduce the chances of some problematic applicants joining the EU, not only on the grounds of the EU's 'enlargement incapacity' but also on the grounds of their insufficient preparation for EU membership.

The Instruments of the EU's Enlargement Policy: Pre-Accession Strategy

As mentioned above, refusing to admit aspiring members to the EU might not only jeopardize the political, security and economic interests of the EU, but it could also undermine the credibility of its principles. Therefore, after setting up a detailed set of entrance criteria for applicant countries, the EU agreed to make a firm commitment to enlargement *vis-à-vis* the aspirant countries. For the first time, the Copenhagen European Council in June 1993 declared that 'the associated countries in Central and Eastern Europe that so desire shall be members of the European Union'. In this regard, the instruments of the Europe Agreement had been inadequate to engineer the declared objective of integration between the EU and the associated members of the CEECs in the European post-Maastricht context. These instruments in the Europe Agreements have been designed only to establish a free trade area progressively between the parties in industrial goods as a means of reducing trade barriers and quantitative restrictions, with the exception of such sensitive products as iron, steel, coal, and textiles. They had also provided a general framework for political and economic cooperation, including the harmonization of legislation in trade (Gower, 1995). Therefore, the EU realized that the Europe Agreement was unsatisfactory and constituted an inappropriate framework for the Copenhagen declaration of an integration process for the CEECs. Hence, the EU decided to initiate a pre-accession strategy for the CEECs with a considerable amount of financial and technical aid.

Subsequently, the Essen European Council in December 1994 adopted a broad pre-accession strategy to bring those countries closer to the EU, taking into account their needs and with the ultimate aim of providing the associated countries with appropriate ways of preparing for their accession to the Union (European Council, 1994). As the Commission stated, the objective of the pre-accession strategy was to be the 'progressive integration of the political and economic system, as well as the foreign and security policies of the associated countries and the Union, together with increasing co-operation in the fields of Justice and Home Affairs, so as to create an increasingly unified area' (European Commission, 1994b). In that extent, the pre-accession strategy incorporated the earlier agreements and commitments of the Europe Agreements and the PHARE, and added new instruments of the 'White Paper' on a single market and 'Structured Relationship' between the EU institutions and the CEECs (Grabbe, 1999, p. 13).

Considering the need for comprehensive and extensive forms of cooperation to accelerate the integration of associated countries into the EU, the EU's pre-accession strategy has enhanced the existing association framework of the Europe Agreements by providing:

- More financial cooperation through the PHARE to support the efforts of the CEECs to meet the accession criteria.
- A new political formula of the Structured Relationship with the EU institutions.
- A kind of action plan in the White Paper on the internal market of the EU to prepare the aspirant countries in Central and Eastern Europe for economic integration in general, and the single market in particular.

Thus, the main theme of the pre-accession strategy is the emphasis that it put on the EU's commitment to the associated countries with the implicit message that all the countries included in the pre-accession strategy would become members of the EU.

The White Paper on the Single Market, the so-called 'Preparation of the Associated States of Central and Eastern Europe for Integration into the Internal Market of the EU', constituted the legal approximation aspects of the integration process in the pre-accession strategy (Ulrich and Wallace, 1996, p. 380). Given that integration into the EU's internal market entailed a complex process involving the harmonization of legislation, norms and standards, the White Paper provided a framework for the associated members to align their legislation with those of the single European market. Indeed, it provided a basic framework for the associated countries to comply with the *acquis communautaire* of the EU's single market by identifying comprehensively the administrative and organizational framework of various sectors of the EU's internal market regulations. It identified the *acquis* of the EU's single market for the creation and maintenance of an internal market in each sector which associated countries needed to adopt. It also underlined the need for adequate administrative and organizational structures to effectively implement and enforce those *acquis* in the CEECs. Indeed, increasing emphasis has been placed on the need to help develop effective administrative, judicial and legal institutions to implement the EU's single market legislation in the CEECs.

In that respect, the EU provided specialized technical and financial assistance for the improvement of public administrative and organizational structure in the CEECs to apply the *acquis* effectively, including a direct and rapid access to the complete and up-to-date EU legislative text, advice from the legal experts on the EU's legal system and the participation of the community programmes with regard to the internal market (Guadisart and Sinnaeve, 1997, p. 67). Basically, the White Paper has served as a guideline for the associated countries to take on the obligations of membership of the Union, and to develop their capacity to cope with the competitive pressure and market forces within the Union. Despite being indicative in character, the White Paper has laid emphasis on the need for the associated members to adopt the EU's internal market legislation in order to join the EU (Preston, 1997). To that extent, the harmonization of law in the field of the internal market is not an ultimate objective itself, but rather an instrument which contributes to achieving the final objective: full integration of the CEECs into the EU (Guadisart and Sinnaeve, 1997, p. 44). Thus, the adoption of the White Paper has become *de facto* a part of EU's conditionality (Grabbe, 1999, p. 14). In fact, compliance with the White Paper seems to be the best way to prepare for EU accession, as the harmonization process contributes in an essential way to the creation of a legal framework for integration. It created a road map for CEECs towards membership as regards internal market of the EU. However, the White Paper did not marginalize the Europe Agreements in this process, it rather dealt with certain areas where the Europe Agreement did not cover (Phinnemore, 1999, p. 109). Thus, the White Paper presents different elements of a wider pre-accession strategy of the EU.

The Structured Relationship and the Political Dialogue envisaged in the Europe Agreements constitute the political dimension of pre-accession strategy. The EU realized that the political dialogue provided for in the European Agreement had been inadequate for involving the CEECs in the various activities of the EU. Therefore, the Structured Relationship was incorporated into the pre-accession strategy of the EU as the political element of the strategy, providing a progressive political integration between the CEECs and the EU. The main objective of such structured dialogue seems to have been the establishment of a 'Structured Relationship' between the associated countries of Central and Eastern Europe and the EU so that associated members are able to be involved as appropriate in the areas of the EU's competence, as well as in cooperation in the CFSP and the JHA – without, however, involving any decision-making concerning them in those areas. This 'Structured Relationship' and 'Political Dialogue', covering many common policies of the EU, especially those with a trans-European dimension, including energy, the environment, transport, science and technology, and the JHA, has already linked the CEECs to the political integration of the EU through joint meetings between the associated members and the EU at various levels. In other words, political and structured dialogues have constituted an important channel not only serving as a forum for cooperation and the exchange of views between the EU members and associated members in the areas of security, defence and foreign affairs, but also giving the associate members 'a sense of belonging to the EU family', as well as providing 'a valuable insight into the workings of the EU machinery' (Graham and Fraser, 1998, p. 19).

The PHARE Programme has constituted the financial and technical aspect of the pre-accession strategy. The PHARE Programme, which was initially designed to accelerate the political and economic transition process in the CEECs, has been extended, in conjunction with the EBRD and the EIB, to cover a number of areas which include the restructuring of agriculture, public administration, the reform of the social services, education, health, the environment and nuclear security. In other words, the PHARE programme has been reorganized to support the associated countries in absorbing the *acquis communautaire*, and to complete market reforms and the medium-term restructuring of their economies and societies with the aim of preparing the associated members for EU membership Indeed, the PHARE programme has been mainly focused on the preparation of the CEE countries for EU membership; for example, a substantial amount of money has been allocated for institution building covering the strengthening of democratic institutions, and public administration to ensure that public services are ready to apply the *acquis* (European Commission, 1997b). As the part of this process, the EU has also offered technical assistance, training and the twinning of institutions and administrations with others in applicant countries. In fact, a number of programmes were created in the applicant countries with the PHARE funding, aimed at improving the court system, training the officials and improving the public knowledge about European integration in the applicant countries (Ram, 1999). In addition, about 70 per cent of PHARE has been channeled towards investment in the applicant countries in order to support the necessary investments for the adaptation of Community *acquis* in the area of infrastructure, covering agricultural restructuring, regional development and investment in human and intellectual capital, investments to support compliance with Community norms in the environment, agriculture, transport and telecommunications, and the co-financing of large scale infrastructure and development of small and medium enterprises (European Commission, 1997b). Consequently, PHARE has played a key role in the integration process between the EU and the CEECs.

This pre-accession strategy described above was further strengthened by the EU in 1997 through the document 'Reinforcing the Pre-Accession Strategy', which provided a more coherent programme to prepare the applicant countries for EU membership and a higher degree of cohesion between the preparations for accession and the negotiations themselves. The primary objectives of this reinforced pre-accession, as indicated in Agenda 2000, were:

First, to bring together the different forms of support provided by the Union within a single framework, the Accession Partnerships, and to work together with the applicants, within this framework, on the basis of a clearly defined programme to prepare for membership, involving commitments by the applicants to particular priorities and to a calendar for carrying them out. Secondly, to familiarize the applicants with Union policies and procedures through the possibility of their participation in Community programmes (European Commission, 1997b).

The Accession Partnership seems to have been the key instrument of 'Reinforcing the Pre-Accession Strategy'. It set out the short term and medium term priorities accorded to each individual candidate. The Accession Partnership has been systematically upgraded to adjust the priorities and to cover all pre-accession assistance (the PHARE, the ISPA, and the SAPARD). It is designed to incorporate all forms of assistance to the concerned countries within a single framework, with particular emphasis on the main problems identified by the Commission in each opinion on the accession applications of the associated members; these included opinions on the improvements in the institutional and administrative capacity of the applicant countries and the bringing of their enterprises into line with Community standards. The other main feature of Accession Partnership has been the national programme for adoption of the EU's *acquis* within a precise timetable.

Furthermore, this Accession Partnership has also provided a new form of financial assistance and instruments for the candidate countries; indeed, not only have the financial resources of PHARE been increased with the reallocation of funds for the institution building and the financing of investment projects, but also new forms of assistance have been provided to the applicants to comply with the *acquis communautaire* of the Union. This increased pre-accession aid, to be granted to the applicant countries from the year 2000, consists of two elements: aid for agricultural development, amounting to 500 ECU million per year and structural aid amounting to 1 billion ECU which would be directed towards the standardization of infrastructure in the applicant countries with those of the EU community in such fields as transport and the environment.[9] In addition, the Accession Partnership has provided other forms of assistance to the applicant countries to enable them to participate in community programmes and machinery to apply the *acquis communautaire* and participate in a number of mechanisms for institutional cooperation (European Commission, 1997b). Clearly, the main objective of this new arrangement for financial assistance and instruments under the Accession Partnership seems to have been intended to mobilize all forms of assistance to the problematic areas in applicant countries identified by the Commission so that they would not create unmanageable problems when the applicant members joined the EU.

To conclude, the pre-accession strategy of the EU has turned the Europe Agreements into a kind of preparatory stage for membership of the EU through a systematic transition as a means of providing closer economic and political cooperation (Christian and Muller-Graff, 1997, pp. 27–40). Thanks to the EU's proactive pre-accession strategy, which has provided the appropriate support for the applicant countries, the CEECs are expected to join the EU eventually. In this regard, the pre-accession strategy has played a twofold role: on the one hand, it has guided the candidate countries to redirect their economic and political systems towards EU norms using the EU's considerable financial aid; on the other hand, it has provided leverage for the EU to influence the political and economic developments in the candidate countries, as the EU has been in a position to judge the progress which the candidate countries have made towards fulfilling the conditions for EU membership. Indeed, the EU has used the accession carrot to persuade and guide them to undertake the necessary reforms for the convergence of their political and economic regimes with the EU norm.

As will be analyzed in Chapter 4 from a comparative perspective, the EU has been inconsistent in applying its pre-accession instruments to all applicants equally. For example, Turkey has attracted an entirely different response from the EU: while the instruments of the EU's policy towards the CEECs have been explicitly linked to their accession to the EU with a comprehensive and clearly defined pre-accession strategy, its policy to Turkey has neither included a firm accession commitment, nor a clearly defined comprehensive accession strategy to support Turkey's efforts to integrate itself with the EU. Although the EU Council at Helsinki revised its policy of containment which declared Turkey to be a candidate for EU membership and agreed to treat Turkey on the same basis as other candidate states, its policy has still lacked adequate instruments to prepare Turkey for EU membership. While the EU has offered Accession Partnership for Turkey, the implementation of this Accession Partnership has not only effectively conditioned settlement disputes between Greece and Turkey, including the Cyprus and Aegean Sea, but also has lacked sufficient policy instruments and financial assistance to stimulate and support policy reforms in Turkey. From this perspective, the Turkish Accession Partnership might become the centerpiece of the EU's containment policy for Turkey to delay her membership bid for the foreseeable future, rather than to prepare her for membership.

The Linkage between the Instruments of Pre-Accession Strategy and the Conditions for EU Membership

The EU's enlargement policy is built on two main pillars: comprehensive and strict conditions for EU membership and a pre-accession strategy for candidate countries which is designed to help and guide these countries to satisfy the stated conditions for EU membership before the accession negotiations start. These two instruments essentially have the same objective: to reduce the perceived costs associated with applicant members' relatively underdeveloped economic and political systems and to minimize any conceivable risks associated with the political and economic instability of the applicant countries by offering them a gradual process of integration with the EU through a pre-accession strategy outside the EU system.

In the meantime, the EU has sought to secure the perceived benefits of the next enlargement through preparing the candidate countries outside the EU mechanism. Therefore, there has been the close parallel between the contents of the economic and political conditions for EU membership and the instruments of the EU's accession strategy.

Firstly, these parallel structures can be seen between the contents and the objectives of the White Paper and the economic requirements for EU membership. In other words, the instruments of the White Paper have been designed to prepare the CEECs to satisfy the economic criteria for EU membership. Indeed, the purpose of the White Paper is to help the CEECs to become capable of fulfilling the economic criteria for EU membership, namely the possession of a functioning market economy and the capacity to cope with competitive pressure within the Union. The objective of the White Paper is also strongly connected to preparing the applicant countries to meet the condition of being able to take on the obligations of full membership and acceptance of the *acquis communautaire*. In this respect, the White Paper is a road map for the CEECs towards meeting economic criteria for EU membership.

The same objective has been envisaged through the political instruments of the EU's accession strategy. In fact, there has been a strong correlation between the Structured Relationship instrument of the EU's pre-accession strategy and the political conditions for EU membership, as the latter's objectives are closely connected to the preparation of the CEECs to fulfil the political conditions for EU membership. Instruments of the Structured Relationship and Political Dialogue between the EU and the CEECs have made a valuable contribution in helping applicant countries' efforts to align their political and human rights system with the EU's system and norms, as well as providing a progressive alignment of these countries with the CFSP. They have also provided a useful forum for the promotion of mutual confidence and for contributing to the diplomatic settlement of bilateral issues between candidate members, thereby stimulating the good neighbourhood agreements on borders and on the treatment of ethnic minorities. As a result the Structured Relationship has constituted the most important part of the CEECs' preparation for fulfilling the *acquis* of the politics of the Union.

The same linkage can be seen in the objectives of the PHARE and the institutional and administrative aspects of the requirements for EU membership. In fact, the PHARE financial and technical assistance and the CEECs' participation in Community programmes and mechanisms have constituted the aspects of financial and technical cooperation in the pre-accession strategy. The financial and technical assistance of the EU through the PHARE has been designed to support the applicants' efforts to meet the conditions of acceptance of the *acquis communautaire* and to support their ability to take on the obligations of full membership. In this respect, the purpose of the PHARE programmes is also closely connected to the EU's desire to support the applicant countries' efforts to fulfil the political conditions of having stable institutions, guaranteeing democracy and protection for minorities. A number of programmes and some financial assistance have been devoted to strengthening the democratic institutions and the improvement of human rights in the applicant countries, such as the European Democracy Fund, designed to assist the development of human rights and to promote civil society and democratization in the CEECs. This seems to have not only reduced the risks associated with the economic and social instability of the applicant members, but also to have affected even permanent institution building and the explicit encouragement of specific political and legal reforms in these countries.

The Accession Partnership, which is the main instrument of the pre-accession strategy, has furthered the level and effectiveness of EU's support for the CEECs. By taking the needs of each country, the Accession Partnership provided further financial, legal and technical support for the CEECs to help them to meet the criteria for accession. It has reoriented the pre-accession strategy towards short-term and medium-term priorities to be meet by the applicant country. The Accession Partnership has thus become the single programming framework of EU's support for candidate countries.

In conclusion, the instruments of the EU's pre-accession strategy have provided appropriate support for the applicant countries to satisfy the conditions for EU membership. Given that all the CEECs started from a very low level of economic and political development, they have for the most part met the political and economic conditions for EU membership; in fact, they expect to join the EU eventually. In this respect, the comprehensive and appropriate instruments of the EU's pre-accession strategy have not only played an anchoring role in the applicant's efforts to satisfy the conditions for EU membership, but have also provided an opportunity for the EU to influence internal developments in the applicant countries.

Conclusions

This chapter has shown that the EU's enlargement policy has a number of stated objectives:

- Political objective to enhance democracy throughout the continent.
- Security objective to stabilize Europe and prevent any possible conflict.
- Economic objective to create a vast European single market.
- History and identity objectives to create a European identity and reunite the divided Europe.

While it is difficult to rank the importance of these stated objectives of the EU's enlargement policy, they all appear to be fundamental to both EU and all candidates. Therefore, a consistency on the part of the EU in applying its enlargement instruments to all applicants equally appears to be important for the success of the EU's enlargement policy. This is partly because applying a hard line policy approach to the weaker candidate(s) could not only undermine the attainability of the EU's objectives, but also undermine its policy credibility to stimulate candidates' preparatory efforts to comply with criteria for accession. However, it does not suggest that the EU should not apply the principle of conditionality in which all applicants need to fulfil the criteria for accession. In other words, excluding the weaker candidate(s) from the conduct of accession negotiations (not from the enlargement process) until they met the necessary criteria should not be interpreted as a policy of inconsistency on the part of the EU.

As the analysis through the chapter suggests, the EU has developed a gradual and an adaptive enlargement policy, designed to deal with the costs/risks and benefits factors. As far as the perceived benefits of the next enlargement are concerned, economic, security and political interests and benefits constituted the main reason for the EU to launch its current enlargement policy. In other words, the perceived political, security and economic benefits associated with the next enlargement of the EU, provided it is well prepared, seem to be vital for both the EU and the applicant countries. In this respect, considering that all the applicants, including Turkey, share similar economic security and political interests in joining the EU, the inclusion of all applicants in the enlargement process (not in the accession process) appears to be important, not only for the credibility of the EU's stated objective of 'equal treatment', but also for the perceived benefits of overall enlargement policy. That implies that the EU's own economic, social, security and political interests require a similar policy response from the EU to the applicant countries, because the exclusion of any applicant country might jeopardize the declared objectives of EU's enlargement policy, or even the excluded applicant(s) might have adverse political and economical implications for the EU. However, 'equal treatment' policy does not imply the early accession of problematic applicants to the EU, including Turkey. It does not also imply that the EU should place all applicant countries in the same lane and apply precisely the same policy instruments to all applicant countries, but at least every applicant country should be supported and motivated through a clear EU accession strategy.

As regards the costs/risks factors, they concern not only financial implications of the accession of a number of relatively underdeveloped countries for the EU budget, but also their implications for the deepening process in the EU. While the costs/risks concerns of the next enlargement for the EU are important issues and thus they might challenge the enlargement process of the EU, the perceived effects of such costs/risks factors appear to be manageable, owing to the EU's new enlargement strategy. The EU has sought to minimize the perceived costs/risks concerns of the next enlargement through introducing a gradual and an adaptive enlargement strategy towards the CEECs and through introducing substantial reforms in its policies and institutions to make them more flexible and adjustable to the greater diversity promoted by the next enlargement.

Thus, the EU has introduced a detailed set of conditions for EU membership, designed to force the applicant countries to undertake the necessary economic and political reforms outside the EU, so that the cost of accepting them into the EU will be minimized. However, the criteria for EU membership represent general principles rather than standard enlargement norms equally applicable to all applicant countries. In other words, conditions for EU membership seem not have been precisely defined, leaving considerable scope for different interpretations of these conditions. The vagueness and imprecision of these requirements for EU membership can explain why the EU has lacked a norm of behaviour in its enlargement policy, as the EU might apply these conditions more strictly to some applicants than others, with consequent political repercussions. Accordingly, the vagueness of these conditions might be used by the EU, or some of its member states, as a pretext to delay or put back the prospects of membership of some problematic applicants: a particular case would arise if there was an applicant whose accession would pose economic and political risks and costs to the EU, such as Turkey. This implies that vagueness of conditions for membership can constitute a basis for the EU to take a different approach towards some applicants, if necessary.

Moreover, there is some vagueness about the conditionality of the EU's enlargement policy. First, while the EU's conditionality for membership obviously clarifies what an applicant country has to do to fulfil membership criteria before joining the EU, it still remains unclear to what extent the candidate must fulfil the conditions in order to be included in the pre-accession strategy of EU's enlargement policy (inclusion in the pre-accession strategy does not imply an inclusion in the accession negotiations process). This is particularly important for the Turkish case, since the EU has made Turkey's inclusion in the enlargement process conditional on Turkish progress towards fulfilling those criteria. Secondly, while the various economic, political and technical conditions for EU membership may well all be required, it is not clear which criteria for admission is the most important. Thus, it is difficult to rank the importance of the accession criteria. Nevertheless, an observation can be made to identify which criteria really matter by looking at the EU's policy *vis-à-vis* each individual applicant. In this respect, the Turkish case provides a good example to show that political criteria are much more important than the economic criteria. Indeed, as is seen throughout the book, the EU's policy towards Turkey has concentrated more on political issues and political conditionality, and less on economic issues. This is why the costs/benefits analysis cannot itself provide a good enough analytical framework for the purpose of this study.

The pre-accession strategy constitutes the second pillar of the EU's adaptive enlargement policy, aimed at lessening the perceived risks of reversals in the applicant states, associated with political, social and economic instability in these countries. In fact, the pre-accession instruments were designed to support and guide the applicant countries to make their economic and political systems gradually converge towards the EU norm, supported by substantial financial aid. Under the pre-accession strategy for the candidate countries, the EU has provided Accession Partnerships which set out the short term and medium term priorities accorded to each individual candidate. The Accession Partnerships have been systematically upgraded to adjust the priorities and to cover all pre-accession assistance (the PHARE, the ISPA, and the SAPARD). Thus, the pre-accession strategy has provided leverage for the EU to influence political and economic developments in the candidate countries. This is not only because the EU has been in a position to judge the progress which the candidate countries need to make before they fulfil the conditions for EU membership, but also because all the applicant members are eager to join the EU and thus want to satisfy the EU over their efforts to reform.

However, it appears that the EU has been inconsistent in applying its pre-accession instruments to all applicants equally. For example, as will be seen in the analysis throughout the book, particular problems in the CEECs seems to have elicited a positive response from the EU in the shape of a clear strategy for accession on the grounds that economic, political and social reforms in these countries must be supported. However, the EU's treatment for Turkey has lacked this and thus has been inadequate to influence the process of reforms in Turkey, although the issues in Turkey and the CEECs have been very similar. The EU's policy post-Helsinki seems to have been more effective in influencing policy developments in Turkey. Nevertheless, while the Helsinki Summit declared Turkey to be a candidate for EU membership and agreed to treat Turkey on the same basis as other candidate states, its policy has still lacked adequate policy instruments to prepare Turkey for EU membership. To be explicit: the principle contention of this book is that the EU has lacked standard enlargement norms equally applicable to all applicant countries.

The proposed characterization of the EU's enlargement norm developed in this chapter will provide a comparative framework to examine this hypothesis. Thus, the remaining chapters will analyze the EU's enlargement policy *vis-à-vis* Turkey by focusing on particular issues (or obstacles) to Turkey's membership of the EU from the comparative perspective, with a view to addressing the following questions.

- Has Turkey been treated differently from other applicant members?
- To what extent has the EU's treatment of Turkey been compatible not only with the EU's enlargement motivations but also the policy objectives of Turkey with regard to enlargement?
- To what extent have the EU's policy instruments towards Turkey been adequate to prepare Turkey for EU membership, and why has the EU been reluctant to apply the same enlargement policy instruments and accession commitment to Turkey as it has applied to the CEECs?
- Why has the EU been less effective in influencing the domestic policy choices and encouraging specific political and legal reforms in Turkey than in the other countries?

Notes

1   The Commission estimated that the first six new members, assuming they join in 2002, would receive 53.8 billion ECU between 2002 and 2006. For this, see European Commission (1997) 'Agenda 2000: For Stronger and Wider Union' COM (97) final, *Bulletin of the European Union*, Supplement 5/9, CEEC Brussels, pp. 9–10.

2   This gradual continuation of reforms begun in 1992 has not only been related to the next enlargement of the EU, but there have also been an external pressures on the EU to liberalize its CAP by making further reductions in price support through the Uruguay Round.

3   For a detailed analysis about the economic programme of Turkey, see *Financial Times*, 'Survey on Turkey', 20 November 2000.

4   For a detailed analysis about the flexible and differentiated integration, see *Flexible Integration towards a More Effective and Democratic Europe* (1995), Center for Economic Policy Research, London, pp. 51–77.

5   For instance, according to the Amsterdam Treaty, EU will 'avail itself of the WEU', and the WEU 'will elaborate and implement' decisions and actions of the EU. As a result, it appears that the WEU is legally subordinated to EU.

6   For the CEECs, accession to the EU would give them grounds for claiming that they were part of European identity and had returned to their original identity, Europe, as they deemed that Communism had forcibly repressed their European identity during the Cold War era. For Turkey, joining the EU is the confirmation of its European identity.

7   For example, the leaders of the European Christian Democrat Parties, including the German Chancellor, Prime Ministers of Spain, Italy and Belgium, declared that the European Union was a civilization project, based upon Christian tradition and values that Turkey does not belong to, cited in the *Economist*, 5 March 1997. Indeed, it is only in connection with Turkey that cultural issue is mentioned as a problematic factor in the context of the enlargement debate, as the Dutch Foreign Minister, Hans Van Mierlo, stated that 'there is a problem of a big Muslim State. Do we want it in Europe', cited in Wood, Pia Christina (1999), 'Europe and Turkey: A Relationship under Fire', *The Mediterranean Quarterly*, winter, No. 10.

8   The 1995 enlargement of the EU to include Austria, Finland and Sweden was different from the previous Mediterranean enlargements in the sense that they had a very short transition period to adopt the EU's *acquis*.

9   For more details on the new financial instruments of the EU for the enlargement, see European Commission (1997b), Agenda 2000.

Chapter 3

The EU-Turkey Association: A Flawed Instrument?

Introduction

The EU-Turkey Association, which is the second association agreement of the EU, was originally intended to pave the way for EU membership through successive stages. It sought to provide a pre-preparatory stage for Turkey to ready itself for EU membership through a systematic transition by providing closer economic and political cooperation. Nevertheless, the EU-Turkey Association has failed to achieve the declared political and economic objective of the agreement. This is partly because of Turkey's failure to fulfil her obligations arising from the Agreement by undertaking the necessary economic and political reforms to bringing its economic and political system to converge with that of the EU.

However, the failure of the Association has been due mainly to the EU's unwillingness to upgrade the instruments of the Agreement in accordance with the developments in European integration. In other words, although the EU realized that the instruments of the Association Agreement had been inadequate and had constituted an inappropriate framework for the declared political objective of the Agreement, it has been reluctant to upgrade them with a view to promoting the EU membership of Turkey; rather it has made an effort to reactivate it as a part of its containment policy, designed to strengthen EU-Turkey relations, while delaying the possibility of actual Turkish membership for the foreseeable future. Even the EU's policy instruments after the Helsinki Summit with the Accession Partnership appear to be limited to reorient the EU-Turkey Association towards full membership. All the instruments available under the Accession Partnership are designed to contribute to Turkey's closer relationship with the EU rather than being oriented towards membership of the EU. This explains why the instruments of the EU-Turkey Association have been inadequate to engineer a progressive kind of integration of Turkey into the EU in the post-Maastricht European Union and even before.

The objective of this chapter is to assess the association politics of the EU in general and the EU-Turkey Association in particular. This is important for the purpose of the book because: first, it will provide a brief historical perspective of EU-Turkey relations showing the objectives, instruments and implementation of the EU-Turkey Association. Second, it will set up some norms for comparison between different versions of the EU's association policy, in particular its policy towards the CEECs and towards Turkey.

This chapter will characterize the EU's association policy for the European states by identifying the political and economic motives behind its association politics. In this respect, specific reference will be made to the EU's new association policy for the CEECs. This analysis will allow a comparison of the instruments of the Europe Agreements and Ankara Agreement and thus in turn will provide some grounds for assessing whether the EU's association policy towards Turkey has been different from that of its association policy for the CEECs. Consideration will then be given to the contents and characteristics of the EU-Turkey Association by looking at both Turkey's and the EU's motivations for establishing the Ankara Agreement (the AA) and the instruments and objectives of the EU-Turkey Association. Apart from this, the chapter will look at the implementation of the AA up to Turkey's membership application in 1987 and explore the reasons behind the failure to implement the Agreement. Then, it will consider the motives behind Turkey's early application for EU membership, as an alternative to reactivating the AA. Also, it will examine the EU's effort to improve the EU-Turkey Association instruments as part of its containment policy for Turkey, as an alternative to Turkey's immediate membership challenge. Finally, the chapter will evaluate the Helsinki process in EU-Turkey relations. In this respect, the EU's revised containment policy instruments under Accession Partnership Document will be analyzed to see whether they have been sufficient in the European post-Maastricht context to facilitate a progressive kind of integration leading to Turkey's EU membership.

The Characteristics of the EU's Association Policy: Motivations, Interests and Instruments of the EU's Association Policy

Motivations and Interests

For both the EU and the applicant countries, economic, political and security considerations have played an important part in establishing association links. For the EU, security and political considerations are often considered to be more important than economic considerations in concluding association agreements with European states. Indeed, the security considerations of the EU played an important part in its original association agreements with Greece and Turkey, subsequently extended to Cyprus and Malta during the Cold War. A similar argument holds true for the EU's association policy *vis-à-vis* the CEECs, as new political, societal and environmental security challenges to the EU from the CEECs began to predominate and compel the EU to create Europe Agreements with these countries. The EU's desire to extend its political influence through the establishment of close relations with the other European countries seems to have been another important political element in motivating its association policy. It is particularly related to the EU's aim to effect further democratization processes in the associate countries. This has been a particular case for the Europe Agreements with the CEECs, as the EU has intended to anchor the CEECs in a democratic Europe by reinforcing the principles of democracy and human rights in these countries through the association links. To illustrate, Article 6 of the Europe Agreement with Romania signifies the importance of human rights and the principles of democracy in the EU's association policy, noting that 'respect for democratic principles and human rights inspire the domestic and external policies of the Parties and constitute essential elements of the present association' (European Commission, 1994a). Political and security considerations have been the main characteristics of the EU's new association policy towards the CEECs, designed to prepare them for full membership not only economically but also politically as a means of closer and continuing institutional political links with the Union.

Although the EU's economic interest in its association policy towards the associate states seems to have been less important than the security and political considerations, it constitutes an important aspect of the EU's association policy, since it provides an increased economic interaction through the creation of trade, with more trading opportunities in goods and investment for the EU members.

As far as the applicant countries are concerned, they were specifically interested in four benefits from their association with the EU. Firstly, most associate members consider the association links with the EU as a preparatory stage implying a further agreement which might lead to EU membership. Secondly, the association agreement is considered a useful mechanism for the applicant countries to pursue their foreign policy objectives. For instance, Turkey regarded it as an important mechanism for achieving her objective of being recognized as a European state. This has also been the case for the CEECs. Thirdly, the association agreements of the EU provide an important input for internal political development in the associate countries; they need a strong anchor in their political transformation and in their process of democratization. The last benefit concerned the EU as a source of funds, financial and technical assistance, trade concessions and the perceived foreign direct investment, which are all necessary for their economic development.

The Characteristics of the EU's Association Agreements

The EU has offered three forms of association framework for European countries:

- The original association framework of the EU, based on 'ad hoc' forms of cooperation and made available on a country-by-country basis.
- Association agreements with the EFTA countries in which economic factors rather than political motives and interests were the determinant factors behind the agreements. These agreements envisaged the participation of the EFTA states in the European Economic Area (the EEA).
- The new generation of EU association agreements for the CEECs, namely, the Europe Agreements, designed to respond to the needs of the CEECs in the 1990s (Croft, and Redmond, 1999, pp. 64–65).

The main characteristic of the association agreements concluded with the European states is that they all – either initially or eventually – came to form a pre-preparatory stage in the path to EU membership. Although the Association Agreements with Cyprus, Malta, the EFTA states and the Europe Agreements with the CEECs were initially designed for the purpose of free trade between the parties through eliminating the custom tariffs affecting the trade between the parties – the so called European Economic Area – they have all been upgraded in accordance with the needs of these countries in their preparation for EU membership. It is quite clear that any participant in the EEA is welcome to join the EU as a full member whenever they wish. Hence, the EU's association policy with the European countries could in principle be considered a form of pre-preparatory stage of the membership process through a systematic transition as a means of providing closer economic and political cooperation.

Secondly, all association agreements of the EU create equivalent rights, obligations, common actions and special procedures binding the parties in order to pursue a progressive integration between the associate members and the EU. In fact, as the first step, all the association agreements were intended to establish a free trade, or customs union with the EU by progressively reducing trade barriers and harmonizing the legislation in relation to the operation of the economy. However, the EU's association policy has been protective in character and all associate members have had to accept exclusions from some part of the EU's common policy. Criticism has been directed against the restrictions of all the association agreements, including Europe Agreements, imposed on trading in sensitive products, namely, agriculture, textiles, steel and iron, all of which account for a significant part of the associated members' exports to the EU.

Thirdly, associate countries are expected to participate and share in the objectives of the Union. The political doctrine of the association policy of the EU with the European states requires that the associate countries which desire to join the EU should commit themselves to the values and political objectives of the Union and participate in certain of the objectives of the EU.

Finally, as compared to other trade and cooperation agreements of the EU, association agreements provide a high level of institutional structures and structured relationships and the highest level of political dialogue. Therefore, the establishment of an association agreement provides for the associate members a closer and more privileged relationship with the EU.

However, it should be noted that the contents and instruments of the EU's association agreements with the European countries are similar, but not identical. For example, the contents and instruments of the Ankara Agreement are very similar to those of the Athens agreement of Greece. Both agreements envisaged the creation of a customs union with a view to eventual membership of the EU. The EU's association agreements with Cyprus and Malta are identical to one another, designed to eliminate the customs tariffs affecting the trade between the parties with a view to the progressive creation of a customs union. However, these agreements do not contain any reference to eventual membership of the EU; hence, they are less comprehensive than those with Turkey and Greece. As far as the EU's new form of association agreements with the CEECs is concerned, the instruments and contents of the Europe Agreements formed a special association framework; they are even more comprehensive than the EU's original association agreements with Greece, Turkey, Malta and Cyprus. In fact, although the EU's new association policy towards the CEECs presents similar characteristics to those of its earlier form of associations, the former differs from the latter in the sense that they extended beyond the traditional association agreements by adding provisions regarding extensive political and cultural dialogue and cooperation, with the aim of deepening cooperation in areas of common interest, particularly with regard to security and democratization. In addition, they contain more comprehensive and detailed provisions concerning the harmonization and coordination in economic and related policies with the EU. As some scholars describe them: 'these in a sense amounted to reinvention of the earlier form of association which had become discredited' (Croft and Redmond, 1999, p. 66). The objectives of Europe Agreements are progressively to establish free trade in industrial goods over a ten-year period, to reduce trade barriers such as tariffs and quantitative restrictions with the exception of such sensitive products as iron, steel, coal, and textiles and to harmonize the laws in relation to operation of the economy (Gower, 1995). Furthermore, the Europe Agreements have been strengthened through structured dialogue, the EU's extensive financial and technical assistance for the CEECs and pre-accession strategy.

Has the Association Policy of the EU Worked?

One can easily assume that the objectives of the association agreements can only be attained if the concerned parties fulfil their obligations and if instruments of the associations are upgraded in accordance with developments within the EU. However, the experience of the EU's association policy suggests that some association agreements have been problematic and difficult to implement in practice. For example, although the contents and the instruments of the EU's association agreements with Greece and Turkey were intended to serve as a useful preparatory phase for EU membership, their success in doing so was not only determined by the full implementation of reciprocal rights and obligations by the concerned parties, but also the political will of the EU. As will be analyzed throughout the following section, the EU-Turkey Association has failed to serve as a useful preparatory phase for Turkey's accession to the EU, because neither the EU nor Turkey have been able to fulfil their obligations, and also the EU has been reluctant to upgrade the instruments of the Association Agreement. As far as the Greek case was concerned, the Athens Agreement had not worked as it was envisaged, either. In fact, it was the main reason why Greece applied for membership before the completion of the final stage of the Athens Agreement, as an alternative to reactivating the Association Agreement, and why the EU accepted her application. Both parties realized that the Association Agreement was unsatisfactory and constituted an inappropriate framework for the relationship (Redmond, 1994, p. 8).

Having realized the shortcomings in its original association policy, the EU has made a considerable effort to develop Europe Agreements into a useful preparatory phase for further agreement leading to accession. Indeed, while the EU initially was careful not to set up any timetable or make a direct reference to the prospects for the CEECs of EU membership in the original Europe Agreements with these countries, it changed its policy by declaring that 'the associated countries in Central and Eastern Europe that so desire shall become members of the European Union' (European Council, 1993). This implied that accession to the EU would be possible as soon as an associated country was able to assume the obligations of membership by satisfying the membership requirements of the EU. Besides, the EU promised the CEECs that it would help to achieve this objective. Soon after this declaration, the EU initiated a pre-accession strategy to prepare these countries for EU membership at the Essen European Council in 1994. This was because the EU realized that the Europe Agreements were unsatisfactory and constituted an inappropriate framework for relations with the CEECs, prompting the EU to initiate a pre-accession strategy for the CEECs with considerable financial and technical aid. Furthermore, the EU strengthened the Europe Agreement and the pre-accession strategy by attaching Accession Partnership and the reinforcement of pre-accession aid to them. All this indicates that the EU has made considerable effort to upgrade the instruments of the Europe Agreement, by taking the needs of the CEECs into account so that Europe Agreements have been able to prepare them for a further agreement leading to accession.

To conclude, the original association agreements of the EU have never worked and thus have failed to achieve their declared objectives.[1] This is because firstly, the concerned parties could not fulfil their obligations. Secondly, the success of the association was bound by the political will of the EU and its determination to reactivate the association by taking the needs of the associate countries into account. This is particularly important because the EU has been under systematic transformation with the aim of establishing an economic, monetary and political union. Hence, the instruments of its association policy need to be changed, or upgraded in accordance with such developments within the EU, so that the associated members could benefit and prepare themselves for EU membership, as has been the case for the Europe Agreements with the CEECs.

Another conclusion to be drawn from the above analysis is that the EU could use association agreements as the framework for its containment policy for certain countries about which the EU has reservations to do with their prospects for EU membership (Redmond, 1994). In fact, the EU could easily criticize an associate country on the grounds of its failure to fulfil its obligations arising from the association agreement, and thus would justify its unwillingness to upgrade the instruments of the association agreement.

This has been the case for the EU-Turkey Association: the EU has used the Ankara Agreement as the framework for its containment policy, not for Turkey's accession to the EU. In fact, the EU has been reluctant to upgrade the instruments of the EU-Turkey Association, by taking the needs of Turkey into account, which explains why the EU-Turkey Association has been inadequate in the European context post-Maastricht to set in motion a progressive kind of integration with a view to Turkey's EU membership. This is a key argument supporting the main argument of the book that Turkey has been treated less generously than other applicants have, as far as EU membership is concerned.

The Characterization of the EU's Association Policy towards Turkey

This section of the chapter will assess the Association Agreement aspect of the EU-Turkey relations by looking at:

- Both Turkey's and the EU's motivation for establishing the agreement.
- The instruments and objectives of the EU-Turkey Association.

The EU's and Turkey's Motivation for Establishing the Association Agreement

Like all other association agreements, political, security and economic interests played an important part in both Turkey's and the EU's motivation for establishing agreement with the EU, although the first two factors were more important than the economic one. For Turkey, two traditional concerns, Westernization and the Greek factor, have always preoccupied Turkish policy-makers. Turkey regarded the association link with the EU as an important asset for its foreign policy objective of Westernization. In this respect, Turkey considered being a member of all the European institutions as the confirmation of its European identity. As a result, she applied to join all the European political, military and economic organizations: Turkey became a member of the Council of Europe and the OECD, signed the European Convention on Human Rights and also joined NATO. Finally, becoming a member of the EU seemed to Turkey to be a logical consequence of its modernization and Westernization policies. Therefore, from the very beginning of the creation of the EU, Turkey has showed a keen interest in becoming integrated with Europe. For instance, in 1957, a few months after signing the Treaty of Rome, the newly elected Turkish Government devoted an important part of its foreign policy objectives to the EU and underlined the political will of Turkey to take part in European integration.

For Turkey, the Association Agreement, providing an important institutional, economic and political link, was seen as a vital step towards the realization of Turkey's ambition to become an integral part of Europe. A senior Turkish diplomat, Teyfik Saracoglu, who negotiated Turkey's application for associate membership, confirmed this argument by stating that 'the main concern of Turkey was not to be excluded from the European integration process which might eventually lead to political union' (cited in Aybak, 1995, p. 84). Due to the objective of Europeanization, which required closer relations with the EU, Turkey applied for associate membership of the EEC in 1959, shortly after the Treaty of Rome in 1957. The EU accepted Turkey's application and signed the Ankara Agreement with Turkey. Thus, the EU with this Agreement recognized the Europeanization objective of the Turkish Republic.

The Greek factor constituted an important political motive behind the Turkish application to the EU as an associate member; this was, to a large extent, connected to consciousness of long standing hostile relations with Greece. Indeed, Turkey's application to the EC was mainly a response to a similar application made by Greece. As Tsakaloyannis puts it, 'had it not been for Greece's application, it would have taken Turkey much longer to decide what kind of relationship to establish with the six' (Tsakaloyannis, 1980, p. 43). The timing of the Turkish application for associate membership of the EU was to do with Turkey's traditional concern about Greek diplomacy, because Turkey was full of anxiety that Greece would use its association tie with the EU against Turkey, in order to gain more concessions with regard to its bilateral disputes with Turkey. The tradition of Turkish foreign policy required that Turkey had to be represented on each and every platform where Greece was represented, to prevent it from using the political and economic leverage resulting from its new relationship with Europe against Turkey (Birand, 1978, p. 52). To be fair, such anxiety of Turkey over Greece was not totally groundless:

for instance, the Greek Prime Minister, talking about the way in which Greek membership of the EU would affect Greece's relations with Turkey over the issues between the two countries, stated:

> It is certain that our membership of the Community will place our country in a favourable position to face the problems which concern us, such as Cyprus and our relationship with Turkey (cited in Tsakaloyannis, 1983, p. 126).

The security consideration was another reason behind the Turkish application for associate membership of the EU. During the Cold War era, Turkey's foreign policy formulations were, to a large extent, shaped by fear of the Communist threat from the Soviet Union. Thus, Turkey saw EU membership as another means of attaching totally to the emerging Western alliance, although the EU had no institutionalized security policy at that time; it did not, therefore, provide a genuine security guarantee for its members. In reality, the competence of the EU was at the time little more than economic in nature, and could only provide an opportunity for Turkey to attach herself to her Western alliance more firmly through institutionalizing economic ties and political relations.

Apart from these political and security considerations, there were economic factors that prompted the Turkish application to the EU. These economic interests included the benefits of a preferential EU market for her exports and the need of foreign economic aid, as well as the expectation of direct capital investment from the members of the EU (Muftuler, 1992, p. 77). Indeed, Turkey urgently needed foreign currency to implement its economic development programme. Therefore, supplementing its financial aid from the EU, through the preferential EU market for Turkish agricultural products, such as figs, tobacco and dried grapes, would be a sensible way of obtaining foreign currency (Aybak, 1995, p. 84). Turkey considered the associate link with EU as a crucial economic integrative mechanism that would accelerate her economic development (Baysan, 1984, pp. 78–92). It was believed that an Association Agreement with the EU would provide economic benefits for Turkey and would reduce the economic disparities between Turkey and the EU. In addition, the prospect of free movement of workers was also an economic motive behind the Turkish application, because she saw this as a means, not only of reducing her huge unemployment level, but also of gaining foreign exchange in the form of guest worker remittances (Kramer, 1988, p. 337).

On the European Union side, security and political considerations were often considered to be more important than economic ones in establishing an Association Agreement with Turkey. Indeed, security considerations became the most important in that Turkey was regarded as the Southern pillar of NATO. Hence, Turkey's ties with the EU were important for Western European security as Turkey had a role to play not only as a barrier against Soviet expansion towards Southern Europe, but also as a bridge between Europe and the Middle East (Kramer, 1988, p. 339). In other words, the EU considered that close links with Turkey were necessary for European security arrangements and would help to achieve the political and strategic aims of strengthening NATO's southern flank by stabilizing Turkey's internal economic and social situation. Ensuring the economic stability of Turkey by supporting her economic development and improving the standard of living was an essential prerequisite for the preservation of its political stability.

Furthermore, the EU's effort to pursue a policy of balance *vis-à-vis* Turkey and Greece was also related to the security considerations of the EU's policy towards Turkey. After concluding the Association Agreement with Greece, the EU decided to respond positively to the Turkish application for associate membership of the EU. This was because the EU was being very careful to calculate the delicate balance between Turkey and Greece. Although the Commission was reluctant to offer a similar association agreement for Turkey on the grounds that the state of the Turkish economy was not appropriate for an associate relationship of a reciprocal kind on the basis of a customs union, the Council was aware of the sensitivity of the balance between Turkey and Greece and the insistence of Turkey on the establishment of an identical association pattern to that of Greece (Aybak, 1995, p. 94). The President of the European Council at the time of the Turkish application for associate membership, Emilio Colombo, affirmed the Greek factor, by stating that:

> It was of the utmost importance to the EC at that time that Greece and Turkey should have been treated equally because of their position in south-eastern Europe *vis-à-vis* the Soviet Union (cited in Birand, 1987, p. 79).

This stance of the EU reflects Turkey's geo-political importance for the EU as a security asset in the circumstances of the Cold War. Another factor behind the EU's decision to have an association agreement with Turkey was related to the EU's desire to extend its influence through the establishment of close relations with the countries of Europe. Indeed, the first generation of the association policy of the EU was the reflection of 'the EU's desire to win friends' in its formative years when it was uncertain about what direction the EU would take in future (Redmond, 1994, p. 8). Therefore, the EU's first generation association policy seemed to encourage European countries which were not yet willing, or not able, to join the EU, as a means of offering them an associate membership which might eventually lead to EU membership (Aybak, 1995, p. 90). Consequently, Turkey, as one of the first countries which sought associate membership of the EU, took advantage the above-mentioned objective of the EU. In addition, after de Gaulle's rejection of the UK's membership application, the EU tended to use the Turkish application to give an impression that the EU was an 'open Community' rather than 'closed shop' (Bourguignon, 1990, p. 52).

The EU's economic interest in its association policy with Turkey was clearly less important than its security and political interests. Given the backwardness of the Turkish economy, Turkey had a relatively unimportant position at that time in the EU's external economic relations, in terms not only of trade relations, but also of foreign investments (Kramer, 1987, p. 338). The superiority of political and security considerations over economic ones was attested by Commissioner Jean Rey, who stated that:

> Greek and Turkish association treaties entail sacrifices from those Community states producing the same things, but they have accepted this interference with the equilibrium of the Community structure in view of the political importance of such association links in the process of European integration (cited in Aybak, 1995, p. 96).

Finally, Turkey applied for associate membership in 1959. The negotiations of the Association Agreement took nearly three years, which indicated that the Turkish application was a problematic one. The reasons that it took so long were: firstly, the military intervention in Turkish domestic politics on 27 May 1960, which created a negative atmosphere as regards the suitability of Turkey as an associate member. Secondly, the different views on the contents of the agreement: while Turkey asked for the inclusion of a customs union clause in the Association Agreement with an automatic transition after a short preparation period, and a deadline for full membership, the EU was reluctant to comply with Turkey's demand on the grounds of the incompatibility of the Turkish economy with that of the EU.[2]

Therefore, the EU intended to offer only a cooperation agreement for Turkey, with agricultural trade concessions and financial assistance. However, Turkish policy-makers were aware of Turkey's strategic importance for the EU and thus used it as a bargaining chip to obtain an identical association agreement with that of the Athens Agreement of Greece.[3] Finally, the Association Agreement of Ankara was signed by the parties in September 1963 and ratified by Turkey and the member states, in accordance with the procedure laid down in Article 238 of the EEC Treaty. According to the Ankara Agreement, the customs union would be established in stages, and in addition, Turkey succeeded in gaining a written promise giving her the prospect of full membership, along with financial aid and some unilateral concessions for her agricultural products.

In conclusion, the above analysis generates some important points, which have implications for the argument of the book. Firstly, establishing the EU-Turkey Association Agreement was not based so much on both parties having mutual economic interests and motives, but rather on Turkey's desire to use the EU as a helpful mechanism in its domestic politics and foreign policy objectives. Given that the competence of the EU was mostly economic in nature, one may infer that Turkey's expectation in this respect was not realistic. Secondly, although the EU had reason to be reluctant to establish an Association Agreement with Turkey, it was bound to respond to Turkey's request for the sake of security. There are also important implications here for the argument of the book, because the security factor could provide some explanation why the EU has shown reluctance to upgrade the instruments of the Agreement since Turkey's security importance has been subject to modification since the Cold War ended.

The Objectives and Instruments of the Ankara Agreement

At a superficial level, the Agreement provided Turkey with an association structure with the anticipation of full membership; indeed, the content of the Ankara Agreement covered not only trade matters but also certain political objectives of the Union.[4] More specifically, it appeared to serve as a useful preparatory stage for a future agreement that would lead to accession. As Lasok puts it, 'the objective of the Ankara Agreement is far more ambitious because, in addition to the customs union, it envisages several other areas of economic co-operation and serves as a preparatory stage to the membership of the Community' (1993, p. 27).

The preamble of the Ankara Agreement recognized the ultimate political objective of the Agreement; it reads, 'the support given by the EC to the efforts of the Turkish people to improve their standards of living will facilitate the accession of Turkey to the Community at a later date' (Ankara Agreement, 1964). Article 28 of the Ankara Agreement makes it clearer:

As soon as the operation of this Agreement has advanced far enough to justify envisaging full acceptance by Turkey of the obligations arising out of the Treaty establishing the Community, the contracting parties shall examine the possibility of the accession of Turkey to the Community (Ankara Agreement, 1964).

However, this should not be interpreted as an automatic transition from associate member to the status of full member; such a progression or transition is dependent on concrete conditions being achieved and on the political decision of the contracting partners. In fact, Article 28 of the Agreement provides a prospect of membership or examination of the possibility of accession, rather than a guarantee of admission, even if the concrete conditions of association were achieved (Lasok, 1993, p. 37).

To achieve this declared political objective, the Ankara Agreement envisaged a progressive integration through the establishment of a customs union serving as the final stage of integration; hence, the customs union was considered the most important instrumental 'integrative task, *a sine qua non* of the association process' (Aybak, 1995, p. 102). This progressive and gradual process of integration would be achieved in three stages: a preparatory stage, a transitional stage and a final stage (Article 2(3), Ankara Agreement). During the preparatory stage, Turkey, with the aid of the EU, was to strengthen its economy so as to enable it to fulfil the obligations which would devolve upon it during the transitional and final stage (Article 3(1), Ankara Agreement). The preparatory stage, which would last five years, was designed to strengthen Turkey's economy and involved the introduction of tariff quotas for Turkish agricultural products under the Preferential Tariff Quotas, and of 175 million ECU in loans to assist Turkish economic development under the Financial Protocol (Article 2, Financial protocol). During the transition period, the EU and Turkey would progressively establish a customs union, and align their economic policies more closely by abolishing all customs duties on imports and exports and of charges having an equivalent effect, quantitative restrictions and the adoption of the common customs tariff of the EU covering all goods in trade (Article 10, Ankara Agreement). In addition, the transitional stage covered the gradual integration of specific sectors, notably the free movement of labour and freedom of settlement for professions and services (Articles 12–14, Ankara Agreement). It also foresaw Turkey's observance of EU rules on competition, taxation, the approximation of laws, the balance of payments, the coordination of economic policies, the rate of exchange and capital transactions for commercial purposes (Articles 14–20, Ankara Agreement).

The Additional Protocol laid down the details of both parties' commitment to timetables for tariff reductions by Turkey and trade liberalization.[5] The Additional Protocol envisaged asymmetric trade liberalization: while the EU was obliged to abolish all customs duties and, with equivalent effect on imports from Turkey in industrial products immediately on its entry in 1973 (except for sensitive products, such as textiles, agricultural and oil products and steel), Turkey could implement its reductions in stages.[6] Although it was asymmetric in character, criticism can be directed against the restrictions that the EU had imposed on the trade in sensitive products – an area in which Turkey had a comparative advantage. These accounted for almost two-thirds of the Turkish exports to the EU. In fact, as will be seen in the next section, the benefit of the Association Agreement was undermined by safeguard clauses, the exclusions of sensitive products from trade and the effective erosion of similar concessions that were given to non-associates under the EU's GSP and Mediterranean policy. The Additional Protocol of 1971 also envisaged a gradual introduction of the free movement of workers by 1986 and immediate complete equality of treatment by the EU members to Turkish workers and safeguards for their social security benefits (Article 40, The Additional Protocol, 1971). In addition, the Protocol declared the gradual abolition of restrictions on the freedom of establishment and services (Article 41). Furthermore, the agricultural products were in principle included in the Agreement, but Turkey had to align her agricultural policy with that of the EU (Articles 31–35, The Additional Protocol, 1971).

As far as the institutional structure of the EU-Turkey Association is concerned, it provides a high level of structured relationship and the highest level of political dialogue, aimed at strengthening the necessary cooperation and promoting a closer and privileged relationship between the parties (at least in theory). Such high-level institutional structures of the Agreement distinguish it from the mere cooperation and trade agreements of the EU with third parties. The main institution of the EU-Turkey Association is the Association Council. Its powers include the periodical review of the functioning of the Association, settlement of disputes in relation to the application or interpretation of provisions in the Agreement and the taking of appropriate steps to promote and to strengthen the necessary cooperation and contact with the institutions of the EU.[7] Basically, the Association Council is the main institution, which allows the transfer of the provision of Agreement to a legal obligation; hence, the progressive development of EU-Turkey relations and the implementation of the Association Agreement is in the hands of the Council.

The other important institution is the Joint Parliamentary Committee that provides a link for parliamentary cooperation, thereby helping to ensure democratic accountability for relationships. The JPC is intended to contribute, through dialogue and debate, to better understanding between Turkey and the European Union in the area of politics. Since the late 1980s the European Parliament has taken a decisive role in the EU's external relations, therefore, Turkey cannot ignore its opinion and requests. For example, the EP has become a decisive actor in EU-Turkey relations. It has expressed its views in the form of reports or resolutions and examined the annual report of the Council of Association with recommendations concerning the implementation of Association Agreement. In fact, it has managed to block the implementation of the Financial Protocol on the grounds of violations of human rights and disputes with Greece over Cyprus and Aegean Sea issues.

In conclusion, the objectives and instruments of the Ankara Agreement and the Additional Protocol seem to have included all aspects of the EU's objectives and its policies. Thus, the instruments of the Association Agreement arguably seemed to be adequate to serve as a useful preparatory stage for the further integration of Turkey into the EU, leading to accession in the context of pre-Maastricht Europe. In other words, it was not only an association for the purpose of Turkish economic development, but as a pre-accession association aimed at facilitating Turkey's preparation for the EU. Indeed, the final stage of the Ankara Agreement envisaged the formation of a customs union and closer coordination of the economic policies between the EU and Turkey; given these, the contracting parties would examine the possibility of the accession of Turkey to the EU. Therefore, the EU-Turkish Association was supposed to be a preliminary to the eventual accession of Turkey to the EU.

However, as previous experiences of the EU's association policy suggest, the objectives of the association can only be attained by the implementation of their instruments. On this account, the implementation of the Ankara Agreement can be determined not only by the concerned parties' capacity to assume obligations entailed by the Agreement, but also their political will to proceed and change it in accordance with the developments within the EU. Therefore, the rest of the chapter will assess the extent to which the parties have achieved the objectives of the Ankara Agreement.

The Implementation of the Association Agreement up to Turkey's Membership Application of 1987

In the preparatory stage, Turkey was under no obligation either to reduce its tariff on imports originating from the EU or to adjust its external tariffs with those of the common customs tariff of the EU (Ugur, 1995, p. 79). Turkey had contractual rights to obtain aid from the EU, but the EU had reciprocal rights to control use of the financial aid for the objectives of the Agreement (Lasok, 1993, p. 28). The preparatory stage proceeded smoothly. During this period, members of the EU countries reduced customs duties on Turkey's exports. As a consequence, Turkey's trade with the EU increased. In addition, Turkey received a credit from the EU for the purpose of economic development. Moreover, there was a large increase in the number of Turkish workers in the EU countries, which constituted one of the main sources of Turkey's foreign currency reserves.

These positive effects of the preparatory stage on the Turkish economy encouraged the Turkish Government to continue with the next stage. The Turkish Government believed that a greater opening of the EU market to exports of Turkish agricultural and textile products, and securing the free movement of Turkish workers with new financial aid would accelerate the development of the Turkish economy. Political motives also played an important role in Turkey's early application to begin the transitional stage. Firstly, Turkey expected better political and economic concessions from the EU following the military take-over in Greece. At the time, Turkey considered that the economic imbalance between the Ankara Agreement and the Athens Agreement with the EU could be restored, as the Athens Agreement foresaw the establishment of a customs union beginning with a transitional stage, since it did not contain a preparatory stage. In addition, closer links with the EU were also considered a necessary policy choice to obtain diplomatic support from the EU members in the Cyprus crisis, as a counterbalance against the USA diplomacy over the Cyprus issue (Bourguignon, 1990, p. 53).

Secondly, developments in external relations of the EU in the late 1960s were also the driving force behind Turkey's request to start the transition stage of the Association Agreement. The EU was becoming the centre of attention; the United Kingdom, Denmark and Norway had applied for EU membership, it might therefore have been easier for Turkey to gain some concessions from the EU before the first enlargement. Furthermore, the emergence of the EU's Mediterranean Policy, based upon trade and cooperation agreements with financial aid and preferential treatment to the countries in the region, was one of the main reasons behind the decision of Turkey's early application to begin the transitional stage. Turkey was anxious about concessions given by the EU to these countries, which had harmed Turkish exports to the EU. As a result, Turkish policy-makers believed that an early start to the transitional stage would be beneficial not only politically but also economically for Turkey and thus applied to the EU to start the transitional stage two years earlier than had been planned.

However, the economic structure of Turkey was not appropriate for the transitional stage of the Agreement. In fact, Turkey's economy was not only strongly protected by import substitution instruments, but also based heavily upon state involvement. Consequently, it was not ready to enter the transitional stage of the Association Agrecment, as the latter required reciprocal obligations and liberal economic policies. But, Turkey ignored the incompatibility of the Turkish economy with that of the EU in the belief that early application was necessary in the country's political interests. This indicated that the driving force behind the early Turkish request to start the transitional stage was not economic, but political,[8] although the transitional stage foresaw purely economic integration between the parties through the liberalization of trade. Basically, it seemed that Turkey was unrealistic in trying to meet the contractual obligations arising from the transitional stage of the Ankara Agreement.

For its part, the EU was initially not enthusiastic about Turkey's request to negotiate the transitional stage, on the grounds that the Turkish economy was not ready for a reciprocal kind of relationship. Yet, the EU was bound to lose its reluctance and to take a positive view of Turkey's request, for reasons of security (Ilkin, 1990, p. 40). Because of the increasing instability of the Mediterranean basin, due to the Arab-Israeli dispute and the military regime in Greece, the EU came to the reluctant conclusion that the political stability of Turkey had to be supported and encouraged as a means of supporting its economic development through further economic aid and preferential treatment for Turkish exports to the EU. In addition, the EU assumed that a negative answer to the Turkish request would have held back the process of Westernization in the country. Finally the negotiations, which began in 1968, were concluded with the signing of the Additional Protocol on 23 December 1970 and came into force in January 1973. The Additional Protocol modified the Ankara Agreement and regulated the transitional stage, aimed at the eventual establishment of a customs union by 1995 for the free circulation of goods, persons, services and capital between Turkey and the EU.

Through the transitional stage of the Ankara Agreement under the Additional Protocol, Turkey and the EU were under mutual and balanced obligations to establish progressively a customs union (Article 4, the Additional Protocol, 1971). In other words, both parties were under obligation to remove customs duties and charges having an equivalent effect, as well as eliminating quantitative restrictions and measures having equivalent effects in trade between the parties. In this respect, the EU's obligations were to abolish customs duties and charges and all quantitative restrictions on imports from Turkey (Articles 9 and 24, The Additional Protocol). However, some exceptions were made: the EU retained the right to charge import duties on some oil products above a fixed quota, and to implement a phased reduction of duties on imports of particular textile products from Turkey. Obviously, the AP was protective in character since it imposed restrictions on trading in sensitive products, namely, agriculture, textiles, steel and iron, all of which account for a significant part of Turkey's exports to the EU. The Additional Protocol also foresaw further financial aid to Turkey and there were provisions designed to ensure the free movement of workers by 1986 (Articles 36–41, The Additional Protocol).

As far as Turkey's obligations were concerned, Turkey was to reduce custom duties and charges made on EU exports to Turkey. According to the Protocol, Turkish imports from the EU were divided into two lists. Those products in which Turkey would achieve international competitiveness relatively early, were placed on a 12-year list to be achieved by 1985, while others, which were considered as uncompetitive, were put on a 22-year list. Duties and imports on commodities on the 22-year list would be reduced to zero by 1995 (Article 1, The Additional Protocol). In addition, Turkey was to eliminate the use of quotas on Turkey's imports from the EU in accordance with a liberalization list, and all quota restrictions were to be removed by 1995 (Article 25, The Additional Protocol). Furthermore, Turkey was to adopt the common customs tariff of the EU during the transitional stage (Article 17, The Additional Protocol). Lastly, Turkey was to align her agricultural policy with the CAP of the EU, if the free movement of agricultural products was to be achieved (Article 33, The Additional Protocol). The Protocol also provided for closer harmonization of economic policies between the parties, including competition and taxation.

With regard to the implementation of the Additional Protocol, the first three years did proceed as planned.[9] The EU abolished the nominal tariff rates on imports of industrial products originating from Turkey. The EU granted Turkey a preferential zero tariff rate on products, accounting for 37 per cent of Turkey's agricultural exports to the EU in 1973, and partial preference for other products, accounting for a further 33 per cent of the total Turkish exports. Moreover, the EU provided credit of ECU 577 million under the Second and the Third Financial Protocol for the development of the Turkish economy (Togan and Yilmaz, 1994, p. 3). For its part, Turkey made the first tariff reduction of 10 per cent for the products in the 12-year list and 5 per cent for the products in the 22-year list. Turkey also reduced the quota restrictions on its imports from the EU in accordance with the EU's consolidated liberalization list. Goods on this list accounted for 40 per cent of total imports from the EU in 1976 (Togan and Yilmaz, 1994, p. 4). After 1976, Turkish-EU relations ran into problems. Thus, the implementation of the transitional period did not proceed as planned, due to a number of specific external and internal factors affecting the Turkish-EU relationship. These included the first enlargement of the EU, the oil crisis, the effect of Turkey's military intervention in Cyprus, the EU's Global Mediterranean Policy and the prospect of Mediterranean enlargement (Bourguignon, 1990, p. 55). Indeed, the EU's Global Mediterranean Policy,[10] adopted in 1975, provided similar concessions to the other countries in the region, whose exports competed with Turkey's exports, particularly in the agricultural sector. The EU signed various kinds of association, trade and preferential trade agreements on a bilateral basis with all the countries, except Libya and Albania, in the Mediterranean.[11] These provided for preferential trade arrangements, agricultural concessions and financial cooperation to those countries.

Consequently, the concessions and other benefits that had been provided for Turkey under the Ankara Agreement were gradually undermined. According to a senior Turkish diplomat:

> Algeria and Spain received 65% to 75% tariff cuts in the agricultural and textiles sector, and for Israel, the EU provided better terms than Turkey on 53 items. These preferences for third parties affected Turkish exports to the EU to the extent of $200 million annually (Eren, 1977, p. 30).

In addition, the EU provided similar tariff preferences for textiles and manufactured agricultural products to developing countries under the Generalized System of Preferences, which also jeopardized Turkey's export of such products to the EU. Furthermore, the first enlargement (the UK, Denmark and Ireland) and the prospective Mediterranean enlargement of the EU (Greece, Spain and Portugal) affected EU-Turkey relations in the 1970s. Turkey was concerned about the political and economic implications of these for herself (Bourguignon, 1990, p. 55). For example, the accession of the UK extended the EU's external relations to the countries where the UK had colonial links. This affected, directly or indirectly, Turkey's agricultural exports to the EU, as was the case for the export of Turkish textiles to the EU, because the UK put unilateral restrictions on Turkish exports of cotton yarns, which played a significant part in total Turkish exports. Basically, Turkey saw all these developments as a means for the EU to deny its special status. She claimed that Turkey had a special Association Agreement that was beyond trade and commercial matters and covered the political objectives of the EU. In this regard, she asserted that Turkey deserved better treatment than countries that had simple trade and cooperation agreements without any substantial obligation. However, Turkey's criticism was partial and one sided and thus cannot wholly explain why she failed to fulfil her obligations under the Ankara Agreement.

There were other external factors affecting the EU-Turkey Association, including oil shocks and the international economic crisis during the 1970s which caused protectionist tendencies in the EU. The economic recessions had two important implications for Turkey: firstly, the imports to the EU from Turkey decreased dramatically because the EU countries showed considerably more hesitation in liberalizing imports of her agricultural products. Secondly, the flow of Turkish workers to the EU countries was stopped, due to economic and social concerns of member states of the EU (Penrose, 1981, p. 64). In fact, the EU members, in particular Germany, took various measures to reduce the number of Turkish workers, which resulted in the decline of workers' remittances.[12]

It is true that although all the above-mentioned factors undermined the benefits of the Association for Turkey, the main reason behind the fruitlessness of the transitional period was Turkey's incapacity to fulfil the obligations resulting from the Agreement. This was because Turkey had failed to make its economic policy converge towards the EU standard. Turkey's economic structure with its import substitution policy was incompatible with European integration, as Ugur suggests:

> European integration was to transcend the nation state on the basis of an essential liberal economic policy. This protectionist bias inherent in import-substitution prevented Turkey throughout the 1970s from complying with the provisions of the Additional Protocol (Ugur, 1999, pp. 5–6).

Consequently, shortly after the Additional Protocol (the AP) came into force, Turkey requested the EU to delay her obligation to gradually reduce tariffs. This was because Turkey's Third Five Year Development Plan, covering the period between 1973 and 1977, was not compatible with her obligations under the AP with regard to the gradual tariff reduction and the alignment of her external tariff with that of the EU's common external tariff (Ugur, 1999, p. 67). Admittedly, Turkey made some limited progress in fulfilling its obligations: she twice reduced her tariff rates, 10 per cent each time, for imports originating from the EU in 1973 and 1976. Nevertheless, after these two reductions, the progress in reducing quantitative restrictions on imports from the EU came to an end during the late 1970s. For example, Turkey postponed its obligation to the EU in relation to the tariff reductions in 1977 and 1978, referring to Article 60, which gave a general safeguard provision. In addition, Turkey was not able to align her customs tariff with that of the EU's common external tariff. Turkey also did not make substantial efforts to align her agricultural policy with that of the CAP (Kramer, 1996, p. 207). According to the AP, Turkey was to eliminate her quantitative restrictions within 22 years and was to adjust her agricultural policy in accordance with the EU's CAP. But Turkey failed to fulfil her obligation; consequently the EU enjoyed virtually no preferences in agricultural trade with Turkey (Aybak, 1996, p. 131).

As a result, Turkish officials realized that Turkey's economy was not suitable for contractual relationship, as her continually growing trade deficit with the EU undermined her economic and political structures.[13] As a result, she requested the revitalizing of the Association, including the suspension of her obligation for the period of 1978–1983 and demanding a substantial amount of financial assistance and concessions for Turkish export of agricultural and sensitive industrial products to the EU (Agence Europe, 13 October 1978, No. 2538). One of the main reasons for the Turkish Government's request for revitalizing the Association Agreement was because Turkey ran into a series of economic and political problems during the late 1970s. Indeed, a shortage of foreign currency, a high level of inflation, widespread unemployment and external debts caused the most severe economic crisis in the history of the Turkish Republic.

As regards the political system, the Turkish Parliament and the Council of Ministers were not able to operate, due to weak and short-lived minority coalition governments, which included representatives of the two extreme right wing parties. In addition, clashes between the extremist left wing and right-wing political groups using arms worsened the social tension and political situation in the country (Hale, 1994). As a result, the EU came to the reluctant conclusion that there was a need for additional economic aid for Turkey and more tariff preference for Turkey's exports to the Union. These were necessary policy instruments for stabilizing Turkey and for supporting a pro-Western force in the country after the Soviet intervention in

Afghanistan and the revolution in Iran (Bourguignon, 1990, p. 57). Finally, the EU prepared a package which was accepted by the Association Council on June 1980, in which the following concessions were granted to Turkey: gradual tariff concessions on Turkish agricultural exports; some improvement in social conditions and job opportunities for Turkish workers and financial aid of 600 million ECU (Aybak, 1996, p.148). Nevertheless, the military coup of 12 September 1980 put an end to the implementation of this package. In other words, the military intervention in Turkish politics resulted in the suspension of the Association Agreement until democratic rules had been applied and the political and human rights situation had been improved. In the meantime, Turkey's relationship with the EU was frozen.

Consequently, the main conclusion to be drawn from the above analysis is that the transitional stage of the EU-Turkey Association under the Additional Protocol did not result in the progressive integration as it had been intended. This was not only due to the incapacity of Turkey to fulfil her obligations under the Agreement, but also to do with the EU's failure to minimize the effects of development and changes occurring in its external and internal policies on the EU-Turkey Association.

Secondly, the lack of mutual understanding between the parties about the nature and the objectives of the Association constituted another main reason for the failure of relations. Indeed, although the EU-Turkey Association foresaw progressive economic integration, Turkey wanted to see it as a political gain and underestimated the economic objectives of Agreement. Finally, the instruments of the EU-Turkey Association were not able to propel a progressive kind of integration, because neither party make necessary efforts to rebuild them according to the changes and developments in European integration.

Turkey's Early Membership Application as an Alternative to the Association

Following the return to elected civilian government after the military regime of 1980–83, Turkey's relationship with the EU showed signs of normalization. Although the EU was anxious about Turkey's political eligibility not only as an associate member, but also, in particular, as candidate for full EU membership, it sought ways to re-activate the EU-Turkey Association after the military coup. In fact, the EU considered that maintaining working relations with Turkey was necessary for the security, political and economic interests of the EU. Likewise, the continuing relations with the EU were also essential for Turkey on the same accounts. Therefore, both sides expressed willingness to continue working towards a strengthened relationship, but with differences about its direction, prospects and objectives.

For its part, Turkey tended to express its wish to apply for EU membership as an alternative to reactivating the EU-Turkey association. As part of its preparation for EU membership, Turkey started to undertake political and economic reforms: the new civilian Government lifted the political restrictions and began to pursue a strategy of abolishing the influence of the military on politics (Evin, 1994, p. 35). As a result, several regulations promulgated during the military regime (1980–83) were abolished and new laws and constitutional amendments were introduced which allowed, to some extent, the elements of civil society and power groups to participate in the political process in Turkey. On the economic front, a liberalization programme was introduced to modernize and to open the Turkish economy to the world economy, which was in stark contrast with Turkey's import-substitution economic policy during the 1960s and 1970s.

The outward and market-oriented transformation that Turkey undertook was based on policies, designed to restrain the growth of domestic demand and on structural reforms to increase supplies through an improved allocation of resources. These included a gradual decrease in the share of the state in the economy; encouraged entrepreneurial activity; promoted the role of market and price mechanisms; and, most importantly, opened the economy to the world market (Muftuler-Bac, 1997, p. 100).

Consequently, numbers of reforms were introduced in the areas of trade, banking and taxation. In addition, the quota system was abolished in the Turkish import regime. As a result, Turkey eliminated the use of quotas on all imports from the EU. This was a kind of signal of Turkey's willingness to apply for EU membership. In fact, Turkey's changes to her economic policies, convergence towards the EU standard was seen as a necessary policy to reactivate relations as a means of accelerating Turkey's accession to the EU. As the Turkish Prime Minister at that time, Turgut Ozal, explained, the main motivation behind Turkey's economic reforms and economic liberalization programme was 'to facilitate Turkey's integration into the EU as a full member' (Muftuler, 1995, p. 85).

The reason for Turkey's wish to apply for EU membership as an alternative to reactivating the Ankara Agreement was because Turkey felt that the Association Agreement was unsatisfactory and constituted an inappropriate framework for relations with the EU. Turkish officials believed that Turkey's political, economic and security interests would be best served if she joined the EU. Another accelerating motivation in Turkey's desire to apply for EU membership was to do with internal developments within the EU. That is, the Single Act of 1986 signalled a completely new qualitative dimension of integration in the economic sphere, with the aim of completing the internal market. Consequently, Turkish officials felt that the deepening process of the EU would make Turkey's future accession increasingly difficult; hence, they considered that an early application for membership would be pragmatic.[14]

Added to this, the perceived effect of the EU membership on domestic stability and democratization process in the country was also a driving force behind the Turkish decision to make an early application. By analogy with the previous Mediterranean enlargements of the EU, in which the accession of Greece, Spain and Portugal to the EU were seen as means of consolidating the democratization process and political developments in these countries, Turkish policy-makers were expecting similar treatment from the EU.[15] Indeed, the example of the Mediterranean enlargements of the EU on the democratization process in Greece, Spain and Portugal constituted an important point of reference in Turkey's justification of its application and its efforts to gain political support from the EU for it. Related to this, security interdependence between the parties was useful for Turkey, making her membership bid more attractive and acceptable to the EU. Turkish officials underlined the effect of Turkey's political stability on European security. As an example, the Turkish Prime Minister, Turgut Ozal, stated that:

A democratic and politically powerful Turkey was in the interests of Europe. Therefore, the EU should promote its own interests by helping Turkey in its effort to make further democratization (*The Guardian*, 25 June 1987).

As this shows, Turkey tended to put forward the argument that a rejection of its application for membership would be prejudicial to its efforts to democratize and attach itself economically and politically to Europe, which might jeopardize European security and political interests in the region. Soon after the relationship with the EU began to normalize, Turkey applied for membership of the EU in 1987, although it was not yet ready to meet the conditions dictated by the EU. The Commission opposed Turkey's early application for EU membership on the grounds that Turkey could not easily be integrated into the EU, as the economic and political situations within the country were not adequate for membership. The Commission also mentioned the persistence of disputes with a member state and the lack of a solution of the Cyprus problem as obstacles to Turkey's EU membership bid (European Commission, 1989a). Basically, the Commission suggested that it would be premature for Turkey to become a full member, as she was neither ready nor mature enough to fulfil the obligations arising from full membership, particularly since the declared political and economic objectives of European integration after the introduction of the Single Act (European Commission, 1989a).

As is seen from its *avis*, the Commission did not reject Turkey's request, but delayed indefinitely the prospect of Turkey's accession to the EU: as it stated, 'The EU should under no circumstances close the door to Turkey forever and the time may came when both the Community and Turkey will be in a position to consider accession without major risk' (*Agence Europe*, 2 December 1989). The main implication of the Commission's opinion on Turkey's application for EU membership was that the EU wished to pursue a containment policy towards Turkey, designed to strengthen EU-Turkey relations through reactivating the AA, while delaying Turkish membership for the foreseeable future.

The Council approved the Commission's containment strategy and asked the latter to prepare proposals to specify what the instruments of the containment policy should be. In June 1990, the Commission issued the Matutes Package, which was purely designed to contribute to the modernization of Turkey's economy and to allow Turkey to move as close to the Community as possible. It proposed the completion of the customs union by 1995, which included a reduction of the tariff system, better access for the export of Turkish agricultural products and textiles, the promotion of industrial and technological cooperation, resumption of financial co-operation and the strengthening of political and cultural links (European Commission, 1990). In particular, the Commission envisaged intense cooperation in the areas of macroeconomics and monetary policy, industry, agriculture, service, transport, energy and the environment. The main objective of this Package was 'to assist Turkey in its modernization with the aim of reducing the gap in development which separates it from the Community and better integrating the country into the economic, social and political fabric of Europe' (European Commission, 1990). It offered Turkey the chance to reactivate the EU-Turkey Association through completion of the customs union with the strengthening of political and cultural links (European Commission, 1990, p. 3). The Commission believed that strengthening the Association Agreement would enable both partners to enter on the road towards increased interdependence and integration.

The Matutes Package provided the main base for the EU to implement its containment policy for Turkey. In fact, the instruments of the Package were well suited to the EU's containment policy for Turkey, designed to strengthen EU-Turkey relations, while delaying the possibility of actual Turkish membership in the foreseeable future. It set up proposals for intensive cooperation and the further development of relations with Turkey through the completion of the customs union. Obviously, the instruments of the Package were not only far beyond being sufficient to prepare Turkey for the EU membership, but also lacked a degree of clarity, certainty and evenhandedness as far as Turkey's membership was concerned. Interestingly, the Matutes Package did not add a new instrument to the existing Association Agreement; in fact, measures contained in the Package were less than what the original Association Agreement envisaged. For instance, it did not have new measures and new policy instruments or programmes in the areas of agriculture, services and free movement, which were all components of the Ankara Agreement. Furthermore, it lacked policy instruments for the political aspects of EU-Turkey relations. Although the EU underlined the importance of entering on the road towards increased interdependence and integration in the areas of politics and security, ironically, its package did not contain suitable policy instruments or a structured framework for deepening the cooperation in these areas. Similarly, given that the EU emphasized the political issues, including Turkey's political system and human rights situation, as obstacles impeding Turkey's accession to the EU, its package lacked the necessary policy instruments or programmes to support and encourage Turkey to fulfil the *acquis politique* of the Union in this respect. This all supports the argument that the EU put forward the Matutes Package as the main instrument of its containment policy for Turkey to serve as an alternative to membership. In fact, there was no firm commitment in the Package to go any further in the direction of full membership (Redmond, 1993, p. 51).

Although the Matutes Package was not implemented due to the decision of Greece to block it, it formed the main basis for the EU's subsequent relations with Turkey. The Commission prepared a 'Working Programme' in January 1992 as a substitute for the Matutes Package, which envisaged similar instruments. In line with this Working Programme, both parties had agreed on the establishment of a customs union at the Association Council meeting in November 1992 (*Agence Europe*, 10 November 1992, No. 5854, p. 4). Thus, the Council asked the Commission to prepare a strategy for it. In response to the Council's request, the Commission prepared guidelines under which Turkey would have to take the following measures:

- To remove surcharges on imports from the EU.
- To reduce tariffs and align its tariffs with those of the EU's common customs tariffs.
- To harmonize its agricultural sector with the CAP.

These measures were very close to the measures and instruments in the Matutes Package. Following this, the Association Council meeting in November 1993 agreed on the completion of the customs union by 1995. In this respect, Turkey started to accelerate the process of adjustment towards a customs union: she attained 80 per cent to 90 per cent reduction in her customs tariffs with the EU. In addition, she made a 70 per cent to 80 per cent alignment towards the EU's common customs tariff. Turkey also abolished surcharges on imports of 2600 products (Ugur, 1995, p. 347). In fact, Turkey made important steps towards the establishment of a customs union that was confirmed by the EU at the Association Council Meeting in December 1994, stating that Turkey was economically eligible to have a customs union with the EU (*Agence Europe*, 19 December 1994). Finally in March 1995, the Association Council took a decision to conclude a customs union with Turkey, followed by the approval of the European Parliament in December.

Nevertheless, the EU's policy towards Turkey has been inconsistent with its policy to the CEECs: while it sought ways in which to reactivate the EU-Turkey Association Agreement through a containment strategy without implying Turkish membership, it pursued an opposite policy approach to the CEECs, on the grounds that the CEECs efforts to gain EU membership must be supported and encouraged by taking their needs into account. The EU realized that the Europe Agreements were unsatisfactory and constituted an inappropriate framework for relations with the CEECs. In fact, these instruments in the Europe Agreements were, with the exception of such sensitive products as iron, steel, coal, and textiles, designed to establish free trade progressively between the parties in industrial goods as a means of reducing trade barriers and quantitative restrictions. As a result of this, the EU made considerable efforts to upgrade the instruments of the Europe Agreement to make sure that these were able to serve as a useful preparatory phase for a further agreement leading to accession. For example, the EU brought a pre-accession strategy into existence as part of the Europe Agreements. The Essen European Council in December 1994 accepted a broad pre-accession strategy to bring those countries closer to the EU, as an appropriate way of preparing the CEECs for accession to the Union by taking their needs into account (European Council, 1994). The EU's pre-accession strategy has enhanced the Europe Agreements by providing more financial co-operation through the PHARE to support the CEECs in meeting the accession criteria, a new political formula of the Structured Relationship with the EU institutions, and a kind of action plan in the shape of a White Paper on the internal market of the EU to prepare the CEECs for economic integration. In this respect, the main theme of the pre-accession strategy seems to have been the emphasis that it put on the EU's commitment to the associated countries with the implicit message that all the countries included in the pre-accession strategy would become members of the EU.

The EU's treatment of Turkey has been inequitable when compared to its treatment of the CEECs: while the objective of the EU's policy towards the CEECs has been explicitly linked to their accession process to the EU with a comprehensive and clearly defined pre-accession strategy, its policy *vis-à-vis* Turkey has not included such a firm accession commitment. This implies that the prospect of Turkey as an EU member was not even considered.[16] In fact, Turkey was seen only as an adjacent country with which cooperation should be intensified on the basis of an Association Agreement with political dialogue. By way of illustration, during the negotiations of the customs union, not only was the EU careful not to mention the issue of Turkey's membership, but it also avoided any direct reference to the effect of such an agreement on the possibility of Turkey's membership. From this perspective, the instruments of the customs union suited the EU's containment policy for Turkey well, since these instruments seem to have been fully compatible with the EU's declared objective of anchoring Turkey into the EU as a stable and secular country, displaying a distinct preference for delaying the prospects of Turkish membership for the foreseeable future.

The objectives of the EU's containment policy towards Turkey became clearer in Agenda 2000 of the Commission: this proposed some measures for intensifying the customs union and political dialogue with Turkey with a view to reinforcing the relationship between the parties, while effectively excluding Turkey from the enlargement process on political grounds (European Commission, 1997b). The EU Council at the Luxembourg Summit in December 1997 endorsed the Commission proposal by placing Turkey in a special lower category of its own, without implying eventual Turkish membership. The effect of this decision of the Council was to put off Turkey's full membership indefinitely. To satisfy Turkey without implying membership, the European Council invited Turkey to participate in the European Conference and asked the Commission to prepare a strategy, the so-called European strategy, for Turkey. All these efforts by the EU were part of its containment policy. In fact, upon the request of the Council, the Commission proposed this European strategy for Turkey in March 1998, in order to deepen the customs union and extend it to services and agricultural sectors (European Commission, 1998a). It also advocated closer co-operation in many fields, such as industrial cooperation, telecommunications, transport, energy and technological research.

The EU Council at the Cardiff Summit in 1998 accepted the European strategy for Turkey. Yet, its instruments were far beyond what was needed to prepare Turkey for accession to the EU; in fact, it reiterated the old commitments of the EU's previous proposals. In this respect, there was inconsistency between the EU's policy towards the CEECs and that towards Turkey: while the former was explicitly linked to the CEECs' efforts to join the EU, the latter included neither a firm accession commitment, nor a clearly defined comprehensive accession strategy to support Turkey's efforts to join the EU. Indeed, intensifying the existing instruments of the Association Agreement and strengthening the customs union were key terms in describing the EU's strategy for Turkey, which lacked financial resources and proper perspectives for gaining membership of the EU; as Turkey's Ambassador to the EU, Akyol, puts it, the strategy has been insufficient to bring Turkey's relations to the desired level.[17]

The Helsinki Process: Revision of the Containment Policy

It appeared that the EU's containment policy of Turkey was not sufficient to generate grounds on which the parties could build their relationship as regards the mutual interests. In other words, the policy of containment failed to produce a working relationship between the EU and Turkey as the latter found the EU's policy instruments inadequate and incompatible with its policy objective of EU membership. Given the importance of the relationship to both sides – from political, economic and security points of view – Turkey and the EU sought to find a way to maintain a working relationship with a better prospect for membership in the long run. From this perspective, the Commission recommended the European Council to declare Turkey to be a candidate state (European Commission, 1999b, p. 35). Finally, at the Helsinki Summit, the EU recognized Turkey as a 'candidate state destined to join the union'. Furthermore, the Helsinki European Council offered a prospect of an accession strategy as it stated: 'Building on existing European Strategy, Turkey will benefit from a pre-accession strategy to stimulate and support its reforms' (European Council, 1999a). At the Helsinki Summit, the EU proposed the following instruments for Turkey:

- Establishment of an Accession Partnership.
- Establishment of a single framework for coordinating all sources of EU financial assistance.
- Enhancing political dialogue, with emphasis on progress towards fulfilling the political criteria for accession, including improvement of human rights and rapprochement between Greece and Turkey.
- The possibility for participation in Community programmes and agencies (European Council, 1999a).

The Helsinki process has brought up a new dynamism and development in EU-Turkey relations with regard to the prospects of membership. The EU has not only restored its relations with Turkey, but has also increased the prospects of closer relations. This has generated positive developments in EU-Turkey, particularly in the sense that it has encouraged Turkish policy-makers to undertake some policy reforms in order to facilitate the convergence of Turkey's laws and Constitution towards EU standards. In addition, it has brought new inputs into Greece-Turkey relations, thereby encouraging Greek-Turkish rapprochement. Moreover, the institutional framework of the Association has started to function. The EU-Turkey Association Council met for the first time in three years in Luxembourg on 11 April 2000 and it adopted two important political decisions:

- Establishment of eight subcommittees under the Association Committee to monitor progress with the priorities of Accession Partnership and approximations of legislation (European Commission, 2000a, p. 7).
- Opening of negotiations aimed at the liberalization of services and mutual opening of procurement markets between the Union and Turkey (European Commission, 2000a, p. 7).

Like the Association Council, the EU-Turkish Joint Parliamentary Committee met in June after being suspended for three years and adopted a joint resolution for the first time. In addition, the Customs Union Joint Committee has met several times to exchange views on functioning the customs union.

More importantly, upon the request from the European Council of Feira, the Commission prepared a proposal for Council regulation on assistance to Turkey in the framework of pre-accession strategy, aimed at coordinating all sources of EU financial assistance to Turkey within a single framework in July 2000 (European Commission, 2000d). Furthermore, the Commission started to prepare the Accession Partnership

Document for Turkey, hence during the preparation of the accession partnership the exchange of views and consultation processes between the parties was increased. For example, the Commissioner responsible for enlargement, Gunter Verheugen paid an official visit to Turkey in March 2000; the aim of this visit was to observe the Turkish position on the draft Accession Partnership (Hurriyet, 22 March 2000).

Finally, the Commission finalized its proposal of the Accession Partnership for Turkey and issued it in November 2000 (European Commission, 2000e). The Document defines strategy, identifying short term and medium term priorities, intermediate objectives and conditions that Turkey is required to fulfil as part of her preparation for membership.

This Accession Partnership provides the basis for a number of policy instruments, aimed at helping Turkey in her preparations for membership. It also provides a framework within which Turkey could prepare a National Programme for the adoption of the *acquis*.

The Council of Ministers has approved the Accession Partnership and identified short term and medium term priorities and intermediate objectives, with emphasis on progressing towards fulfilling the political criteria for accession with particular reference to human rights, the Cyprus problem, as well as bilateral issues between Greece and Turkey over the Aegean Sea. Notably, under the enhanced political dialogue and political criteria, Turkey is required to take a number of measures. These include:

- Reform of the Turkish human rights system and review of the Turkish Constitution and other relevant legislation to ensure rights and freedoms of all Turkish citizens are granted in line with the standards, including ratification of the International Covenant on Civil and Political Rights and the International Covenant on Economic, Social and Cultural Rights.
- Guarantee cultural rights for the minorities, including the use of their mother tongue in conformity with practices in EU member states.
- Preventing torture and ill-treatment with a full respect for human rights.
- Lifting the death penalty with the signing and ratifying of the Protocol No. 6 of the European Convention of Human Rights.
- Review of the constitutional role of the National Security Council with a view to make it an advisory body to the government.
- Reforms in judiciary system to improve functioning and efficiency of the judiciary, including the state security court in line with international standards.

With regard to bilateral disputes with Greece over the Aegean Sea and Cyprus issue, Turkey is required to support the UN Secretary General's effort to bring the process of finding a comprehensive settlement of the Cyprus problem to a successful conclusion. In addition, the Accession Partnership made a reference to jurisdiction of the ICJ in the Aegean Sea issue (European Commission, 2000e). On the Economic front, the Accession partnership set a range of recommendations to adopt and implement the *acquis communautaire* in the field of internal market, taxation, agriculture, transport, energy, transport, environment and regional policy.

As is seen from the above analysis, the EU's policy post-Helsinki appears to have been different from its previous policy in many ways: it has not only recognized

Turkey as a candidate for accession, but also has offered an Accession Partnership for Turkey, known as a road map to the accession. This has restored EU-Turkey relations and thus has increased the prospects of closer relations through the Helsinki Declaration. This seems to imply that there have been some positive changes on the part of the EU with regard to the prospect of Turkish membership, compared with the ambiguities and hesitations of its previous policy of containment.

However, the EU's policy post-Helsinki appears to have shortcomings, which raise doubts about the attainability of the EU's policy in the medium and long term. The first concern is the ambiguity of the conditions contained in the Helsinki Document and Accession Partnership. Although the EU's policy post-Helsinki has generated positive development in EU-Turkey relations, it has effectively delayed the eventual Turkish membership for the foreseeable future by firmly making the prospects of Turkey's accession conditional on settling a number of political issues, including the disagreements with Greece, improvements in human rights and the solution of the Kurdish issue (European Commission, 2000e). The deputy Head of the Turkish Unit at the Commission, Van der Meer, confirmed this:

> The decision of the Helsinki Summit to declare Turkey as a candidate state should be interpreted as a changing of the EU's conditionality policy towards the prospects of Turkey's membership. (Interview with Van Der Meer, Deputy Head of the Turkish Unit in the European Commission, 16 June 2000, Brussels).

A member of the European Parliament, Richard Balfe, also underlined this: 'the successes of the Helsinki process is conditional on the progress of Turkey in settling the political issues between Turkey and the EU'.[18] However, this is not to criticize the conditionality of the Accession Partnership as regards the prospects of Turkish membership, and certainly it is not to deny that the political issues are major obstacles to Turkish membership. As indicated in chapter 5, Turkey has a number of political issues to be solved prior to the negotiations for accession. If she wants to join the EU, Turkey has to accept the conditions contained in the Accession Partnership. Nevertheless, there seem to be uncertainties and vagueness over the terms of Accession Partnership as regards conditions for the prospect of Turkish membership, thereby providing some grounds for doubts about the feasibility of the implementation of the Accession Partnership. Considering the implementation of the Accession of Partnership is firmly conditional upon Turkey's progress towards fulfilling the political criteria, the ambiguity of these conditions could cause reciprocal conflict over the terms of Accession Partnership and, thus the Accession Partnership Document could easily became another dead letter in the history of EU-Turkey relations.

Moreover, the Accession Partnership has lacked sufficient financial assistance to stimulate and support policy reforms in Turkey (European Commission, 2000d). The amount of annual ECU 177 million financial assistance offered by the Commission's proposal in the framework of Association Partnership has fallen far short of the amount made available to other countries. For example, the financial instrument of Accession Partnership did not include Turkey in the ISPA and SAPARD programmes (Special Accession Program for Agricultural sector and Rural Development), designed to restructure the agricultural sectors in the applicant countries and develop infrastructures in line with the EU standards. Considering the relevant financial instruments offered for the CEECs, an increased amount of pre-accession aid has been granted to the CEECs for agricultural development, amounting to ECU 500 million per year under the SAPAD and for structural development, with ECU 1 billion annually to align infrastructure standards of the CEECs with those of the EU in many areas under the ISPA (European Commission, 1997b). The amount offered for Turkey seems to have fallen far short to prepare Turkey for EU membership even in the long run.

Furthermore, the proposed amount of an annual ECU 177 million for the next five years has not added a new instrument in the existing financial framework in EU-Turkey relations. In other words, the proposed amount of financial assistance is limited to resources, which was already granted to Turkey under the MEDA programmes and European Strategy for Turkey. This implies that the EU assistance provided for Turkey under the MEDA programmes and measures to intensify the EU-Turkey customs union foreseen in the European Strategy will be used for pre-accession purposes. As the proposed framework regulations stated, 'this regulation has no financial implications' (European Commission, 2000d). The Commission's proposal on assistance to Turkey rather established a single framework for coordinating these financial instruments of EU assistance under the Accession Partnership. From this perspective, it appears to be inappropriate to maintain parallel funding structure, which was already established in the past, in a clearly comprehensive and targeted accession strategy for Turkey.

As is seen from the contexts of the Helsinki Agreement and the Accession Partnership, the EU has revised its containment policy to the extent that a close special relationship could be developed in a constructive and inclusive manner with a prospect of Turkish membership in the long run. In other words, the EU's declaration of Turkey as a candidate along with the Accession Partnership appears to have been as part of its efforts to reactivate EU-Turkey relations after the Luxembourg Summit decisions, which damaged these relations to the extent that they were at their lowest point since Turkey's application for EU membership in 1987. The objective of the EU's revised policy post-Helsinki was twofold: first, the EU considered that the revised policy of containment would encourage Turkey in its effort of economic and political reform and would generate incentives in rapprochement process between Greece and Turkey. Second, it could provide the grounds on which the parties could maintain continued working relationships without alienating politically and strategically important countries. Nevertheless, the EU's revised policy of containment has remained to oppose the prospect for opening negotiations with the EU in the foreseeable future. In this respect, the EU has not substantially changed the objective of its previous containment policy towards the prospects of Turkey's membership. In fact, the revised containment policy of Turkey would appear to be the most likely basis for relations in the foreseeable future. For example, Turkey still remains outside the accession process, involving all the applicant countries, and there is little reason to expect a reversal in the EU's position. Moreover, the Nice Summit conclusions on institutional reforms for an enlarged EU support the above contention: although all 12 candidate counties were included in proposed institutional reforms of the EU, Turkey was excluded from any of the EU's plans for the post-enlargement future. This appears to be inconsistent with the EU's recognition of Turkey's stature as an equal candidate for accession through the Accession Partnership.

Conclusions

The chapter has suggested that the association politics of the EU cannot serve alone as a useful preparatory phase for a further agreement of the associate state leading to accession, as has been the case for the Athens Agreement with Greece and the Europe Agreements with the CEECs. In fact, Greece applied for EU membership as an alternative to reactivating the Athens Agreement and the CEECs asked the EU to upgrade the instruments of Europe Agreement with the view to its EU membership. Thus, the EU has made substantial efforts to upgrade the instruments of the Europe Agreements in preparing the CEECs for full membership. Consequently, Europe Agreements have been reoriented towards eventual full-membership with the appropriate framework of the pre-accession strategy.

In the case of the Turkish Association, the EU-Turkey Association has never proceeded as was envisaged. There seem to have been a number of reasons for the failure of the Agreement, which included the lack of parallelism in the parties' interpretations of the ultimate objective of the Agreement and the incompatibility of their policies with the objectives envisaged in the Association Agreement.

Nevertheless, the failure of the Association has been due mainly to the EU's unwillingness to upgrade the instruments of the Association Agreement in accordance with the developments in European integration. More precisely, the EU has tended to see the AA as the framework for its containment policy rather than a pre-accession strategy, because it has serious reservations about Turkey's prospects of EU membership on political and economic grounds. Although the EU realized that the instruments of the EU-Turkey Association have been inadequate in the European context post-Maastricht to act as a progressive kind of integration with a view to Turkey's EU membership, it has been reluctant to reorient the EU-Turkey Association as part of pre-accession and accession process, as it has done for the CEECs. Even the EU's policy instrument after the Helsinki accord appears to be limited to reorient the EU-Turkish association towards full membership. That is, all the instruments available under the Accession Partnership are designed to contribute to anchor Turkey firmly within the future architecture of Europe, rather than being oriented towards membership of the EU.

This leads to a main conclusion: the EU has perceived the EU-Turkey Association framework as a basis for its containment policy rather than as a basis for preparing Turkey for EU membership. Admittedly, the domestic, political and economic situations, combined with its size, seem to make her membership prospect less unattractive to the EU than the applicants in the CEECs. In this respect, the EU has used the inadequacy of Turkey's political and economic structures, along with her bilateral disputes with Greece to legitimize its reluctant approach to reorient the instruments of the EU-Turkey Association towards membership. It does not mean to say that these issues should not be considered major obstacles to Turkish membership, it rather suggests that this does not seem a sufficient reason for the EU's different treatment of Turkey; in fact, it cannot explain why similar political and economic issues in the CEECs have attracted an entirely different response on the part of the EU from those in Turkey.

It is not sufficient to argue that Turkey is different from, and by implication a more difficult case than, other applicants: some of them started from an even lower base than Turkey but with the appropriate support from the EU through the pre-accession strategy, they are expected to join the EU eventually. In fact, once the EU realized that the Europe Agreements were unsatisfactory and constituted an inappropriate framework for the relations with the CEECs, it made considerable effort to upgrade the instruments of the Europe Agreements in accordance with the objectives of the European integration in the post-Maastricht context with a broad pre-accession strategy which has brought the CEECs closer to the EU. However, this has not been the case for Turkey: the EU has used its Association Agreement as a base for its containment policy for Turkey.

This suggests that there has been inconsistency between the instruments of the EU's association policy towards the CEECs and its association policy *vis-à-vis* Turkey: while the former has been explicitly linked to the CEECs accession process to the EU with a comprehensive and clearly defined pre-accession strategy, the latter has not included such a firm accession commitment and policy instruments to prepare Turkey for accession. Thus, the contribution that the Turkish-EU Association has played in preparing Turkey for accession to the EU has been far less than the contribution of the Europe Agreements for the CEECs in this respect. The implication of this is that the EU's containment policy towards Turkey has not only been inadequate, but also less effective in terms of preparing Turkey for EU membership than its association policy towards the CEECs has been.

Notes

1   It is an interesting suggestion that the Association agreement does not necessarily prepare the applicant country for EU membership. The UK, Denmark, Ireland, Spain, Portugal, Austria, Norway Finland proceeded to full membership without an association agreement. The EFTA countries did not need an association framework to proceed to EU membership as they had, to a large extent, harmonized and aligned their economic and related policies with those of the EU before they applied for EU membership; however, this was not valid for the Spanish and Portuguese cases as their economy was relatively backward, but even they proceeded to full membership without the association framework.

2   In fact, Turkey's economic structure at that time made it ineligible for an associate relationship, which required reciprocal rights. Turkey's economy was mainly agricultural with nearly 80 per cent of her labour force employed in the agricultural sector and the GDP per capita was just $180 USA, in comparison to the EU's average of $2800. For this, see Mehmet Ali Birand (1987), *Turkiyenin Ortak Macerasi*, p. 147.

3   Eventually, the final stage of negotiations started in 1963, centring on an establishment of the customs union: while Turkey was in favour of an automatic transition towards the customs union through a short preparation period, the EU insisted on a long transition period before the creation of the customs union and suggested that the transfer from one stage to another should be decided by the progress being achieved by Turkey, rather than being automatic transition. For a detailed analysis of the negotiations of the Ankara Agreement, see Tekeli and Ilkin (1993), *Turkiye and Avrupa Toplulugu* (Turkey and European Community), Umit Yayincilik, Ankara, pp. 134–188.

4   The last paragraph of the Preamble reveals the political character of the Association, which reads: 'the parties resolved to preserve and strengthen peace and liberty by joint pursuit of the ideals underlining the Treaty establishing the European Community', see European Commission (1964) 'Agreement Establishing an Association between the European Economic Community and Republic of Turkey', *Official Journal of European Communities, L.1217*, Brussels.

5   The Additional Protocol also included some provisions for the coordination or alignment of economic and related policies, such as the gradual harmonization of taxation in trade, capital transactions, the gradual alignments of Turkey's competition rules with the EU's competition rules. It provided financial aid for Turkey during the transitional period, as Turkey needed in order to fulfil her obligations.

6   For this, see Arts, 8, 10, 11 of The Additional Protocol.

7   For this, see Articles 24(2), 25 and 27 of the Ankara Agreement.

8   The dilemma of politics versus economics can be seen in the debate between the Ministry of Foreign Affairs and the State Planning Organization on the advantages and disadvantages of the transitional stage: while the former, as the main advocate of Turkey's European destiny, believed that the transitional stage would accelerate Turkey's participation in European integration, the latter opposed it on the grounds that the Turkish economy was still at the stage where protection was necessary; hence, competition with the EU would harm the Turkish economy.

9   In 1974, having assessed the progress of the Association in every aspect, the Association Council expressed its satisfaction and stated that 'one day Turkey would be called upon to became a full member of the Community', cited in *The Twenty second Review of the Council's Work* (1974), General Secretariat of the Council of the European Communities, Brussels.

10   For more detailed analysis of the EC's Mediterranean policy, see Gingsberg, Roy Howard (1993), The European Community and the Mediterranean in Juliet Lodge (ed.), *Institutions and Politics of the European Union*, Frances Pinter, London, pp. 154–167.

11   The EU's Global Mediterranean Policy was to a large extent related to the EU's concern over the political situation in the region (i.e., tension between Israel and the Arab states, the increasing naval presence of the Soviet Union and the EU's dependency on oil).

12   For example, Germany imposed a recruitment ban on foreign workers from non-EU members and other countries soon followed suit. Turkey interpreted these measures as the non-fulfillment of obligation as regards the free movement of workers, which was scheduled to begin on December 1976 and would be completed by 1986.

13   For detailed information about the debate among the Turkish officials on Association agreement during the late 1970s, see Cayhan, Esra (1997), *Turkiye-Avrupa Birligi iliskileri ve Siyasal Partilerin Konuya Bakisi* (Turkey-EU Relations and the Positions of the Political Parties on the Subject), Boyut Maatbacilik, Istanbul, pp. 198–240.

14   Interview with Korkmaz Haktanir, the Turkish Ambassador to the UK and the former Undersecretary of the Foreign Ministry, London, 12 July 2000.

15   In the interview with Haluk Illicak, senior Turkish diplomat at the Turkish Embassy in London, he reaffirmed this argument, stating that after the military intervention to Turkish politics, Turkey expected similar concern from the EU as they had showed in Greece, Spain and Portugal, 14 March 2000, London.

16   It is interesting to note that for the CEECs, the words 'preparing for accession' are used in a number of conclusions of the European Council Summits, in official documents of the Commission and in a number of resolutions of the European Parliament. But such wording is not used in the Turkish case; any reference to the membership application or preparation for membership seems to be carefully avoided.

17   Interview with Nihat Akyol, Turkish Ambassador to the EU, 16 June 2000, Brussels.

18   Interview with Richard Balfe, Member of the European Parliament, 20 June 2000, Brussels.

Chapter 4

Economic Instruments of the EU's Policy for Turkey in a Comparative Perspective with the CEECs

Introduction

Experiences of the Turkish Association have fallen short of expectations and have not provided a framework for developing a strategy with a view to preparing Turkey for accession. Thus, the EU proposed to enhance the EU-Turkey Association, centred around building relations on the customs union with intensifying financial cooperation and strengthening political dialogue. However, this policy of containment on the part of the EU failed to produce a working relationship with Turkey and thus became unattainable. As a result, the EU revised its containment policy, in an attempt to reassure its longest standing associate of its European vocation. While the EU has been actively engaging in preparing the CEECs for accession, it developed a European Strategy for Turkey. Arguably, although it was designed to prepare Turkey for EU membership, it did not add any substantial new instrument to the existing framework of the customs union, but extended it to intensify the relations in the agricultural and the services sector, as well as strengthening cooperation in several other areas (European Commission, 1998a). Consequently, Turkey remained outside the accession process on political grounds. Finally, at the Helsinki Summit in 1999, the EU recognized Turkey as a candidate country and offered an Accession Partnership for her. Building on the existing customs union, the offered Accession Partnership contained enhanced political dialogue and financial assistance to Turkey in the framework of pre-accession strategy with political conditions that Turkey needs to fulfil. All this development implies that the instruments of the pre-accession strategy for Turkey, including the Accession Partnership, have been centred on the customs union. By implication, the instruments of the customs union have become the key features of the EU's pre-accession strategy for Turkey in relation to her preparation for the EU's single market in the long run.

Therefore, this chapter will consider whether the instruments of the customs union have been appropriate for pre-accession strategy, with a view to preparing Turkey for accession. The chapter argues that the customs union has constituted the central part of the EU's containment policy, rather than being the key feature of the pre-accession strategy for Turkey as regards her integration into the EU's single market. Thus, the main contention of this chapter is that there has been inconsistency not only between the EU's declaration confirming its commitment to Turkish membership and its containment policy for Turkey, but also between the

EU's policy instruments towards the CEECs and those towards Turkey. Essentially, the EU's containment policy for Turkey, including the customs union, has lacked the necessary instruments to prepare Turkey for accession to the EU.

To support this argument, the chapter will first explore both the EU's and Turkey's motivations and interests in completing the customs union and try to answer the question of why the customs union was the preferred policy for the EU. Then, it will evaluate the contents and characteristics of the customs union. Finally, this chapter will offer a comparative analysis of the EU's policy towards the CEECs and its policy *vis-à-vis* Turkey in the context of enlargement. This comparative analysis will shed light on the question as to whether Turkey has been treated in a different way from other countries.

The Customs Union: as the Central Part of the EU's Containment Policy

After the EU's opposition to Turkey's early application for EU membership in late 1989, both the EU and Turkey sought ways, not only to reactivate the EU-Turkey Association, but also to upgrade it in accordance with the developments in the EU. This indicated the willingness of both parties to continue working towards a strengthened relationship. In this respect, the debates were primarily centred on the completion of a customs union between the two parties. After the Commission issued its opinion on Turkey's request for EU membership to the Council of Ministers on 5 February 1990, the Council approved it and asked the Commission to prepare specific proposals for strengthening cooperation with Turkey. In June 1990, the Commission adopted the Matutes Package, which proposed completion of a custom union by 1995. This has become a central part of the EU's containment policy for Turkey which has the declared objective of strengthening EU-Turkey relations by bringing Turkey closer to the EU as much as possible, at the very least on economic grounds, while delaying the prospects of Turkish membership in the foreseeable future. However, it is necessary to look at the EU's and Turkey's motivations and interests in completing the customs union.

The Customs Union as Part of Turkey's New Strategy for Gradual Integration with the EU in the Long Term

After the EU's opposition to Turkey's early application for EU membership, Turkey was left with no alternative but to pursue more gradual integration with the EU. The completion of a customs union constituted the most important feature of Turkey's gradual integration approach. This was also the economic aspect of a legal requirement arising from the Association Agreement in which the second stage of the transitional period foresaw the establishment of a customs union. Indeed, Turkey had tended to see the completion of a customs union as the final phase of her association before accession to the EU. Hence, Turkey's motivation to conclude the customs union with the EU was primarily based upon the political assumption that this customs union would strengthen Turkey's position in its demand for membership. From this perspective, at the beginning of the negotiation process,

Turkey was determined to make a firm link between the customs union and the prospects for its membership, and thus refused to see the customs union as a substitute for membership. It came as no surprise, then, that the Turkish Foreign Minister, Murat Karayalcin, stated at the Association Council meeting in December 1994 that:

> The customs union is not an end in itself. It should and will serve as a stepping-stone to the realization of the final objective of the Association Agreement, which remains my Government's long-standing goal (Minutes of the 35th Meeting of the EC-Turkey Association Council, 1994, p. 28).

The Turkish Foreign Minister, Karayalcin, further stated:

> Our expectations from the successful completion of the customs union are not limited strictly to economic considerations; indeed, the CU represent a reaffirmation of the objective of Turkey's full membership in the European Union; thus it is not a substitute, but a stepping stone towards full membership (Minutes of the 35th Meeting of the EC-Turkey Association Council, 1994, p. 28).

The Turkish Government counted on the assumption that the customs union would strengthen Turkey's position in its demand for membership: after the signing of the customs union, the statement of the Turkish Prime Minister, Tansu Ciller, confirmed this before the start of the Dublin summit in 1996, as she asserted:

> As well as being the oldest associate member and the only member of NATO, Turkey is the only country, which has achieved a degree of integration represented by the customs union (Milliyet, 14 December 1996).

Another political motive behind Turkey's insistence on the completion of the custom union was related to the domestic conflict between those of pro-Western and Islamic tendencies in Turkish society. The Islamic movement, which had grown strongly, was beginning to look as though it might be able to offer a feasible alternative to Turkey's 'European vocation'; the customs union with the EU was therefore seized upon as a timely means of reasserting the primacy of the objective of Westernization. In other words, Turkish officials believed that the completion of the customs union would help to restrain the fundamental Islamic movement and enhance Western values in Turkish society (Hic, 1995). In fact, one of the main arguments they presented to the EU during the completion of the customs union was that if it were rejected, it would strengthen anti-Western tendencies in Turkish society and give grounds for opposing Turkey's ties with the West.

On the economic front, Turkey considered the customs union as a key economic instrument which would bring closer economic integration with the EU. In fact, Turkish officials tended to see the customs union as a pre-accession strategy for Turkey to prepare its economy for EU membership. Furthermore, they believed that the customs union would accelerate Turkey's effort to modernize and liberalize her economy. Since the mid 1980s, when Turkey launched an economic liberalization programme to prepare the Turkish economy for integration with the EU, Turkey has been compelled to undertake a series of structural reforms in order to create a fair and competitive environment for a market economy. The Turkish Prime Minister at that time, Turgut Ozal, explained the main motivation behind this economic liberalization programme was 'to facilitate Turkey's integration into the EU as a full member' (cited in Muftuler, 1995, p. 85).

Turkey's other economic motivation for wanting the customs union was related to internal economic developments within the EU. Post-Maastricht European integration has opened a completely new qualitative dimension of integration in the economic sphere; hence integration with such a dynamic and well-integrated internal single European market requires a complex process of harmonization of legislation, norms and standards.

Given that the scope of the customs union which foresaw not only the removal of tariff barriers between the EU and Turkey for industrial goods, but envisaged the harmonizing of the structure, standards and legislative framework of the Turkish economy, the completion of the customs union was seen by Turkey as an essential mechanism which provided a framework in which Turkey could participate in the single European market. Turkey considered the completion of the customs union to be a means of assisting her to adopt the parts of the EU's *acquis* which related to the single European market.

In conclusion, to a significant extent, the customs union was perceived in Turkey as not really being about economic integration, but rather more in terms of being a political and strategic decision; hence it was seen as a halfway house to the EU.

In other words, it constituted the biggest step forward to fulfilling Turkey's desire for membership that had ever been taken. Considering that the scope of the customs union involved not only the economic objectives of preparing Turkey for the European single market, but entailed political objectives by increasing political dialogue and introducing structured relationship, Turkey saw the customs union as a kind of pre-accession strategy, which would bring her closer to the EU from many perspectives and thus would make her accession to the EU more achievable and feasible.

The Customs Union as Part of the EU's Containment Policy for Turkey

The EU remained reluctant to endorse the Turkish view, which saw the customs union as an important step towards full membership (Toksoz, 1996, p. 75). In fact, the EU considered customs unions merely as an economic agreement as part of a legal requirement arising from the Association Agreement. Consequently, the EU perceived it as part of reactivating the existing Association Agreement, rather than a final step towards Turkish membership. While the EU accepted that the agreement of a customs union was the completion of a requirement arising from the Association Agreement, it avoided any reference to Article 28 of the Agreement,[1] which foresaw the eventuality of Turkish membership. However, it is interesting to note that the EU started to negotiate the customs union with Turkey after it had committed itself to bringing the CEECs into the EU through the enlargement strategy for these countries. This was one of the main reasons why Turkey had made an effort to make some reference to the issue of Turkish membership during the negotiation of the customs union. Nevertheless, despite Turkey's insistence, not only was the EU careful not to mention the issue of Turkey's membership during these negotiations, but it also avoided any direct reference to the effect of such an agreement on the possibility of Turkey's membership. While the EU committed itself fully to a policy of enlargement to take in the CEECs, Malta and Cyprus at the Copenhagen European Council in June 1993, and initiated a pre-accession strategy to prepare these countries for EU membership at the Essen European Council in 1994, the prospect of Turkey as an EU member was not considered.[2] It was seen only as a neighbouring country with which cooperation should be intensified on the basis of an association agreement including political dialogue.[3]

In truth, the EU basically saw the customs union as a mechanism for its containment policy for Turkey and thereby as a means of strengthening EU-Turkish relations to include institutional cooperation, political dialogue and financial cooperation. Thus, Hans van den Broek, the Commissioner responsible for the external relations of the EU, indicated the EU's motivation for the conclusion of the customs union when he said:

> The customs union represents closer relations with Turkey offering wide-ranging cooperation in many areas. It will make it possible to re-launch relations with Turkey and promote harmonization with European values (*Agence Europe*, 15 March 1995).

Primarily, the customs union agreement carried the implicit message to Turkey that the EU was reluctant to commit itself to open its doors further to Turkey and saw the customs union as an end in itself. From this perspective, it seems appropriate to ask why the EU wanted the customs union. What were the EU's motivation and interest in the completion of such an agreement?

The main motives behind the EU's decision to conclude a customs union agreement with Turkey can be explained in the context of security and economic factors. Given the EU's declared objective of anchoring Turkey into the EU as a stable and secular country with a large market, the EU's approach to the customs union was mainly dominated by economic, strategic and security considerations (Ugur, 1999, p. 243). The importance of Turkey for Europe as a security asset compelled the EU to maintain a special relationship with it; from this perspective, the customs union was seen as a mechanism which would anchor Turkey to the West in a highly unstable region. For example, the Foreign Secretary of the UK, Douglas Hurd, stated that:

> It is extremely important to maintain a partnership with Turkey. Whether one thinks of the Balkans or the dialogue on human rights, or the Soviet Union, or the Middle East, or Cyprus, relations with Turkey are indispensable (*Financial Times*, 20 December 1994).

Therefore, the EU had an interest in developing close relations with Turkey through a customs union, involving institutional cooperation and political dialogue, as well as the reestablishment of financial cooperation. Another security consideration was the EU's concern about the negative effects of rejection of the customs union on Turkey's domestic politics. Indeed, after the EU's opposition to Turkey's early application for EU membership, any delay in complementing the customs union would have been perceived as a lasting rejection of Turkey both by political circles and public opinion. In addition, the EU believed that the customs union would boost the democratization process in Turkey. The EU also hoped that customs union might lessen Turkish anger over the fact that the EU had committed itself to opening accession negotiations with Cyprus and Central and Eastern European countries.

As far as the economic motivation of the EU was concerned, the customs union foresaw the free circulation of industrial products between Turkey and the EU. In other words, Turkey had to further align itself with the EU in economic terms. It virtually eliminated tariffs on industrial goods from the EU and also extended the majority of the EU's regulations on trade and competition to Turkey. Such economic integration would give a major boost to EU exports to Turkey, due to the reduction of tariff barriers. The EU showed a keen interest in the conclusion of the customs union on the grounds that it would offer European enterprises a new and important consumer-oriented market, which was already, in 1995, the EU's tenth biggest trade partner. In addition, the EU would be able to use Turkey as an export base for the Middle East, the Black Sea region and Central Asia. Improved opportunities of cooperation between Turkish and European firms would enable them to penetrate and to cooperate in those markets.

In conclusion, both the EU and Turkey had different expectations and motivations behind the completion of a customs union. Turkey tended to interpret it as the final step in the process of moving towards full membership. It was seen as a kind of pre-accession strategy that would bring Turkey into the EU in the long run. The EU, however, saw it as the necessary instrument to re-launch relations with Turkey and the customs union effectively constituted a prominent part of the EU's containment policy for Turkey which was designed to strengthen EU-Turkey relations, while postponing the possibility of actual Turkish membership into the foreseeable future. Such different motivations and interests between the parties constituted the main reason why EU-Turkey relations since the inception of the customs union have been politicized, particularly when it comes to the issue of Turkey's membership. As the EU's Ambassador to Turkey, Michael Lake observed:

> The customs union created misconceptions on both sides. The European side felt that Turkey would be preoccupied with making it work and not press for full membership for the time being, while Turkey had the misconception that the customs union was a stepping stone towards full membership in the next year or two (*International Herald Tribune*, 24 February 1997).

The implication of this for the argument of the book is that although Turkey was desperately eager for an affirmative answer from the EU with regard to its membership expectations through the establishment of the customs union, the EU responded reluctantly to the latter's request. In fact, it developed an alternative policy for Turkey (of which the customs union constituting the most important part), which can best be described as a containment policy and a substitute for membership; indeed, the policy lacked the necessary instruments to support Turkey's preparation for accession to the EU.

The Characteristics and Contents of the Customs Union: A Kind of Pre-Accession Strategy for Turkey?

The significance of the customs union between the EU and Turkey clearly goes beyond the economic sphere. Its contents not only include commercial and trade matters, but it is also supplemented by further measures, including an intensive political dialogue, the development of further cooperation and the resumption of financial cooperation. Hence, these instruments form a strategy intended to bring Turkey closer to the European Union. It forms a special link between the EU and Turkey in which Turkey takes part in some EU systems and participates in the objectives of the EU. Yet, the question still remains as to whether the customs union is able to serve as a pre-accession instrument for Turkey's membership, or whether it is a substitute for it. Therefore, this section will assess the contents of the customs union and their implementation, and argues that the instruments of the customs union have not been comprehensive enough to support the integration process of Turkey with the EU.

The customs union has three dimensions: the economic dimension (in industrial goods), the political dimension and the financial dimension. The economic dimension involves:

- The elimination of customs duties, quantitative restrictions and measures of equivalent effect on trade in industrial goods between Turkey and the EU and the alignment of Turkish customs tariffs with those of the common customs tariffs of the EU in industrial products (Articles 4 – 11, Decision No 1/95 of the EC-Turkey Association Council, 1995).
- The harmonization of Turkey's commercial policy with that of the common commercial policy of the EU, involving a progressive adoption by Turkey of the EU's preferential trading arrangements with certain third party countries (Article 12).
- The alignment of Turkish legislation with that of the EU in the areas of competition rules, the protection of intellectual, industrial and commercial property, including patents and anti-piracy law, and copyright (Article 31).
- Abolition of the voluntary restraints arrangements limiting the export of Turkish textiles to the EU.

Furthermore, the EU and Turkey resolved to intensify cooperation in some areas which are not covered by the customs union, including intensification of industrial cooperation and promotion of investment, and EU support for the adoption by Turkey of the *acquis communautaire* in the areas, such as the environment, telecommunications, energy, transport, agriculture, science, consumer protection and the JHA (Neuwahl, 1999, p. 39).

As is seen from the above, the scope of the customs union foresees not only the removal of tariff barriers between the EU and Turkey for industrial goods, but envisages the harmonization of the structure, standards and legislative framework of the Turkish economy. In this regard, it appears that the completion of the customs union could provide a framework for Turkey to participate in the single European market as a means of assisting her to fulfil the economic *acquis* of the single

European market. Since the customs union came into existence, Turkey has made important progress in liberalizing her external trade: customs duties and other charges, quantitative restrictions and measures having an equivalent effect have all been abolished. In fact, she has already fulfilled most of its undertakings concerning the harmonization of customs legislation, including the common external tariff of the EU (European Commission, 1998b, p. 4). As the Commission indicated, there are no longer any quantitative restrictions and measures of equivalent effect on trade on imports or on exports in the industrial sector in trade with Turkey (European Commission, 1998b, p. 5). Internal taxes can no longer be used as an indirect protection mechanism, nor can tax rebates be used as export subsidies. In addition, Turkey's competition policy and intellectual property legislation is to be harmonized with that of the EU (Neuwahl, 1999, p. 40).

In addition, the customs union requires Turkey's full adoption of the EU's common commercial policy, involving a progressive alignment of Turkey's tariffs system with the EU's common customs tariff and adoption of preferential agreements with third countries (Article 16, Decision No 1/95 of the EC-Turkey Association Council, 1995). Turkey has made significant progress in this respect and, indeed, the Commission, in its regular report, noted that Turkey's commercial policy was largely aligned with the EU policy (European Commission, 1999a, p. 4). For example, negotiations on a Free Trade Agreement with Poland were concluded in July 1999 and, in fact, Turkey has signed Free Trade Agreements with all EU candidate countries, as well as with FYROM. Also negotiations with the Magreb and the Mashreq countries have been in progress.

Furthermore, the customs union also requires that Turkey's competition law, the rules of state aid control and other relevant parts of regulations all be harmonized with the relevant parts of the *acquis communautaire* of the single market of the EU. Turkey is also obliged to adopt the EU legislation and international convention on intellectual property rights. As Article 31 of the customs union states: 'The parties confirm the importance they attach to ensuring adequate and effective protection and enforcement of intellectual, industrial and commercial property rights' (Article 13, Decision No 1/95 of the EC-Turkey Association Council, 1995). Accordingly, Turkey has made some progress in protection of intellectual, industrial and commercial property rights and the Commission confirmed it: 'Turkey has undertaken significant progress in aligning her economic legislation, notably in the fields of competition and intellectual, property' (European Commission, 1999a). However, as the Commission indicated, progress still remains to be made to full conformity of approximation on the *acquis* in relation to the protection of copyrights and neighbouring rights in satellite and cable broadcast, patents and industrial designs (European Commission, 1999a, p. 22).

Another area where some problems have still been encountered in practice is the alignment of taxation. While the CU envisages the harmonization of the tax system and has called for the parties to take necessary measures to prevent unfair internal taxation on the products of the other party, further alignments still need to be made. A more sustained effort is required in particular with regard to excise duties, as well as the elimination of supplementary tax for certain imports (European Commission, 1999a).

As can be seen from the contents of the customs union, the agreement amounts to less than what the original Ankara Agreement envisaged. Indeed, the customs union is limited in the sense that Turkey is excluded from some of the crucial aspects of the EU's single market: it does not offer progressive integration with the EU in the areas of agriculture, services and free movement of persons, which are all components of the European single market. However, it must be recognized that the progressive establishment of free movement of persons will be difficult, as the increasing population of young people and Turkey's weak economy could lead to a significant migratory influx from Turkey to the EU. Thus, the establishment of free movement for workers will require a long transition period and must take account of *inter alia* the social and economic conditions and requirements in Turkey and the employment situation in the EU. Nevertheless, the customs union does not contain any provisions or commitments about how this would be achieved. The Commission, in its report, recognized this; 'the issue of free movement of workers needs to be subject of mutual consultations, but no progress has been made in that respect' (European Commission, 2000a, p. 35).

Furthermore, the customs union does not envisage progressive integration of the Turkish agricultural sector with the EU and lacks adequate financial and technical cooperation instruments to cope with the adaptation of Turkey's industrial sector to new competitive situations. The main concern has been related to the incompatibility of the Turkish economic structure with the EU in general and industrial sectors in particular. Although the customs union introduced the progressive removal of duties and charges on industrial imports from the EU over the five years, the macro economic conditions of Turkey were, and still are, poor and certainly require more time under an appropriate policy to adapt to the common external tariff policy of the EU and the abolition of import tariffs on industrial goods from the EU. For instance, Spain and Portugal achieved the abolition of import tariffs in seven years and had a six years transition period in which to adapt for the customs union of the EU, but had voting power and full access to structural funds as soon as they joined the EU.

Thus, it can be argued that the customs union creates an unequal balance in trade between Turkey and the EU in favour of the EU. As is shown in Table 4.1, since the customs union came into effect, Turkey's trade deficit increased from US$5.872 billion in 1995 to $11.59 billion in 1996 and continued to increase to $12.622 billion in 1997 and to $10.27 billion in 1998. After rising dramatically in the first year, the trade deficit between the partners has continued to increase slightly in favour of the EU, despite declining to $8.08 billion in 1999, which was the result of the earthquakes in August 1999.

However, the negative consequences of the customs union for Turkish trade with the EU have been inevitable in the short term because of the heavily misshapen structure of the Turkish economy. The benefits of the customs union for Turkey are largely dependent on Turkey's economic policy and, therefore, it would be wrong to attribute the negative economic consequence of the customs union entirely to the agreement. In fact, chronic mismanagement of the Turkish economy by successive governments has seriously weakened not only the potential benefits of the customs union, but also the prospect for Turkish accession to the EU on economic grounds. Macroeconomic instability, including instability of the exchange rate and unfavourable economic climate, combined with a lack of structural economic reforms on the part of Turkey with a high level of public expenditure and political instability, has created serious concerns about any prospect of Turkey's participation in the European single market and the EMU (The European Commission, 2000a).

Moreover, the significant trade deficit between the EU and Turkey can be largely explained by the fact that Turkey has imported mainly industrial products from the EU, while she has exported mainly agricultural and textiles products to the EU. Therefore, it could be argued that the inclusion of agricultural products in the customs union would have reduced the huge trade deficit between the parties. In fact, agriculture is the sector where Turkey has a comparative advantage; it could easily export to the EU to reduce the huge trade deficit. But, the EU has retained its barriers on Turkish agricultural exports. According to Turkey, the EU has raised its level of protection for basic agricultural products, which has had the effect of increasing the level of the agricultural component in processed agricultural products and reducing the competitive edge of Turkish exports in the European market.[4] Apart from the agricultural products, the textile industry has been also subject to quotas where Turkey has a comparative advantage.

Table 4.1   Turkey's trade with the EU since the customs union

Year	Import (US$ billion)	Change (%)	Export (US$ billion)	Change (%)	Trade deficit	EU's share (%)
1995	16.95	–	11.078	–	5.872	48.7
1996	23.138	36.5	11.548	4.2	11.591	51.9
1997	24.870	7.5	12.248	6.1	12.622	49.6
1998	24.075	-3.2	13.498	10.2	10.275	51.5
1999	22.419	5.58	14.333	6.2	8.086	53.1

Sources: Devlet Istatistik Enstitusu in March 2000 and Ticaret Mustasarligi Bulteni in June 2000.

In addition to the trade deficit, the loss of tariff revenue from imports has become another issue. Considering that 17 per cent of Turkey's tax revenue originated from duties placed on industrial imports, the customs union has caused the loss of tax revenues amounting to approximately $2.6 billion annually, which is almost equivalent to the financial support promised by the EU in five years.

On the other hand, Turkish policy-makers recognized that improving the structure, standards and adjustment of the legislative framework of the Turkish economy in line with the EU, including harmonizing the Turkish competition policy and intellectual property legislations with that of the EU, should attract more foreign direct investment (FDI) in Turkey. They believed that increased FDI could, therefore, reduce the costs arising from the loss of revenue and the trade deficit with the EU. As the Turkish Foreign minister, Murat Karayalcin, said at the EU-Turkey Association Council meeting in 1995:

> Substantial increases in flows of private direct investment will help to alleviate some of burdens that Turkey will incur (The Minutes of the 36th EU-Turkey Association Council, 1995).

However, the substantial increase in direct investment has not materialized as had been hoped. This has been partly due to Turkey's political and macro economic policies which have not encouraged the FDI in Turkey. Although Turkey has undertaken some necessary structural adjustment to integrate herself into the single market of the EU with the large domestic market, the macro-economic situation with a high rate of inflation and the political instability have undermined these efforts (Loewndahl, H. and Loewndahl, E., 2000). In addition, the rise of political Islam, the Kurdish issue and the political disputes with Greece have all adversely affected the decisions of foreign investors. Of course, another factor is that the lack of commitment and lack of accession credibility in the EU's policy towards Turkey might well have had a negative effect on FDI in Turkey. In contrast, the EU's enlargement strategy *vis-à-vis* the CEECs incorporating a high degree of accession credibility has brought them significant positive economic effects, including increased FDI, economic growth and rapid progress in their economic reforms.

To conclude, the instruments of the customs union have not been comprehensive enough to act as a pre-accession instrument for Turkey's membership, and thus cannot provide the necessary support to integrate Turkey into the EU. This implies that a more effective customs union, by taking the needs of Turkey into account, with more comprehensive instruments than the existing customs union, would be necessary if membership of Turkey was considered to be attainable in the foreseeable future. The rest of the chapter will explore the question as to what extent the EU's containment policy for Turkey, including the customs union and Accession Partnership Document, has been incompatible with the latter's membership expectations? This will be analyzed from a comparative perspective, comparing the EU's pre-accession instruments for the CEECs with its containment policy instruments for Turkey. This comparative analysis contributes to the main argument of the book, as it provides some evidence to suggest that Turkey has been treated in a different way from other applicant countries.

A Comparison of the EU's Containment Strategy for Turkey and its Pre-Accession Strategy for the CEECs

The EU's containment policy towards Turkey, including the customs union and Accession Partnership, seems to have been primarily concerned with trade liberalization and creating the conditions for the free-movement of industrial goods, along with commitment to political dialogue and financial cooperation measures, conditional on Turkey's making progress in human rights and improving relations with Greece. Thus, the EU's policy instruments indicated in the above have lacked the credibility that would be afforded by strategy which explicitly incorporated the prospect of Turkish accession to the EU. In fact, although the EU always underlined the main problems impeding Turkey's accession to the EU, its policy does not seem to have focused much on resolving these problems. Even the recently accepted Accession Partnership is not appropriate for developing a strategy to prepare Turkey for accession. Although the instruments of the EU's policy towards Turkey, including the customs union, will establish the deepest possible economic integration in the area of industrial products, it is limited in the sense that Turkey has been excluded from many of the crucial aspects of the EU's single market. This implies that the EU's policy *vis-à-vis* Turkey has fallen well short of a pre-accession strategy for Turkey to bring her into the EU in the long run.

However, the EU's policy towards the CEECs has been more generous: it clearly has been comprehensive enough to act as a pre-accession instrument for their accession to the EU. The Europe Agreements and the EU's pre-accession strategy for CEECs, enhanced by accession partnership and reinforcement of pre-accession aid, have covered a comprehensive range of policy areas and set out a very ambitious agenda for the CEECs, which is explicitly linked to the latter's accession to the EU. In this respect, the EU's role in the CEECs has gone beyond just economic aid to include and support the legal harmonization process, institution-building, democratization and the explicit encouragement of specific political and legal reforms, as accession partnership and reinforcement of pre-accession aid of the EU have given priority to addressing the main problems which might impede the CEECs' accession to the EU. With appropriate support through the pre-accession strategy, the EU has guided and even directed or catalyzed the reform process of the CEECs. Therefore, a comparison of the EU's enlargement policy towards the CEECs and its policy *vis-à-vis* Turkey suggests that there has been inconsistency between the two in terms of instruments, effectiveness and accession credibility. In other words, the CEECs have attracted an entirely different response from the EU with the form of clear policy instruments and accession commitment, while the EU's policy towards Turkey has lacked the necessary instruments to help and support Turkey's preparation for membership of the EU.

The following section of the chapter will analyze the EU's policy instruments towards Turkey and the CEECs in preparation for the EU's single market, the CAP and financial and technical cooperation. This comparative analysis will shed further light on the question of whether Turkey has been treated in a different way than the others.

The EU's Policy towards Turkey and the CEECs in Relation to the EU's Single Market

As far as preparation for the single market of the EU is concerned, while some similarities can be seen in the EU's policy towards the CEECs and Turkey in terms of instruments for liberalizing trade between two parties, the general contents of the former seem to be more comprehensive and structured than the latter: for example, the pre-accession strategy has been accompanied by the White Paper on the preparation of the CEECs for integration into the EU single market. The White Paper provides not only a basic framework for the *acquis communautaire* with regard to trade liberalization in industrial goods, but also covers all aspects of the single market. Although the White Paper is indicative in character, and hence not legally binding, it became a *de facto* part of the EU's conditions for the CEECs to join the EU. Indeed, it provides a main basis for the Commission in its assessment of the CEECs ability to take on obligations of membership (Grabbe, 1999, p. 14). In this regard, the White Paper establishes a general framework for regulatory alignment for the CEEC in a large number of the EU's common policies, including the free-movement of services, the gradual implementation of free circulation of basic agricultural products, the right of establishment, free movement of persons, safe movement of industrial products, social policy, agriculture, transport, audiovisual, environment, telecom, taxation and financial services.

The White Paper provides a basic framework for the *acquis communautaire* with regard to the respective sectors of the single market and the chronological order for the adaptation of the legal provisions. In each sector, the White Paper divides the legislation into Stage I measures which set out the basic policies for the functioning of the single market and the instruments required to implement them, while Stage II details the implementation of the single market rules (Grabbe, 1999, p. 14). In total, the White Paper details 23 areas, ranging from the free movement of capital and services to consumer protections, where the CEECs would eventually have to align domestic law to that of the EU (Phinnemore, 1999, p. 108). In addition, the Commission established a Technical Assistance Information Exchange Office to advise the CEECs on aligning their legislation with the internal market of the Union (Avery and Cameron, 1998, p. 18). Basically, the White Paper presents the administrative and organizational framework for each section of the single market to enable the CEECs to adopt the EU's legal legislation, norms and standards efficiently and thus develop capacity to cope with competitive pressure and market forces within the Union.

However, as indicated in the previous section, the contents of the customs union are primarily concerned with liberalization of external trade relations between parties and creating conditions for the free-movement of industrial goods. Unlike the White Paper, the customs union lacks the regulatory framework for implementing all aspects of the EU single market, which is of critical importance for the preparation of EU membership. Indeed, the customs union appears to fall short of the EU's White Paper of pre-accession strategy for the CEECs in many ways. Although the instruments of the customs union push economic integration further in the area of industrial products than the instruments of the White Paper, the former is not as comprehensive as the latter. Some of the crucial aspects of the EU's single market were excluded from the objectives of the customs union. It does not contain any provisions for the gradual implementation of free circulation of basic agricultural products, the right of establishment and the free movement of services and free movement of workers, nor any move to a single currency. Even though the full establishment of the free movement of workers appears to be difficult and requires a long transition period, the study of alternative strategies for the development of relations in the fields of agriculture, the right of establishment and free movement of services would be necessary, not only for the proper functioning of the customs union, but for Turkey's adaptation to the EU's *acquis* with a view to the future accession of Turkey to the EU. In addition to this, the customs union does not provide a sufficient instrument to integrate Turkey with the EU's policies and allow the possibility of Turkey's participation in Union programmes.

Although the Commission's proposal of European Strategy for Turkey in 1998 recognized the need for new instruments to bring Turkey closer to accession, its contents seem to have fallen short of Turkey's preparation for membership in many ways (European Commission, 1998a). The European Strategy for Turkey principally has proposed broadening relations, designed to deepen the customs union as a means of extending it to some areas of the EU's common policies, such as the service and agricultural sectors. It has advocated closer cooperation in fields such as telecommunications, macroeconomic dialogue, industrial cooperation and investment, scientific and technological research and participation in Community programmes (European Commission, 1998a, p. 3). However, unlike the White Paper of pre-accession strategy for the CEECs, it has lacked the regulatory framework for implementing the EU single market, which is of critical importance for the preparation of EU membership.

Arguably, the Accession Partnership is designed to prepare the country for EU membership. In essence, however, the prospect for contributions that it would play in promoting Turkish accession to the EU appears to be limited. This is because its declared intermediate objectives, priorities and conditions and its financial instruments have not been comprehensive enough for developing strategy with a view to preparing Turkey for accession. That is, the Accession Partnership of Turkey lacks appropriate policy instruments and sufficient financial support to enhance the existing framework of the EU-Turkey Association, including the customs union and European Strategy for Turkey so as to reorient it towards eventual membership. The Accession Partnership broadly deals with the areas, such as taxation, fisheries, transport and environment, energy and telecommunications. Nevertheless, it does not contain any provisions as regards important aspects of the European Single Market, such as the right of establishment and the free movement of services and free movement of workers.

The EU's Policy towards Turkey and the CEECs in Relation to the EU's Common Agricultural Policy in the Context of Enlargement

Agriculture is also part of the single European market, and hence, the alignment of the agricultural sector of the applicant countries with that of the CAP is seen as fundamental to the success of the European single market in an enlarged Union. Comparing the EU's policy towards Turkey and its policy *vis-à-vis* the CEECs in terms of preparing them for the CAP suggests that the former has been much clearer and comprehensive than the latter, since the EU's policy *vis-à-vis* the CEECs has a more transparent strategy with policy credibility and a firmer commitment in supporting these countries' efforts to align their structure with that of the EU than its policy towards Turkey.

The CEECs and Turkey have similar characteristics; consequently, extension of the Common Agricultural Policy in its present form to the CEECs and Turkey would create similar difficulties for the EU. For example, the CEECs and Turkey have a large agricultural sector; consequently, they would greatly increase the agricultural potential of the EU in many aspects. The CEECs would increase the current EU's agricultural land area by 43 per cent (Ardy, 1997, p. 119). Turkey's accession to the EU would lead to enlarging the useable agricultural area of the EU by 22 per cent (European Commission, 1989b, p. 20). The number of people employed in the agricultural sector in an enlarged Union with CEECs would be increased by nearly 210 per cent, while Turkey's accession to the EU in present form would increase the number employed in the agricultural sector by nearly 170 per cent. The number of workers employed in the agricultural sector in both Turkey and the CEECs appears to be high, with 42.3 per cent and 24.5 per cent respectively, as compared to an EU average of 4.3 per cent (Eurostat, 1997). In addition, the share of agriculture in the GNP is 8.6 per cent for the CEECs and 16 per cent for Turkey. Indeed, the share of the Turkish agricultural sector in the GNP is the third highest among the applicant countries after Bulgaria with 21.1 per cent and Romania with 17.6 per cent (European Commission, 1999b). Furthermore, both Turkey's and the CEECs agricultural sectors can be considered relatively underdeveloped with relatively poor productivity. Therefore, such relatively large and underdeveloped agricultural sectors in the CEECs and Turkey would create a tremendous burden on the CAP, although it is difficult to assess the effect of their participation on the CAP, as it is not clear what the structure of the CAP will be at their accession. For the CEECs, the Commission estimated that the enlargement to include the CEEC-10 would add ECU 11 billion to the agricultural expenditure of the EU (Ardy, 1997).

As is seen from the above analysis, Turkey and the CEECs have similar structural problems in the field of agriculture. Therefore, extension of the Common Agricultural Policy in its present form to the CEECs and Turkey would create similar difficulties for the EU. In fact, the EU has underlined the incompatibility of the Turkish and the CEECs' agricultural sector with that of the EU's CAP and recognized the need for fundamental reforms to restructure the agricultural sector in these countries.[5] For the CEECs, the EU has developed a gradual approach to integrate the CEECs' agricultural sectors with the EU, with a parallel reform strategy. The EU has offered a preparation strategy for the CEECs, providing gradual, but increasingly close involvement in the CAP before accession starts. At the same time, the EU has initiated reforms to enable the CAP to continue to function effectively in an enlarged Union by means of reorientation of the CAP with less focus on price support and more on direct income support, as well as on rural development and environmental policy and further adjustments in the current support policies (European Commission, 1997b).

Contrary to its policy towards the CEECs, the EU's policy towards Turkey, including the customs union, European Strategy for Turkey and Accession Partnership, has lacked pre-accession instruments and a structural programme for the Turkish agricultural sector. Though the customs union provides that parties should commit themselves to move towards the free movement of such products, in accordance with special rules which should take into account the common agricultural policy of the EU, it seems that such commitment has not been accompanied by the necessary instruments or programmes to proceed towards the free movement of agricultural products. This is important in the sense that the necessary instruments or programmes would provide a framework with which to guide Turkey to implement fundamental reforms of its agricultural sector, thereby hastening Turkey's ability to assume the obligations of membership in regard to the *acquis* of agriculture. The EU offered only an assurance for Turkey in which it would take into account Turkey's agricultural interests in developing its agricultural policy. In return, Turkey would adjust its policy to adopt the common agricultural policy measures required to establish freedom of movement in agricultural products (Articles 24–27 of Decision No 1/95 of the EC-Turkey Association Council, 1995).

Turkey's relatively large agricultural sector, combined with a low level of income and a huge number of workers employed in the agricultural sector, would create a tremendous burden on the EU's budgetary resource under the existing structure of the Common Agricultural Policy of the EU. However, it should be noted that Turkish agricultural output consists predominantly of vegetable products, which account for 65 per cent of the total products, and Mediterranean products, while the EU's agricultural price support is much greater for northern products, such as meat, milk and diary products (Redmond, 1993). Consequently, Turkish agricultural products would receive only limited support under the current Common Agricultural Policy of the EU. After all, it is difficult to assess the effect of Turkey's participation on the CAP, because it is not clear what the structure of the CAP will be at the time of Turkish accession. In fact, the EU has already initiated reforms to enable the CAP to continue to function effectively in an enlarged Union by means of reorientation of the CAP (European Commission, 1997b). By implication, considering the long-term prospect for Turkey's accession to the EU and the reformed CAP by the time of Turkish accession, the budgetary implication of Turkish accession would not be too costly.

As indicated in the above, Turkey's participation in the CAP would require a long-term transition period, but such a transition period would also depend on the progress Turkey has made in aligning its agricultural policy with that of the CAP. During this period, the EU might provide financial and technical support for the incorporation of Turkey into the existing Community legislation on agriculture. In addition, a regular dialogue on technical cooperation, providing know-how, appears to be essential to identify the main issues in Turkey's adoption of the CAP. Although the Commission proposal of European Strategy for Turkey recognized the need for measures to help Turkey adopt the existing Community legislation on agriculture, it did not provide any new instruments or a regular dialogue at a technical level to prepare Turkey progressively for the CAP (European Commission, 1998a). Finally, the Accession Partnership recommended Turkey to complete preparations for the *acquis* in agricultural and rural developments. It also identified some specific needs of Turkish agricultural structure to comply with EU standards. These included developing a functioning land register, animal identifications system, implement environment, structural and rural development measures and establishing an appropriate alignment strategy for veterinary and plant health Community legislation (European Commission, 2000e). Yet, these provisions and priorities in the Accession Partnership are not detailed enough to provide a road map for Turkey's preparation for the CAP in the long run. Besides, it has lacked financial and technical assistance to support Turkey's preparation for complying with *acquis* of the EU in this respect.

The EU has essentially been more favourable towards the CEECs than Turkey. The EU has supported the structural adjustment process of the agricultural sector in the CEECs through the pre-accession strategy (Ardy, 1997, pp. 107–129). Technical and financial assistance has been provided for structural reforms and rural development in these countries. In addition, the EU has strengthened the pre-accession strategy, the so-called reinforced pre-accession strategy, which envisages more financial support for the CEECs to prepare them in adopting the CAP (European Commission, 1997b). For example, the PHARE investment support has been particularly concentrated with agricultural restructuring to adapt the infrastructure to the EU *acquis*, including the support for the alignment of norms and standards with those of the EU and the support for the development of regional, social and rural policies similar to those developed in the EU. In addition, the 'twinning project' – as part of the institution building process under pre-accession assistance for the CEECs – has provided substantial aid to the CEECs' development of modern and efficient administrations with the structures, human resources and management skills. In this respect, one of the main areas in which the Twinning Project concentrates has been agriculture, including harmonization of the CEECs' legislation with EU legislation, training of veterinarians, food quality and consumer protection, the interaction between agricultural products and the environment, environmentally friendly control methods, and sustainable agriculture.

More importantly, as part of the pre-accession assistance, the EU initiated the Special Accession Programme for Agriculture and Rural Development, designed to help the CEECs with the problems of structural adjustment in their agricultural sectors and rural areas, as well as in the implementation of the *acquis communautaire* in the CAP and related legislation (European Commission, 1997b). Furthermore, the EU has set up a programme and established a dialogue through a Joint Committee in order to prepare the CEECs for the CAP as a means of helping these countries to bring their farm policy in line with the CAP.

To conclude, Turkey has been treated differently in the enlargement process of the EU. In fact, there has been inconsistency between the EU's policy towards the CEECs and that towards Turkey: while the EU has sought ways to hasten the CEECs participation in the CAP with substantial financial assistance, its containment policy towards Turkey has lacked a firm commitment, policy credibility and adequate instruments to prepare the latter for participation in the CAP. In other words, similar issues in the CEEC have attracted an entirely different response from the EU, with the shape of a clear policy instrument and accession commitment on the grounds that reforms to restructure the agricultural sector in these countries must be supported and encouraged. However, the EU's containment policy for Turkey, including the customs union and Accession Partnership, has fallen short of preparing Turkey for participation in the field of the CAP.

The Financial and Technical Cooperation Aspects of the EU's Containment Policy in a Comparative Perspective with the CEECs

Financial protocols have been part of the EU-Turkey Association Agreement with the aim of accelerating the development of the Turkish economy. However, not only the amount envisaged in Financial Protocols of the EU-Turkey Association, including the customs union and the Accession Partnership, but also the failure to implement them exemplifies the fact that the EU's policy towards Turkey has been insufficient for the purpose of the progressive integration of Turkey with the EU in the context of post-Maastrich Europe.

The First Financial Protocol in 1963 was ECU 175 million for the financing of investment projects in Turkey for a five-year period (Article 2 of the Financial Protocol, Ankara Agreement, 1963). Although the amount seems very limited in today's values, at that time it constituted a substantial amount to the Turkish economy, considering that Turkish annual exports were around $400 million (Kabaalioglu, 1998, p. 133). The Second Financial Protocol was accepted in accordance with the Additional Protocol in 1971 in which the amount of ECU 195 million was granted to Turkey to cover a period of five years (Article 3 (2), Financial Protocol, 1971).

Similarly, the Third Financial Protocol, with the aim of increasing the productivity of the Turkish economy was agreed in 1977. It allocated the amount of ECU 310 million for the period until 1980 (Kabaalioglu, 1999, p. 122). The Fourth Financial Protocol was agreed in which the EU made a commitment of ECU 600 million of financial aid for the period of five years beginning in 1980. However, this has never materialized for many reasons, mainly, the suspension of the Association Agreement due to the military coup of September 1980, breaches of human rights in Turkey and Greek objections.

The Commission in its opinion on Turkey's early application for EU membership underlined the importance of the EU's financial support for the Turkish economy, stating that 'financial co-operation should be revitalized by releasing the resources of the Fourth Financial Protocol' (European Commission, 1989a). Yet, it has gained a political character. Consequently it has been consistently suspended for the above-mentioned reasons.

When the customs union was agreed, the EU reaffirmed its commitment to resuming financial aid to Turkey. In fact, it recognized that Turkey needed 'substantial financial resources, in particular long term loans and technical assistance, in order to adapt its industrial sector to the new competitive situations created by the customs union'.[6] Thus, the EU offered special cooperation measures for Turkey in which it would help Turkey's effort to strengthen its social and economic structure and to improve the competitiveness of Turkey's economy, as well as to consolidate democratic principles and the development of a civil society.

Basically, the aim of the financial cooperation was to help alleviate the negative effect of the structural adjustment process so as to integrate Turkey into the single market of the EU. In this respect, the financial cooperation of the customs union consisted of the following elements:

- Budgetary resources of ECU 375 million to be provided for Turkey over a five-year period starting in 1996.
- Access to ECU 300–400 million of EIB loans under the Mediterranean Policy for the financing of infrastructure projects in the fields of environment, energy, transport and telecommunication.
- Loans of up to ECU 750 million over the period 1996–2000 to improve the competitiveness of the Turkish economy.
- Additional EIB loans of ECU 750 million over the five years from the budgetary resources and loans which the EU would make available from 1996 to all Mediterranean countries.
- At Turkey's request and if Turkey needed, the EU, in coordination with international financial institutions, could examine the feasibility of

exceptional further medium term macro-economic financial assistance, linked to the execution of IMF approved programmes (Declaration of the EU-Turkey Association Council on the Financial Cooperation, 1995).

As is seen from the above, the envisaged amount of the EU's financial assistance to Turkey under the financial cooperation of the customs union was approximately ECU 2.5 billion. Such an amount of declared financial support seemed to be insufficient for the needs of Turkey in structurally adjusting to its integrating into the single market of the EU. More interestingly, though the Commission issued a proposal for a Council decision on assistance to Turkey in the framework of pre-accession strategy, it is limited to resources that were already granted to Turkey under the customs union, the MEDA programmes and European strategy for Turkey (European Commission, 2000d). The proposal has rather established a single framework for coordinating these financial instruments of EU assistance as the part of the Accession Partnership Document.

When comparing the EU's financial support for the CEECs to its financial support for Turkey, many discrepancies can be seen. First, the objective of the EU's financial support for the CEECs has been explicitly linked to their accession process to the EU. Indeed, the main objective of the financial support granted in the framework of the pre-accession strategy under the PHARE programmes, structural instrument (the ISPA) and the agricultural instrument (the SAPARD) is to assist the CEECs in their preparations for joining the EU. All these financial sources have been closely oriented to accession. However, the EU's commitment to resume financial aid to Turkey does not seem to have included such a firm accession commitment to Turkey. In fact, the EU's financial support has been principally related in general to the development of the Turkish economy and the harmonious expansion of trade and in particular to the strengthening of Turkey's economic structure to cope with the customs union (Declaration of the EU-Turkey Association Council on the Financial Cooperation, 1995). Even the proposal of the Commission for a Council regulation on assistance to Turkey in the framework of pre-accession strategy has lacked sufficient financial instruments to support Turkey in her preparation for EU membership in the long run.

Second, the EU's financial support to the CEECs has been more comprehensive and wide-ranging than its support for Turkey. While the initial aim of the PHARE was to support the political and economic reforms in the CEECs, its scope has been extended to cover other projects in the restructuring of agriculture, public administration, education, health, environment and nuclear security. The financial aid offered by the EU under the PHARE programmes has included these areas:

- Consumer protection: designed to help the establishment of institutions and legislation, in order to harmonize consumer protection in the CEECs with the EU standard.
- Harmonization of standards and technical regulations: aimed at building knowledge and facilitating implementation of the EU' norms and standards and copyright protection.
- Intellectual property: directed to support the development of trademark, patent and industrial design protection.

- Customs and statistics: aimed at drafting EU-compatible customs legislation, with a focus on easing transport and trade, helping the CEECs to create the statistical base necessary for a market economy.
- Public procurement: designed to support modifying public procurement legislation through legal advice, training and documentation in the CEECs.
- Environment: intended to support building a legal environment framework for the CEECs in line with the EU's environmental standard.
- Competition and state aid: support for drafting new laws with regard to state aid to industry by providing training and documentation (European Commission, 1995d, pp. 15–16).

Furthermore, the PHARE programme has been reorganized in accordance with Agenda 2000 of the Commission. In fact, the scope of PHARE has been extended to the building of the institutions and to the financing of investment projects. From 1998, 30 per cent of PHARE assistance has been allocated for institution building aimed at strengthening democratic institutions and public administration in the Central and Eastern European Countries, including technical assistance, training and the twinning of institutions and administrations. Priority has been given to areas such as finance, agriculture, environment, justice and home affairs. The rest of PHARE, which accounts for 70 per cent of total assistance, has been allocated to the investment programmes in the CEECs. This has sought to support the necessary investments as regards the adaptation of the *acquis* of the EU in the area of infrastructure, agricultural restructuring and regional development, including investment in human and intellectual capital, investments to support compliance with Community norms in the environment, agriculture, transport, telecommunications and the co-financing of large scale infrastructure, as well as the development of small and medium enterprises (The European Commission, 1997b).

Moreover, the two new pre-accession financial instruments were made available for the CEECs: the structural pre-accession instrument (the ISPA) and the agricultural pre-accession instrument (the SAPARD). For the period between 2000 and 2006 an increased amount of pre-accession aid has been granted to the CEECs for agricultural development, amounting to ECU 500 million per year under the SPARD; and for structural development, with ECU one billion annually to align infrastructure standards of the CEECs with those of the EU in many areas, such as in the transport and environmental spheres (The European Commission, 1997b). Furthermore, the reinforced accession strategy has provided other forms of assistance for the CEECs to help them to participate in EU programmes (The European Commission, 1997b).

Nevertheless, the EU's commitment to financial support to Turkey does not seem to have been as comprehensive or wide-ranging. It has not provided adequate financial and technical support for Turkey to absorb the *acquis communautaire* of the EU and to complete market reforms and the medium-term restructuring of its economy to create the conditions required for future membership. In other words, while the EU's financial and technical support for the CEECs has given priority to the main problems impeding these countries' accession to the EU in accordance with the Commission's opinion, the EU's financial cooperation measures for Turkey have principally tended to support the adaptation of Turkey's industrial sector to new competitive situations, including the improvement of infrastructure linkages with the European Union and reducing the difference between the Turkish economy and that of the Union. That is to say that the EU has not offered financial and technical support for numerous areas that constitute a barrier to Turkey's membership prospects, such as agricultural development and structural adjustment. The Commission proposal in 1998 for releasing EU financial assistance to Turkey, designed to support Turkey's inclusion into the European rules of origin system and her participation in regulations on transit, as well as support to improve efficiency of Turkey's public sector, has not been comparable with that of the PHARE for the CEECs. Even the proposal of the Commission for a Council regulation on assistance to Turkey in the framework of pre-accession strategy in June 2000 has lacked a sufficient financial instrument to stimulate and support policy reforms in Turkey for its preparation for membership (European Commission, 2000d). To illustrate, it does not make any reference to the prospect for Turkey's inclusion in the ISPA (Instrument for Structural Policy for Accession) and the SAPARD (Special Accession Programme for Agricultural Sector and Rural Development), designed to restructure the agricultural sectors in the applicant countries and develop infrastructures in line with the EU standards.

Third, the failure by the EU to resume its commitment to the financial support of Turkey and the EU's full implementation of its commitment *vis-à-vis* the CEECs has provided more supporting evidence that Turkey has been treated unfavourably. The implementation of the Fourth Financial Protocol had already been frozen since 1980 for well-known reasons. In addition, although at the time of the establishment of the customs union, the EU made a commitment to Turkey, including a special package of ECU 375 million in budgetary aid and a package of EIB loans totalling ECU 750 million, the EU Council has been unable to attain the required unanimity to adopt the framework regulations for the special customs union budgetary aid of ECU 375 million, owing to Greek objections. Similarly, the EIB has been unable to act on the invitation made by the Council in December 1995 to grant loans of ECU 750 million to Turkey as envisaged in the declaration made by the EU on financial cooperation (The European Commission, 1996, p. 3). In accordance with the request of the European Council Summit in Luxembourg in 1997, the Commission adopted the European Strategy for Turkey in which the implementation of financial cooperation was one of the main elements. The Commission underlined the urgent need for the adoption by the Council of financial regulation regarding Turkey. However, Greece blocked the approval of the proposed financial cooperation with Turkey on the grounds of Turkey's failure to maintain good relations with Greece (*Agence Europe*, 28 April 1998). Therefore, the Commission adopted a new proposal to resume financial aid to Turkey, totalling EUR 135 million. The Cardiff Summit of the EU favourably received it in 1998, as it was a development aid based on Article 235 of TEU; thus, unanimity is not required for it. Greece reacted harshly to this Commission initiative and claimed that it presented a dangerous precedent, and that it would refer the matter to the Court of Justice in Luxembourg (*Agence Europe*, 22 October 1998).

This indicated that the EU could find ways to dismiss the Greek objection so long as the member states are determined to carry on. The EU's financial commitment to Turkey is part of the Agreement and thus the EU should have found ways to disregard Greek objections for financial cooperation with Turkey. Therefore, it does not seem the Greek objection is a good reason for treating Turkey unfairly in this respect. Another reason for the failure of the implementation of the EU's financial commitment to Turkey is the breach of human rights. In particular, the EP has made the approval needed for implementing the EU's financial commitment to Turkey conditional upon respect for principles of liberty, democracy, respect for human rights and the rule of law. For example, the EP called on the Commission and the EU Council of Ministers to block all appropriations set aside the project in Turkey under the MEDA programme (European Parliament, 1996a). Although the MEDA was prepared to support the Mediterranean countries, including Turkey, in their development efforts, this support has not been properly introduced in the Turkish case. Although Turkey's failure to undertake the necessary policy reforms in human rights has provided some grounds for the EU's hesitation towards the implementation of financial cooperation with Turkey, it cannot provide sufficient reasons why Turkey has been treated differently from the other applicant countries, as they have similar problems.

As mentioned above, unlike Turkey, the CEECs have already attained successful financial and technical cooperation with the EU despite the inadequacy of their human rights and political systems. During the period between 1990 and 1993, ECU 3285.7 million were made available to the CEECs. Similarly, for a period between 1994 and 1996, ECU 3350.5 million were allocated to the CEECs from the PHARE programme (The European Parliament, 1999, p. 16). Since then, the totals have continued to increase: for example in 1996, ECU 6600 million were made available to the CEECs.[7] In addition, complementary to PHARE, the Luxembourg Summit of the EU decided to increase substantially pre-accession aid and to allocate ECU 520 million aid in annually to the agricultural sector, as well as new structural instruments which allocated ECU 1 billion per year for the period between 2000 and 2006 (The European Commission, 1997b).

It should be noted that although the EU has made the implementation of all instruments of European Agreements, including financial aid, conditional upon compliance with the requirement of respect for democratic principles and human rights, this conditionally has not been applied to any country in the CEEC as strictly as it has been applied to Turkey. While the EU has always highlighted a number of problems to do with the treatment of minority rights and the functioning of institutional democracy in the CEECs, it has continued to provide financial support for them with a view to influencing their route to integrating with the EU; hence, suspension of financial cooperation, or their exclusion from the accession strategy seems to have been considered by the EU as a policy of last resort.

For example, while the EP and the Commission always underlined that Slovakia's political situation presented a number of problems to do with treatment of Hungarian minorities and in the functioning of institutional democracy, the EU continued to provide financial support for Slovakia with a view to influencing the Slovakian route to integrating with the EU. Even following the EU's strong criticism of undemocratic practices in Slovakia in 1994 and in 1995, no suspension of financial cooperation occurred (Grabbe, 1999, p. 11).

Therefore, it can be argued that the EU's condition on the implementation of financial cooperation with Turkey seems to be applied more strictly than its policy towards the CEECs. This has even been the case for the decision-making procedure of financial cooperation: as regards the CEECs, the PHARE financial regulations at the Council are taken by majority decisions, as the Council Regulation[8] stipulates:

> The Council shall at any time take appropriate steps with regard to any pre-accession assistance granted to any applicant countries, acting by qualified majority on a proposal from the Commission, where the commitments contained in the Europe Agreement are not respected and the progress towards fulfillment of the Copenhagen criteria is insufficient (Article 4 Council Regulation, 1998).

Nevertheless, the EU's insistence on the rule of unanimity for the financial regulations relating to Turkey can be regarded as an indication of the way in which financial cooperation between the EU and Turkey has became politicized.

In conclusion, the above analysis has suggested that the EU has explicitly linked all financial sources for the CEEC to their accession process to the EU. The PHARE is the EU's most important financial and technical support instrument in preparing the CEECs for the next enlargement of the EU by means of helping the CEECs to comply with *acquis* of the Union in many areas. In fact, while the initial phase of the PHARE programme was demand-driven in order to support the economic and political transformation in the CEECs, it has became an accession instrument with a focus closely on accession requirement in accordance with priorities set by the Commission. For Turkey, in contrast, the EU's commitment to resume financial aid neither includes such a firm accession commitment to Turkey, nor one comprehensive enough to support the integration process of Turkey as she prepares for accession to the EU. The EU's commitment to financial support for Turkey has more closely focused on the general development of the Turkish economy than on accession requirements. In addition, the financial cooperation between Turkey and the EU has become politicized for the above-mentioned reasons; thus, it has caused another issue. Therefore, the failure to implement financial cooperation seems to have introduced a credibility issue in EU-Turkey relations. A former EU Ambassador to Turkey, Michael Lake, underlined this credibility issue, arguing that the failure by the EU to implement the declared financial aid to Turkey 'continues to damage the Union's credibility'. He further stated that:

> It is not money which counts, the loss is psychological and political; it saps trust and confidence in the relationship (cited in Kabaalioglu, 1999, p. 128).

Similarly, the Turkish Prime Minister, Tansu Ciller, stated that:

> The importance of the failure to implement the financial commitment was more than a question of the amount at stake, which is rather small amount in proportion to the whole of the Turkish economy, but rather the fact that the EU had not honored its commitments under the customs union (cited in Neuwahl, 1999, p. 49).

The Helsinki process has brought some improvements in the financial support of the EU for Turkey. Since the Helsinki Summit, which made Turkey a candidate for EU membership, the Commission has taken some measures to establish a single framework for coordinating all sources of EU financial assistance for Turkey. First, the Commission submitted the Proposal for a Council decision on assistance to Turkey in the framework of pre-accession strategy. As noted in the above, although the Commission's proposal is limited to resources that were already granted to Turkey under the customs union, the MEDA programmes and the European Strategy for Turkey, it was important in that the new pre-accession strategy makes a strong commitment to provide Turkey with these financial resources. The Proposal envisages an annual figure of EUR 177 million for the next five years, of which EUR 127 million corresponds to Turkey's share of MEDA programmes, EUR 45 millions for social and economic development and five million to support the customs union. However, as is seen the amount provided for Turkey in the framework of pre-accession strategy, the envisaged financial instrument appears to be insufficient to support Turkey in her preparation for EU membership. Indeed, the amount offered for Turkey seems to have fallen far short of the amount made available for the CEECs, as an annual figure granted to the CEEC in the framework of the pre-accession strategy under the PHARE, the SPARD and the ISPA has reached EUR 3.12 billion (European Commission, 2000f). Moreover, the content of the Commission's proposal on financial assistance to Turkey is not closely oriented to accession, as it has been for the CEECs.

Conclusions

As the above analysis suggests, the instruments of the EU's pre-accession strategy, consisting of the Association Agreement, the customs union, the European strategy for Turkey and the Accession Partnership Document, have not been closely oriented to prepare Turkey for accession. In this respect, rather than being pre-accession strategy, the EU's policy towards Turkey has been better described as a containment policy: a policy designed to establish a framework for diverse form of cooperation and integration with Turkey for the foreseeable future, with a promise of full membership of the EU in the long run but without an appropriate instruments to deliver it. In this respect, the customs union, strengthened by a European Strategy for Turkey and Accession Partnership Document, has constituted a prominent part of this policy, as the EU believed that it could anchor Turkey into the EU as a stable and secular country. This implies that the EU genuinely desires to continue building on its relations with Turkey on economic grounds with a strengthened institutional cooperation, but also implies that there has been inconsistency between the EU's declaration confirming its commitment to the Turkish membership and its actual policy. Despite the EU's repeated assertions of the eligibility of Turkey for EU membership and recognition of Turkey as a candidate for EU membership at the Helsinki Summit, the instruments of its policy have fallen short of achieving this commitment. To illustrate, considering that a clear transparent and targeted accession strategy requires a sufficient pre-accession aid, financial sources provided for Turkey in the customs union and Accession Partnership have not only been inadequate to support Turkey's preparation for accession, but also not closely oriented to accession. This explains why Turkey has been treated differently from the other applicant countries.

Although the EU's containment policy, including the customs union, has reactivated the EU-Turkey Association and resulted in an increased economic interdependence in trade, it has not provided a similar degree of integration in the other aspects of the European single market, because its instruments have fallen well short of what is required to prepare the way for EU membership. For example, the instruments of the customs union were limited to cover a specific aspect of single market, however, some of crucial parts of the EU's single market were excluded. The customs union has not offered progressive integration with the EU in the areas of agriculture, services, free movement of persons, environment and transport, which are all components of the European single market. This supports the chapter's contention that there has been inconsistency between the EU's policy towards Turkey and its policy for the CEECs: while the objective of the EU's policy towards the CEECs has been explicitly linked to their preparation for the EU's single market, including the establishment of adequate implementation and enforcement mechanism with sufficient financial support, its policy towards Turkey has neither included a clearly defined accession strategy to support Turkey's preparation for the internal market of the EU, nor a sufficient financial and technical support to achieve this. By implication, Turkey has been treated differently.

The overall conclusion is that the instruments of the EU's containment policy, including the customs union and Accession Partnership, have been inadequate for Turkey's preparation for membership. Thus, a comprehensive policy framework – a clear transparent and targeted accession strategy – is needed in policy areas outside the customs union and Accession Partnership Document to stimulate and support Turkey's efforts towards adoption of the *acquis* of the European single market with a view to accession. Moreover, incorporating the *acquis* of the European single market into Turkish legislation is not sufficient in itself; there is also need for credible and effective implementation and enforcement of this *acquis*. Thus, it will require a comprehensive framework within which Turkey's preparation for the EU's internal market will be supported by way of helping it to develop the capacity to implement the EU's *acquis* (through institutions building) and to mobilize the investment needed to bring its industry and its infrastructures up to the EU standards (through investment support structural adjustment facilities), as well as to support Turkey for tackling the issue of economic and social cohesion through the SPARD (Special Accession Programme for Agriculture and Rural Development) and the ISPA (Instrument for Structural Policies for pre-Accession), as has been the case for the CEECs.

Notes

1   Article 28 of the Ankara Agreement stipulates that 'as soon as the operations of the Agreement has advanced far enough to justify envisaging full acceptance by Turkey of the obligations arising out from the Treaty establishing the Community, the contracting parties shall examine the possibility of the accession of Turkey to the Community'. For this, see 'Agreement Establishing a Association between the European Economic Community and Republic of Turkey', *Official Journal of European Communities,* L.1217, Brussels.

2   As regards the CEECs, Cyprus and Malta, the term of preparing for accession were used in the conclusions of the European Council summits, in official documents of the

Commission and in a number of resolutions of the European Parliament, Nevertheless, there was not any reference to the membership application or preparation of membership as regards Turkey.

3   For this, see European Council (1995) *Presidency Conclusions,* Madrid, 15–16 December, General Secretariat of the Council, Brussels.

4   See, Ministry of Foreign Affairs (1998) *A Proposal of Turkey: Strategy for Developing Relations between Turkey and the European Union* (Ministry of Foreign Affairs website: www.mfa.gov.tr).

5   For this, see each of the Commission's avis as regards the capacity to take on the obligations of membership in the agricultural sectors.

6   For this, see Declaration of the EU-Turkey Association Council on the Financial Cooperation*, Decision No 1/95 of the EC-Turkey Association Council on the Customs Union*, CE-TR 106/1/95, General Secretariat of the Council, Brussels.

7   For this, see the debates of the European Parliament, *Official Journal of the European Parliament*, No 4–503/48, 25.6.97.

8   For this, see Article 4 Council Regulation, 622/ 98, *Official Journal of European Union*, LC 278, 12 April 1998, Brussels.

Chapter 5

The Political Aspects of the EU's Policy Towards Turkey in the Context of a New European Political Order

Introduction

It is widely believed that Turkey's failure to implement its commitment to make its political and human rights system converge with that of the EU has provided legitimate grounds for the EU's differentiated policy towards Turkey. However, this does not seem a convincing argument for the EU's different treatment of Turkey; in fact, it cannot explain why similar political issues in the CEECs have attracted an entirely different response on the part of the EU from those in Turkey. The EU has guided and even directed and catalyzed the political reform process in the CEECs through its pre-accession strategy and through its extensive membership requirements in relation to the stability of institutions, the guaranteeing of democracy and respect for human rights. However, the EU has taken a different approach to similar political issues in Turkey: its response to these issues seems not only to have been more rigid and critical, but also has lacked the necessary instruments to help the democratization process and improvement of the human rights system in Turkey. This difference between the EU's treatment of Turkey and of the CEECs has generated different results in the CEECs and in Turkey. That is, the EU has been more effective in influencing the policy reforms and outcome of these reforms in the CEECs than it has in Turkey, since the EU's clear commitment to the prospect of the CEECs' membership of the EU has forced the CEECs to undertake the necessary political reforms. However, the EU has been less effective in influencing a similar process in Turkey because of its reluctance to offer the country a similar accession instruments and membership commitment. In order to support the above argument, this chapter looks at:

- The emergence and development of the EU's political identity with reference to the characteristics of the EU's human rights policy towards the third parties.
- Issues in the Turkish political system and its human rights regime.
- The EU's policy towards Turkey in two phases: first, before Turkey's application for membership in 1987; second, since the Turkish application for membership with a focus on two particular issues: the customs union and Turkey's membership challenge with a special reference to the post-Helsinki developments in EU-Turkey relations.
- The EU's response to similar policy issues in Turkey and the CEECs.

The New European Political Order and Pan European Identity

Since the late 1980s, the European Community has gradually transformed itself into the EU with the aim of establishing an economic, monetary and political union as well as asserting a European identity. Hence, the post-Maastricht political order of the EU, in many ways, differs from its earlier form in that it has become involved in forming a European identity from a political point of view. Thus, political convergence has become as important as economic convergence in European integration.

All of these structural changes occurred in the late 1980s and the objectives of European integration have compelled the EU to take on more political responsibilities than ever. Before this, the EU was little more than an economic organization. Consequently, economic factors and considerations were more important than political considerations in EU politics, in particular in its external relations. In fact, the founding Treaties of the European Union did not make explicit reference to the political or social competence of the Union. For example, there was no explicit reference to respect for human rights or the principle of democracy either in the Treaty of Paris or in the Treaty of Rome. Therefore, human rights and social and political issues did not constitute an important part of the EU's external relations. Although the enlargement process towards countries in Southern Europe in the 1970s and the efforts of the EP compelled the EU to assume more political responsibilities for maintaining democracy in Southern Europe, the EU still lacked instruments to pursue coherent human rights in its external relations.

Since the late 1980s, the EU has started to take on political responsibilities as the result of internal and external factors. As regards internal factors, it has been realized that the further deepening of the EU, with the aim of establishing political Union, can only proceed in parallel with common European political values. In addition, the objective of bringing the Union closer to its citizens requires the firm application of transparency, principles of democracy, equality, social justice and respect for human rights at a European level. Furthermore, due to the advance of integration in the area of economics, involving the free movement of persons, goods, capital and services, people's lives are increasingly more affected by the EU's legal structure and activities, thereby creating a variety of additional human rights-related challenges for EU citizens. Therefore, the social and political dimension of European integration has become one of the main subjects on the agenda of the EU.

Apart from these internal factors, there have been external considerations that have compelled the EU to take on more political responsibilities. Since the end of the Cold War, and the disintegration of the Communist bloc in Eastern Europe in the late 1980s, there has been a process of re-structuring an international system in which human rights, fundamental freedoms and respect for democracy, as well as the supremacy of law, have become some of its more defining features. Furthermore, the dissolution of the Communist bloc in Eastern Europe has brought out important political and security implications for the EU. The countries of Eastern Europe and of the Balkans have been fully engaged in forming their own national identity in a difficult transition process, which has resulted in conflicts in some countries, along with the reappearance of claims by various national minorities, which were suppressed under the old regimes, and disputes over territorial borders. These have presented disturbing elements for European security.[1] Therefore, the EU has been assuming increased responsibility for promoting respect for human rights and the principles of democracy and minority rights issues in several transitional countries. For example, the emergence of the EU's strongly activist human rights policy towards the CEECs after the collapse of Communism in Europe was reflected by the statement of the Irish Foreign Minister, Gerard Collins, during the Irish Presidency in 1990: he stressed that an effective human dimension in the EU's policy *vis-à-vis* the CEECs was necessary due to the fact that it had far reaching implications for strengthening peace and security in Europe (cited in Ugur, 1999, p. 208). In addition, given the fact that almost all Eastern and Central European countries have became interested in joining the Union, the EU has demanded that the potential members must respect human rights and principles of democracy, as a political basis for their membership.

In parallel to these internal and external developments, the principles of democracy and human rights have become a defining feature of the new European political order and sense of identity. In other words, since the late 1980s, the EU has begun to establish its own common values and objectives in a political sense, thereby assuming responsibility for promoting its own sense of identity. In this respect, the Single Act of 1987 was an important step towards the creation of a European political identity, making explicit reference to human rights and the principles of the EU in the preamble, which states that:

Members are determined to work together to promote the democracy on the basis of the fundamental rights recognized in the constitutions and laws of the member states, in the Convention for the Protection of Human Rights and fundamental rights and the European Social Charter (The Preamble of the Single European Act, 1987).

Furthermore, the Single Act also explicitly made reference to the importance of human rights in the EU's external relations, which stipulates that:

The EU is 'aware of the responsibility incumbent upon Europe to aim at speaking ever increasingly with one voice and to act with consistent solidarity in order to more effectively protect its common interests and independence, in particular to display the principles of democracy and in compliance with the law and with human rights to which they are attached, so that together they make their own contributions to the preservation of international peace and security, in accordance with the undertaking entered into by them within the framework of the United Nations Charter'(The Preamble of the Single European Act, 1987).

Apart from the Single Act, the Treaty on European Union, which came into force in 1993, has furthered the establishment of European political identity by making the principles of democracy and human rights a fundamental part of the European integration process. In fact, many articles in the TEU make direct reference to these political values. For instance; Article F of the TEU emphasizes 'the importance of systems of government founded on principles of democracy, respect for fundamental rights, protection of human rights and fundamental freedoms' (Treaty on European Union). Finally, the Amsterdam Treaty furthers these principles and defines the European Convention on Human Rights and Fundamental Freedoms as the main source of a definition of human rights. Furthermore, the Amsterdam Treaty also envisages the enforcement mechanism for any infringement of the founding principles of the Union by member states. 'If there is a serious and persistent breach of those principles in any member state, the concerned member states may find certain of its rights suspended' (Article 6(1) the Amsterdam Treaty). The Amsterdam Treaty also enables the Union to take appropriate action to combat any form of discrimination based on sex, racial or ethnic origin, religion or belief, disability, age or sexual orientation. To sum up, all these developments indicate that the EU has been turning into a political entity. In fact, a progressive evaluation of the principles of liberty, democracy and respect for human rights reflects the building of a constitution by the EU. In this regard, the EU is no longer only motivated by economic considerations, but is creating an identity determined by political values and social ideals.

Human Rights in the External Relations of the EU

In line with these developments, human rights provisions and the principles of democracy have been gradually introduced into the EU's external relations. For instance, the inclusion of human rights provisions, the rule of law and democratic principles and respect for human rights have become an increasingly important determinant feature in the EU's external relations in general and its enlargement policy in particular. The Treaty on European Union makes explicit reference to respect for, and promotion of, these principles in its development cooperation policy; stating that the EU's policy in this area 'shall contribute to the general objective of developing and consolidating democracy and the rule of law, and that of respecting human rights and fundamental freedoms' (Article 130u, the Treaty on European Union). In addition, these principles constitute the primary objective of the Common Foreign and Security Policy, as outlined in Article J-1 (2) of the TEU, which reads that one of the objectives of CFSP is 'to develop and consolidate democracy, the rule of law, and respect for human rights and fundamental freedoms' (The Treaty on European Union).

Apart from Treaty articles, the European Council has made a number of references to the principles and values mentioned above. For example, the Luxembourg European Council Summit in June 1991 referred to the political dimension of the EU's external relations, declaring that 'respect for and the promotion and safeguarding of human rights are an essential element in international relations and one of the cornerstones of European cooperation, as well as in relations between the European Union and third countries'. The declaration also states that:

> The different ways of expressing concern about the violation of rights, as well as requests designed to secure those rights, cannot be considered as interference in the internal affairs of the state and constitute an important and legitimate part of their dialogue with third countries (Bulletin EC, 6–1991, Point 1.45, pp. 17–18).

A similar concern can be seen in regard to the Lisbon European Council of 1992 in that it has stressed the strengthening of democratic principles and institutions; and respect for human and minority rights are referred to as the main objectives of the EU's external relations (European Council, 1992). Again the Luxembourg European Council in 1997 declared that promoting and safeguarding human rights and fundamental principles of democracy throughout the world constitute an important and legitimate part of their external relations (European Council, 1997). Similarly, the Presidency conclusions of Vienna in December 1998 reaffirm the protection and promotion of human rights at national, regional and global level as the main feature of the EU's external activity (European Council, 1998a).

The European Parliament has particularly played a pioneering role in raising political issues in the EU's external relations. Considering its recently extended powers and responsibilities in the post-Maastricht era of European integration, owing to the SEA, Maastricht and the Amsterdam Treaties, the EP has increased its involvement in the decision-making process, including assent to accession to EU membership and assent to the conclusions of all trade, cooperation and association agreements of the EU with third countries. As a result, it has taken an important role in promoting human rights, minority issues and principles of democracy as an integral component of EU policies *vis-à-vis* external domains. In fact, the EP has been a decisive agent in the formulating of the EU's external relations with third parties. It has played an important role in drawing the attention of the Commission and the Council through its resolutions and its reports on countries that aspire to accede to, or get financial assistance from the EU. Moreover, it has instruments for exerting pressure on the Commission and the Council to make explicit reference to human rights and principles of democracy as far as they concern the EU's external relations. The EP has not only condemned the continuing violations of human rights and the resurgence of ethnic and regional conflicts in many countries in a number of its resolutions, but has firmly made the EU's agreements with third countries conditional on the fulfilment of EU criteria as regards human rights and principles of democracy, as has happened in the cases of Greece and Turkey.[2] For example, the EP has made the approval needed for implementing the EU's financial and technical aid to third countries conditional upon respect for principles of liberty, democracy, respect for human rights and fundamental freedoms, as it intends to set up a mechanism for the enforcement of human rights in the countries which have contractual relations with the EU.

The Commission, equally, has also underlined the importance of respect for the principles of democracy and protection for human rights in the EU's contractual agreements with third parties. It issued a communication of 23 May 1995 entitled 'the inclusion of respect for democratic principles and human rights in agreements between the Community and third countries', referring to the political instrument with a clause defining human rights as an essential element of the EU's contractual relations with non-member countries (European Commission, 1995e). The Council approved the Commission's communication with a suspension mechanism to be included in the EU's agreement with third parties, so as to enable the Community to react immediately in the event of violations of human rights and breaches of principles of democracy. As a result, contractual agreements signed between the EU and third parties have became one of the main instruments of the EU in promoting its political identity and protecting human rights and fundamental freedoms in those countries.

In conclusion, the EU has been seeking to implement its trade and financial instruments to promote human rights and principles of democracy in the countries that have a contractual relationship with the EU. Since the early 1990s, the EU has included a conditional clause, the so-called human rights clause, in its bilateral trade cooperation and association agreements with third countries, such as the Europe agreements, the Mediterranean agreements and the Lomé Convention. For example, respect for democratic principles and human rights constitute an essential element of the Europe Agreements with Romania (European Commission, 1994a). The Barcelona Declaration, which was adopted at the Euro-Mediterranean Conference in November 1995, has also made reference to the political objectives of the EU in its relations with the Mediterranean Countries. It states that the political objective of the Mediterranean Agreements are to promote 'human rights and fundamental freedoms and guarantee the effective legitimate exercise of such rights and freedoms, including freedom of expression, freedom of association for peaceful purposes and freedom of thought, conscience and religion, both individually and together with other members of the same group, without any discrimination on grounds of race, nationality, language, religion or sex'. The same considerations are presented in the Fourth Lomé Convention signed between the EU and 69 Asian, Caribbean and Pacific Countries in 1989, which made specific references to human rights and principles of democracy in the body of the text, and which also stipulated that 'the allocation of EU funds to these countries depends upon the progress in developing human rights and on the application of measures of the convention' (Napoli, 1995, p. 306).

Similar concerns are presented in the Council's regulations for technical assistance and financial cooperation that contain explicit references to respect for human rights and democratic principles as an essential element of cooperation.[3] For example, the Council Regulation of 1992, which deals with economic cooperation and financial and technical assistance to the developing countries in Asia and Latin America, underlines that 'the Community attaches the greatest importance to the promotion of human rights, support for the process of democratization and good governance'. Another illustration of this is the Council Regulation on assistance to the applicant countries of Central and Eastern Europe in the framework of the pre-accession strategy. Article 4 of the regulation stipulates that 'should the commitments contained in the Europe Agreement not be respected, or progress towards the fulfilment of the Copenhagen criteria not be sufficient, the Council, on a qualified majority in favour of a proposal from the Commission, may take appropriate steps with regard to any pre-accession assistance granted to an applicant state' (European Council, 1998b).

As far as the enlargement policy of the EU is concerned, adopting the principles of democracy and respect for human rights is a necessary condition for membership of the EU. In fact, these are common values and ideals that determine the eligibility of any European state for EU membership. Although the Treaty of Rome did not make a direct reference to respect for human rights and principles for the democracy as a precondition for EU membership, a certain level of commitment to the promotion of these values was regarded as a major requisite for membership. For example, the Biskelbach Report of the Political Committee of the European Parliament stipulated that 'only states which guarantee on their territories truly democratic practices and respect for fundamental rights and freedoms can become members of our Community' (cited in Pridam, 1991, p. 215). When the Southern European Countries declared their wish to join the EU in the 1970s, the EP's efforts to insert political values in the EU's external relation compelled the EU to declare that respect for human rights were the political basis of EU membership (Brewin, 1986, p. 195). The EU has increased its concern in this respect not only because all the CEECs and Turkey are interested in joining the EU, but also because the EU has been turning into a political union. As a result, the European Council at the Copenhagen Summit agreed that:

> Membership requires the applicant countries to have stable institutions able to guarantee democracy, the rule of law, human rights, respect for and protection of minorities (European Council, 1993).

Similarly, The Amsterdam Treaty, amending Article O of the Treaty on EU, provided that:

> The union is founded on the principles of liberty, democracy, respect for human rights and fundamental freedoms, and the rule of law, principles which are common to the member states (Article 6(1), The Amsterdam Treaty).

That is, membership of the European Union is expressly conditional upon respect for such principles, which are basic features of European identity. For this reason, the European Commission's Agenda 2000 reaffirms that membership of the European Union requires that the candidate country has to fulfil the political criteria laid down in the Copenhagen Council Summit (European Commission, 1997b). In fact, the European Council Summit in Luxembourg on December 1997 confirmed once again that 'compliance with the Copenhagen political criteria is a prerequisite for the opening of any accession negotiations' (European Council, 1997). Each accession partnership therefore includes a conditional clause, to be applied in the event of an applicant country's breaching the principles of democracy and human rights. More recently, the Helsinki Summit of the EU reaffirmed that candidate countries 'must share the values and objectives of the European Union as set out in the Treaties' (European Council, 1999a).

To conclude, it is obvious that any aspirant country needs to fulfil basic political conditions for membership. This is one of the reasons for the EU's strong and rigid human rights policy towards Turkey since she declared her wish to join the EU. Such a political stand of the EU is itself a considerable leverage in promoting democracy and human rights in countries that aspire to join the EU. In fact, the EU can wield influence in the domestic policy choices in the applicant countries, providing an explicit encouragement for specific political and legal reforms as regards democracy and human rights.

Hence, the rest of the present chapter will analyze the EU's approach to political issues in Turkey by looking at these following questions:

- To what extent has the EU's treatment towards Turkey been compatible with not only the EU's enlargement motivations, but also its policy towards the CEECs?

- Why has the EU been less effective in influencing the domestic policy choices and encouragement of specific political and legal reforms in Turkey than in the other countries?

Characterization of Turkey's Political System

Turkey's bid to join the EU has brought it under close scrutiny from the EU. The latter has identified areas in which Turkey needs to undertake policy reform in order to make its standards convergent with those of the EU. These are as follows:

- Restrictions on full participatory democracy.
- The role of the military in Turkish politics.
- Breaches in human rights, including, torture and other cruel, inhuman, or degrading treatment or punishment and arbitrary arrest and detention.
- The Kurdish issue.
- Existence of the death penalty.

As far as the credentials of Turkey's parliamentary democracy is concerned, the EU's criticisms of Turkey are primarily centred on Turkey's slow progress towards democratization, her limits on full political participation and constitutional restrictions on civil society, notably on the creation of political parties and other associations. A good example is the decision made by the Constitutional Court to close the Islamist Refah Party (The Welfare Party) and ban several of its leaders, including a former Prime Minister, Erbakan, from engaging in political activity for five years. Moreover, freedom of association and assembly is not fully respected in Turkey either. NGOs' activities have still been under close scrutiny by the State Security Court, which limits the freedom of NGOs and associations (The European Commission, 2000a, p. 17).

One of the main reasons behind the inadequacy of the Turkish political system seems to have been a lack of social or institutional pluralism and inadequacy of political participation by social groups. In other words, the societal transformations in many aspects of life have been imposed from above, rather than through the inner dynamic of Turkish society.[4] As a result, the civil societal elements in Turkey have not yet been strong enough to act as agencies of social coordination through horizontal relations of adjustment and exchange, which lead the way to participatory democracy (Heper, 1994, p. 13). Moreover, maintaining the tradition of a strong state image has been the main feature of Turkish politics, inherited from the Ottoman Empire. That is, the political elite has viewed a centralized strong state as vital for the indivisibility and integrity of the Turkish Nation State (Heper, 1994).

Despite some progress undertaken by Turkey in recent years, a well-functioning parliamentary democracy has not yet reached the level required in a pluralist democracy. In other words, although the basic features of a democratic system exist in Turkey, there are serious shortcomings in many areas and, thus, Turkey's record on upholding the rights of the individual and freedom of expression falls well short of standards in the EU. The Commission's recent report of November 2000 towards meeting the *acquis* confirms this:

Although Turkey has most of the basic features of a democratic system, her parliamentary democracy has not reached the level required in a democracy. Turkish Constitutions and her human rights system have not been compatible yet with democratic principles in many respects (The European Commission, 2000a, pp. 10–19).

Similarly, the Most recent Commission's report on Turkey suggests that, 'Turkey is slow implementing the institutional reforms needed to guarantee democracy and the rule of law' (The European Commission, 2001). Moreover, the Accession Partnership Document issued by the Commission in November 2000 reaffirms the incompatibility of Turkey's democracy with the Copenhagen criteria and urges Turkey to review her Constitutions and other relevant legislation, with a view to guaranteeing rights and freedoms of all Turkish citizens in conformity with EU standard (The European Commission, 2000e).

Whenever credentials of Turkish parliamentary democracy are evaluated, the role of the army in Turkish politics is identified as a problem. The role of the army, which is incompatible with Western democratic practices, reflects the authoritarian tradition of Turkey, at odds with European political norms. The military have intervened three times in the short history of recent Turkish politics (in 1960, 1971 and 1980 respectively). It still plays a crucial role in the political system, as was made all too apparent to the Government in 1997 led by the Islamic Refah (Welfare) Party.

The army considers itself the guardian and ultimate protector of the secular nation-state against the Islamist and separatist Kurds. It has succeeded in legitimating its role in politics on the grounds of instability in the country, caused by political Islamic and separatist Kurdish movement. A declaration by the Chief of Military Staff before the general election of December 1995 clarifies this, 'the Turkish armed forces are the most effective guarantor of the Turkish republic, which is secular, social and lawful' (Milliyet, 24 December 1995). Turkish Constitution allows the army to play a civil role and to intervene in every area of political life. Under the Turkish Constitution, even though the National Security Council is a supervisory body and its recommendation is not binding, the army is allowed to play a civil role and to intervene in many areas of political life. As the Commission Regular Report in 2000 acknowledges:

> Its conclusions, statements or recommendations continue to strongly influence the political process. At present the views of the National Security Council in practice seriously limit the role played by the government (European Commission, 2000a, p. 14).

This implies that the role of the military in the Turkish political system is not compatible with the concept of a liberal democracy. As a result, the EU opposes the strong position of the military in Turkish politics and cites it as firm evidence that the development of Turkish democracy at the present time falls short of Union standards. In fact, the Accession Partnership Document urges Turkey to 'align the constitutional role of the National Security Council as an advisory body to the Government in accordance with the practice of EU member states' (European Commission, 2000e, p. 11).

Another area to which the EU attaches importance in its relations with Turkey is that of human rights. Although Turkey has made some progress towards modifying its legal institutions – having ratified almost all conventions for the protection of human rights, including the European Convention for the Prevention of Torture – its human rights regime has frequently been the subject of discussion in international humanitarian circles. Turkey has failed to prevent torture and ill treatment of its citizens. The Report by the European Committee for the Preventation of Torture and Inhuman or Degrading Treatment and Punishment (CPT) states that, 'a considerable number of Turkish citizens had been subject to various forms of torture and ill-treatment at the hands of police officers' (European Committee for the Preventation of Torture, 2000). However, the Turkish Government recognized this; during the debate in the Turkish Parliament in 1995, the Justice Minister, Firuz Cilingiroglu, stated that, 'torture was a widespread practice in particular during periods of custody when the detainee did not enjoy legal protections' (cited in European Commission, 1996). More recently, in May 2000, the Human Rights Commission of the Turkish Parliament issued six long and detailed reports documenting the persistence of torture (TBMM Insan Haklari Inceleme Komisyonu, 2000).

This all indicates that the Turkish human rights system has not yet reached the EU's standard. Respect for basic fundamental rights remains problematic. Freedom of expression is not fully assured and the freedom of press and freedom of opinion is subject to numerous restrictions (Amnesty International, 2001). In fact, journalists, politicians, writers, trade unionists and NGO workers have been charged or sentenced for their statements due to excessively narrow interpretation of the Constitution and other relevant articles concerning the unity of the state, territorial integrity and secularism (Amnesty International, 2001). Moreover, disappearances of individuals and extra-judicial executions have been recorded on many occasions and the excessive use of force by security forces has resulted in many human rights violations (Human Rights Watch Report, 2002). As the Commission has stated:

> Many of the cases recorded are so precisely documented that there is no doubt about the responsibility of the police authorities. These cases put into question the effective control and supervision of the security forces. Appropriate standards of discipline are lacking for these officials (European Commission, 2000a).

Basically, Turkey needs to undertake the necessary measures in order to comply with the Copenhagen criteria of respect for human rights. As the Accession Partnership indicates, 'Turkey should strengthen legal and constitutional guarantees for the right to freedom of expression in line with article 10 of the European Convention of Human rights and it should undertake all necessary measures to reinforce the fight against the torture practices and improve the functioning and efficiency of its judiciary' (European Commission, 2000e).

Another area in which the EU attaches greater degree of importance in its relations with Turkey is the issue of minority rights, namely the Kurdish issue. In fact, many of the current human rights problems in Turkey are linked to the long-standing Kurdish issue. The Kurdish issue is perhaps the most important task to solve for Turkey because it involves concern over security against separatism. Since the early 1980s, Turkey has been fighting an armed rebellion by the so-called Kurdistan Workers' Party (PKK), which advocates achieving independence from Turkey. Members of the PKK have frequently resorted to terrorist activities aimed at both civilian and government targets. In return, Turkey has responded with force to the PKK activities, which in turn has resulted in serious human rights violations (Human Rights Watch Report, 2002). Moreover, due to the strong rebellious actions by the PKK against the indivisibility of the country, Turkey has introduced the 'State of Emergency Regime' for some provisions in the southeastern region of Turkey.[5] The State of Emergency Law exempts judicial review of acts carried out by administrative authorities and security forces. For example, the emergency region Governor has powers to confiscate publications and limit the rights of city council assemblies. Maximum police detention periods can be extended from seven days to ten days within the declared emergency regions. Thus, such actions have resulted in serious human rights violations by the security force in the region (Human Right Watch Report, 2002).

The EU has criticized Turkey on the grounds that it has resorted to the military option over the Kurdish issue, and not attempted a political solution. The Union also criticizes Turkey for not applying the Copenhagen criteria of respect for protection of minorities to the Kurdish minority. Turkey's approach to the concept of what constitutes a minority has been, to a large extent, shaped by the Turkish State doctrine of the indivisibility of the Turkish nation and State. That is, 'the nation and the nation-state form an inseparable whole, which, if coupled with the principle of political democracy and the rule of law, renders meaningless any differentiation between citizens based on ethnic criteria' (Kramer, 1997, p. 220). Indeed, the Turkish State doctrine is manifested in Article 10 of the Turkish Constitution, which reads:

> All individuals are equal without any discrimination before the law, irrespective of language, race, color, sex, political opinion, philosophical belief, religion and sect, or any such consideration (Article 10, Turkish Constitution).

Turkey takes the view that constitutional citizenship is the basic principle upon which the Turkish Republic was founded. According to this interpretation, there is no need to grant minority status to people of different ethnic origins in the country, except for cases mentioned in the Treaty of Lausanne. Turkey acknowledges the existence of different ethnic groups, including Kurds, but it rejects their legal status as a minority (Kramer, 1997). According to the Turkish view, all ethnic groups together constitute the Turkish nation and are first-class citizens enjoying equal rights.[6] However, the Turkish approach on minority rights, more precisely on the Kurdish issue, seems to be incompatible with those of the emerging consensus about the treatment of minorities in the EU. Indeed, the Copenhagen criteria for respect for protection of minorities requires that Turkey, if she wants to join the EU, should fully respect the cultural identity and cultural diversity of the Kurdish people. For example, the Accession Partnership document asks Turkey to remove any legal provisions forbidding the use by Turkish citizens of their own mother tongue on TV/ radio broadcasting and to lift state emergency in the South-East, as well as to ensure the cultural rights for all her citizens, irrespective of their ethnic origin, as a means of abolishing legal provisions preventing these rights, including in the field of education (European Commission, 2000e).

The existence of the death penalty in the Turkish Penal Code also causes concern in EU-Turkey relations. Although Turkey has carried out no executions since 1984, she has not signed the Sixty Protocols to the European Convention on Human Rights. Thus, the EU wants Turkey to harmonize its own judicial system with the European Convention on Human Rights through lifting the death penalty. In particular, the EU has showed strong concerns over the case of Abdullah Ocalan, sentenced to death, although not immediately executed owing to an appeal to the European Court of Human Rights (ECHR).

To conclude, Turkey's human rights system, part of her legal system and her Constitution all fall far short of standards outlined in Copenhagen political criteria for EU membership. Thus, Turkey needs to undertake the necessary measures in order to comply with these criteria if its Accession Partnership is to prosper.

Therefore, one could take the view that the EU has treated Turkey differently due to the latter's human rights records, as Turkey has not met the Copenhagen political criteria yet. However, this book does not suggest that the EU should have started the accession negotiations with Turkey before she meet the necessary requirements. Certainly, it does not suggest early Turkish accession and the EU's tolerance for Turkey's failure to undertake the necessary policy reforms towards converging her political system with the EU. It rather argues that the EU could have used a more effective policy approach and instruments in order to influence domestic politics and policy reforms in Turkey, by providing a clear accession strategy and clear accession commitment. Given Turkey's vulnerability and her eagerness for EU membership that represent the strongest confirmation of Turkey's political identity, the EU could have applied an accession carrot more effectively to influence Turkey's domestic politics, in relation to democratization and human rights. This has been the case post-Helsinki of EU-Turkey relations, as Turkey has shown a positive response to the EU's demands in many ways with regards to human rights and democratization, including the cultural rights for minorities. Therefore, the rest of this chapter will examine the EU's policy towards Turkey since the EU's delay of Turkey's membership expectations, as a result of the Commission's negative opinion in 1989.

The Development of the EU's Policy towards Political Issues in Turkey

In EU-Turkey relations, one of the main problematic areas to which the EU always makes reference is doubt about Turkey's democratic credentials, breaches of human rights and the Kurdish issue. The EU member states and its institutions, particularly the EP, frequently state that closer relations with Turkey and the prospect of Turkish membership depend essentially upon Turkey's progress in democratization and the observing of human rights.

Therefore, the primary objective of this section will be to analyze the EU's approaches to the political issues in Turkey from a comparative perspective. This is important for the purposes of this chapter because it will enable us to consider to what extent the EU has pursued a consistent policy with regard to democracy and human rights. This will be done by looking, first, at the EU's policy approaches to political issues in Turkey in different cases, namely the military regime, customs union and Turkey's membership; and second, at the EU's policy approaches to similar policy issues in the CEECs in the context of enlargement. In this regard, the first part of the section will analyze the EU's approach to political issues in Turkey, covering the period between 1980–1987. Then, the second part will evaluate the EU's policy after Turkey officially declared its wish to join the EU in 1987. The third part will analyze the EU's approaches to political issues in Turkey and the Turkish Government's response to the EU's demands in the context of the customs union agreement. Finally, the last section will analyze the extent to which the Helsinki process in EU-Turkey relations has been effective in influencing internal politics in Turkey.

The EU's Policy Approaches to the Military Regime and Afterwards: 1980–1987

Although the limitations of Turkey's parliamentary democracy and its breaches of human rights attracted widespread outcry in the 1960s and 70s, the EU adopted its critical and rigid human rights policy only after the military came to power in 1980, and then intensified its criticism after Turkey officially declared her wish to join the EU in 1987. The deficiencies of Turkish democracy in the 1960s and 1970s, including restrictions on human rights, did not significantly influence EU-Turkey relations. As an example, the negotiations leading to the Association Agreement of 1963 and to the Additional Protocol of 1971 took place in the aftermath of military intervention in 1960 and 1971. Moreover, the restrictions on human rights and lack of elements of participatory democracy in Turkey did not constitute important issues in the implementation of the Association Agreement and the Financial Protocol until the military intervention of 1980. This was due partly to the strategic interest of the EU at the time in its relations with Turkey and the fact that Greece's withdrawal from NATO's military command in 1974 had increased Turkey's importance as a security asset to the EU. The low profile of the EU's human rights policy *vis-à-vis* Turkey during the 1960s and 70s was also to do with the EU's lack of policy instruments and institutional framework to apply a coherent and consistent human rights policy in its relations with third countries (Ugur, 1999, p. 216).

The EU first started to investigate human rights violations and raise the issue of democratization in Turkey after the military coup of 1980. In response to this, the Commission issued a statement, declaring that, 'it was following the developments in Turkey with the greatest concern and hoped to see human rights full respected' (*Agence Europe*, 13 September 1980, No. 2977). The EU foreign ministers also made a statement that the relationship between the EU and Turkey depended upon Turkey's military government fulfilling three conditions: 'the re-establishment of democratic institutions, observing human rights and respect for the lives of political prisoners' (*Agence Europe*, 17 September 1980, No. 2979). These statements appeared to imply a soft response and thus were hardly regarded as an effective condemnation of a military takeover. As Dagi suggests, 'the statement issued by the Council of Ministers was more a reassurance to the new regime and less a condemnation of the military intervention' (Dagi, 1993, p. 129). Even the European Council took the view that there was no need to suspend the EU-Turkey Association Agreement or the recently agreed framework of the Financial Protocol, as they believed that relations with Turkey should be maintained (Bulletin of European Communities, 9/10, 1980, Point 3.9.23, p. 52). This was partly because they seemed to be satisfied by the assurance of the military regime that the restoration of parliamentary democracy would take place as quickly as possible (Ugur, 1999). It was also partly because they wanted Turkey within the sphere of influence of the EU, as a total isolation of the military regime from the EU would not be compatible with its political and security interests in Turkey.

The European Parliament, however, took a more critical view; it adopted a resolution, stating that the current situation in Turkey was not compatible either with Turkey's commitment under the provisions of the European Human Rights Convention or its Association Agreement with the EU. Therefore, the EP warned that 'the suspension of relations would be considered if Turkey did not return to democratic rule as soon as possible' (*Agence Europe*, 18 September 1980, No. 2980). Basically, the EP tended to take a more critical policy stance towards Turkey than member states and the Commission did: while the EP was keen to suspend the EU-Turkey Association Agreement immediately after the military regime, the Commission and several member states, including Germany, the UK and Italy, wanted to continue to implement the Association Agreement with Turkey (Ugur, 1999). Even the Commission declared that 'it would be a more realistic policy to maintain the association relations with Turkey taking the view that democracy would be restored as quickly as possible' (*Agence Europe*, 18, September 1980). In fact, despite the military regime, the EU-Turkey Association Council (AC) meeting was held at ambassador level and the AC agreed that existing legal, political and economic ties should be continued (Bulletin of the European Communities, 1980, 12/1980, p. 83).

Throughout 1981, the EU tended to harden its policy stance towards Turkey by emphasizing the importance of restoring parliamentary democracy and respect for human rights. Although, after joining the EU, the presence of the Greek members in the EU was one factor in increasing degree of the EU's criticisms over Turkey, the EU's move to take a more concrete and critical approach to Turkey was primarily because the military regime failed to undertake the necessary measures to restore key democratic institutions. Moreover, there still remained widespread violations of human rights, although it had given assurances to the EU that democracy would be restored as quickly as possible. Furthermore, the growing concern about the breaches of human rights in European public opinion compelled the EU to take a firm stand against a number of unlawful actions by the military regime in Turkey (Birand, 1986, pp. 423–424). As a result, the EP issued a resolution, which called on the Commission and the EU Council to notify Turkey that the Association Agreement would be suspended if Turkey did not turn to democracy within two months (Ugur, 1999, pp. 220–221). Finally, for its part, the EP froze relations by dissolving the Joint Parliamentary Committee until the Turkish Parliament had been fully elected by direct universal suffrage (European Parliament, 1982).

Due to strong pressure from the EP and several EU member states, particularly Denmark, France, the Netherlands and Greece, the EU Council in January 1982 gave notice to Turkey that Turkey must as soon as possible take the necessary measures for the reestablishment of institutional democracy, as well as for protection for human rights, if she wanted to have maintained the association relations.[7] Indeed, the EU expressed its disapproval of the developments in Turkey mainly through resolutions and declarations and adopted certain measures to put pressure on Turkey to become more democratic (Muftuler-Bac, 1997, p. 79). Moreover, the EP and the Commission sent a clear message to Turkey that the military regime was not recognized as the lawful government of Turkey, hence the restoration of democracy was a pre-requisite for the normalization of relations. For example, the Commission issued a statement in December 1981, stating that 'it would not recommend the Council to continue the financial aid, as envisaged in the fourth Financial Protocol, as a sanction against Turkey for having arrested the leaders of political parties' (Bulletin EC, 12/1981, p. 67). The release of aid under the Financial Protocol was made conditional on Turkey's progress towards the restoration of parliamentary democracy. Basically, the EU tended to use financial instruments to exert more pressure on Turkey over a rapid return to democracy and respect for human rights.

The messages mentioned above seemed to be taken seriously by Turkey. For example, the Turkish Foreign Minister paid an official visit to EU officials to assure them that Turkey was taking the necessary action to resolve the political issues which hampered relations between Turkey and the EU (Bulletin EC, 1/1982, p. 42). Certainly, Turkey's policy-makers realized that maintaining a relationship with the EU was very important; thus, they undertook some reforms towards the restoration of institutional democracy. A Constitution was drafted in September 1982 and was approved by a majority vote of 91.37 per cent, and in addition the next parliamentary election date was fixed as November 1983 (Ugur, 1999, p. 222). Although the new Constitution was highly restrictive, it was an important step towards the reestablishment of a constitutional democracy. After this, elections were again held in Turkey in November 1983.

Nevertheless, the steps taken by Turkey to restore democracy did not satisfy the EU. It expressed its disapproval about the way in which the process of establishing political parties had taken and about the restrictions on the selection of parliamentary candidates, which the EU considered undemocratic and unrepresentative (Birand, 1986). For example, the EP issued a resolution in May 1984, stating that the parliamentary elections and constitutional developments were of only limited significance; hence, only measures leading to the re-establishment of democracy and respect for human rights could bring about the normalization of relations between Turkey and the EU (the European Parliament, 1984). Most importantly, the Balfe Report of the Political Affairs Committee in 1985 suggested that Turkey's human rights practice was still far from complying with the most elementary standards and condemned the practice of torture and restrictions on former politicians and trade unionists. As a result, it recommended a further suspension before re-activating the EU-Turkey Joint Parliamentary Committee (European Parliament, 1985a, p. 25).

However, it is interesting to note that although the EP seemed to take a critical and coherent human rights policy towards Turkey, its effectiveness was restricted by some EU member states' soft policy stance. Indeed, the Council of the EU could not pursue a coherent and consistent human rights policy. This was due to the divergence that existed within the member states of the EU (Ugur, 1999, pp. 218–226). For example, the UK, Germany and Italy refrained from taking strong action against Turkey, as they believed that a strong policy stance could alienate Turkey from the Western alliance in a period of political uncertainty in the region surrounding Turkey. In contrast, Denmark, the Netherlands and Greece (for different reasons) were concerned about the human rights violations in Turkey, and thus were in favour of a firm policy stand towards Turkey being more in line with the views of the EP (Ugur, 1999, p. 219).

After the civil government came to power in 1983, Turkey tended to take the EU's criticism more seriously, and in consequence made remarkable progress in democratization and improvements in human rights. This was because Turkish policy makers realized that Turkey needed the help of Europe not only for economic reasons to release the blocked aid and to increase textile and agricultural exports, but also for political reasons to increase the level of cooperation. Therefore, Turkey decided that the normalization of relations with the EU was a priority policy, even though it required the implementation of conditions that were imposed by the EU. In this respect, following the return to an elected civilian government after the military regime of 1980–83, the newly elected civilian government sought closer ties with the EU; hence, it made a greater effort to satisfy the demands of the EU on political grounds. As a first step in this direction, the Turkish Foreign Minister paid an official visit to the Commission in January 1984 in order to inform the EU about the political reform package of the new Government. During the visit, the Commission made it clear that the normalization of EU-Turkey relations depended on the continuation of the process with regard to democratization and human rights (Bulletin EC, 1/1984, p. 97).

The new Turkish Government lifted political restrictions and started to pursue a strategy of eradicating the influence of the military on politics (Evin, 1994). As part of the democratization process, a radical democratic programme was introduced, designed to eliminate a number of anti-democratic clauses associated with the Constitution of 1982. Several regulations promulgated during the military regime (1980–83) were abolished and new laws and constitutional amendments were introduced which allowed, to some extent, the elements of civil society and power groups to participate in the political process in Turkey. For example, restrictions on trade unions and associations and the forming of new political parties were abandoned. Furthermore, Article 4 of the 1982 Constitution, which banned political activity by former party leaders, was rescinded. A partial amnesty was declared which led to the release of the detainees of the Peace Association trials with another 31,000 prisoners. These all improved Turkey's image in Europe. Indeed, the European Commission on Human Rights dropped the case against Turkey by agreeing on a friendly settlement; Turkey began to chair the OECD and was offered the postponed presidency of the Council of Europe (Dagi, 1993, p. 217). Even the EP was taking note of the normalization of EU-Turkey relations in its resolutions.[8]

All the reforms mentioned above were also part of Turkey's preparations to apply for EU membership. The membership of the EU was expressed as the ultimate aim of the first Ozal Government programme. This was because Turkish policy-makers realized that instead of solely relying on any circumstantial military alliance with the West, Turkey should be integrated structurally into Europe through membership of the EU. The Prime Minister, Turgut Ozal, stated the motive behind the economic and political reforms of the 1980s, which was to facilitate Turkey's integration into the EU as a full member (Ozal, 1991, p. 8). In addition, there was a wide consensus among the Turkish policy-makers that Turkey's membership of the EU would guarantee the durability of the Turkish democracy and lessen the prospects of another military intervention, as was the case in southern Europe for Greece, Portugal and Spain. From this point of view, the Ozal Government, in an attempt to gain support from the EU, based its argument on the grounds that Turkey's membership would consolidate the parliamentary regime and improve the concern for human rights. In a speech to the EU ambassadors, Ozal tended to reinforce his argument by suggesting that 'if the EU wanted Turkey to have a viable and durable democracy, the best way of doing this was political integration of Turkey into the EU'; he stated:

> What we need is encouragement for the further consolidation of democracy and strengthening the respect for human rights (cited in Dagi, 1993, p. 220).

As seen from the above analysis, Turkey's determined effort to normalize relations with the EU, with a view to full membership, after the military coup, increased the EU's leverage over promoting human rights and the development of institutional democracy by linking the normalization of relations with the progress Turkey had made in these areas.

In particular, the EP listed a number of conditions for the reestablishment of the EU-Turkey Association by identifying specific areas where Turkey needed to take measures. For instance, the EP's resolution on the human rights situation in Turkey in October 1985 underlined the necessary reforms for the establishment of institutional democracy and protections of fundamental rights which included the removal of restrictions on freedom of political activity and trade union rights, freedom of expression, the granting of the right of individual appeal to the European Commission of Human Rights and the abolition of the death penalty (European Parliament, 1985b). A similar concern can also be seen in its resolution in December 1986, as it declared that the Community was not yet justified in fully normalizing its relations with Turkey, therefore, it called on Turkey to continue progress towards the full restoration of parliamentary democracy as the condition for normalization of EU-Turkey relations (European Parliament, 1986a).

As far as the member states of the EU are concerned, although divergence about the practicality of a critical human rights policy towards Turkey still remained an issue, all the member states were concerned about the human rights situation in Turkey. Therefore, they were in favour of a slightly more coherent and firmer human rights policy stand towards Turkey than their earlier policy stance. Indeed, the Council of the EU started to issue a more critical statement towards Turkey, calling for a full restoration of parliamentary democracy and the protection of fundamental rights. For example, during his official visit to Turkey in 1985, even the Chancellor of Germany, who tended to take a less critical policy stance towards Turkey, stated that the normalization of the EU-Turkey Association was virtually dependent on Turkey's continued progress towards the full restoration of parliamentary democracy and respect for human rights (Financial Times, 3 May 1985).

In addition, during the preparation of the EU-Turkey Association meeting in September 1986, member states, particularly Denmark, the Netherlands, France and Luxembourg insisted on including the human rights situation in Turkey on the agenda of the meeting. As a result, the President of the Council, Geoffrey Howe, the Foreign Secretary of the UK, conveyed the common position of the EU member states, by underlining the importance of the human rights situations in the normalization of EU-Turkey relations (Bulletin of the EC, 9/1986, Point 2.2.19).

When the Turkish Government declared openly its intention to apply for membership during the visit of the Turkish Prime Minister in February 1986, the EU began to take a more rigid and critical stance towards Turkey by underlining the political and human rights situation in Turkey, along with her disputes with Greece. From this perspective, Turkey became more vulnerable to pressure from the EU; in fact, her aspiration to join the EU provided a political justification for the EU's interference in Turkish politics. In addition, Turkey's wish to apply for membership increased European public interest in developments in the domestic politics of Turkey, which led to continuing public scrutiny of Turkey's human rights record. In particular, the EP tried to keep the political issue on the agenda as Turkey began pressing for membership. In fact, just after Turkey's application for membership, the EP issued a resolution on Turkey, stating that Turkey's policy towards the Armenians, Kurds, Greece and Cyprus, along with the lack of parliamentary democracy and respect for human rights were insurmountable obstacles to considering the possibility of Turkey's accession to the EU (European Parliament, 1987a). The EP used these vexed questions as a pretext to discourage Turkey's membership expectation by sending a message to Turkey through its resolution that she should not rush towards full membership.

Turkey was aware of the need to improve the image of the country by making further reforms in the direction of parliamentary democracy and human rights. In line with this, two months before its official application, Turkey accepted an individual petition to the European Commission of Human Rights (the ECHR) in January 1987, in expectation of joining the EU (Cameron, 1988, pp. 887–925). This was a decisive gesture by the Turkish government to show that it was genuinely committed to improving its human rights situation in line with the EU norms. In fact, it was a sign of Turkey's readiness to collaborate with the EU to undertake the necessary policy reforms required by the EU. To support this, for the first time since the military regime an Amnesty International team was allowed to study prison conditions in the city of Adana on 14 April 1987 (Dagi, 1993, p. 249). As a parallel move, the day after Turkey's application for membership, a law abolishing the long-criticized penalty of internal exile was passed and some constitutional amendments were introduced to lift the ban on former political party leaders.

In conclusion, during the period between 1980 and 1987, the EU seemed to take a constructive human rights policy stance *vis-à-vis* Turkey by guiding her towards improving her standard. Although some member states and the EP tended to take a more critical stance and showed their anxiety over the slow progress of Turkish democracy and human rights, the EU generally sought ways of re-establishing relations after the military coup. This low profile human rights stance of the EU towards Turkey can be explained in the context of three main factors. The first was related with the defence and security interests of the EU in maintaining relations with Turkey in the belief that strong criticism of the country could encourage anti-Western tendencies that would distance Turkey from Europe. Secondly, the gradual introduction of democratic reforms by the new civilian government elected in 1983, and some improvements in the human rights situation, gave a clear indication that the restoration of democracy was in progress, which reduced the grounds for strong criticism by EU institutions and the member states (Ugur, 1999). Thirdly, although the EP tended to assume a more critical and high profile stance towards Turkey, the member states assured the EP that this would stimulate anti-Western sentiments in Turkey and thus discourage its democratization process.

Another conclusion that can be drawn from this section is that after the EU learned of Turkey's intention to join the EU, the EU started to pursue a more coherent and a stronger human rights policy towards Turkey. It was not only the EP that continued to follow this strong line, the Commission and member states were also in favour of taking a more active and critical policy stance towards Turkey by attaching greater importance to democratization and respect for human rights as a condition of the prospect of Turkey's membership. Even some member states that were in favour of the normalization of EU-Turkey relations started to relinquish their soft policy after they received Turkey's request to join the EU.

The above analysis also suggests that the Turkish Government, and even the military regime, responded positively to the European concerns and criticism. This was because Turkey was concerned to maintain closer relations with the EU, not only for entirely economic reasons, but also for political, security and ideological reasons; and in addition expected to join the EU one day. In particular, after Turkey declared her intention to apply for membership, the Turkish Government became more vulnerable and more responsive to the issues raised by the EU. Thus, Turkey introduced some constitutional changes, abolished martial law, declared amnesty for political prisoners, held a referendum that consolidated democracy and lifted political bans on former political leaders, and accepted an individual petition to the ECHR. These measures all showed Turkey's readiness to collaborate with the EU to undertake the necessary policy reforms required by the EU with regard to human rights and democratization.

The EU's Policy Approaches to Turkey's Application for EU Membership

The timing of Turkey's application for full membership was interesting in that it occurred in the same year that the EU began to establish an active human rights policy as part of its external relations. In fact, relationships between the EU and third countries have become increasingly more politically oriented since the late 1980s. By implication, since Turkey's application for membership in 1987, the EU's approach to political issues, including human rights in Turkey, has become more visible and more coherent than before.

Accordingly, Turkey's quest to join the EU not only made her more vulnerable and more responsive to EU influence, but also made the concern of the EU a source of greater pressure for the Turkish government, thus increasing EU leverage in the areas of democracy and respect for human rights. Almost all of the member states have begun to take firmer and more critical policy stances towards Turkey, and thus they appear to have made their policy approaches converge with that of the EP. This new activist move by the member states has enhanced the effectiveness of the EP in adopting a more coherent and consistent policy towards Turkey.

Consequently, Turkey's determined efforts to establish a closer relationship with the EU for the purpose of membership have brought its human rights record, the

Kurdish issue and the credentials of Turkey's political system to the forefront of the EU agenda in its relations with Turkey.

EU efforts to highlight political issues in Turkey were intensified during the period between Turkey's application for membership and the Commission opinion on the request, because the EU was well aware of the vulnerability of Turkey to the Commission's *avis*. In particular, the EP sought to influence the forthcoming Commission opinion on Turkey's membership by attaching greater importance to the political issues in EU-Turkey relations. In fact, from 1987 onwards, the European Parliament began to intensify its critical stance towards Turkey. Shortly after Turkey applied for full membership, the EP issued a very sensitive resolution, stating that Turkey should recognize 'the Armenian genocide' and that the Armenian question must be resituated within the framework of the EU-Turkey Association. It also pointed out that democracy cannot be solidly implemented in Turkey unless she recognized the genocide of 1916 (European Parliament, 1987a). Given the sensitive nature of the Armenian Question, the timing of the resolution and Turkey's application for membership were interesting in the sense that the EU was sending a sign to Turkey through the EP that her application for membership would not be well received, on political grounds.

Furthermore, this resolution was important to show that minority rights were about to emerge as an important policy issue in EU-Turkey relations, including Kurdish ones. In fact, the EP adopted another resolution that called for Turkey to recognize the basic rights of members of the Kurdish minority living in Turkey and asked the Commission and the Council to put more pressure on Turkey to recognize the rights of the Kurdish minority (European Parliament, 1988). The Kurdish issue was also the subject of its resolution in March 1989 which put forward a conditional clause for strengthening the EU-Turkey relations, stating that the extension of the present Association Agreement with Turkey could only be considered when democracy was fully restored and minority rights, including those of the Kurdish minority, were fully recognized by the Turkish Government (European Parliament, 1989a). The Parliament went further with these conditions in its resolution in May 1989 by linking the prospect of Turkish membership to the solutions of these policy issues; it stated that:

> Turkey's membership of the EU was not conceivable without full democratization, including freedom of opinion and association, and respect for basic human rights as well as the full recognition of minority rights (European Parliament, 1989b).

The member states also expressed their anxieties about the political issues in Turkey's domestic politics, including the human rights and Kurdish issues through the Council of Ministers and in their bilateral meetings with Turkish officials. For example during the Turkish President's official visit to Germany, human rights in Turkey were widely discussed and German President, Weizsacker, conveyed the message to his counterpart, Kenan Evren, that continuing allegations about human rights in Turkey were damaging EU-Turkey relations (Milliyet, 19 October 1988). France took a more critical stance towards Turkey; for instance, the French National Assembly organized a conference to highlight Turkey's human rights record and called for an end to political imprisonment and a general amnesty (*The Times*,

27 November 1987). Furthermore, in an attempt to gain support, the Prime Minister, Turgut Ozal paid an official visit to France in December 1988 during which Turkey's human rights record was widely discussed (Milliyet, 7 December 1988). Even the UK, which tended to pursue a quiet diplomacy over the Turkish political issue, expressed openly her concern about the issue of human rights in Turkey; in fact, the human rights situation in Turkey and its implications for EU-Turkey relations constituted the main item of the meeting between the Turkish President and Prime Minster Thatcher in April 1988 (*The Times*, 22 April 1988). However, despite their increasing concerns over political issues in Turkey, individual member states were careful not to voice strong and open criticism of Turkey. They tended to play down human rights issues during their bilateral contacts (Dagi, 1993, p. 289). But they used the EP and Council of Ministers to express their concerns over the developments in Turkish politics.

For her part, while awaiting the Commission opinion, Turkey was under considerable constraint to make its membership bid more acceptable to the Commission in political terms. Turkish policy-makers realized that the unsatisfactory state of Turkish parliamentary democracy and lack of recognition of fundamental human rights were obstacles to their application for membership. Hence, they increased their efforts to make some improvements to the political system. Meanwhile, in an attempt to gain support, Turkey intensified her diplomatic efforts *vis-à-vis* the Commission and individual member states. Following the application of Turkey for membership in 1987, the Turkish Prime Minister, Turgut Ozal, made an official visit to the Commission. His meeting with the President of the Commission provided an opportunity for a discussion on human rights in Turkey (Bulletin of EC, 3–1988, Point 2.2.25). The Turkish Prime Minister visited the Commission again in May 1989, when the developments in democracy and the human rights situations in Turkey were discussed (Bulletin of EC, 6–1989, Point 4.3.27). The intention of Turkish officials was to inform the Commission of recent developments in these areas, and to convey the message that the Turkish government was making efforts to bring human rights and parliamentary democracy in Turkey up to the European standard. In addition, the Turkish President made official visits to the UK and Germany in April and October 1988 respectively, and the Turkish Prime Minister visited France in December 1988 and the UK in 1989, to state that the Turkish government was determined to undertake the necessary policy reforms in the areas of human rights and democratization.

Turkey did indeed make some progress towards bringing her legal system towards convergence with European norms; such as her ratification of certain important human rights instruments against torture and mistreatment. For instance, Turkey introduced the individual rights of petition for Turkish citizens to the European Commission of Human Rights in January 1987. In addition, Turkey ratified the UN Convention against Torture and other Cruel, Inhuman, or Degrading Treatment of Punishment. Furthermore, she ratified the European Convention for the Prevention of Torture and Inhuman or Degrading Treatment in 1988; in fact, Turkey was the first country to ratify it. Her ratification of these conventions allowed individual Turkish citizens to appeal to the European Commission on Human Rights and also allowed them the right to protest if they had been tortured. The prohibition on the use of torture or any other inhuman treatment or punishment was also inserted in the Turkish Constitution: Article 17 of the Turkish Constitution clearly states that 'no one shall be subjected to a penalty or to treatment incompatible with human dignity'.

Turkish policy-makers, while rejecting calls for total abolition, also took account of European lobbying over the death penalty, which became a widely discussed issue in Turkey. The Turkish Parliament did not ratify 200 impending death sentences, partly owing to EU influence (Dagi, 1993, p. 296). Furthermore, some amendments were made to the Penal Code, reducing the maximum detention period without charge from 15 days to 24 hours and increasing the access of lawyers to detainees. Apart from these legal developments, Turkey has taken important steps towards an institutionalized human rights system. A number of governmental and non-governmental organizations have been established in Turkey in response to the growing popular advocacy of democratization and to EU pressures. The Turkish Assembly established a Human Rights Commission and the Ministry of Human Rights was created in 1991. In addition, a number of human rights NGOs were formed, with the aim of improving the human rights record in Turkey. These are indications of the country's vulnerability to EU influence.

All these developments were undertaken after Turkey applied for EU membership and thus seemed to be part of Turkey's preparation for joining it. Nevertheless, the EU found Turkey's efforts to be unsatisfactory. This was confirmed by the Commission's negative opinion on Turkey's official application for accession in 1989: its *avis* on Turkey's request stated that 'although successive reforms had resulted in a parliamentary democracy closer to Community models, the political situation in Turkey was not adequate for membership' (European Commission, 1989a). As Ugur put it, 'The Commission opinion on Turkish membership was essentially a catalogue of political reservations dressed in some economic and diplomatic jargon' (Ugur, 1999).

In conclusion, after Turkey applied for EU membership, it became more vulnerable and more responsive to EU influence. In other words, Turkey's aspiration to join the EU provided an opportunity for the EU, particularly for the EP, to increase its influence on specific political and legal reforms in Turkey with regard to human rights and democratization. From this perspective, the EU was well aware of Turkey's vulnerability to its demands, thus, it listed a number of conditions that Turkey needed to fulfil. In fact, the EU not only began to raise more political issues – which included abolition of the death penalty, recognition of the rights of minorities, the release of political prisoners, restoration of full trade union and association rights, the eradication of torture in detention and in prisons and the full restoration of institutional democracy – but it also directed Turkey towards aligning her political and human rights system with that of the EU.

From Turkey's point of view, her long-standing political objective of joining the EU made her more vulnerable to the influence of the EU that compelled her to adopt a more responsive policy as regards human rights and democratization. To a greater extent, Turkey showed readiness to collaborate with the EU to undertake the necessary policy reforms listed by the EU; in fact, she did not ignore the European critics but responded positively to them and put forward her argument to persuade the Europeans of her commitment to improving her political system and human rights observance.

Another conclusion that can be drawn from this evidence is that after Turkey applied for EU membership, the EU started to pursue a more coherent and a stronger human rights policy towards her. It was not only the EP which continued to take a strong line; the Commission and individual member states were also determined to take a more active and critical policy stance towards Turkey by attaching greater importance to democratization and respect for human rights and minority issues as a condition for the Turkish membership. This was because the EU tended to send a message to Turkey that her political fitness to join the EU was rather distant; thus her membership was not conceivable for the foreseeable future. From this perspective, the insufficiency of Turkey's political system and human rights system was used as a legitimizing factor by the EU to delay the prospect of Turkey's accession to the EU. In fact, by stipulating very sensitive issues, such as the Armenian questions and the Cyprus problem, as pre-conditions for the consideration of Turkey's membership, the EU used these vexed questions as a pretext to discourage Turkey's membership expectations, with the intention of delaying her membership for the foreseeable future.

This all indicated that Turkey's desire to join the EU has been a driving force behind the progress she has been made since the civilian government came to power in 1983. Therefore one can assume that that the EU could have acted as a steadying influence on further progress in democracy and human rights in Turkey by offering her a clear prospect of membership.[9] The customs union case supports this argument because Turkey's determined effort to conclude customs union with the EU provided an opportunity for the EU, and particularly for the EP, to increase its influence on specific political and legal reforms in Turkey. In fact, the EU's willingness to have a customs union with Turkey accelerated the process of democratization and improving human rights.

Moreover, the positive development in EU-Turkey relations after the Helsinki Summit has encouraged political and legal reforms in Turkey. However, it should be noted that Turkey's failure to undertake the necessary policy reforms to make convergence its human rights system with the EU has not only increased the EU's concern about the appropriateness of Turkey as a candidate for EU membership, but have also undermined Turkey's own effort and commitment to achieving EU membership. The next section will then identify the deficiencies of Turkish democracy and its human rights regime.

The EU's Policy towards Turkey during the Completion of the Customs Union Agreement

After the EU's opposition to Turkey's early application for EU membership in late 1989, both the EU and Turkey sought ways, not only to reactivate the EU-Turkey Association, but also to upgrade it in accordance with the developments in the EU. In this respect, the debates were primarily centred on the completion of a customs union between the two parties. After the Commission issued its opinion on Turkey's request for EU membership to the Council of Ministers on 5 February 1990, the Council approved it and asked the Commission to prepare a specific proposal for strengthening cooperation with Turkey. In June 1990, the Commission adopted the Matutes Package, which proposed the completion of a custom union by 1995.

However, the EU made it clear that the completion of the customs union was conditional upon Turkey's progress to align its political and human rights system towards that of the EU. This implies that the progress towards the establishment of a customs union between Turkey and the EU was bound up with Turkey's response to the EU's political prerequisites. Therefore Turkey was under the close scrutiny of the EU. Meanwhile, Turkey's determined efforts to conclude a customs union along with the EU's clear commitment to establish a customs union increased the EU's leverage over Turkey, exerting more influence on her to undertake the necessary political reforms. In particular, the scope of the EU for defining and pursuing consistent policy approaches to political issues in Turkey became more visible and decisive. The EU identified the main policy issues in Turkey, which included the unsatisfactory state of Turkish parliamentary democracy, the lack of recognition of basic human rights, and the Kurdish issue. Therefore, the next section will explore these two questions:

- To what extent did the EU influence the domestic politics of Turkey by offering the clear prospect of a customs union?
- To what extent did Turkey respond positively in meeting the EU's requirements for concluding a customs union?

On her part, Turkish policy-makers realized that the European political order had been changing. Hence, they recognized the need for political reforms to align Turkey's political system with that of the new European political order. In other words, they were aware that the successful completion of the customs union depended upon Turkey's performance in the field of parliamentary democracy, human rights and the Kurdish issue. For example, at the meeting of the Turkish Foreign Minister and the Minister responsible for European Affairs with Turkish ambassadors from 12 EU countries, the question of human rights was underlined as the most important issue in EU-Turkey relations, including the completion of the customs union and Turkey's chance of membership of the EU (Dagi, 1993, p. 293).

Accordingly, Turkey made certain changes to eliminate a number of anti-democratic measures, which had been introduced by the military government. In this respect, Articles 141 and 142 of the Criminal Code, which banned any form of association or propaganda with the purpose of establishing communist, dictatorial or racist regimes, were repealed. Similarly, Article 163 of the Criminal Code, which banned any kind of association or propaganda with the aim of transforming Turkey's basic social or political order in conformity with any religious principles and beliefs, was also repealed in 1991 (Ozbudun, 1994, p. 46). In addition, some measures were initiated in order to improve Turkey's human rights situation and to find a solution to the Kurdish issue.

Furthermore, a reform of judicial procedure was introduced in 1992, stipulating that in the future suspects should only be held for 24 hours before being charged, and granting them the right to ask for the presence of lawyers during preliminary interrogation. Moreover, within the Turkish Grand National Assembly, a Human

Rights Commission was formed, and the members of this Commission participated in a meeting of the Turkish-EU Joint Parliamentary Committee.

More importantly, for the first time in modern Turkish history, Turkey officially recognized the 'Kurdish reality' and accepted the need for further legislative and constitutional reforms. As a first step, a ban on the use of the Kurdish language was lifted and restrictions on Kurdish cultural activities were alleviated; in fact, for the first time, Kurdish people were allowed to celebrate Nevruz (a Kurdish national celebration) openly.

Although Turkey undertook some reforms to prevent human rights violations and to recognize 'Kurdish reality', the member states and the EU institutions were not satisfied with the progress she had made. It intensified its criticism, mainly concentrated on the Kurdish issue. Because of public sensitivity about this issue, and in response to the contemporaneous rise of nationalist and Islamist political movements, Turkey proved reluctant to bow to the EU's demands in this respect. The fact is that that the EU was less influential in relation to Turkey's policy on Kurdish matters. This was not only because of the political sensitivity of the issue in Turkish public opinion, but also because of the way in which the EU had approached it. In particular, Turkey did not welcome the EP's strong reaction and policy approach to the Kurdish issue. In most of its resolutions, the EP recommended cultural rights for the Kurdish people as a solution to the issue, including official Turkish recognition of the cultural, social and political rights of the Kurds. In its resolution in 1996, the EP stated:

> The Kurdish issue can only be resolved by guaranteeing their rights to speak, write, publish and testify in courts of law in the Kurdish language, and to be educated in that language; by abolishing the state of emergency in the Southeast and by removing provisions which directly or indirectly discriminate against persons, groups or associations due to their language or ethnic origin (European Parliament, 1996a).

Another characteristic of the EP's approaches to the issue was its language, which appeared to be extremely critical. Although it heavily condemned Turkey's policy on the Kurdish issue, it did not seem to address any strong disapproval of the terrorist actions of the PKK in its resolutions. In fact, similar terrorist actions by ETA (Basque Country and Freedom) and by the IRA (Irish Republican Army) had attracted an entirely different response from the EP in that it used a more stricter and critical tone in its condemnation of the ETA (Basque Country and Freedom) and the IRA (Irish Republican Army) than in its condemnation of the PKK's terrorist activities.[10]

Although the member states and the Commission to a large extent shared the EP's critical approach to Turkey concerning the Kurdish issue, they tended to be more diplomatic in their criticism and showed some degree of understanding of Turkish concerns with regard to Kurdish separatism and human rights. They underlined the need for a political solution to the Kurdish problem as a means by which Turkey should recognize the legitimate aspirations of the Kurdish people, on the basis of their own collective, political, social and cultural identity. In fact, the member states addressed their concern over the Kurdish issue through the EU-Turkey Association Council meetings and through the EU Council statements. These called on Turkey to resolve the Kurdish issue by political means, with full respect for human rights, the rule of law in a democratic society and in full accordance with Turkey's commitments as a member of the Council of Europe. For example, in meetings of the EU-Turkey Association Council in April 1997, the Presidency statement on behalf of the European Union underlined that:

> The EU is aware of the extent of the problem Turkey is facing in the south-east, but the fight against terrorism must be conducted with due respect for human rights and the rule of law, and calls for a political solution. Turkey should have no doubt that the Union upholds the territorial integrity of Turkey and all countries in the region, and condemns terrorism (Bulletin of the EU, 4–1997, Point 1.4.74).

For its part, the Commission took a similar stand, which can be noticeable in a number of its reports, all underlining that Turkey should find a political and non-military solution to the problem of the southeast. A civil solution could include recognition of certain forms of Kurdish cultural identity and greater tolerance of the ways of expressing this identity provided that it does not advocate separatism or terrorism (European Commission, 1998b).

It appears that the Turkish approach on the Kurdish issue was incompatible with that of an emerging consensus over the treatment of minorities in the EU. Given the EU's strong criticism, coupled with increased terrorist activities by the PKK, Turkey showed extreme reluctance to bow to the EU's influence on this issue. The Turkish Court decision to dissolve the Kurdish Democracy Party (DEP) in June 1994 and the trials of the DEP representatives were an important indication that the EU was having a limited influence on Turkey's policy choices in this respect. Dissolving the DEP and the trials of its members occurred at the time when Turkey was pressing for the customs union.

However, Turkey's determined effort to conclude the customs union made the concern of the EU a source of greater pressure for her. The EU intensified its efforts to highlight the Kurdish issue as a condition for establishing a customs union with Turkey. For example, the President of the Commission, Jacques Delors, condemned the decision of the Turkish Court by declaring that 'this kind of behaviour could not be considered appropriate within the context of Turkey's integration with Europe'. He also added that 'the customs union agreement should not be signed with Turkey without guarantees that Turkey would respect human rights and find a political solution to the Kurdish problem' (*Financial Times*, 19 December 1994).

The EP took an even a more critical stance; it suspended the meeting of the Joint Parliamentary Committee in October 1994 and declared that a peaceful political solution to the Kurdish issue and progress in respect for human rights were a firm expectation of the new contractual relationship between the European Union and Turkey.[11] The European Council took a similar position: at the Essen Summit, held in December 1994, made a declaration in which the sentences of the DEP representatives were condemned (The European Council, 1994). In addition, on behalf of the EU Presidency, Germany's Foreign Minister, Klaus Kinkel, stated that 'If Turkey wants to have a customs union, it must not turn a cold shoulder to everything Europe stands for' (*Financial Times*, 15 December 1994).

Therefore, during the preparation for the customs union at the Turkey-EU Association Council meeting in October 1994, the EU Ministers told their Turkish counterpart, Murat Karayalcin, that they were concerned about Turkey's treatment of the Kurdish population and breaches of human rights and asked Turkey to make some improvements in these areas before the completion of the customs union (Milliyet, 18 December 1994).

Despite all of the difficulties and negative developments, on 6 March 1995, the EU-Turkish Association Council agreed to the completion of a customs union between Turkey and the EU. Although the EU members reminded Turkey that it had to find a political solution to the Kurdish problem and improve her human rights record, they did not oppose the completion of the customs union on the grounds of human rights and the Kurdish issue. On the contrary, the leading members of the EU, namely Germany, France and the UK, had lobbied for the customs union by pressing reluctant countries to support it. For example, during her presidency, France in particular was determined to see the customs union completed; thus it pressed Greece to abandon its objections (*The Economist*, 12 February 1995). Tony Blair, the leader of the Labour party in the UK, asked the British Labour MEPs to vote for the customs union (*Financial Times*, 23 November 1995). Similarly, Germany announced its full support for the planned customs union between the European Union and Turkey (*Financial Times*, 6 December 1995).

In essence, despite negative developments on the Kurdish issue and the breeches of human rights in Turkey, member states took constructive approaches towards it. Their positive attitudes towards the completion of a customs union can be explained in terms of the EU's containment policy objective of anchoring Turkey to the EU, as a stable and secular country with a large market, while keeping a clear preference for delaying the prospects of Turkish membership in the foreseeable future. Considering Turkey's importance for the EU as a security and economic asset, the customs union constituted the most important part of the EU's containment strategy, as it was assumed that such an arrangement would tie Turkey to the EU. For example, the Foreign Secretary of the UK, Douglas Hurd stated:

> It is extremely important to maintain a partnership with Turkey. Whether one thinks of the Balkans or the dialogue on human rights, or the Soviet Union, or the Middle East, or Cyprus, relations with Turkey are indispensable (*Financial Times*, 20 December 1994).

He also supported the completion of the customs union on the grounds that the customs union would boost the democratization process in Turkey, as he suggested:

> The Turks are taking quite substantial measures to legislate on human rights, the rights cause would not be advanced 'one jot' by refusing a customs union (*Financial Times*, 20 December 1994).

Given that a secular and democratic Turkey is an essential for European security, both the member states and the Commission assumed that the establishment of a customs union would tie Turkey to the EU. This indicates that the EU's human rights policy is not consistent and is determined by its containment policy objectives rather than by its human rights norms.

As mentioned above, the customs union agreement between Turkey and the EU was subject to the assent procedure of the EP in which the Parliament had a right to approve the agreement, or refuse to give its assent. Therefore, the EP made it conditional on Turkey's progress to align its political and human rights regime with

EU standards. For example, the EP appealed to the Turkish Government to undertake a fundamental reform of its Constitution, in order to better guarantee the protection of democracy and human rights. To be precise, the European parliament put forward three specific conditions to be met by Turkey for its approval of the customs union. First, Turkey had to make constitutional amendments in order to eliminate legal and constitutional restrictions on civil society and political participation, which included freedom of association and the freedom of trade unions. Second, Turkey had to change or abolish Article 8 of the Anti-Terror Law, which forbade the issue of written or verbal propaganda and demonstrations which had the aim of violating the political, legal, social, secular and economic order of the country so as to impair the integrity of the Republic of Turkey, its territory and its nation. Finally, all the DEP representatives who had been jailed were to be released (The European Parliament, 1995a).

In response to the demands of the EP, the Turkish government managed to pass 17 constitutional amendments, which increased the opportunity for democratic participation, including the lifting of restrictions on associations and trade unions to conduct political activities. In addition, the political parties were allowed to broaden their activities, including granting the rights to set up wings for young people and women, to open offices abroad, to establish links with associations and international organizations. Furthermore, members of the Turkish Parliament were given greater rights, such as the right to change party and to appeal to a constitutional court if their parliamentary immunity was restricted. Moreover, greater financial and administrative powers were given to local authorities.

Apart from these, the following changes were made: restrictions on civil servants' collective bargaining and joining trade unions were abolished; restrictions on the participation of students and teachers in political life were removed; the minimum age of right to vote was lowered from the age of 21 to the age of 18 (European Commission, 1995b).

Basically, the constitutional amendments of Turkish constitutions have provided greater scope for civil society to participate in political activities, as well as greater safeguards for the rights and guarantees accorded to members of the Turkish Parliament (Ozbudun, 1996). Some amendments to Article 8 of the Anti Terrorism law were also made. The most substantial change introduced in this Article was consideration to judge the intention behind the act. The previous version of Article 8 automatically condemned any written or spoken propaganda, meeting or demonstration that impaired the integrity of the state, its territory and its nation. Obviously, Article 8 was directed primarily at 'thought crime', such as curtailing the exercise of the right to freedom of information and freedom of expression (Ozbudun, 1996, 135). On 27 October 1995, the Turkish Parliament amended Article 8, in which the prison sentence for 'separatist propaganda' was reduced from between two and five years to between one and three years and might be converted to a fine; the notion of 'intentionally' and 'explanatory memorandum' was introduced, allowing judges to implement the new law in the light of the European Convention on Human Rights. Basically, the amendment to Article 8 distinguished between those who were involved in acts that impaired the integrity of the state and those who merely expressed their views about the Kurdish issue and human rights.[12]

Turkey considered all these to be a message for the EU that they were making the necessary reforms to fulfil the EU's demands.

As regards the EP's third condition, to release the DEP representatives who had been sentenced on the grounds of their involvement in the PKK activities, the Turkish Appeal Court ruled on the request for a review of the judgment taken by the Ankara Security Court. As the result of an appeal, two of the defendants were released but the other four were sentenced to 15 years in jail. Turkey defended herself against the criticism from the EU member states and from the EP on the grounds that those concerned could appeal to the European Court of Human Rights. The Turkish Government declared that, in accordance with its obligation as a signatory of the European Convention on Human Rights, she would accept the Court's decision.

The member states and the Commission reacted favourably to these new reforms and considered these conducive to Turkey's application for the establishment of a customs union. The Commission noted that, despite the growth of terrorism and political difficulties linked to the forthcoming election, the progress made by Turkey to bolster democracy and the rule of law lent credence to Turkey's renewed commitment to democratization and respect for human rights and complied with its obligation as a signatory to the European Convention on Human Rights (European Commission, 1995b). Nevertheless, the EP considered these changes as inadequate and insufficient. It took the view that Turkey's constitutional amendments were not sufficient, that Article 8 of the Anti Terrorism Law was still in effect and that the DEP parliamentarians were still not free. Therefore, the Parliament reaffirmed its position on the importance of the consolidation of democracy and the respect for human rights in the context of closer relations between the EU and Turkey, including the customs union. In this respect, Pauline Green, the leader of the Socialist Group in the EP, warned Turkey that, 'Turkey's approval of a package of constitutional amendments would not alone guarantee that its customs agreement with the European Union was ratified'. In this regard, she put special emphasis on Turkey's need to cancel Article 8 of the Anti-Terrorism Law and the release of the DEP representatives: in her statement, 'we have to be sure that changes are made' (*Financial Times*, 25 July 1995). Similarly, a report prepared by Carnero Gonzalez for the Committee on Foreign Affairs, Security and Defence Policy, suggested that:

> The current political system in Turkey is, no matter how you look at it, an incomplete democracy lacking notably in mechanisms essential for very important fundamental freedoms to be exercised (European Parliament, 1995b).

Despite all these negative developments in Turkish politics, the EP ratified the customs union agreement in the session of 13 December 1995 with a resolution, calling on Turkey to take further concrete steps toward democratization and the improvement of human rights and the Kurdish issue. The change in the position of the EP on the ratification of the customs union was largely due to pressure from the member states on the MEPs.[13] An argument used by the member states to persuade their deputies in the EP was that rejection of the customs union would cause a sudden halt in the process of democratization, and an increase in radical nationalism and Islamic fundamentalism in Turkey.[14]

In addition, intensive lobbying efforts by the Turkish Government on the member states to gain their support had a more positive impact on the ratification of the customs union by the EP. For instance, it was only after a meeting between the British Labour Leader, Tony Blair, and the Turkish Foreign Minister, Deniz Baykal, in November that the Socialists, with 217 members by far the largest group in the EP, in December 1995 decided that they would vote in favour of the customs union.[15] As a result, the intensive lobbying efforts by the Turkish Government and pressure from the member states' governments and political parties left the EP in a self-contradictory position in its demands. Pauline Green, speaking for the Socialist Group, opened her statement by saying that, 'whichever way Socialists vote today they will do so in sorrow, with heavy hearts and without enthusiasm' (*Agence Europe*, 7 December 1995).

In conclusion, as the above analysis suggests, Turkey's wish to conclude the customs union with the EU enabled the latter to exert pressure and to some extent compelled the former to respond positively to the political requests by the EU. This implies that the EU played a steadying role in hastening Turkey's effort to align her political and human rights systems with those of the EU by using the customs union as leverage in Turkey's democratization process. Meanwhile, the EU's clear commitment to the establishment of a customs union provided the necessary motivations for Turkish policy-makers to undertake some important reforms in the Turkish constitution and its human rights regime.

However, the EU had a limited effect on some specific policy issues in Turkey, the Kurdish issue and that of human rights. This was mainly because the EU did not pursue a consistent and effective policy approach to them. More specifically, the EU was determined to conclude a customs union with Turkey as a part of its containment policy towards that country. Such determination on the part of the EU made it restrain its criticisms towards Turkey and reduced its leverage to exert sufficient pressure on Turkey to undertake the necessary policy reforms. In fact, despite the EU's earlier statements on the link between the establishment of the customs union and improvements in Turkey's human rights and the Kurdish issue, it relinquished its earlier critical policy stance and even showed greater enthusiasm than Turkey for the establishment of the customs union.

Although the EP made a determined effort to link the establishment of customs union with Turkey's progress in specific areas of human rights and the Kurdish issue, its effectiveness was limited by the member states' and the Commission's determination to a customs union with Turkey. This was because the EU member states and the Commission saw the establishment of a customs union as a policy course that was necessary in order to develop closer relations with Turkey. Therefore, they appeared to ignore the inadequacy of Turkey's political and human rights regime. This observation supports the contention of the book that that there has been inconsistency in the EU's approaches to policy issues in Turkey, and that its policy towards the country has been determined by the objective of a containment policy.

To support the above argument, the following section will examine the EU's policy approach to the same policy issues in Turkey in the light of Turkey's membership challenge from a comparative perspective with the EU's policy approaches to similar policy issues in the CEECs.

Turkey's Membership Challenges after the Customs Union and the EU's Human Rights Policy in a Comparative Perspective

After establishing the customs union agreement with the EU, Turkey became even more assertive in its demands for membership. It argued that, apart from being the most senior associate member, it is also the only country to have achieved such a degree of economic integration with the EU through the customs union. Turkey's efforts to join the EU have brought close European scrutiny, which has made Turkey more vulnerable and more responsive to the EU's requirements in many areas. Meanwhile, Turkey's eagerness to join the EU has provided political and even a legal-procedural justification for the EU to interfere in Turkish domestic politics. In fact, it appears that it is not only the EP that has taken a strong line towards Turkey, but member states and the Commission have started to follow this strong line; their criticisms have in fact became harder.

In these circumstances, Turkey made an effort to undertake further reforms in her political system and human rights situation so as to make her membership prospects more viable and more attainable. These included reducing the areas subject to emergency regulations and a government programme aimed at reducing cases of mistreatment and creating an increased supervision of potentially troublesome situations. In addition, the Interior Minister initiated a programme of random unannounced inspections of police facilities to ensure compliance with proper procedures, to observe the condition of prisoners, and to check for any inappropriate devices or equipment that may be being used in interrogation (the European Commission, 1998b). Indeed, through this procedure, public inspectors and supervisors can inspect security forces more frequently and widely with administrative and punitive measures in order to prevent torture by security forces. Furthermore, Missing Persons Bureau was created to investigate allegations of missing persons more efficiently and methodically, in the light of international standards (the European Commission, 1998b).

Although the EU described all these measures as a positive step towards further democracy and respect for human rights, it considered Turkey's progress to be inadequate, noting that these measures had not brought about any significant progress towards democratization or greater respect for human rights, nor a political settlement of the Kurdish issue. More interestingly, contrary to their human rights policy stance *vis-à-vis* Turkey during the process of the completion of the customs union, the member states (along with the EP) began to assume a more rigid and critical policy stance whenever the issue of Turkish membership came up for discussion, by making a firm link between the consideration of Turkey's accession to the EU and Turkey's full attainment of the Copenhagen criteria.

This high profile policy of the EU was seen at successive European Council Summits, in the Commission's Agenda 2000 document and in a number of EP resolutions. Agenda 2000 clearly excluded Turkey from the enlargement process on political grounds and offered a special relationship instead, involving strengthened political dialogue at the highest level (European Commission, 1997b).

The Luxembourg European Council Summit in December 1997 approved the Commission's opinion on the prospect of Turkey's membership, and hence excluded Turkey from the EU's enlargement process on the same political grounds

(European Council, 1997). For example, the President of the European Council, Jean-Claude Juncker, defended the EU's position at the Summit by referring to Turkey's human rights record and the Kurdish issue: he said, 'it cannot be that a country where torture is still practised has a place at the European Union table' (*Financial Times*, 23 November, 1997). The German Foreign Minister, Klaus Kinkel, took the same view, stating that 'Turkey's accession into the European Union was not possible because of its human rights violations and the Kurdish problem in the Southeast part of Turkey' (*Turkish Daily News*, 30 November, 1997). Consequently, the effect of the Luxembourg decision was to put full Turkish membership off indefinitely. At the Summit, Turkey was the only country among the 13 candidates that was deemed not yet visibly on the path to membership.

This was not the case for Romania and particularly for Slovakia: although the Commission's opinion on the Slovak Republic's application for EU membership stated that the political situation was not satisfactory in terms of the stability of its institutions and respect for human rights and minorities, the EU provided a clear and more favourable prospect for Slovakia, as it was, at least, included in the enlargement process in the second group of countries with a reinforced enlargement strategy, designed to prepare all the candidate countries for EU membership (European Commission, 1997d). Indeed, though Slovakia's human rights policy and its approaches to the Hungarian minority were not compatible with the EU norms since Slovakia denied minority rights for the Hungarians, forming 10.7 per cent of its population (its government even banned bilingual signs on local roads and signature of names in Hungarian in birth registers in 1996), the EU allowed Slovakia to benefit from the accession strategy and gave it clear commitment to accession to the EU (Ram, 1999, p. 63).

However, the EU's policy towards Turkey was far being compatible with its enlargement objective of encouraging and persuading Turkey to undertake the necessary reforms for fulfilling the Copenhagen conditions. In other words, a more effective policy with moderate criticisms and a clear commitment to Turkey's membership would have been more influential in improving human rights in Turkey. This all supports the argument that there has been considerable inconsistency between the political motivation behind the EU's enlargement policy towards the CEECs and its policy approach to Turkey. A similar political problem in the CEECs seems to have attracted an entirely different response from the EU on the grounds that the democratization process and recognition of human rights must be supported and encouraged in the countries of Central and Eastern Europe. However, the EU's approach to similar political issues in Turkey seems not only to have been inflexible and more strict, but also has lacked the necessary instruments to help the democratization process and improve the regard for human rights in Turkey. This is one of the main reasons why democratization efforts have been more successful in these candidate countries than in Turkey.

As argued above, the EU's approaches to political issues in Turkey have been more rigid and critical than its approaches to similar political issues in the CEECs. Although the EU has made the implementation of all instruments of European Agreements and pre-accession strategy, including financial aid, conditional upon compliance with the requirement of respect for democratic principles and human rights, this condition has not been applied to any country in Central and Eastern

Europe as strictly as it has been applied to Turkey. While the EU has always underlined that the political situation in these countries presented a number of problems to do with the treatment of minority rights and in the functioning of institutional democracy, it has continued to provide financial support for them with a view to advocating their route to integrating with the EU; hence the suspension of financial cooperation, or their exclusion from the accession strategy seems to have been considered by the EU as a policy of last resort.

Although Romania and Bulgaria (not to mention Hungary) have similar political problems to do with human rights and respect for minorities, they have benefited from the EU's accession instruments. For example, the Magyar minority in Romania (approximately 1.7 million) and the Turkish community in Bulgaria, estimated at approximately ten per cent of the population, have not enjoyed full respect for their minority rights as required by the EU (Foucher, 1994). But both have benefited from the EU's support through its enlargement instruments. In addition, the Gypsies, who constitute a significant minority not only in Bulgaria and Romania, but also in all other countries in the CEEC, have not been integrated in the societies in which they live.[16] Indeed, the Gypsies who are estimated at more than five million throughout Central Europe seem to have been targets for social and racial violence as well as victims of social exclusion (Foucher, 1994, p. 42). Serious human rights violations and the treatment of Gypsies in Romania were particularly addressed by the Commission's opinion on Romania's application for EU membership, which states that:

> The Gypsies, who account for a considerable percentage of the population (1.5 million), are the victims of discrimination in many areas (European Commission, 1997f).

Despite this, Romania has benefited from the EU's accession instruments. This indicated that the EU has given too little attention to the minority issues concerning the Gypsies.

Similar minority issues have arisen in Estonia and Latvia, as the Commission opinions on the issue has indicated that the Russian-speaking non-citizens have been facing difficulties in integrating into Estonian and Latvian societies (European Commission 1997g). Nevertheless, all those countries mentioned above, have been treated more favourably than Turkey. In fact, the EU's policy towards these countries has been explicitly linked to their accession process to the EU with a comprehensive and clearly defined pre-accession strategy. A recent comparative study of EU financial support for democratic reform in Turkey and Poland suggests that the latter country has received much more support for democratic transition than the former has since the end of the Cold War (Lungen, 1998). For example, a considerable amount of money has been allocated to the democratization process in the applicant countries through the pre-accession strategy and the PHARE programme. A number of non-governmental organizations were created in the CEECs with the aim of encouraging the human rights situations in these countries that were mostly funded by the EU. In addition, the EU has encouraged political developments in these countries by not only offering them clear prospects for EU membership, but also working closely with them to help them to improve their human rights regimes and their parliamentary democracy.[17] There have been particular links between the efforts by Romania and Hungary to resolve their minority issues and their membership expectations from the EU (Ram, 1999). So far this has not been the case for Turkey: the EU's policy *vis-à-vis* Turkey has included neither a firm accession commitment, nor a clearly defined comprehensive accession strategy to support Turkey's efforts to resolve minority issues and to align its political and human rights system with that of the EU.

The Slovakian case offers the clearest support for the above argument. The EU's concern over Slovak political developments started in 1994, even before the EU initiated its accession strategy to prepare the CEECs for integration into the EU at the Essen Summit in December 1994. For example, due to the political developments in Slovakia in September 1994, the German Embassy, on behalf of the Presidency of the European Council, gave the first official *demarche* to the Slovak Government in November 1994 (Henderson, 1999). One year later, the representatives of France, Germany, Italy, Spain and the Commission, on behalf of the EU, represented their second *demarche*, which called for Slovakia to fulfil its obligations arising from the Association Agreement with the EU and under the Copenhagen criteria (Henderson, 1999, p. 232). Moreover, although the President of the Commission at the meeting with the Prime Minister of Slovakia underlined that respect for democratic principles and human rights was an essential part of both the EU's Association Agreement with Slovakia and its participation in the pre-accession strategy of the EU, the EU did not suspend the implementation of financial cooperation. In fact, Slovakia continued to benefit from the programmes of assistance and instruments in the EU's pre-accession strategy. This implies that the EU's human rights policy stance seems to have been inconsistent in the sense that its policy towards the Slovak Republic has been more favourable and constructive than its policy to Turkey.

Comparing the EP's resolutions regarding Turkey and Slovakia supports the above observation: the resolution issued by the EP on the Slovak Republic in 1995 gave a mild warning to the country, which stated that:

> If the Slovak Republic continue to follow policies which show insufficient respects for democracy and human rights and rule of law, it will be necessary for the European Union to reconsider its programme of assistance and financial cooperation under the European Agreement which might have to be suspended (European Parliament, 1995c).

The language used in the resolution was not strong; in fact, it did not call on the Commission and the Council of Ministers to block all appropriations set aside in the Europe Agreement. Another example of the European Parliament's soft stance is that, despite serious breaches of human rights and minority rights in the country, it overwhelmingly supported the Council and Commissions' decisions to conclude an Additional Protocol to the Europe Agreement between the EU and Slovakia in 1996; it stated that:

> Although there are serious problem with the country's Hungarian minority and with functioning institutional democracy which are totally not acceptable for us, we must open up the Community programmes and financial instruments to participation by Slovakia, with a view to deepening and strengthening of contact and of the common political ground between Slovakia and the European Union (European Parliament, 1996c, p. 6).

In the case of Turkey, in a number of its resolutions, the EP has called for suspension in the implementation of the Financial Protocol between the EU and Turkey. For example, the EP called on the Commission and the EU Council of Ministers to block all appropriations set aside for the project in Turkey under the MEDA programme (European Parliament, 1996a). This indicates that the EP had taken a rigid policy stance by making the approval needed for implementing the EU's financial commitment to Turkey conditional upon respect for the principles of liberty, democracy, respect for human rights and fundamental freedoms. In fact, the EU issued a list of demands on fulfilling the financial commitments in the context of the customs union. The EP even blocked Turkey's participation in European programmes, such as Leonardo, Socrates Youth and the coordinating of Turkey's efforts in the field of democracy, the rule of law and human rights. This seems to be contradictory to the EU's enlargement objective of promoting European values in Turkey.

The above argument might be questioned on the grounds that the EU's more rigid human rights policy has been due to the lack of progress on Turkey's part with regard to improvement in its human rights record, its political system and the Kurdish issue.[18] In fact, there seems to be room for the argument that the EU has taken a more rigid human rights policy towards Turkey because her human rights record and treatment of minorities are worse that those in the applicant countries. Though the above argument seems to provide some reasonable grounds for the EU's different treatment towards Turkey, it seems to be only a partial explanation why Turkey has been treated differently from the other applicants in the enlargement context. Some of the CEECs started from an even lower base than Turkey; they started to benefit from the EU's accession strategy with a clear accession commitment eventually. As Melanie Ram argues, Romania started from the lowest possible base in the denial of human rights, lower than any other applicant countries, but she has benefited from the EU's accession strategy since 1994 (Ram, 1999). The EU has financially supported a number of NGOs and programmes in Romania through the PHARE, covering the strengthening of democratic institutions and public administration to prepare Romania to fulfil political and legal membership requirements.

As illustrated in the above, the Slovakian case is another good example in that respect: the EU has used the accession carrot and accession instruments to influence internal policy development in the country. Like Romanian and Slovakian cases, the EU could have used the accession carrot to persuade Turkey to take the necessary reforms to align its political and human rights regime towards that of the EU norm. Given Turkey's 'European vocation' objective and hence its eagerness for EU membership, which has made her open and vulnerable to EU influences, the effectiveness of the EU's human rights conditionality on Turkey might have been strengthened by the EU's firm commitment to Turkey's accession to the EU, as a means of providing a pre-accession strategy for Turkey. In fact, as is seen in the following section, the EU's relatively positive policy approach to the prospect for Turkish membership at the Helsinki Summit in 1999 supports the above contention.

EU-Turkey Relations Post-Helsinki: Has the Accession Carrot Influenced the Domestic Politics of Turkey?

The EU realized that the Luxembourg decision to exclude Turkey from the enlargement policy was incompatible, not only with its containment policy objectives, but also with its enlargement objective of promoting democratization and political transformation in the applicant countries. Hence, the EU considered that a more effective policy approach to Turkey would be one that was similar to that used in the case of the CEECs; such a policy would not only encourage Turkey to undertake the reforms necessary to comply with the political criteria for membership, but would also provide a legitimate opportunity for the EU to apply leverage to Turkey in that respect, as in the case of the CEECs. Thus, the EU finally recognized Turkey as a candidate country at the Helsinki Summit in December 1999.

The Helsinki process has brought forward a new dynamism and further developments in EU-Turkey relations: it has encouraged Turkish policy-makers to undertake some policy reforms in order to make Turkey's laws and Constitution draw closer to EU standards. Most importantly, political parties, officials, NGO and other civil organizations have engaged in public debate on many human rights issues, including the Kurdish one. For example, the High Co-ordination Council on Human Rights, attached to the Prime Minister's Office, issued a report that contained proposals for constitutional and administrative reforms to bring improvements in human rights observance in Turkey (Basbakanlik Insan Haklari Yuksek Kurulu, 2000). The Report identified short-term and medium-term priorities and objectives of policy reforms to comply with the Copenhagen political criteria for EU membership. These included:

- Changes in the Turkish Constitution and other relevant legislation, with the view to ensuring freedom of expression and improving the human rights situation.
- Constitutional amendment to modify the role of the National Security Council;
- Abolition of the death penalty.
- Amendment of law 3984, which regulates radio and television broadcasting and powers of the Radio and Television Supreme Board.
- The establishment of a judicial policy and the abolition of incommunicado police detention.
- The establishment of an ombudsman to facilitate investigation and prosecution of public officials and to combat domestic violence.
- Changes in the Press Law and the Panel Code, to remove restrictions on the freedom of thought and expression.
- Finally, the Report suggests that, in order to bring it in line with requirements of democratic society, the necessary measures should be taken in the framework of collective freedoms, especially legislations concerning the freedom of association, freedom of demonstrations and freedom of trade unions (Basbakanlik Insan Haklari Yuksek Kurulu, 2000).

This Report is important in the sense that the Turkish Government accepted it as a framework within which Turkey would carry out political reforms, in order to comply with the political Copenhagen criteria. On the basis of this report, the Turkish Government accepted a number of policy objectives for reform and legislation, with a view to satisfying the Copenhagen political criteria. These included the adoption of new legislation on working rights, freedom of association and right to demonstrate, the development of freedom of thought and expression, the operation of the judicial system and the elimination of regional disparities in eastern and south-eastern Anatolia (European Commission, 2000a, p. 10).

This provided some evidence not only for Turkey's vulnerability to EU's influence but also of EU leverage to encourage policy reforms by dangling the carrot of accession. Indeed, the effect of prospective EU membership on the democratization process in Turkey seems to becoming more apparent; a number of important constitutional and legal changes have already been made since the EU Helsinki Summit. The Security Court law in Turkey was amended and in effect removed military judges from state security courts. A law on the Prosecution of Civil Servants and other Public Employees was passed by Parliament, as well as amendments to the Turkish Penal Code. The numbers of provinces under emergency rule was reduced from six to four.[19] In addition, the amendments to the Penal Code were introduced to facilitate complaints about torture and ill treatment, and to enable them to be dealt with more effectively. Moreover, human rights education was incorporated in the curricula of police academies, while an amnesty for journalists was introduced in May 2000 (European Commission, 2000a, p. 10).

Besides, in August 2000 Turkey signed the International Covenant on Civil Rights and Political Rights (ICCRP) and the International Covenant on Economic Social and Cultural Rights (European Commission, 2000a, p. 11). A month later, Turkey also signed the UN Convention of the Rights of Women and Convention of the Rights of Children in September 2000 (Duner and Deverell, 2000, p. 6). More recently, a number of articles of the Turkish Constitution were amended by Parliament in December 2001. These changes covered a wide range of issues, introducing new provisions on matters such as freedom of thought and expression, the strengthening of civil authority in the National Security Council, limiting the scope for capital punishment in the Turkish Penal Code, the lifting of restrictions on broadcasts in the Kurdish language and reducing the maximum period of detention for suspects (European Commission, 2001). This Constitutional reform related to the Copenhagen political criteria and was thus intended to fulfil the objectives set out in Turkey's Accession Partnership.

However, there are many areas where Turkey still needs to improve. For example, there are a number of restrictions on freedom of thought, freedom of press and freedom of association. Furthermore the death penalty should be abolished. Although the moratorium on the death penalty has been maintained and the revision of Article 37 has limited capital punishment to cases of terrorist crimes, and offenses committed in wartime or when war seems imminent, the amended Article 37 still fails to conform with Protocol 6 to the European Convention on Human Rights, which does not allow for any reservations. Ecevit's Government seems to be in favour of the abolishment of the death penalty in the medium term. For example, the Turkish Prime Minister, Ecevit, has publicly announced his personal opposition to the death penalty (Milliyet, 16 February 2002). Similarly, the Justice Minister, Hikmet Sami Turk, stated:

Turkey, as a member of Council of Europe and a candidate for full EU membership, should make the appropriate amendments to its judicial system. The abolishing of the death penalty should be debated within this framework. Turkey should harmonize its own judicial system with the trends in the European system and tendency in Europe against the death penalty (*Turkish Daily News*, 30 December 1999).

With regard to the protection of minorities, the Helsinki process has brought the Kurdish issue onto the agenda of the Turkish public. The use of the Kurdish language in education and broadcasting has since prompted an unprecedented public debate, particularly at the time of the visit of EU Commissioner Gunter Verheugen in July 2000.[20] Apparently, the Government has chosen to solve the Kurdish issue within a cultural framework, conceding the right to communicate and publish in Kurdish. Indeed, recent constitutional changes to Articles 26 and 28 removed the provisions forbidding the use of languages prohibited by law. This allows languages other then Turkish to be used in communications, publications and broadcasts. Nevertheless, no languages other then Turkish is allowed for teaching purposes, except where officially authorized by the Ministry of Education. Therefore, Constitutional amendments appear to be inadequate for the full enjoyment of cultural rights. As the Commission report on Turkey states:

> There has been no real improvement in the real enjoyment of cultural rights for all Turks, irrespective of their ethnic origin (European Commission, 2001, p. 32).

But although Turkey has been reluctant to grant unrestricted rights to use the Kurdish language in broadcasting and education on the grounds that it could foster separatism and encourage PKK activities, it has made some positive responses to EU demands in this respect. Even the army, which initially was critical of the use of Kurdish in broadcasting, has changed its stance. As the Guardian observed, 'a powerful army chief signalled that he could accept the Kurdish language broadcast – a key demand by Brussels' (*The Guardian*, 22 December 2000). When the Commission issued the Accession Partnership Document for Turkey, which proposed to remove any legal provisions forbidding the use by Turkish citizens of their mother tongue in TV/radio broadcasting, the Government took a favourable approach to the EU's demand in that respect. For example; after the Cabinet discussed the Accession Partnership Document, the spokesperson of the Government, Sukru Gurel, said, 'except for the Cyprus issue, there has been a harmony between Turkey and the EU in political conditions set in the Accession Partnership'. He also added, 'the differences should not be considered problems' (Sabah, 10 November 2000).

These positive developments and the political willingness to reform on the part of Turkey do not suggest that the country is ready for accession negotiations with the EU. The recent Commission report on Turkey states that:

> Though it is beginning to make progress in some areas, Turkey does not yet meet the Copenhagen political criteria and is therefore encouraged to intensify and accelerate the reforms (European Commission, 2000, p. 33).

Turkey still needs to strengthen its democratic structures and the rule of law and human rights observance in order to satisfy the criteria for accession. More importantly, the success of the constitutional and legal amendments that have been passed is largely dependent on their effective implementation. Otherwise, the result may simply be cosmetic changes to satisfy the EU, as has occurred many times in the past.

However, Turkey needs a clearer accession commitment and more appropriate instruments than those offered by the current EU policy. There needs to be both financial and technical support from the Union, aimed at training officials, improving the public knowledge about the European democratic values and bolstering institution building, thus encouraging Turkey to strengthen its democratic institutions and public administration, and apply political *acquis* in full. The Accession Partnership issued in November 2000 is important in this respect, since it not only identifies short- and medium-term priorities, objectives and conditions that Turkey must fulfil before the accession negotiations start, but it also sets out the EU's obligations to provide the appropriate instruments and support geared to the specifics needs of Turkey. On the basis of this document, in March 2001 Turkey prepared its own National Programme for the Adoption of the EU *Acquis*, (the NPAA) which identified short- and medium-term priorities in order to comply with the requirements of the Accession Partnership.

However, it is still too early to make an assumption about how the new phase in the relations between Turkey and the EU will impact on the progress of democratization. Some vagueness still exists in the declared priorities of the National Programme for the Adoption of the EU's Copenhagen political conditions, which might continue to pose problems in the implementation of the Accession Partnership document. Thus, the latter could still turn out to be another 'dead letter' in the history of EU-Turkey relations.

The decisions taken in Helsinki, which offered Turkey candidate country status and the opportunity to benefit from the pre-accession strategy, have encouraged both political and legal reforms in Turkey. The decisive factor in this process has been the prospect of EU membership, which was not the case before the Helsinki Summit. As Gunter Verheugen of the EU Commission stated:

> I should make it clear that the Helsinki Process has revealed the first positive signs of political willingness for reform in Turkey. Helsinki has also promoted debate among the Turkish public on the conditions for EU membership, a debate which is supported and encouraged by the forces for reform in Turkey (Verheugen, 2000).

In many ways, Turkey has responded positively to the EU's demands with regard to human rights and democratization, including the Kurdish issue. The recent developments in respect of constitutional reforms can be considered clear evidence of this. These reforms were intended to fulfil Turkey's Accession Partnership priorities, and thus they are part of the country's National Programme for the Adoption of the *acquis* of the EU. As the European Parliament suggests:

> Turkey has made a genuine start in moving closer to European standards, *via* the National Programme for the Adoption of the Acquis in March 2001, although the list of reforms is

still vague as to the timetable for implementation and the exact scope of the proposed measures (European Parliament, 2001).

This observation supports the contention of the book that if the EU had started to treat Turkey more seriously following her application for EU membership in 1987, as it did with the CEECs, then Turkey would have been more responsive and would have been in a better position to satisfy the political criteria for accession.

Conclusions

Since the late 1980s, the EU has begun to push the principles of democracy and human rights to the top of the agenda of its external relations. This can be explained in the context of internal and external factors. As regards the internal factors, the EU has promoted human rights and the principle of democracy as part of the new European identity. Secondly, since the Single Act of 1987, the institutionalization process of the EU's decision policy-making process has provided increased roles for the EU institutions in the EU's external policy formulations. Consequently, the EP has tended to assume a significant degree of activism in promoting the political values of European identity in the EU's external relations. As for the external factors, after the collapse of the Communist regime in Europe, almost all the European countries have become interested in joining the EU. Given the levels of their political system and issues concerning national and ethnic minorities in those countries, the EU had to introduce strict political conditions to be satisfied by the applicant countries before membership was feasible. The logical explanation of such strict political criteria is that applicant countries must be sufficiently developed in political terms before their accession, in order to prevent their internal problems becoming a burden upon the EU. In fact, according to the Copenhagen criteria, the countries applying for membership must first prove that they would not pose any political and security problems for the EU. Therefore, over the past years the EU has progressively increased the scope of its political conditions for EU membership, since it realized that political convergence is needed as well as economic convergence for achievable enlargement.

As far as the Turkish case is concerned, whereas the above developments have affected the EU's human rights policy towards Turkey, there have been other factors that have shaped the EU's policy as well. Firstly, Turkey has failed to put into action the necessary political reforms to fulfil the Copenhagen criteria. The lack of a political solution for the Kurdish issue, the breaches of human rights and the immaturity of political democracy in Turkey have caused a series of problems in EU-Turkey relations. Nevertheless, there seems to have been inconsistency in the EU's human rights policy towards Turkey in that conditionality has been less visible in relation to maintaining or upgrading the EU-Turkey Association, while it has been too rigid and firmly effective over the issue of Turkish membership. Indeed, the EU has tended to take a moderate and constructive policy stance in relation to maintaining the relationship (seeming to tolerate the inadequacy of Turkey's political and human rights regime). This was the case during the normalization of EU-Turkey relations after the military regime and for the customs union agreement.

This suggests that its policy approaches to the political issues in Turkey have been, to a large extent, determined by its containment policy objective which requires closer relations with Turkey, while delaying Turkish membership for the foreseeable future, a policy which, in fact, seems to have been fully effective in delaying Turkish membership. The successive EU Council Summit declarations and Commission reports have already verified this argument. For example, after the Luxembourg decision, which effectively delayed Turkish membership indefinitely on political grounds, the EU made a clear effort to bring Turkey back into closer relations with the EU at the Cardiff Summit in 1998, but showed reluctance to recognize Turkey as a candidate state with appropriate policy instruments to prepare Turkey for EU membership. It rather proposed a 'European Strategy' for Turkey to make its containment policy more attractive as a means of deepening the customs union through extending it to services and agricultural sectors.

However, the EU has pursued a critical and rigid human rights policy *vis-à-vis* Turkey over the issue of membership as means of delaying Turkey's accession to the Union in the foreseeable future. Although the lack of progress on Turkey's part with regard to improvement in its human rights records and its political system have provided some grounds for the EU to adopt a reluctant approach to Turkish membership, it cannot explain sufficiently why the Union has been unwilling to offer an appropriate accession strategy to Turkey in order to prepare the country for membership in the long run. Although post-Helsinki policy of the EU towards Turkey appears to be moving in that direction, the implementation of the Helsinki process and Accession Partnership still seem doubtful. Though the EU Council in December 2000 has offered the Accession Partnership for Turkey, it has conditioned Turkey's benefit from pre-accession strategy on Turkey's progress towards fulfilling the political criteria. This implies that the vagueness surrounding the political condition in the Accession Partnership might still be used as a pretext to effectively delay or reduce the chances of Turkey's membership. Indeed, the conditions of uncertainty in the Accession Partnership are likely to continue to prevail in the EU-Turkey relations. Therefore, it might not be totally wrong to argue that the Helsinki process has brought the EU's containment strategy back on track, which has not only restored EU-Turkey relations after the Luxembourg Summit, but also has increased the prospects of closer relations with Turkey.

The other characteristic of the EU's human rights policy towards Turkey is that the political motivation behind the enlargement strategy has been different in Turkey's case as compared with that of the CEECs. That is, there has been inconsistency between the democratization motivation of the EU's enlargement policy towards the CEECs and its policy *vis-à-vis* Turkey. One of the main objectives of the EU's enlargement policy towards the CEECs has been to promote and defend democracy and human rights in these countries. Therefore, all applicant countries, including those who have not yet fulfilled the Copenhagen criteria, have benefited from the EU's enlargement policy since 1994. In other words, the EU has used the accession carrot to persuade the CEECs to undertake the necessary political reforms to fulfil the accession criteria, by granting extensive financial and economic support. Consequently, it has played a major role in hastening their efforts to improve their political and human rights systems. Meanwhile, the EU's policy towards Turkey has lacked such instruments and accession commitments. Even the

Helsinki process did not involve a clear commitment in the direction of Turkish membership in the foreseeable future.

To conclude, the analysis of the EU's policy towards Turkey suggests that there has been inconsistency not only within its policy towards Turkey but also between the EU's policy towards the CEECs and that towards Turkey in terms of policy instruments, effectiveness and commitment of the EU's approaches to political issues in the CEECs and those to similar issues in Turkey. The analysis of the EU's policy towards Turkey also supports the secondary contention that the EU has been less effective in influencing the developments of Turkey's domestic politics. A more effective policy would have taken the needs of Turkey into account and would therefore have been more influential on developments in Turkey's domestic politics.

Notes

1   In addition, the economic collapse and heavy transition costs to large sections of society in these countries have caused the upsurge of nationalism and populist feelings, thereby creating ethnic tensions.

2   For a detailed analysis of the EP's role in the EU's external relations, see J. Ellas (1990), 'The Foreign Policy of the European Parliament', *The Washington Quarterly*, Vol. 13, No. 4.

3   For this, see, for example, Council Regulation, No. 443/92, on 'Financial and Technical Assistance to, and Economic Co-operation with, the Developing Countries in Asia and Latin America', *Official Journal of European Communities* L 52, 27.2.1992; Council Regulation, No 1279/96, on 'the Provision of Assistance for Economic Reform and Recovery in the New Independent States and Mongolia', *Official Journal of European Communities* L 165, 25 June 1996.

4   For this, see Ilkay Sunar (1996) 'State, Society and Democracy in V. Mastny and R. C. Nation (eds.), *Turkey: Between East and West*, Westview Press, USA, pp. 141–154.

5   According to Turkish Constitution, the Council of Ministers may declare martial law in the case of widespread act of violations and serious deterioration of public order (Article 120).

6   Cemil Karaman (senior Turkish diplomat) interviewed by the Author, 27 December 2001, Ankara.

7   For this, see *Official Journal of European Communities* – databases no. 1–279, January 1982, Office for Official Publications for European Communities, Luxembourg, p. 58.

8   See the debates of the European Parliament, *Official Journal of the European Communities*, No. 2, 346/129–139,10.12.1986.

9   This is even supported by Van Der Meer, Deputy Head of the Turkish Unit in the Commission, interviewed in Brussels, 16 June 2000.

10   For example, with regard to a bomb attack in Barcelona organized by ETA, the EP defined the act as 'a genuine crime against the people for which ETA was solely responsible'. It also underlined that 'any act of terrorism in one Member State affects the others in that it represents an attempt to destabilize our democracies and an attack on the fundamental rights of Community citizens'. For this, see the European Parliament (1987) 'Resolution of the EP on a Bomb Attack in Barcelona by ETA, *Official Journal of the EC* C 246, 4.9.1987, p. 65.

11   For this, see *Official Journal of the EC*, C 305, 31.10.1994, p. 95.

12   Under the original Article 8, many writers, journalists and publishers were sent to court and jailed on the grounds of their views on Kurdish and human rights issues. However,

amendments to Article 8 allowed the release of all prisoners who were detained under the original Article 8, as a result, approximately 80 prisoners were released.

13 The Party leaders of leading member states asked their representatives in the EP to vote for the ratification of the customs union. More precisely, Germany, France and the UK had lobbied for the customs union by pressing the deputies in the EP to support it.

14 In fact, the governments and political party leaders in many member states briefed their representatives in the EP, stating that a rejection of the customs union by the EP would be prejudicial to the pro-Western and pro-European policy of Turkey, as the custom union was seen as Turkey's last chance in affirming its European identity.

15 Richard Balfe, a member of the European Parliament and a member of the EU-Turkey Joint Parliamentary Committee, interviewed in Brussels, 20 June 2000.

16 For this, see the Commission opinion on both Bulgaria's and Romania's applications for EU Membership, *Bulletin of the European Union*, Supplement 8/97 for Romania and Supplement 13–97 for Bulgaria.

17 See, for example, Joint Programme between the Commission and the Council of Europe (1997) *Assistance with the Development and Consolidation of Democratic Security: Cooperation with the Countries of Central and Eastern Europe*, SG/INF (97) 2.

18 Richard Balfe, member of the EP and of the former EU-Turkey Joint Parliamentary Committee, interviewed in Brussels, 20 June 2000, defended this argument.

19 For this, see Address by Foreign Ministry of Turkey, Ismail Cem, at the 39th Turkey-EU Association Council Meeting in Luxembourg', 11 April 2000 (website of Turkish Foreign Ministry: www.mfa.gov.tr).

20 The main aim of his visit to Turkey was to observe the reaction of the Turkish Government on the draft proposal of Accession Partnership Document.

Chapter 6

The Greek Factor: The Ultimate Obstacle to Turkish Membership?

Introduction

To some extent, the same consideration can be observed in Greece and in Turkey in relation to their foreign policy objective *vis-à-vis* the European Union. Both countries' relations with the EU have rather been driven by their efforts to call one another to account, and have been dictated by their long-standing mutual hostility. Indeed, the timing of the Turkish application for associate membership can be viewed in the context of Turkey's traditional concerns about Greek diplomacy, in that it feared that Greece would use its association with the EU to its disadvantage, in order to gain more concessions with regard to the issues between them. This was also the case for Greece: her traditional concern over Turkey constituted an important element in the decision of the Greek government in 1959 to negotiate an association agreement with the EU and apply for full membership in June 1975 (Christakis, 1993, p. 20).

Since she joined the EU in 1981, Greece has pursued a policy, which implies that improvement in EU-Turkey relations, and Turkey's accession to the EU, should depend upon the settlement of disputes between Greece and Turkey. Given the complexity and 'high politics' character of these disputes, Turkey has opposed Greece's view on the grounds that the issues between the parties are bilateral in character and the EU should not concern itself with them. Consequently, the perennial Greek-Turkish conflicts have widened to become an issue in EU-Turkey relations. The Greek objections which have sought to link the feasibility of Turkish membership with the settlement of the Cyprus and of the Aegean Sea issues have gained particular importance, as far as the question of Turkey's membership is concerned.

The aim of this chapter is, therefore, to assess how the difficult bilateral relations between the two sides have become another source of conflict between Turkey and the EU. First, these following questions should be considered:

- To what extent has Greece gained the position of agenda settler with regard to the implementation of the EU-Turkey Association by using its institutional links with the EU?
- To what extent has Greece been effective in delaying Turkey's accession to the EU?
- To what extent has the EU's policy towards Turkish membership been effective in influencing Turkey's policy with regard to bilateral issues with Greece?

This chapter argues that although Greece has, to some extent, had the power to modify the EU's policy, it has not been especially effective when it comes to the implementation of the EU's containment policy for Turkey, as this requires a close relationship with Turkey to be maintained. However, Greece has been fully effective over the issue of Turkish membership due to the convergence between the linkage politics of Greece, which have sought to link the feasibility of Turkish membership with the settlement of the Cyprus and of Aegean Sea issues, and the objective of the EU's containment policy of delaying Turkish membership. The secondary argument is that the EU's rigid linkage of the settlement of the Cyprus and the Aegean Sea issues with the prospects of Turkish membership have meant that it has been less effective in influencing both Turkey and Greece and encouraging them to take a more constructive policy stance towards the settlement of these issues. In other words, it seems that the EU policy of conditionality has not been compatible with a key objective of its enlargement policy, which is to create political stability throughout Europe. It could be argued that the EU could have used the accession carrot more effectively to influence both Turkey and Greece by pursuing a more balanced policy *vis-à-vis* the two countries and by injecting a degree of clarity and accession commitment in its policy towards Turkey, as the latter would have encouraged Turkey to take a more constructive policy stance over the Cyprus and Aegean Sea issues.

This chapter will, first, present a brief analysis of the issues between two parties. It will then examine the Greek accession to the EU and Turkey's response to it. The chapter will move on to analyze the extent the Greek membership affected EU-Turkey relations and the way in which the EU approached the issues between Turkey and Greece during the period between 1981 and 1987. Moreover, the chapter will consider Greece's efforts to link the feasibility of Turkish membership with the settlement of the Cyprus and Aegean Sea issues after Turkey declared its wish to join the EU. This will be done by looking, first, at both Greece's and the EU's response to Turkey's membership application; and second, at the EU's efforts to pursue its containment policy for Turkey in the 1990s. Finally, the last section of the chapter will consider Greek-Turkish relations after the Helsinki Summit in 1999.

The Issues Between Turkey and Greece

The disagreements between Turkey and Greece are many and complex; therefore a detailed and technical assessment of them would go beyond the objectives of this book. However, a brief outline of these issues is necessary to better understand how they have become such a decisive factor in EU-Turkey relations. The issues between Turkey and Greece include:

- The Cyprus question.
- Sovereignty and control over the Aegean Sea.
- The treatment of Greek and Turkish minorities in the two countries.
- The provision of arms by Greece to its islands in the Aegean Sea.

These are issues of high politics; hence, compromises or concessions over these issues seem to be very difficult for both Greece and Turkey.

The Cyprus Question

Cyprus is the main issue between Greece and Turkey. In fact, the outbreak of the Cyprus crisis was the main reason preventing them from constructing cooperative and peaceful relations. Despite a number of negotiation attempts under the UN auspices and the high level of international concessions on the elements necessary for such a diplomatic settlement, the Cyprus issue still remains an issue between the parties yet to be resolved. The failure of the international community, including the UN, the EU and the USA, was related with the containment of Soviet influence during the Cold War in the Aegean and Eastern Mediterranean. In fact, both the EU and the USA were intent on keeping Turkey and Greece within the Western Alliance; hence they were careful not to show favour to one party or another. Their policies were designed to prevent a possible Greek-Turkish war and general hostilities between Greece and Turkey, and not to develop a realistic framework for a settlement.

After the end of the Cold War, there seems to have been a policy difference between the EU and the USA over Cyprus: while the USA's involvement in the issue seems to have been dictated by Turkey's importance as a security asset to the USA in the region,[1] the EU's policy has, to some extent, been shaped by the Greek presence in the EU. Greece has used its EU membership as a bargaining counter in broader negotiations with Turkey. Therefore, the presence of Greece has made it difficult for the EU to pursue a balanced policy in relation to the Cyprus issue, as Greece takes part in its decision-making process of the EU. However, the main reason behind the failure to reach agreement between the parties seems to have been caused less by the complexity of the constitutional and territorial problems between the two communities than by the disinclination of Turkey and Greece to work actively for a settlement. This reflects the psychological characteristics of the Cyprus issue among Greeks and Turks, inherited from history, which constitutes an obstacle to finding a rational solution since any compromise, or even concession, is seen as an injury to national pride by both the Turkish and the Greek public.

Since the Turkish military intervention in 1974, there have been several unsuccessful meetings between the leaders of the two communities with the UN Secretary General.[2] At present, it seems that the main problem between the two sides lies in a different approach to the negotiation of a settlement for Cyprus. In other words, each community's understanding of sharing the island's sovereignty is fundamentally different. While the Turkish Cypriots support the idea of a confederation with the political equality of the two Cypriot peoples,[3] the Greek side supports a bi-zonal and bi-communal federal state with a single sovereignty and single citizenship, providing a strong protection for the Turkish minority.[4] Finally, the Cyprus application for EU membership and the positive response of the EU to it has made the Cyprus issue even more complicated. As a counterbalance policy, Turkey declared that the Turkish Republic of Northern Cyprus (the TRNC) would be integrated with Turkey if Cyprus joined the EU without a political settlement.[5]

The strong reaction by Turkey to the EU's decision was also related to its exclusion from the enlargement process.

Basically, the Cyprus issue remains the most serious and unresolved issue between Turkey and Greece. More importantly, this conflict has a 'spill-over effect' into the other areas of disputes, including sovereignty claims over the Aegean Sea and minority problems. Moreover, the Cyprus conflict between Greece and Turkey has inevitably had an impact on the national perceptions and behaviour of both countries, which cannot help but make their relationship more susceptible to conflict (Aybak, 1995, p. 162).

Sovereignty Issues over the Aegean Sea

Sovereignty disputes over the Aegean Sea include territorial claims over the Sea, the continental shelf, territorial waters and air space. Although all these issues seem to be separate, they are closely related to each other in a complicated legal and political fashion. The continental shelf dispute constitutes the most important issue among the Aegean problems. Greece claims that the islands and islets are entitled to have their own continental shelves. She bases her argument on the regulations of the 1958 and 1982 Conventions on the Law of the Sea.[6] The Convention provided Greece with legal support for its position since it provides that islands can be the basis for the calculation of both continental shelf rights and a standard 12-mile limit for territorial seas, which effectively enlarges Greek sovereignty to the entire Aegean seabed. Given that there are more than 2000 Greek islands, islet rocks and other geographical formations in the Aegean Sea, one can easily compute the gain for Greece if the regulations of these conventions were strictly applied to all the islands in the Aegean Sea (Wilson, 1979). For its part, Turkey, conversely, claims that the Aegean Sea has some *sui-generis* special features, as it is a semi-enclosed sea with islands and islet rocks. Therefore, the regulations of 1958 and the 1982 Conventions of the Sea should not be applied to the Aegean Sea. For this reason, Turkey has never signed the Convention and strongly objects to the Greek claims on the grounds that granting shelf rights to islands would preclude them from shelf rights in the Aegean. She claims that due to the unique nature of the Aegean Sea, islands should not have their own continental shelves because intervening international waters make the islands discontinuous from the Greek mainland.

Another territorial dispute related to the Aegean Sea is the issue of territorial waters since the signing of the 1982 International Conventions on the Law of the Sea by Greece. According to Article 3 of this Convention, Greece is entitled to extend its territorial waters up to 12 miles. Therefore, being a signatory of this Convention, Greece intends to implement this Article as regards the Aegean Sea. Greece has used the International Conventions on the Law of the Sea to assert her right to extend her territorial waters from six to 12 miles. Turkey, as we have seen, adopts a contrary position. She bases her argument on the 1923 Treaty of Lausanne, which she interprets as intending a balance of benefits through the limitation of coastal maritime jurisdictions and making the bulk of the Aegean available for the common benefit of both countries.

In addition, Turkey also makes reference to Article 300 of the Convention on the Law of the Sea to support her case that stipulates that littoral states shall not use their rights to the detriment of their neighbours in an abusive manner.[7] Conventions on the Law of the Sea also make reference to areas of special circumstances, where factors such as particular history and geography may be taken into account. This is highly relevant for the Turkish side (Wilson, 1979, pp. 138–139). Consequently, Turkey objects to the intention of Greece to apply the Law of the Sea to the islands of the Aegean Sea. In fact, in response to the Greek ratification of the Law of the Sea Convention, Turkey declared in 1995 that the Greek extension of both the continental shelf and Greek territorial waters would be a *casus belli*.

In principle, while Greece supports the solutions reached through international law and the courts, Turkey wishes to propose bilateral talks before recourse to international mediation.[8] Greece brought these issues to the International Court of Justice in The Hague in 1976 but the Court ruled in 1978 that it lacked the jurisdiction to deal with the issue in the absence of Turkey unless both parties came to the Court together. Upon the Greek application to the United Nations in 1976, the United Nations Security Council issued a resolution stating that the parties should first try to negotiate, and then, if they could not reach a compromise, should use a judicial and arbitration mechanism, including the International Court of Justice (Aybak, 1995, p. 164). All these decisions, including the stance of the UN and the decision of the ICJ, seem to be far less than what Greece was expecting; therefore, Greece tended to take advantage of its position inside the EU to gain acceptance of its own position in its bilateral disputes with Turkey by linking the improvements in EU-Turkey relations and the issue of Turkish membership of the EU to Turkey's recognition of the ICJ's jurisdiction on the issue. Considering Turkey's eagerness to join the EU, Greece has gained diplomatic leverage over Turkey that may influence the latter to make some concessions in return for the prospect of EU membership.

The Treatment of Greek and Turkish Minorities in Both Countries

The last issue between the two parties involves their respective minorities living in both countries. The Greek Orthodox population in Turkey numbers about 10,000, whereas the Turkish minority in Greece stands at 130,000 (Bölükbası, 1993, p. 43). These minorities were exempted from earlier population exchanges and are protected under the Treaty of Lausanne. However, the breakdown of relations over the Cyprus crisis and other issues between Greece and Turkey has created a hostile environment for the minorities in both countries. Both countries accuse each other of discriminating against their national minorities. Greece claims that thousands of Greeks were forced to emigrate to Greece due to Turkey's discriminatory policies, including a 1942 capital tax imposed on non-Muslim businessmen and those Greek nationals, who had been allowed to reside in Turkey under Treaty of Lausanne (*The Economist*, 12 July 1986). In addition, Greece has often raised the restrictions imposed on the status of the Orthodox Church and on the Greek educational establishments in Turkey as violations of the Treaty of Lausanne.[9]

Turkey, for its part, claims that Greece has mistreated the Turkish community living in Greece. In fact, the ethnic conception of the Greek nation does not accept the distinctive identity and right of self-expression of the Turkish community in Greece. For example, according to the Greek Constitution, the Turkish community is classified as a Muslim minority. On this basis, Greece in 1991 closed down the

Turkish cultural associations on the grounds that there were no Turks in Greece, but only Muslim Greeks. Turkey also claims that restrictions imposed on Turkish schools and on education and Greece's intervention in the appointment of the religious leader and his status constitute a breach of the Treaty of Lausanne (Bolukbasi, 1993, p. 44).

As can be seen from the above account, both sides follow one another to adjust the balance against each other. In fact, both parties' policies are biased against each other, largely a legacy of their troubled history. The rest of the chapter will trace the way in which these issues between the two sides have turned into another source of conflict in EU-Turkey relations.

The Greek Accession to the EU: The Turkish and the EU's Response

After reintroducing the system of democracy following the collapse of the Junta regime, Greece applied for full membership of the EU in 1975 in the belief that it would strengthen her democracy and economic development and put her in a better position *vis-à-vis* Turkey (Ioakimidis, 1994, p. 4). The application to join the EU was seen by the Greece as a means of political stabilization and development, and of ensuring a process of gradual change in the economy and in the political culture of Greek society and polity (Moschonas, 1997, p. 1). Greece felt that, as regards her relations with the EU, an association link was not sufficient for its political and economic objectives; hence, she applied for membership as an alternative to reactivating the Association Agreement. In addition to this, full membership of the EU would put her in a better position *vis-à-vis* Turkey. In the aftermath of the Cyprus crisis of 1974, Greek policy-makers realized that the strategic balance in the Eastern Mediterranean which had been for many years fairly evenly held between Greece and Turkey was shifting unstoppably in the latter's favour (Barchard, 1985, p. 49).

One of the reasons for Greece's application for full membership was the security concern, notably the negative development of Cyprus and the inadequate NATO response to it. Greek policy-makers believed that NATO had done nothing to prevent Turkey's military intervention in Cyprus. As a result, Greece withdrew from NATO in protest against its policy toward Cyprus. All in all, the best foreign policy course for the Greek policy-makers seemed to be to apply for EU membership to gain a better position *vis-à-vis* Turkey. In fact, having left the integrated command structure of NATO immediately following Turkey's military intervention in Cyprus, Greece believed that membership of the EU was its best counterweight to Turkey's position as Turkey was, according to the Greeks, highly regarded by NATO and the USA. As Tsakaloyannis puts it, 'the EEC provided the right framework to counter NATO's favouring of Turkey which had been dictated by strategic considerations' (Tsakaloyannis, 1981, p. 51). This was confirmed by the statement of the Greek Ambassador to the EU, declaring that 'Greece expected that the EC would favour Greece in the event of Greek-Turkish conflict' (Esche, 1990, p. 111). Finally, the Greek government applied for full membership of the European Union in June 1975.

Turkey, for its part, reacted anxiously to Greece's full membership application to the EU, since she was concerned about the possible effects of Greek membership on her own relations with the EU. For instance, the Turkish Prime Minister, Suleyman

Demirel, interpreted Greece's application as 'a political act aimed at getting a new international platform against Turkey' (*The Economist*, 21 June 1975). He also conveyed a message to the EU stating that, 'the Community should be careful not to upset the delicate balance between Turkey and Greece by treating Greece better than Turkey' (Tekeli and Ilkin, 1993). It was highly likely that in the absence of Turkey, Greek membership would change the EU's balanced policy to one in favour of Greece, which could undermine Turkish security as regards sensitive and important issues such as those of Cyprus and the Aegean. From this perspective, some Turkish policy-makers, including the Turkish Foreign Minister, Turhan Gunes, even considered following suit and applying for full membership in order to maintain the balance with Greece (Tekeli and Ilkin, 1993, p. 239). This could have been a best counter balance policy of Turkey *vis-à-vis* Greece; in fact, it was likely that if Turkey had applied for EU membership, the EU would have felt obligated to accept or reject both Turkey's and Greece's application because of the need to maintain the delicate balance, dictated by the politics of the Cold War.

However, it appeared that applying for membership was not a feasible option for Turkey for several reasons: firstly, the internal political situation would not allow her to take such a drastic step. In fact, the opinion of the political parties was not unanimously in favour of it: the Islamic Milli Selamet Partisi and the ultra-Nationalist Milliyetci Haraket Partisi, which were part of the coalition government, were against closer links with the EU (Ceyhan, 1997, pp. 155–176). Therefore, the existence of anti-EU elements in the Turkish coalition Government, which had only a narrow parliamentary majority to rely on, was one of the reasons preventing Turkey's membership application.

Secondly, Turkey's weak economic structure that was totally incompatible with the EU's economic system was a major barrier to her membership application at that time. Far from meeting the economic requirements of membership, Turkey was even unable to meet the economic obligations of the Association Agreement (Aybak, 1995, p. 169). Apart from this, the Cyprus crisis created an unfavourable climate for Turkey in which to canvass support from the member states for her bid to join the EU.

Therefore, as an attainable policy objective, Turkey was inclined rather to use Greece's application to the EU as a bargaining counter to gain some political concessions from the EU. Turkey strove to strengthen her institutional participation in the European Political Cooperation (the EPC) with political assurances from the EU that Greek membership would not affect EU-Turkey relations. These were all considered by Turkey as essential mechanisms to use against Greece's political pull in the EU (Birand, 1978, p. 60).

As far as the EU's position on the Greek application was concerned, the Commission took a different view on the Greek application from the European Council on economic and political grounds. The Commission mainly concerned the disagreement between Turkey and Greece: the Commission suggested that the EU 'should not became a party to disputes between Greece and Turkey' (European Commission, 1976). It appeared that the Commission recognized Turkish concerns about the possible effects of Greek membership on subsequent relations between Turkey and the EU. In its opinion on Greece's request for membership, the Commission stated that:

> Until now the balance in the Community's relations with Greece and Turkey has found its expression in their identical status as associates, both of them with the possibility of full membership as their final objective, albeit with different timetables (European Commission, 1976, p. 6).

Therefore, in order to maintain the existing balance between the parties, the Commission underlined the need for a formula to ensure that:

> The Greek application for membership would not affect relations between the Community and Turkey and that the rights guaranteed by the Association Agreement with Turkey would not be affected thereby (European Commission, 1976. p. 8).

In principle, the Commission was in favour of the idea that some positive steps should be taken by the parties towards a lasting solution of the disputes before the start of accession negotiations with Greece.

The EU Council, however, disregarded the Commission opinion and soon started accession negotiations with Greece.[10] At the same time, the EU sought to hold parallel talks with Turkey so as to preserve the balance between the two that the Council of Ministers recognized the need to preserve. For example, the EU Presidency at Luxembourg in 1975, where the Greek application was the main subject, gave assurances to the Turkish Government that the Greek application would not affect Turkey's right to EU membership in the future (European Council, 1975). In addition, in March 1976, the EU at the EU-Turkey Association Council meeting pledged itself to keep Turkey fully informed of the progress of their negotiations with Greece with a full assurance that Greek membership would not affect EU-Turkey relations (*Agence Europe*, 2 March 1976, No. 2036). Yet all these assurances by the EU did not appear to satisfy Turkey; she wanted a written guarantee attached to the accession agreement between Greece and the EU that Greece would not veto Turkey's accession to the EU in the future. However, the EU rejected this request (Tekeli and Ilkin, 1993, p. 244).

The other diplomatic effort by the EU to minimize the effect of Greek membership on EU-Turkey relations was to incorporate Turkey in the European Political Cooperation, which was the forum in which member states coordinated their foreign policy. Although Article 76 of the Additional Protocol of Turkey provided political consolation, guaranteeing that the EU would inform Turkey about the political discussions if they were of interest to Turkey, it was limited to political matters related to Turkey and Turkey had no right to participate in the decision, even if the question concerned her (Aybak, 1995). The Foreign Minister of the EU in June 1977 discussed ways to minimize the effect of Greek membership on EU-Turkey relations. The UK and Denmark, along with the Commission, were in favour of Turkey's being incorporated into the EPC, but France and Belgium were opposed to the British proposal on constitutional grounds that stated that only full members were allowed to participate in the activities of the EPC (Tsakalayannis, 1981, p. 144). However, given the strategic importance of Turkey, the EU finally agreed on a two-way information procedure in which Turkey would be informed of the decisions of the EPC throughout the EU presidency, the so-called troika system, in relation to matters relating to Turkey and the eastern Mediterranean (*Agence Europe*, 12–13 June 1978). In addition, the EU Council of Ministers agreed that during the Greek Presidency, the EU's contact with Turkey would be continued by the three party representations so that the predecessor and successor would accompany the Greek representative. This was a kind of insurance for Turkey that the EPC mechanism would not be used in a way which would damage Turkey's interests, as well as making sure that the EU joint decisions would be accurately conveyed to Turkey (Tsakaloyannis, 1981, p. 145). However, this mechanism was a mutual information procedure rather than consultation and Turkey was not allowed to present her views before decisions were taken. Understandably, all the EU's efforts to assure Turkey that Greek membership would not affect the EU-Turkey relations did not appear to satisfy Turkey.

Finally, the Council agreed to the admission of Greece to the EU and asked the Commission to prepare a transition period for Greece. Finally, the member states agreed to open the accession negotiations with Greece at the Luxembourg Presidency in February 1976. During the Greek accession negotiations with the EU, EU-Turkish relations remained dormant. This was due mainly to the internal political situation in Turkey; by implication, Turkey would not be able to pay sufficient attention to the Greek-EU accession negotiations. In fact, Turkey decided to suspend her Association with the EU that made the Greek-EU accession negotiations easier; as one scholar puts it, 'Turkey's decision to suspend the Association was greeted with undisguised relief in Brussels' (Tsakaloyannis, 1981, p. 137). Finally, Greece became a member of the Community in October 1981.

In conclusion, both the EU and Turkey were mainly concerned about the political and security aspects of the likely effect of the Greek membership on EU-Turkey relations. Despite the EU's effort to find ways in which to reassure Turkey, its offer to Turkey to minimize the possible effects of Greek membership on EU-Turkey relations was not satisfactory. In this respect, it was a strategic mistake of Turkey not to have applied for membership at the same time as Greece: if Turkey had applied for EU membership, it would have put the EU in a difficult position, or at least it would have increased Turkey's bargaining power to get more political concessions and assurances from the EU with regard to the Greek effect on EU-Turkey relations. As expected, the Greek accession has had implications for EU-Turkey relations. Before Greece joined the EU, the EU had managed to pursue a balanced policy in its relations with the two associate members. However, since Greece became a member of the EU, it has been difficult for the EU to continue the same balanced policy towards disputes between Greece and Turkey. Given that Greece takes part in the decision-making of the EU as a veto-wielding member, the EU cannot in any case qualify as a neutral participant. Therefore the following sections will explore how the difficult bilateral relations between the two sides have widened to become another source of conflict between Turkey and the EU after the Greek accession to the EU.

Greek Membership: The Ultimate Obstacle to Turkish Membership?

Greek membership has brought a Greek presence to the institutions inside the EU, thereby providing a decisive opportunity for Greece to gain the support of its European partners *vis-à-vis* Turkey. Despite the assurance by the EU that Greece's membership would not affect Turkey's relationship with the Union, the EU has been bound by its decision-making procedure, in which the formulation of the EU's policy *vis-à-vis* Turkey in most areas, including the membership issue, requires the unanimous vote of the EU Council. Consequently, Greece's strong reservations and the conditionality of the solution of its disputes with Turkey has become an important feature of EU-Turkey relations.

When Greece joined the EU, EU-Turkey relations were at their lowest ebb in the history of the EU-Turkey Association, owing to the military coup of September 1980 that resulted in the suspension of the Association Agreement until parliamentary democracy had been introduced. During the period between 1981 and 1987 when Turkey applied to the EU, the influence of Greece on EU-Turkey relations was not entirely effective. This was partly due to the suspension of institutional links between Turkey and the EU; in fact, the suspension of the Association Council and Joint Parliamentary Committee in which Greece could exert pressure on Turkey directly limited Greece's influence on EU-Turkey relations. Secondly, Greece was at the learning stage of Union politics; hence she was not yet ready to formulate a firm policy stance toward Turkey through the EU. Thirdly, Greek policy-makers considered that undermining the assurance given to Turkey by the EU immediately after its accession could create an unfavourable image of Greece inside the Union. Finally, Turkey's acceptance of Greece's return to NATO five weeks after the military coup in 1980 created optimism in Greece that Greek-Turkish relations would improve. The Greek Prime Minister, Constantine Mitsotakis, expressed this optimism, in his statement: 'Turkey's new leadership will face constructively the question of Greek-Turkish relations' (cited in Minnet and Tsakaloyannis, 1979, p. 150).

Apart from this, some member states and the Commission sought to reduce the effect of Greece's edge over Turkey in the EU by using other channels outside the EU mechanism. The most important channels were the bilateral relationships between individual member states and Turkey (Tsakaloyannis, 1981, p. 140). During the official visits of some EU member states to Turkey, they tended to assure Turkey that the EU would not take sides in disputes between Turkey and Greece. For example, the British Foreign Secretary made an official visit to Turkey to discuss the relationship between the EU and Turkey in February 1985 (*Financial Times*, 13 February 1985). This was followed by the German Chancellor's visit to discuss not only ways to restore the association links with Turkey, but also to assure Turkey that Germany would not allow Greece to use the EU mechanism for its disputes with Turkey.

The main reasons for individual member states' efforts to keep up relations with Turkey were strategic. After the military coup in Turkey in September 1980, the member states were even more concerned about the internal and external consequences of the new regime. Consequently, some member states sought ways not only to minimize Greece's political advantage inside the EU, but also they were inclined to make an effort to reactivate the Association Agreement with Turkey so as to keep Turkey-EU relations alive. For instance, in accordance with the agreement of 1979, the EU decided to invite Turkey for consultations within the EPC mechanism in order to lessen Turkey's concerns with regard to Greece's accession to the EU in 1981 (*Agence Europe*, 10 December 1980, No. 3037, p. 4).

Some EU members even used the political consultation mechanism to maintain a political balance in their relations with Turkey and Greece through the EU's inner circle, the so-called directorate, which was a political consultation mechanism between France, the UK, Germany and Italy. This provided a kind of forum for these countries to formulate policies with regard to Greek-Turkish disputes unhindered by Greece's presence (Tsakaloyannis, 1981, p. 142). Besides, some member states, namely Germany, the United Kingdom and Belgium, tried to assure Greece that maintaining relations with Turkey would serve the economic and security interests both of the EU and Greece. These all indicated the political willingness of the EU to find a way to minimize Greece's political advantage inside the EU and to maintain a balanced policy *vis-à-vis* Greece and Turkey.

Although member states tended to minimize the influence of Greece on EU-Turkey relations and avoided taking part in disputes between Turkey and Greece, the political developments in Cyprus and the Aegean Sea made the EU not only feel vulnerable to the influence of Greece, but also made it develop a more coherent policy towards disputes between the parties. Considering that Greece was a part of the EU, it was impossible for the EU not to be involved in Greece's disputes with Turkey. It was particularly the case for the Cyprus issue, as political developments in Cyprus made the EU vulnerable to the increased pressure of Greece in this respect.

Alternatively, Turkey's Cyprus policy, which gave full support to the Turkish Cypriot leadership when they declared the Turkish Republic of Northern Cyprus as an independent state in 1983, was a favourable factor for Greece in facilitating its efforts to gain the agreement of the EU over its stance on the Cyprus issue. Indeed, after the declaration by the Turkish Cypriot leadership of the Republic, the EU expressed its concern over the developments in Cyprus. For instance, at the Luxembourg Council Summit, the EU issued a statement asking Turkey to withdraw her recognition of the TRNC and called on her to exercise influence on the Turkish Community so that they should rescind their decision (European Council, 1984). This statement of the EU members was in fact a turning point, showing that the EU was about to take an activist policy stance toward Turkey in relation to Cyprus. For example, the Council of Ministers at the meeting of EPC in Italy in June 1985 declared that:

> They do not recognize the TRNC, therefore, they do not recognize any so called constitutional developments in Northern Cyprus and that the member states of the EC wish to see a viable solution to the Cyprus problem on the basis of the UN resolution (Bulletin of the EC, 4, 1985, point 2.5.1, p. 104).

In addition, the EP strongly condemned the declaration of the Turkish Cypriot leadership in establishing an independent Turkish Cypriot state: in its resolution of 17 November 1983, the EP declared that they did not recognize the TRNC and called upon Turkey to cooperate with the UN for a lasting solution in Cyprus (European Parliament, 1983).

Although the member states and the EP were about to take an activist policy stance toward Turkey in relation to the way in which Turkey approached the Cyprus issue, they were inclined not to take sides in the conflict. In other words, it might be wrong to suggest that these above declarations of the Council and resolutions of the

EP should be regarded entirely as marking the end of the EU's balanced policy in its relations with Turkey and Greece. Firstly, the increased activism of the member states and the EP should be seen as a sign of their concern over the developments in Cyprus, rather than their taking sides in the issue. In fact, they called upon Turkey to contribute actively to international efforts to achieve a solution. Secondly, the member states and the EP in their respective declarations and resolutions did not explicitly make any direct reference to the effects of the Cyprus issue on EU-Turkey relations. Thirdly, both the EP and the member states were careful not to include other disputes between Greece and Turkey, despite Greece's insistence on the inclusion of the issue of sovereignty over the Aegean Sea with Turkey's recognition of the ICJ's jurisdiction on the matter.

However, Greece began to intensify its effort to Europeanize its other disputes with Turkey. It tended to take advantage of its position inside the EU to gain support in its Aegean Sea issues with Turkey by linking the improvements in EU-Turkey relations with Turkey's recognition of the ICJ's jurisdiction on them. On the basis of Turkey's desire to reactivate EU-Turkey relations with a view to becoming a full member, Greece gained diplomatic leverage over Turkey to influence the latter to make some concessions on these issues in return for the prospect of strengthening EU-Turkey relations. For example, at the EU Summit in the Hague on 26–27 July of 1986, where the member states brought up on the agenda the issue of the normalization of EU-Turkey relations, Greece attempted to insert political conditions, in return for normalizing EU-Turkey relations. Greece strongly resisted the efforts of the member states to normalize EU-Turkey relations, insisting that Turkey must withdraw its troops from Cyprus and show good will to the solution of the disputes in the Aegean Sea (*The Economist*, 12 July 1986). From this perspective, Turkey's strong support for the TRNC as well as its strong objection to Greece's intention to extend its territorial waters up to 12 miles intensified Greece's efforts to make the normalization of the EU-Turkey relations conditional upon Turkey's response to the Greek demands. For example, although the British Foreign Secretary, Sir Geoffrey Howe, as the President of the European Council, tried to convene a meeting of the Association Council, Greece blocked the first serious attempt to reactivate the EU-Turkey Association Agreement on the grounds that all aspects of the Greek-Turkish disputes should be introduced at the AC meeting (Brewin, 1996, p. 39). This policy stance of Greece *vis-à-vis* Turkey indicated that Greece was becoming one of the decisive factors in EU-Turkey relations and thus had the effect of linking its disputes with Turkey to the normalization of EU-Turkey relations.

In conclusion, during the period between Greece's accession to the EU in 1981 and Turkey's application to join the EU in 1987, it became clear that Greece had started to use its membership as a bargaining chip to gain concessions from Turkey over its disputes with Turkey. Although the EU became vulnerable to the influence of Greece, and thus showed signs of a more active and critical policy stance towards Turkey, particularly as regards Cyprus, the increased activism of the EU should not be considered entirely as marking the end of the EU's balanced policy in its relations with Turkey and Greece. This continuation of the EU's more-or-less balanced policy stance towards disputes between Turkey and Greece could be explained in the context of security and other considerations for the EU involving Turkey. The

EU assumed that active participation in the disputes between Turkey and Greece could disturb the Western security structure. Therefore negotiation between the parties under the UN framework was the preferred approach for dealing with the issues.

Secondly, the EU was inclined to normalize the EU-Turkey Association after the civilian government came into power, in fact, the UK and Germany made most effort to activate the Association agreement. Therefore, the EU was aware of Turkey's sensitivity over Cyprus and the Aegean Sea issues, by implication, and it was careful not to worsen the already impaired relations by endorsing Greece's view. Finally, the 'hands-off policy' of the EU towards the bilateral disputes between Turkey and Greece was adopted partly because of the lack of a common foreign policy mechanism within the EU. Although European Political Cooperation (EPC) was aimed at harmonizing the respective foreign policy courses of the member states, the EU could not succeed in formulating and implementing a common policy stance for third parties. In particular, there was a lack of willingness among the member states to follow a common policy stance regarding the Turkish-Greek disputes.

The Greek Factor after the Turkish Application to Join the EU

Following the return to elected civilian government after the military regime of 1980–83, Turkey's relationship with the EU showed signs of normalization. Soon after relations began to return to normal, Turkey declared its wish to apply for EU membership as an alternative to reactivating the Association Agreement. This was because Turkey felt that the latter was unsatisfactory and constituted an inappropriate framework for future relations. In addition, increased efforts on the part of Greece to use its membership as a bargaining counter to gain concessions from Turkey in its disputes with Turkey were also an important factor behind Turkey's wish to join the EU. Turkish policy-makers realized that Greece had started to influence the EU-Turkey relationship; therefore, they believed that becoming a full member of the EU would be Turkey's best policy stance to counter the EU's favouring of Greece.

After Turkey declared its wish to join the EU, Greece began to increase the degree of its criticism of Turkey and urged the EU to take a stronger and more coherent policy towards Turkey than its earlier stance in relation to issues over Cyprus and the Aegean Sea. In this respect, the presence of Greece at the EU institutions provided the relevant institutional powers for Greece to defend her interests in the EU's policy formulation towards Turkey. In addition, Greece was well aware of the vulnerability of Turkey to the EU's view of its membership application; thus, she sought to influence the EU to link Turkey's membership expectations with the settlement of its disputes with Greece. This implies that Turkey's quest to join the EU not only made the EU more vulnerable and more responsive to Greek influence, but also made the concern of the EU a source of active involvement in disputes between Greece and Turkey. Consequently, after the Turkish application for membership, the EU's balanced policy in its relations with Turkey and Greece appeared to be replaced by a policy that tended to favour Greece.

Contrary to their earlier policy stance, not only the EP but also the member states were about to change their policy stance in favour of Greece, asserting that the bilateral disputes with Greece, including the Cyprus issue, affected the whole EU-Turkey relationship. Such a move by the EU was not entirely owing to Greece's presence at the EU institutions and her continued pressure on the member states in connection with its bilateral disputes with Turkey. There were also other factors to be taken into account. For example, since the late 1980s the EU had begun to establish more coherent and cohesive foreign policy objectives in its external relations, and thus by implication the EU compelled itself to take a more active policy stance towards the bilateral issues between Turkey and Greece. In fact, it was almost impossible for the EU not to associate itself with Greece's disputes with Turkey, as Greece was part of the EU.

However, the main thrust of the EU's policy change in relation to Greek-Turkish disputes was related to its unwillingness to entertain the idea of Turkey's EU membership. It seemed that Turkey's accession to the EU would not only constitute a major institutional, political and financial burden on the EU, but also hamper its further political and economic integration (European Commission, 1989a). Therefore, the EU needed a strategy to put off the possibility of actual Turkish membership in the foreseeable future. From this perspective, linkage politics of Greece appeared to be useful for the EU in pursuing its policy preference of delaying Turkey's membership. To be more precise, Greek objections to Turkish accession seemed to be a welcome tool for the EU in allowing Turkish membership to be delayed by referring to the settlement of the Cyprus and of the Aegean Sea questions as pre-conditions for the consideration of Turkey's accession.

This argument gains strength from the fact that some member states attached particular importance to the Greek-Turkish disputes in EU-Turkey relations. For example, Germany, concerned as she was about the flow of immigrants from Turkey, immediately stressed the importance of the Cyprus and Aegean Sea issues in EU-Turkey relations soon after Turkey formally applied for EU membership (*Financial Times*, 28 November 1987). This was followed by other countries: for instance, in response to the Turkish application for EU membership, the British Government had first linked the Turkish application specifically to the Cyprus problem and relations with Greece: the Prime Minister of the UK, Margaret Thatcher, stated that:

> With other member states we shall make sure that consideration of Turkey's application takes full account of all factors relating not only to Turkey itself but to its relation with every Community country including Greece and third states (*Financial Times*, 16 June 1987).

In addition, the Foreign Affairs Committee of the British House of Commons suggested that the Turkish application should be frozen until Turkey made concessions over Cyprus (*The Guardian*, 7 July 1987). France took a more critical line, stating that Turkey should first improve its relations with the member states, including the settlement of its disputes with Greece over Cyprus and the Aegean Sea (*The Times*, 18 July 1987).

For its part, the EP was even more assertive, linking even the reactivation of the EU-Turkish Association with the improvement in Greece-Turkish relations, alongside improvements in human rights. For example, on 10 July 1986 – just after Turkey's declaration of its intention to apply for membership – the EP adopted a resolution, partly the result of the intense activity of the Greek representative in the EP, stating that 'Turkey must be held partly responsible for the situation in Cyprus since the northern part of the Republic of Cyprus was occupied by its troops' (European Parliament, 1986b). More importantly, the EP for the first time officially admitted that Turkey's policy toward Cyprus and the Aegean Sea was affecting Turkey's relations with the EU (European Parliament, 1986b). In addition, five days after Turkey applied for membership, the EP adopted another resolution, which called on Turkey to reach agreement with Greece over the Aegean Sea as a means of bringing them to the International Court of Justice (European Parliament, 1987b). The timing of these resolutions of the EP and the timing of the Turkish application for EU membership were not purely coincidental; in fact, the EP intended to give a discouraging signal to Turkey that it should not apply for EU membership before the accession conditions, including an agreement with Greece, were completely fulfilled.

Such a move and policy change of the member states and the EP towards Turkey encouraged Greece to make a firmer linkage between the issue of Turkey's membership and her bilateral disputes with Turkey. For example, when the Belgian Presidency tried to hold an EU-Turkey Association Council meeting in December 1987, Greece objected to it on the grounds that Turkey should recognize the ICJ's jurisdiction on the Aegean Sea issues and withdraw her troops from Cyprus (*The Guardian*, 14 December 1987). Furthermore, Greece strongly objected to the decision of the Council to apply normal procedures in the Turkish membership application and its request to the Commission to prepare a report on Turkey's membership application. According to the Greek Foreign Minister:

> The decision was hypocritical since the whole of the Community agrees that Turkish accession is not possible, therefore, instead of being hypocrites and hiding behind procedural aspects it would be much fairer for the principle of the Community if a negative answer was given directly to Turkey clearly and concisely (*Financial Times*, 28 April 1987).

Since Turkey applied for EU membership in 1987, Greece has continued to exert pressure on the member states and the EP to make a solid link between the settlement of its bilateral conflicts with Turkey and the strengthening of EU-Turkey relations. For instance, it blocked the EU's attempt to reactivate the EU-Turkey Association and made it conditional on including the questions of Cyprus and the Aegean Sea on the agenda of the Association Council meeting in 1990.

Realizing that Greece was one of the main obstacles to normalizing EU-Turkey relations and to Turkey's full EU membership, Turkey acknowledged that a process of dialogue and rapprochement with Greece was a necessary step to achieving these objectives. In fact, the timing of Turkey's rapprochement with Greece and the timing of Turkish membership application were not coincidental; the most important factor behind this conciliatory approach of Turkey was its desire to join the EU. Consequently, the Turkish Prime Minister, Turgut Ozal, initiated a meeting with his Greek counterpart, Papandreou, in Davos in 1987 and visited Athens in 1988, anticipating that dialogue with Greece would help to overcome Greece's objections to Turkey's full membership application (*The Economist*, 18 June 1988). For its part, Greece realized that Turkey was eager for EU membership; hence, she saw it as a good opportunity to extract concessions from Turkey. As *The Economist* observed:

> Papandreou evidently hoped that he could get enough leverage out of the Turkish Government's eagerness for EC entry to enable him to extract some concession on Cyprus and the Aegean Sea (*The Economist*, 18 June 1988).

Greece continued to pursue a policy of conditionality towards Turkey in return for the normalization of EU-Turkey relations and for the Turkish accession to the EU during the negotiations at Davos. For example, Prime Minister Papandreou stated that 'Greece would oppose Turkey's membership unless she made some concessions on Cyprus and the Aegean Sea' (*The Economist*, 18 June 1988). However, Turkey regarded Greece's demands unacceptable. Both sides' rigid policy stance over the issues left no room for manoeuvre to reach a compromise. For its part, Turkey was not ready to make such a compromise, and there was even no guarantee from the EU that Turkey's accession to the EU would be considered once the issues between Greece and Turkey were resolved.

Basically, although the Greek-Turkish rapprochement, the so-called 'spirit of Davos', brought some improvements in Greek-Turkish relations and created a constructive environment in the area of low politics, such as economic co-operation,[11] the parties were not able to reach agreement on the solution of fundamental political issues. In other words, despite all efforts, Greece continued to object to the normalization of EU-Turkey relations, and to Turkish membership. Greece's continuous attempts to make any new movement in EU-Turkey relations conditional upon the settlement of its disputes with Turkey was seen in its rigid resistance during the preparation for the meeting of the Association Council of 25 April 1988. At the Association Council meeting, Greece succeeded in inserting a conditional clause in the preliminary statement of the meeting, which acknowledged that the Cyprus and Aegean Sea issues affected EU-Turkey relations (*Agence Europe*, 25 April 1988, No. 4771). In return, Turkey strongly reacted to the preliminary statement and boycotted the meeting.

This was also something to bear in mind in the preparation of the Commission's opinion on Turkey's request for full membership. Greece was well aware of the vulnerability of Turkey to the Commission's *avis*, hence it sought to influence the forthcoming Commission opinion on Turkey's membership by attaching greater importance to the Cyprus and Aegean Sea issues in EU-Turkey relations. It used every opportunity to strengthen the link between the issue of Turkish EU membership and settlement of these disputes during the preparation of the Commission's opinion. Consequently, Commission opinion on Turkey's request for accession to the Community identified the persistence of disputes with a member state and the lack of a solution of the Cyprus problem as the main obstacles in the way of Turkey's full membership (European Commission, 1989a).

The main implication of the Commission opinion on Turkey's application for EU membership was that the EU wished to pursue a containment policy towards Turkey, designed to strengthen EU-Turkey relations through reactivating the Association Agreement. Upon submission to the Council, the Commission's opinion was discussed in the COREPER. Although all member states accepted the Commission's proposal as it stood, Greece objected to the Commission's offer to strengthen EU-Turkey relations on the grounds that Turkey must agree to meet certain political conditions before cooperation started: these were the withdrawal of Turkish troops from Cyprus and the bringing of the disputes over the Aegean Sea to the International Court of Justice at the Hague (Ugur, 1996, p. 20). However, the Greek objection was not compatible with the EU's policy objectives of strengthening EU-Turkey relations. The following section will analyze to what extent Greece has been effective in the implementing of the EU's containment policy towards Turkey.

The Containment Policy of the EU: Customs Union and Linkage Politics

Although the EU effectively rebuffed Turkey's application for full membership, at least for the foreseeable future, it sought ways to keep up the relationship. The EU acknowledged that maintaining closer relations with Turkey was necessary for its objective of anchoring Turkey within the EU as a stable and secular country. The EU was constrained to improve its relations with Turkey and started to make efforts at rapprochement and strengthening EU-Turkish relations. Immediately after effectively delaying Turkish membership by accepting the negative opinion of the Commission, the Council in February 1990 asked the Commission to prepare a specific proposal to specify what the instruments of its policy should be. Although Greece objected to the Council's decision to strengthen EU-Turkey relations until Turkey agreed to meet her well-known conditions, the Commission finalized its proposal known as the 'Matutes Package', which envisaged basically the reactivation of the EU-Turkey Association Agreement, including the establishment of a customs union.

However, Greece made it clear that this rapprochement process between the EU and Turkey depended on parallel progress being made in the Cyprus and Aegean Sea issues. She sought to use the EU's rapprochement policy towards Turkey not only as a bargaining counter in the issue of whether Cyprus should join the EU, but also to gain some diplomatic leverage over Turkey with regard to the Aegean Sea issue. Her conditionality was even stronger at the Dublin Summit of the EU in 1990 that linked for the first time at the highest level the question of Turkish membership to Greece's disputes with Turkey. At the Dublin Summit in June, the EU declared that:

> The European Council, deeply concerned at the situation, firmly affirms its previous declaration and its support for unity, independence, sovereignty and territorial integrity of Cyprus in accordance with relevant UN resolution. Reiterating that Cyprus Problem affects the EC Turkey relations and bearing in mind the importance of these relations (European Council, 1990).

As Dinan puts it, 'This was unusually strong support for Greece's position on the issues' (1991, p. 147). Since the Dublin Summit, the Cyprus problem and disputes over the Aegean Sea have become part of the *acquis communautaire* that Turkey must meet before its membership is considered. Turkey immediately reacted against the EU's declaration, stating that since the EU had taken Greece's side on the issues, it had lost any political credibility in the international efforts to achieve a negotiated solution.[12] The Dublin declaration was important in the sense that it suited not only the EU's containment policy preference of delaying Turkey's membership by referring to the settlement of Cyprus and of the Aegean Sea questions as pre-conditions for the prospect of Turkey's accession to the EU, but also it was compatible with Greece's policy objectives as it had made such firm conditions for Turkey. This implies that there had been a degree of convergence between the linkage politics of Greece and the EU's policy objective of delaying Turkish membership.

Greece was also well aware of the EU's determination to re-define EU-Turkey relations through the containment strategy, which made the EU more vulnerable to Greek influence. From this perspective, Greece sought to place the Cyprus application for EU membership on the negotiation table to trade against its approval of the EU's containment policy for Turkey. To be fair, the timing of the Cyprus application did not entirely coincide with the timing of the EU's rapprochement efforts towards Turkey. As a matter of fact, Cyprus applied for EU membership in 1990 soon after the Council had declared the need for strengthening EU-Turkey relations and requested the Commission to prepare a report. In this respect, the rapprochement efforts of the EU towards Turkey in the early 1990s was seen by both Greece and the Greek Cypriot Governments as a good opportunity to place the Cyprus issue on the negotiating table of EU-Turkey relations.[13]

Nonetheless, this move of Greece was severely criticized by Turkey, who argued that the Cyprus application was illegal on the grounds of the 1960 Cypriot Constitution. Article 50 of the Constitution stipulated that Cyprus could not join any international organization or alliance of which both Greece and Turkey were not members. However, the Council ignored the Turkish view and upon receiving the application, asked the Commission to prepare an opinion on it. Consequently, the Cyprus application for full membership, combined with the Greek political bargaining, has made the Cyprus issue more complicated. As a result, the EU has found it increasingly difficult to continue to follow a policy of non-involvement in Cyprus. As a result of Greece's linkage politics, the progress in EU-Turkey rapprochement was slow. Therefore, the EU realized the need to find a way to overcome the Greek objections to the account of its containment policy objectives with regard to Turkey. More specifically, the EU was determined to strengthen its relations with Turkey. This was noticeable in the Lisbon EU Council Summit:

> The Turkish role in the present European political situation is of the greatest importance and that there is every reason to intensify co-operation and develop relations with Turkey, including political dialogue at the highest level (European Council, 1992).

This implies an emerging consensus among the member states that an effort should be made to overcome the Greek objections towards finalizing the customs union and creating intensive political dialogue at the highest level. Such determination from the EU resulted in its putting increased pressure on Greece to lift her objection to the EU's effort in this respect.

Yet it was not an easy task, as the Greeks were determined to connect the rapprochement efforts of the EU with concessions from Turkey on Cyprus and the Aegean Sea issues. For example, the Foreign Minister of Greece underlined this policy of linkage in April 1992; he stated that 'the improvement in EU-Turkey relations was entirely dependent upon the progress towards settling the Cyprus problem and Turkey's recognition of the ICJ's jurisdiction over the Aegean Sea issues' (*Agence Europe*, 27 June 1992, No. 5759, p. 7). Furthermore, Greece refused to yield to pressure from its partners to remove its long-standing objections to the implementation of the Financial Protocols during a meeting of the EU's Foreign Ministers in Luxembourg in 1991: the Foreign Minister of Greece, Samaras, stated that 'Greece would continue to block any EU aid to Turkey until Turkey made the first concession in Cyprus and agreed to bring the issues over the Aegean Sea to the ICJ' (*Financial Times*, 5 March 1991). In fact, the Greek objection was only eliminated in July of 1992 on the horizontal-financing element of the EU's revised Mediterranean policy, from which Turkey partially benefited, in return for an EU declaration confirming its position on Cyprus (Redmond, 1993, p. 39).

Despite Greek resistance, the EU was determined to make an effort to improve relations with Turkey through the establishment of the customs union. On this account, Turkey's intensive efforts to influence member states and the Commission to strengthen the relationship also had a positive impact on the EU to put more pressure on Greece to lift her objections towards EU-Turkey rapprochement.[14] Consequently, the EU sought ways in which to increase its constraint on Greece to change its strong conditionality towards Turkey. Firstly, the EU tended to use Cyprus's accession to the EU as a bargaining chip in its effort to persuade Greece to lift her objection for the strengthening of EU-Turkey relations. This can be seen in the Commission's opinion on the application by Cyprus for EU membership. The Commission proposed that 'if the inter-communal talks between the Greek and Turkish Cypriots did not reach agreement, the question of Cyprus's accession to the Community was to be reconsidered in January 1995' (The European Commission, 1993, p. 24)

Obviously, it was not just by chance that the timing of the completion of the customs union with Turkey by 1995 coincided with that of the reconsideration of Cyprus' accession to the EU in January 1995. It was a package deal policy of the EU. The primary objective of this package deal was twofold; while it intended to push the Turkish Cypriots and Turkey to make an effort to reach agreement by linking the Cyprus issue to the completion of the customs union, it provided, at the same time, considerable leverage for the EU over Greece to reconsider her objection to the establishment of the customs union. Soon after the Commission's *avis*, it become clearer that the EU had been effectively trading off the EU's accession negotiations with Cyprus for Greece's approval of the establishment of the EU-Turkish customs union. For example, during the French presidency, the EU offered a package deal to both Turkey and Greece: as the General Secretariat of the Council stated:

For the purpose of reaching an overall compromise over a general political framework for developing future relations between the EU and Turkey, the EU would start negotiations for Cyprus's accession six months after the end of the intergovernmental Conference, if it ended with unanimous agreement on the proposal for the customs union (*Financial Times*, 8 February 1995).

Secondly, the EU tried to persuade Greece on the grounds that the improvements in EU-Turkey relations were necessary for Turkey's cooperation in the settlement of disputes between the parties, including the issues over the Aegean Sea. Indeed, Greece began to accept that the rapprochement progress of EU-Turkey relations would be beneficial for Greece, as it could make Turkey more amenable to the influence of Greece and of the EU to make some concessions over Cyprus and the Aegean Sea.

In the light of these factors, Greece came to the reluctant conclusion that it could not prevent the EU from proceeding with its containment policy objectives towards Turkey and hence it tried to maximize its gain from the trade-off politics.[15] Indeed, Greece did not object to the meeting of the EU-Turkey Association Council on 8 November 1993, where it was agreed that the process of the completing the customs union between the EU and Turkey was to be finished by the end of 1995 (EU-Turkey Association Council, 1993). In return, Greece announced many times that she would veto the customs union as long as a resolution of the conflict between the Turkish community and the Greek community in Cyprus remained a precondition for Cyprus's accession. For example, although the establishment of the customs union was the main topic on the agenda of the Association Council meeting in December 1994, it was not successful, as Greece maintained her opposition to the completion of the customs union and declared that she would not drop her objection to it, unless a timetable had been set for the start of accession negotiations with Cyprus (*Financial Times*, 21 December 1994).

As the above analysis shows the main factor behind the EU's success in overcoming Greek resistance to the completion of the customs union was the EU's determination to implement its containment policy for Turkey, as the EU believed that it was necessary for the EU's political, security and economic interests in its relations with Turkey. Therefore, some major members sought to make sure that Greece was not impairing the EU's containment policy towards Turkey. For example, the Anglo-German initiative was indicative of this concern of the EU during the presidency of Greece in 1994. The joint visit to Turkey of the British and German Foreign Ministers, Douglas Hurd and Klaus Kinkel, was intended to reassure Turkey that the six-month Greek presidency would not damage EU-Turkey relations. The Foreign Secretary of the UK, Douglas Hurd, described it as 'not a luxury but a necessity', stating that 'they [were] impatient of Greek efforts to block any positive move of the EU in the EU-Turkey relationship in the hope of extorting Turkish concessions on Cyprus and Aegean Sea' (Brown and Mortimer, 1994). However, Greece denounced it as a breach of the Common Foreign and Security Policy (CFSP) and criticized Germany and the UK for not showing solidarity with the principles of the CFSP (*Financial Times*, 20 January 1994). Finally, the EU-Turkey Association Council made the decision to finalize the customs union agreements with Turkey in March 1995 and the European Parliament ratified it on 14 December 1995.

In conclusion, although Greece has, to some extent, had the power to modify the EU's policy towards Turkey, it has not been effective with regard to the implementation of the EU's containment policy for Turkey, as this requires a close relationship with Turkey to be maintained for the sake of the EU's political, security and economic interests in its relationship with Turkey. The negotiations of the customs union case, which is the most important instrument of the EU's containment policy, supported this argument: the EU found a way to push Greece into not objecting to the rapprochement of EU-Turkey relations. Despite Greece's strong objection to the completion of the customs union on the grounds of its political disputes with Turkey over Cyprus and the Aegean Sea, the majority of EU member states managed to dismiss the Greek objection. This implies that Greece's power in EU-Turkey relations is not so strong as to thwart the EU as long as the latter is firmly determined to carry out its policy towards Turkey.

Turkey's Membership Challenge: The Greek Factor as a Pretext for Delaying Turkey's Membership?

Since the customs union came into force, Turkey has sought to keep the question of her inclusion in the next enlargement process on the agenda of Turkey-EU relations. However, the EU has remained reluctant to endorse the Turkish view, and thus was careful not to imply that there were any prospects of Turkish membership in the foreseeable future. In fact, the EU saw the customs union as sufficient for its declared objective of anchoring Turkey within the EU. On this account, the customs union seems to have been offered by the EU as a substitute for Turkey's membership.

From this perspective, the Greek linkage politics, which have sought to link the prospect of Turkish membership with the settlement of the Cyprus and the Aegean Sea issues, have gained particular importance, as it has been highly useful for the EU to allow Turkish membership to be delayed by letting it depend on the settlement of the Cyprus and of the Aegean Sea questions. This implies that there has been convergence between the EU's containment policy objective of delaying Turkish membership and the objective of Greece linkage politics: on the one hand, the EU's approval of Greece policy towards Turkey has increased Greece's diplomatic and political leverage over Turkey by making the prospect of Turkish accession to the EU conditional upon Turkey's concessions in the bilateral issues with Greece. On the other hand, Greece's strong objection to Turkish membership has provided some grounds for the EU to support and justify its policy objective of delaying Turkish membership in the foreseeable future.

However, this playing into one another's hands between the EU and Greece in their policies over the issue of Turkey's membership cannot be seen when it comes to the improvement of the EU-Turkey relations. In other words, it seems that there has been some inconsistency in the EU's policy approach to the Greek-Turkish disputes: while the EU has approached certain political issues positively when it comes to its policy objective of strengthening EU-Turkey relations, the same issues have attracted an entirely different response from the EU when it comes to the issue of Turkish membership. This implies that the EU's policy approaches to the Greek-Turkish disputes have been shaped by its policy preference. In fact, contrary to the EU's policy during the establishment of a customs union, in which almost every member state and the Commission made substantial efforts to overcome the Greek objections, the EU has not only been hesitant in making an effort to mitigate the Greek objections to Turkey's accession to the EU, but has approved Greece's linkage politics to undermine Turkey's membership expectations, by linking the feasibility of Turkish membership with the settlement of Cyprus and Aegean Sea issues. Take an example from the Turkey-EU Association meeting in November 1996: in response to Turkey's request for inclusion in the enlargement strategy of the EU, Hans van Mierlo, the Dutch Foreign Minister and President of the Council, stated that the prospects of Turkey's accession to the EU depended on an improvement in relations between Greece and Turkey (Bulletin European Union, No. 10–1996). This was just what the Greeks had been trying to get Turkey to do in the disputes between them.

The EU's use of Turkey's disagreement with Greece for delaying the prospect of Turkey's accession to the EU can also be seen in the Commission's Agenda 2000. Although it acknowledged that the customs union was functioning effectively, demonstrating Turkey's ability to adapt to the economic *acquis* of the EU in many areas, it cited Turkey's disagreements with Greece over Cyprus and the Aegean Sea, as two of main reasons why Turkey should be treated differently from other countries in the context of enlargement. The Commission simply recommended a deepening of relations with Turkey, using the Association Agreement and customs union as the foundations for proposed closer political and economic relations, without implying anything about the prospects of Turkish membership (European Commission, 1997b). A Commission Communication on the further development of relations with Turkey implicitly stated that the disputes between Turkey and Greece and the Cyprus questions were to be resolved before any consideration of accession negotiations with Turkey (European Commission, 1997a, p. 5). By implication, the Commission effectively avoided the question of when Turkish membership should be offered by making it conditional upon the establishment of good neighbourly relations with Greece, including settlement of the Cyprus question.

However, the EU does not seem have been entirely candid in explaining its differentiation policy towards Turkey on the grounds of Greek objections to the prospect of Turkey's membership. The deep fragmentation and diversity among the member states with regard to the likely effect of Turkish membership on the EU's political and economic integration has resulted in a lack of any clear enlargement policy of the EU *vis-à-vis* Turkey. This constitutes the main reason why the EU has shown extreme caution in dealing with the question of Turkey's membership. From this perspective, the Greek objections to Turkish accession have been highly useful for the EU in delaying Turkish membership. For example, the Luxembourg Summit of the EU in 1997 effectively rejected the candidacy of Turkey on the grounds of Turkey's disputes with Greece. Although most members of the EU were as reluctant as Greece to accept Turkey as a candidate, on the grounds that Turkish membership would be disadvantageous not only for the EU in the political, economic and cultural senses, but also for their own interests, they did not want to be seen to show such reluctance during the preparation of the Luxembourg Summit. Therefore, they tended to use the Turkish-Greek disputes and strong Greek objections as a pretext to hide their own disapproval of Turkish membership. The Greek Foreign Minister, Pangalos, clarified this argument by asserting that:

> Our partners have hidden behind Greece by offering Turkey the Greek conditions, which
> they describe as logical on the one hand, and telling Ankara that they themselves support

an upgrading of EU-Turkish relations, on the other. There are other countries in the European Union which have problems with Turkey and which are hiding behind Greece (cited in Bohlen, 1997).

Pangalos's accusation was not groundless; as an example, although Germany had consistently supported the principle of closer relations between Turkey and the EU, she has been very reluctant to consider the Turkish membership on the grounds of the free movement of people and the implications of Turkish membership for further European integration.[16] Therefore, Germany tended to use the Greek-Turkish conflicts as a pretext for her own objections to Turkish membership. As an example, the German Foreign Minister, Klaus Kinkel, stated that 'Turkey's long-standing conflicts with Greece over the divided island of Cyprus and the Aegean Sea must be sorted out before EU membership could be considered' (*Financial Times*, 24 March 1997). In addition, during the visit of the Turkish Prime Minister, Mesut Yilmaz, in his attempt to gain German support for Turkey's inclusion in the next enlargement of the EU just before the Luxembourg Summit, the Chancellor of Germany, Helmut Kohl, specifically made reference to the importance of a lasting settlement of Greek-Turkish disagreements and of a rapid solution of the Cyprus question to the prospect of Turkey's membership (Kramer, 1997, p. 24). The Chancellor's concern about the disputes between Greece and Turkey did not appear to be sincere, as he seemed to be using them as a pretext for his own objections to Turkish membership.

However, the EU has approached the Greek-Turkish disputes and Greece's linkage politics differently when it comes to strengthening EU-Turkey relations. As an example, the EU disapproved of Greece's effort to set up strict conditions for Turkey's participation in the European Conference; it not only tried to find a way to dismiss the Greek objections, but also criticized Greece's rigid conditions over Turkey's participation in the Conference. This was primarily because the European Conference was considered as part of the EU's containment policy, intended to satisfy Turkey without implying membership. Initially, Greece objected to Turkey's participation. As the Prime Minister of Greece, Simitis, stated, Greece was ready to block the participation of Turkey in the European Conference if Ankara was not more cooperative over Cyprus and the Aegean Sea (*Financial Times*, 29 November 1997). However, the EU member states easily managed to dismiss the Greek objections, as they believed that Turkey's participation in the Conference would secure Turkey's cooperation with the EU and strengthen the relationship. Nevertheless, Turkey reacted adversely to the decisions of the Luxembourg Summit and turned down the EU's invitation to participate in the European Conference on the grounds that the Conference was a forum for consultation on broad issues rather than a forum for the enlargement of the EU (*Financial Times*, 15 December 1997). Consequently, Turkey suspended political dialogue with the EU in relation to issues between Greece and Turkey over Cyprus and the Aegean Sea until it was included in the list of candidate countries. [17]

The EU realized that Turkey's decision was not compatible with its policy objective of strengthening EU-Turkey relations yet without implying the offer of full membership in the foreseeable future. As a result, the EU under the British Presidency made a clear effort to bring Turkey back into closer relations with the EU. Upon the request of the Council, the Commission on 4 March 1998 proposed a strategy, the so-called European strategy for Turkey, designed to deepen the customs union and extend it to the services and agricultural sectors. Greece objected to the EU's effort led by the British presidency, to restore EU-Turkey relations and described it as a breach of the principles of the EU. However, the EU member states and the Commission warned Greece to lift its veto against the EU's effort to restore relations. For example, the British Foreign Secretary, Robin Cook, stated: 'we must find new ways to restructure constructive working relations with Turkey' (*Middle East International*, 13 March 1998, p. 13). The French Minister for European Affairs, Pierre Moscovici, took the same line, stating that 'it is necessary to think of a way to bypass the Greek veto: the situation with Turkey cannot remain blocked. The credibility of the EU is at stake' (cited in Wood, 1999, p. 113). Even Germany asked Greece to make a constructive contribution to restore EU-Turkey relations. Thus, Greece was unable to resist the EU's determination and eventually took a more flexible approach towards Turkey.

Greek-Turkish Relations after the Helsinki Summit of the EU

As indicated above, the Luxembourg decision of the EU in relation to Turkey's prospect for EU membership damaged EU-Turkey relations to the extent that they were at their lowest point since Turkey's application for EU membership. Given the importance of the relations to both sides – from the political, economic and security points of view – the EU sought to a way to reactivate its containment policy of Turkey by upgrading Turkey's status from applicant state to candidate state. For example, Germany attempted to upgrade Turkey's status to a candidate country at the Cologne Summit, but this effort failed due to Greek objections. The EU increased its pressure on Greece to persuade her to take a more positive approach towards Turkey. An argument used by the member states to persuade Greece to recognize Turkey's candidacy was that keeping Turkey out of the EU would not serve Greek interests, as it would make the settlement of disputes between the parties more difficult.

For its part, Turkey also made diplomatic efforts to exert pressure on Greece to withdraw its objection to the Turkish candidacy. Given that all other members of the EU expressed their willingness to give Turkey candidate status, the latter was quick to warn Greece of the negative consequences which opposition to the Turkish candidacy would have. As the State Minister responsible for EU affairs, Mehmet Ertemcelik stated; 'It would be difficult to sustain the recent improvement in relations between Greece and Turkey if Athens were to prevent it from becoming a full candidate for membership of the EU' (Norman, 1999).

Accordingly, Greece soon realized that her traditional policy to keep Turkey out was not in her own long-term interests. Greek Foreign Minister, George Papandreou, said:

> Contrary to popular belief, it is in Greece's interest to see Turkey, at some point, in the EU, rather than having it in continual conflict and tension with the bloc and European standards (*The Guardian*, 13 September 1999).

Greece realized that Turkey's reaction to the Luxembourg decisions was not compatible with her own foreign policy objectives, as she had already lost leverage in the EU diplomacy over Turkey. Turkey's reaction to the Luxembourg outcomes had not only strained EU-Turkey relations, but also made more complicated the prospects of settlement of the issues between Greece and Turkey, including the Cyprus issue. Turkey in turn did not cooperate with the EU over Cyprus because the Luxembourg Summit set a date for the accession negotiations over Cyprus to begin. Turkey ended not only most of her formal contact with the EU, but also refused to enter any political dialogue with the EU concerning Cyprus and the Aegean Sea issues. Moreover, she started to take a harder policy stand towards the EU's policy for Cyprus as the EU set in notion the accession process of Cyprus; for instance, Turkey and the TRNC issued a joint Declaration which anticipated a similar integration approach between the TRNC and Turkey in the event that Cyprus joined the EU without a political settlement.[18] Consequently, Greece hoped that Turkey would adopt a more flexible and constructive approach towards a settlement of bilateral issues if a clear prospect for membership were given to Turkey through the recognition of her candidacy. Greece also assumed that prospect of Turkish membership for the EU would also increase her diplomatic and political leverage over Turkey.

However, it should be pointed out that Greece's approval of Turkey's candidacy at the Helsinki Summit of the EU did not imply that Greece had changed its linkage politics in any way; that sought to link the prospect of Turkish membership with the settlement of Greece's bilateral issues with Turkey, including the Cyprus question. Rather, Greece aimed to make a stronger link between the settlement of these issues and the issue of Turkey's candidacy through the EU's declaration at the Helsinki Summit. Consequently, Greece succeeded in attaching political conditions to the approval of Turkey's candidature, including recognition of the ICJ's jurisdiction in resolving the disputes between Greece and Turkey and an assurance that Cyprus would join the EU without political settlement at the Helsinki Summit. The EU Council made it clear that 'If no settlement has been reached by the completion of the accession negotiations the Council decision on accession will be made without the above being a precondition' (European Council, 1999a). The Helsinki Document also urged Turkey to give 'strong support to the UN Secretary-General's efforts to bring the process to a successful conclusion'.

As far as the conditionality of the Aegean Sea disputes on the Turkish accession was concerned, the Helsinki Document made a general reference to Paragraph 4, which urges all the candidate countries 'to make any efforts to resolve any outstanding border disputes and other related issues. Failing this they should within reasonable time bring the dispute to the International Court of Justice' (European Council, 1999a). It also stated that 'the Council will review the situation relating to any outstanding disputes, in particular concerning the repercussions on the accession process and in order to promote their settlement through the International Court of Justice, at the latest by the end of 2004' (European Council, 1999a).

There seem to be some uncertainties and vagueness in the Helsinki Document about these conditions for the prospect of Turkish membership. In other words, the wording and style of the conditions in the Helsinki document leaves room for different interpretation. In fact, both Greece and Turkey seem to have interpreted them differently from their own perspectives. For example, even after agreeing to the EU candidacy, the Turkish Prime Minister, Ecevit, stated that 'we cannot accept any preconditions on Cyprus' (*Financial Times*, 11 December 1999). For Greece's part, after the Helsinki Summit, the Foreign Minister, Papandreou, announced that Turkey's EU prospects depended on the Cyprus solution, as well as on Greek-Turkish relations (Macedonian Press Agency, 18 February 2000). Moreover, the reference to ICJ to resolve any outstanding border disputes and other related issues caused considerable concern in Turkey, and thus she asked the EU to clarify it.[19] The EU was quick to convince Turkey that 2004 was not a rigidly set as time to bring the Aegean dispute to the ICJ, but rather a dateline for revision of the situations by the European Council.

The same vagueness is seen about how effectively the EU had made Turkey's accession negotiation conditional on the solution of the Cyprus issue. The Helsinki document only made a reference to paragraph 9, which urges Turkey to maintain 'strong support for the UN Secretary-General's efforts to bring the process to a successful conclusion'. This seems acceptable for Turkey and, in fact, the Prime Minister of Turkey, Bulent Ecevit, stated that 'our government will continue to support all initiatives aimed at finding peaceful and lasting solutions to the dispute' (*Turkish Daily News*, 16 November 2000).

Accordingly, it seems that the Helsinki Text was a carefully phrased document, designed to satisfy both Greece and Turkey. One observer describes it as follows:

> The Helsinki outcome is a masterly diplomatic document that manages to give Greece what it wanted without going so far as to lead the Turks to conclude that they were being given lessons and lectures. It was enough to protect the Greek Government but also not so much that Turkey would not accept the offer (Philip, 2000, p. 49).

The Helsinki decision seemed to be a strategic move by the EU not only to find a middle ground between Turkey and Greece in order to reactivate EU-Turkey relations, but also to overcome the Greek objections to the Turkish candidacy. Given that the Luxembourg decision of the EU in 1997 had already made membership unattainable for Turkey, and thus soured relationships, the EU upgraded Turkey's status from applicant country to candidate country in an attempt to reactivate its containment policy of Turkey because the cost of Turkey's exclusion is high in security, political and economic terms. Hence, the EU has revised its containment policy – without making substantial changes in its policy objectives – as a means of recognizing Turkey as a candidate country, but delaying Turkish membership prospects in the foreseeable future by attaching firm conditions to it.

However, it should be noted that the Helsinki outcomes have brought new inputs into Greece-Turkish relations, encouraging Greek-Turkish rapprochement, which started after the earthquake in Turkey of August 1999. As the Greek Prime Minister puts it, 'Turkey's EU candidacy marked a historic shift towards the new relationship and Greece and Turkey have the basis for a new relationship' (*Financial Times*, 13 December 1999). Official visits of Greek and Turkish Foreign Ministers to Ankara and Athens respectively resulted in the signing of a number of bilateral agreements in trade, commerce, the environment, tourism, culture and multilateral cooperation with regard to legal immigration, drug trafficking and terrorism. This has created a constructive environment in the area of low politics. In addition, both sides have agreed to establish bilateral committees at a high-ranking administrative level to build mutual confidence. Accordingly, six working groups were set up to search for a solution to fundamental political disputes between the two sides.

Furthermore, upon the proposal by Greece, the two parties initiated a cooperation on EU affairs through the Turkey-Greece EU Committee, aimed at accelerating Turkey's accession process to the EU, as well as improving relations between the two countries (IKV Bulteni, 2000). Moreover, at the level of civil society, a number of NGO and civil society organizations and business associations have engaged in activities aimed at improving the relationship (Hurriyet, 28 February 2000). Another important result of this Helsinki rapprochement is that the parties have agreed to build on the confidence that neither side will use military threats against the other in their disputes in future.

Yet it seems doubtful that successful cooperation in low politics will encourage cooperation in 'high politics' issues in the foreseeable future. Convergence of expectations and interests in the economic field does not seem to have extended to the issues of high politics. In fact, the parties have not been able to reach agreement on the solution of major political issues. The crisis between Greece and Turkey over the status of two Aegean islands during the NATO exercise in October 2000 illustrates this: when Greek warplanes flew over two islands, Turkey reacted on the ground that these islands are under demilitarized statues. As a result, Greece withdrew from the NATO exercise, which for the first time deployed Greek military forces in Turkey as allies (*Financial Times*, 3 November 2000).

Furthermore, the disagreement between Greece and Turkey over the reference to the Cyprus issue and jurisdiction of the ICJ in the Aegean Sea issue in the Accession Partnership Document for Turkey is another case, indicating the limits of Turkish-Greek rapprochement with intend to reach agreement on the solutions of sensitive issues. While the Commission's proposal for the Accession Partnership Document for Turkey was discussed at the General Affairs Council before the Nice Summit of the EU, Greece made an effort to make link the prospect of Turkish membership formally to progress on resolving territorial disputes over the Aegean Sea and Cyprus issue as a means of inserting them as political conditions in the Accession Partnership Document. For its part, Turkey reacted strongly against the Greek attempt: for example, the Prime Minister of Turkey sent a letter to the leaders of the EU member states, stating that Turkey has never accepted any linkage between the solution of the Cyprus issue and bilateral disputes with Greece and its candidacy to the EU beyond the decision taken at the Helsinki Summit (*Financial Times*, 5 December 2000). Finally, the Accession Partnership Document, endorsed by the Council of Ministers, included the same wording as had been written in the Helsinki Conclusions.

This above analysis does not mean to suggest, however, the recent improvement in Greek-Turkish relations would not lead to a broad dialogue between the parties on high politics issues in the long run. The EU's acceptance of Turkey's candidacy for EU membership and improvement in Greek-Turkish relations have already generated some incentives in both sides which might encourage the parties to take a more conciliatory approach to the settlement of their bilateral disputes. In fact, Turkey endorsed the measures suggested in the Accession Partnership Document in relation to the Cyprus issue and disputes over the Aegean Sea in the context of enhanced political dialogue. In this respect, the EU's policy towards Turkey and

Cyprus is important in the sense that EU diplomacy would encourage and even direct the process of Greek-Turkish rapprochement through a more balanced policy towards the issues between the parties.

However, as the Helsinki Text and Accession Partnership Document indicates, there are no substantial changes in the EU's approach towards issues between Greece and Turkey. By implication, the prospect for Turkey's accession is made firmly conditional upon the resolution of the Cyprus problem and bilateral conflicts between Greece and Turkey over the Aegean Sea. As the Accession Partnership implied, accession negotiations can only start once the political criteria for EU membership, including bilateral disputes with Greece, have been fulfilled. Even the implementation of the Accession Partnership that aims to prepare Turkey for EU membership, is firmly conditional upon Turkey's progress towards meeting the political conditions indicated above.

Although the Helsinki process seems to have provided a vision of Turkish membership on a long-term basis, it still doubtful how the Accession Partnership will be implemented to prepare Turkey for EU membership. Given the vagueness of political conditions and different interpretations of such conditions by Turkey and Greece and even by the EU, the bilateral issues between Turkey and Greece are likely to prevent implementing the Accession Partnership accord. In this respect, the main question is whether the way in which the way the EU has approached the issues between Greece and Turkey has been appropriate and compatible with the security objectives of the EU's enlargement policy to stabilize the region through encouraging dialogue between the parties. Particularly, the EU's approach to the Cyprus application seems to have been incompatible with its *acquis* in the CFSP. Even some EU member states – France, Italy and Denmark – have already addressed their concerns over the security implications of Cyprus's accession to the EU (*Financial Times*, 13 December 1999). The Commissioner responsible for the enlargement, Gunter Verheugen, described the accession of Cyprus as being problematic, saying:

> There are a number of big and influential Member States who are already saying that we should not negotiate further with Cyprus because it is clear that Cyprus cannot fulfill the *acquis* in the area of the common foreign and security policy (cited in Nugent, 2000, p. 147).

Indeed, it is likely that without the political settlement Cyprus's accession to the EU would not only harm the EU's cohesion but also would create security problems in Southern Europe, since the accession of Cyprus to the EU could increase the long-standing restraint of the relations between Greece and Turkey. Moreover, given that the EU is formally considering the Cyprus application on the part of whole island, once Cyprus joins the EU as a full member, the EU will became a part of the issue as the island will become an integral part of EU territory which would add complexity to the security issues of the EU.

By implication, Cyprus accession to the EU without political settlement might seriously undermine stability in Southeastern Europe and the Mediterranean. As Nugent puts it: 'The accession of Cyprus will import fierce territorial disputes within the EU borders – a dispute in which the two sides are protected by separate security guarantees from Greece and Turkey' (Nugent, 2000, p. 139). Moreover, the

EU's policy approach to the Cyprus issue seems to have been inadequate to generate sufficient incentives for not only Turkey and the leaders of Turkish Cyprus, but also for Greece and Greek Cyprus to take a more conciliatory approach towards the settlement of the Cyprus issue. For example, Turkey and the leaders of Turkish Cyprus have objected to the accession negotiations of Cyprus with the EU without a political settlement (*The Guardian*, 25 November 2000). Turkey considers that Cyprus membership would further strain EU-Turkey relations; once Cyprus becomes an EU member, she, alongside with Greece, is likely to exercise her veto power to make both the improvement of the EU-Turkey relations and Turkey's prospective membership conditional on the political settlement of Cyprus.

For their part, Greece and the Republic of Cyprus assume that prospect of EU membership would provide an incentive to a settlement of the Cyprus problem. They seems to take the view that if the EU gives a clear accession commitment to Cyprus without precondition of political settlement, then Turkey and the TRNC would adopt a more flexible approach towards a settlement of the Cyprus issue (Theophanous, 2000). It became apparent that the EU has endorsed Greek view on this by not linking the Cyprus accession to a political settlement of the Cyprus issue. The EU Council at Helsinki made it clear that 'If no settlement has been reached by the completion of the accession negotiations the Council decision on accession will be made without the above being a precondition'. As one scholar puts it, 'the EU leaders went closer than they have ever done before to stating that a solution to the Cyprus problem is not absolutely necessary for Cyprus accession' (Nugent, 2000, p. 147). This is what Greece and Cyprus wanted in order to make its linkage politics firmer and more effective. Nevertheless, the question is whether the way in which the EU has approached the Cyprus issue has been appropriate to influence Greece and Cyprus to adopt a more flexible approach towards a political settlement. It appears that there is no reason why Greece and Cyprus should find themselves obliged to show flexibility in settling the Cyprus issue, as the EU's approach towards the question of the proposed Cyprus accession has been in harmony with their policy objectives.

To conclude, the EU's policy post-Helsinki has brought the old containment policy of Turkey back on the track. Although the EU's policy since Helsinki has brought some dynamism into EU-Turkey relations and has boosted the rapprochement in Turkey-Greek relations, it has not been sufficient to generate the necessary incentives to make a dramatic shift on the part of Turkey towards the Cyprus and Aegean Sea issues. Therefore, the analysis in this section suggests that the EU post-Helsinki policy towards Turkey has not changed much from its old policy containment of Turkey with regard to bilateral issues between Greece and Turkey, because the EU allowed Greece to insert political conditions for the prospects of Turkey's accession, including recognition of the ICJ's jurisdiction in resolving the disputes between Greece and Turkey and the solution of the Cyprus issue.

One might argue that the EU's strong conditionality towards Turkey is appropriate and in harmony with its political conditions for EU membership. In fact, there might be room to argue that the EU's strong objection to Turkish membership before the settlement of disputes with Greece is reasonable and compatible with its membership condition that aspirant members have to resolve all their outstanding differences with their neighbours before joining the EU. This argument could even be supported on the grounds of the EU's concern that unresolved political issues between Greece and Turkey would harm the Union's cohesion. However, this is only part of the explanation of the EU's strong objection to Turkish membership on these grounds. Furthermore, it is difficult to explain the EU's policy towards Cyprus: although the latter has similar problem, the EU has proposed accession of Cyprus without a political settlement, with a view that prospect of EU membership would provide an incentive to a settlement of the Cyprus problem.

Thus, it could be argued that the EU's rigid and strong conditionality policy *vis-à-vis* Turkey has been incompatible with its enlargement policy objectives. One of the main objectives of the EU's enlargement policy is to create political stability throughout Europe. On this account, the EU has supported other applicant countries' efforts to resolve their outstanding border disputes and other related issues through its pre-accession strategy and the use of political dialogue. For example, the EU has proposed joint actions, the so-called Stability Pact for Europe, to contribute to the diplomatic settlement of bilateral issues between candidate members and to stimulate good neighbour agreements on borders and on the treatment of ethnic minorities. This Stability Pact for Europe has become part of the CEECs preparation for the fulfilment of political obligations to allow their accession to the EU; thus, it has forced the candidate countries to adopt a more cooperative and constructive attitude towards each other. This implies that the EU has effectively used the accession carrot to persuade the applicant countries to contribute to the diplomatic settlement of their bilateral issues and to stimulate good neighbour agreements on many issues. The EU has encouraged the CEECs to settle their bilateral issues by not only offering them clear prospects of EU membership, but also by working closely with them to find ways towards the resolution of their disagreements. A case in point is the particularly relevant effort by Romania and Hungary to resolve their minority issues and their expectations of membership of the EU. With the common goal of joining the EU as an incentive, they signed a cooperation and friendship treaty, the so-called 'Treaty on Understanding, Cooperation and Good Neighbourliness' (Ram, 1999). The expectation of EU membership was the motivation for its conclusion and it remains a prime cause of the current and future cooperation between Romania and Hungary.

However, this has not been the case for Turkey. The EU's policy of containment towards Turkey, which links the membership prospect of Turkey with the resolution of the latter's disputes with Greece, seems to have made the settlement of Turkey's disputes with Greece even more complicated and difficult. This is partly because Turkey believes that the EU has taken the side of Greece in the bilateral disputes, which makes the EU unsuitable to mediate. This is affirmed by a high-ranking Turkish diplomat: he claims that the EU has taken a one-sided approach in dealing with Cyprus and the Aegean Sea issues without taking the actual nature of the problems into account.[20] This is even implied by Richard Balfe, member of the European Parliament, who says: 'the EU is probably not quite the right actor to mediate the settlement of Greek-Turkish disputes, because the EU is pro-Greek'.[21] In addition, the Deputy Head of the Turkish Unit in the Commission, Van den Meer, hinted at the difficulty for the EU of pursuing a different policy from that of Greece towards Turkey by stating: 'Greece is a member of the EU; hence, the EU has to accommodate the interest of its members in its policy towards Turkey.'[22]

Overall, the EU's policy of conditionality towards the prospect of Turkey's membership seems to have lost credibility in influencing and encouraging Turkey to settle the disagreement over Cyprus and the Aegean Sea issues. This is because Turkey has found the EU's linkage politics and its containment policy unattractive and inadequate to encourage concessions over these issues. The implication is that the EU has not used the accession carrot effectively to influence and encourage Turkey to resolve its disputes with Greece, as it has done for the CEECs. On this account, it could be argued that an alternative policy of the EU to locate Turkish accession negotiations within a more flexible and positive framework of Greek-Turkish relations and to have offered a degree of clarity and certainty about Turkish prospects for membership might have been more effective in influencing Turkey to settle her disagreements with Greece. The post-Helsinki state of EU-Turkey relations appears to support the above contention, as Turkey has shown some signs that it would be willing to bring the continental shelf issue to the ICJ if they fail to reach agreement through dialogue within reasonable time. This indicates that the Helsinki process has provided important incentives for a relatively reconciliatory stand in this respect. Turkey's acceptance of the Helsinki document and Accession Partnership – despite some conditions attached to it on Cyprus and the Aegean Sea – provides some evidence to support the contention that the accession carrot could encourage Turkey to take a constructive approach towards bilateral issues with Greece.

Conclusions

The above analysis suggests that after joining the EU, Greece started to use its position as a bargaining counter to gain concessions from Turkey as regards her bilateral disputes with that country. Thanks to the Cold War politics and security concerns of Europe, the EU made efforts to maintain a balanced policy in its relations with Greece and Turkey until Turkey officially declared its wish to join the EU by applying for EU membership in 1987. Since then, it has become increasingly difficult for the EU to continue to pursue an evenly balanced policy in its relations with Greece and Turkey. This has been, firstly, due to the Greek presence at the institutions of the EU and her veto power in the decision-making of the EU towards Turkey in most areas, including membership and financial cooperation. In other words, EU membership has provided diplomatic and political leverage for Greece over Turkey, as the latter has been eager to intensify its relationship with the EU, with a view to becoming a member. As a result, Greece has managed to push the EU towards accepting the view that Turkey's disagreements with Greece have affected the EU-Turkey relationship.

Secondly, Turkey's uncompromising and rigid policy towards issues over Cyprus and the Aegean Sea has increased Greece's efforts to Europeanize its disputes with Turkey. Considering that Greece has been a full member and that both Cyprus and Turkey have applied for EU membership, it would, by implication, have been almost inevitable for the EU to pursue a policy of non-involvement in the disputes between the parties. Thirdly, since the late 1980s, the EU has been evolving towards political union with Common Foreign and Security Policy objectives that have made the EU more sensitive and responsive to Greek-Turkish disputes. In particular, Greece has consistently asked the EU to act in line with the objectives of the CFSP, as she believed that she was under threat from Turkey.

Although Greece has had some power to modify the EU's policy towards Turkey, this has been constrained and her decisiveness in EU-Turkey relations has depended on the EU's approval of Greece's linkage politics, and on its containment policy objectives for Turkey. More precisely, Greece has been less effective when it comes to the EU's policy objective of strengthening the relations with Turkey, since the EU disapproves of Greece's linkage politics towards Turkey. There have been three main cases that support the above hypothesis. The first was the customs union, which is the most important instrument of the EU's containment policy. Despite Greece's strong objections to the completion of the customs union with Turkey on the grounds of its disputes over Cyprus and the Aegean Sea, the majority of EU member states managed to dismiss the Greek objection. Therefore, the customs union indicated that Greece cannot shift the EU's policy *vis-à-vis* Turkey by herself so long as the member states find it a necessary policy course to implement. The second case was the issue of Turkey's participation in the European Conference. Although Greece initially opposed the EU's invitation to Turkey to take part in the European Conference for well-known reasons, the EU again discounted the Greek objection. This was because almost all the member states wanted to have a close relationship with Turkey. On this account, they believed that Turkey's participation in the European Conference would provide some sort of inclusive arrangement for Turkey in which Turkey could be anchored within the EU, without implying anything about membership. The last case was the Helsinki Summit; when the EU realized that the Luxembourg decisions of 1997 were not compatible with its objective of maintaining closer relations with Turkey, it managed to push Greece towards agreeing that close relations were necessary not only for Greek interests but in the interests of the EU. Therefore, despite initial Greek objections, the EU established a common position of accepting Turkey as a candidate for EU membership.

However, the Greek factor has been fully effective when it comes to the EU's policy objective of delaying Turkish membership itself. This has been due to the convergence between the linkage politics of Greece and the EU's policy objective of delaying the prospect of Turkey's EU membership. Greek objections to Turkish membership seem to have suited the EU preferences and been highly useful when the EU want to slow Turkey down. Since Turkey officially declared its wish to join the EU by applying for EU membership in 1987, the EU has not only begun to take a firm and critical policy stance *vis-à-vis* Turkey regarding the disputes between that country and Greece, but it has also promoted the Greek argument by making the settlement of Cyprus and of the Aegean Sea questions pre-conditions for the prospect of Turkey's accession to the EU. The Helsinki Summit and Accession Partnership Document appear to support the contention that the EU has effectively delayed the prospect of Turkish membership in the foreseeable future by linking the prospects of Turkey's accession negotiations with the settlement of the Greek-Turkish disputes, including the Cyprus issue. This seems a diplomatic design of the EU to use the Greek objection to delay Turkey's membership for the foreseeable future. If the EU really wanted to offer Turkey a more satisfactory strategy – by placing Turkish accession negotiations within a more flexible and positive framework of Greek-Turkish relations from the Helsinki accords – Greek opposition would be discounted.

The secondary argument of the chapter is that the EU's strong conditionality policy *vis-à-vis* Turkey, which has firmly linked the membership prospects of Turkey with the settlement of the latter's disputes with Greece, has not only been unfair but also less effective in influencing the settlement of these disagreements than an alternative policy would have been. The EU's linkage politics towards Turkey have increased Greece's leverage within the EU to Europeanize its disputes with Turkey. Having Europeanized its disputes with Turkey, Greece has not found itself obligated to show flexibility in settling the Cyprus and the Aegean Sea issues. But the EU could have used the Cyprus accession to the EU as a bargaining counter to persuade Greece to take a constructive approach to the settlement of her disputes with Turkey. This might also be the case for Turkey. Instead of pursuing a containment policy, which lacked the necessary instruments and credibility for Turkey's membership prospects, the EU could have used the accession carrot more effectively to influence and encourage Turkey to contribute to the diplomatic settlement of its bilateral disputes with Greece, as it has done for the CEECs.

On this account, it could be argued that an alternative policy of the EU, to locate Turkish accession negotiations within a more flexible and positive framework of Greek-Turkish relations and to have offered a degree of clarity and certainty about Turkish prospects for membership, might have been more effective in influencing Turkey to settle her disagreements with Greece. In fact the post-Helsinki character of EU-Turkey relations appears to support the above contention that the accession carrot (despite some conditions attached to it on Cyprus and the Aegean Sea) has had some positive impact on Turkey's policy in this respect.

Notes

1　For the USA's policy towards Cyprus, see Monteagle Stearns (1992), *Entangled Allies: USA policy towards Greece, Turkey and Cyprus*, Council on Foreign Relations Press, New York.

2　For a detailed analysis of the UN efforts, see S. Bolukbasi (1998), 'The Cyprus Issue and the United Nations: Peaceful non-settlement between 1945–1996', *International Journal of Middle Eastern Studies* Vol. 30, No. 3, Cambridge University Press.

3　For this, see the Statement by Rauf Denktas, President of the TRNC, 3 February 2000, (TRNC Government website: http://kktc.pubinfo.gov.nc.tr).

4　For this, see the Statement by Glafcos Clerides, the President of Cyprus, 2 February 2000, *Cyprus News*, Cyprus High Commission, London.

5　See the statement by the Turkish Foreign Minister, *Turkish Newspot*, No. 32, 7 March 1995.

6　The 1958 Geneva Conventions and the Law of the Sea state that islands shall be entitled to their own continental shelves, but Turkey did not sign these conventions, and hence is not party to them.

7　Article 300 of the Conventions on the Law of the Sea reads as follows: 'Parties shall fulfil in good faith the obligations under this convention and shall exercise the rights, jurisdictions and freedoms recognised in this convention in a manner which would not constitute an abuse of rights.'

8   For a detailed analysis of the Greek view, see Theodore C. Karioatis (1990) 'The Case for a Greek Exclusive Economic Zone in the Aegean Sea', *Marine Policy Journal*, Vol. 4.

9   See the statement by the Greek Foreign Ministry in *The Financial Times*, 14 September 1989.

10   This positive response of the Council was due partly to the intensive lobbying efforts by the Greek Government on the member states and the explicit support of the President of France for the Greek application.

11   As a result of the Davos meeting, Greece ratified the accession protocol, thereby binding it to Turkey's Association Agreement with the EU. In addition, Greece and Turkey agreed to establish economic and political communities at ministerial level. The economic committee was to explore economic cooperation including trade, tourism and communication; the political committee, for its part, was to search for a solution of fundamental political disputes between the two sides. Another important result of this Davos rapprochement is that both parties agreed to build on the confidence that they would not use military threats against each other over their disputes in future.

12   See the Statement of the Ministry of Foreign Affairs, in *Turkish Newspot*, No. 28, 12 July 1990, p. 6.

13   In addition to this, the timing of the Cyprus application was also related to its aim to link the prospect of the EFTA enlargement to Cyprus's application for EU membership. After the application of Austria for membership in June 1989 and the prospect of the membership applications of Norway and Finland, Greece and Cyprus hoped that the Cyprus application would be processed with those of the EFTA countries. In fact, Greece tended to use the EU's EFTA enlargement as a bargaining chip for the issue of Cyprus membership. The statement of the Foreign Minister of Greece, Pangholas, supported this observation: 'Cyprus was raised as an enlargement issue before enlargement with the Scandinavian countries. In the normal course of events – if the Cypriot leadership and the Greek leadership hadn't made serious mistakes – it could have been included in the Sweden, Finland, Austria and Norway package and would now be a member of the European Union', cited in *Cyprus Bulletin*, 15 November 1996, Vol. XXV.

14   For example, the Turkish Foreign Minister, Erdal Inonu, paid an official visit to Brussels in February 1993 and met with the President of the European Council and of the Commission. During the meeting, they discussed ways to improve relations, including the completion of a customs union and the issue of Turkey's EU membership. For this, see *Agence Europe*, No. 6102, 25 February 1993.

15   In this context, the proposed EU-Turkey customs union agreement and the next enlargement of the EU to include Central and Eastern countries provided an immense opportunity for Greece to use it as a bargaining chip to give Cyprus a timetable for entry. In fact, Greece repeatedly warned the other EU member states that she would veto the next enlargement of the EU if Cyprus' accession were delayed. For this, see, 'The EUI Country Risk Service Report: Greece', *The Economist*, 16 June 1998, p. 8.

16   Given a sizeable Turkish minority in Germany, which has not yet integrated successfully with German society, a more important reason for the German objection might be the fear that Turkey's membership would result in an unmanageable flood of immigrants. In addition, the Turkish accession would be a huge burden on the EU budget and the common policies of the EU.

17   See the statement by the Turkish Foreign Ministry in the *Turkish Daily News*, 22 December 1997.

18   See the Joint Declaration between President of Turkey and President of the TRNC, 20 January 1997, available at (http//kktc.pubinfo.gov.nc.tr).

19   Paavo Lippnen, Prime Minister of Finland, sent an official message to Turkey that it does not constitute a requirement, but rather a set out date when the EU council would review the situations relating to outstanding disputes. For this, see the Press statement by the

Prime Minister of Turkey following the decision at the Helsinki Summit on Turkey's candidature to the EU, 10 December 1999.
20 Interview with Korkmaz Haktanir, the former Under-secretary of the Ministry of Foreign Affairs and Turkish Ambassador to London, in London on 12 June 2000 and interview with Dr Nihat Akyol, Turkish Ambassador to the EU, on 20 June 2000.
21 Interview with Richard Balfe, 20 June 2000, Brussels.
22 Interview with Van Den Meer, 16 June 2000, Brussels.

Chapter 7

Security Aspects of the EU's Relations with Turkey

Introduction

For both the EU and Turkey, security considerations have played an important part in their policy formulation *vis-à-vis* each other. During the Cold War era, Turkey's foreign policy was, to a large extent, shaped by the fear of the Communist threat from the Soviet Union. It was the 'Soviet threat' to Turkish territorial integrity and demand for political influence in the wake of the Second World War that forced Turkey to join all kinds of organizations in the Western bloc during the Cold War era. From this perspective, she applied for associate membership of the EU. Since the end of the Cold War, security factors have continued to be an important component of EU-Turkey relations; in fact, Turkey's security assets have not only constituted solid grounds for the EU to make an effort to maintain closer relations with Turkey, but it has also provided a strong argument for Turkey to make her membership more acceptable to the EU.

This chapter will present an analysis of EU-Turkey relations from the security perspective. It will, first, evaluate the security aspects of EU-Turkey relations during the Cold War structure. It will then analyze the security interdependence between the EU and Turkey and particular focus will be placed on Turkey's importance as a security asset for the EU in the post-Cold War European security order. Furthermore, it will consider the EU's policy towards Turkey in the light of the evolving of the Common European Security and Defence Policy (the CESDP) after the post-Maastricht European integration. Finally, the chapter will look at the EU's enlargement policy in the security context and compare the EU's policy towards Turkey with its policy towards the CEECs, with emphasis on political and structured relationship and cooperation.

Security Factors in EU-Turkey Relations during the Cold War

Given the character of the Cold War and the security objectives of Western unity, which rested primarily upon the communist threat, Turkey was very careful in calculating the security benefits of having closer relations with the EU. After joining NATO in 1952, closer relations with the EU were regarded as the necessary policy choice for Turkey's security needs. She considered the EU as another ground on which to base her attachment to the emerging Western alliances, even though the EU had no institutionalized security policy at that time; it did not, therefore, provide a comprehensive security guarantee for its members. Turkey believed that the EU would provide an opportunity for Turkey to attach herself to her Western alliances more firmly through institutionalizing the economic ties and political relations with the EU.

As regards the European Union, security considerations were often considered to be more important than other factors in establishing institutional links with Turkey through the Association Agreement, as the latter was regarded as the southern pillar of NATO. Turkey's ties with the EU were important for Western European security because Turkey had a role to play not only as a barrier against Soviet expansion towards Southern Europe, but also as a bridge between Europe and the Middle East. Consequently, the EU viewed Turkey an extremely important asset for European security. This is because, firstly, Turkey could check Soviet naval access to the Mediterranean as she controlled the strategically important Straits (Aybak, 1994, p. 252). Secondly, Turkey could act as a barrier against the extension of Soviet political influence in the Middle East in which Western Europe had vital economic and political interests. Thirdly, 'Turkey was seen as a buffer zone; potentially bottling up the Soviet navy in the Black Sea, tying up Warsaw Pact forces along NATO's southern flank, and serving as a staging ground for counterbalance against the Soviet Union' (Kuniholm, 1991, p. 34). Such importance as Turkey had for Western security made the EU need to pay attention to the political and economic developments in Turkey, and hence Turkey's request from the EU. In fact, it was the security concern on the EU's part which impelled it to accept Turkey as an associated member of the EU on the grounds that Turkey's economic and political stability and her Westernization process had to be strengthened for the sake of the EU's security and political interests (Maurizio, 1983, p. 53). As one Turkish scholar observed: 'the ultimate objective of the modern Turkish republic was to be recognized as a European state. The Cold War structure guaranteed the realization of that goal' (Muftuler, 1996, p. 255).

After establishing an associate membership link with the EU, Turkey tended to use her security assets as a bargaining for economic and political gains from the EU in the course of reviving the conditions of its Association with the EU. This was particularly the case during the late 1970s when the USA suspended its military and economic aid after Turkey's military intervention in Cyprus in 1974. As a result, Turkey became a reluctant Atlantic ally (Dankward and Penrose, 1981, p. 10). Therefore, as an alternative policy, Turkey sought to develop closer ties with the EU and its member states when she became disappointed with the USA for its neglect of Turkish security interests. Indeed, Turkey began to see herself more clearly as a member of the European component of NATO, and sought to attract European military and economic aid to compensate for the reduced aid from the USA (Kramer, 1988, p. 337).

During the late 1970s, the political developments occurring in Turkey's backyard strengthened her bargaining power in her economic and political demands from the EU. The Iranian revolution resulted in the removal of a key player in the Western security structure against Soviet expansionism, which increased the security concern of West about political Islam, since Iran was likely to be a destabilizing factor in the Middle East. Furthermore, the Soviet invasion of Afghanistan revived the fear of Western alliances regarding Soviet expansionism to the south through Asia and the Middle East (Önis, 1995, p. 52). These developments occurring so closely to Turkey further increased the value of Turkey's strategic position to the Western alliances that consequently made the EU vulnerable to Turkey's political and economic demands. For instance, the EU was obligated to offer special treatment for Turkey as regards the EPC mechanism in 1978: the EU agreed to have a two-way information procedure in which Turkey would be informed of EPC decisions by a troika system through the existing presidency as well as the previous and next presidency of the EU. Furthermore, the EU promised additional economic aid to Turkey, supplemented by an increasing preference for Turkey's agricultural exports to the EU. With this, the EU aimed to stabilize Turkey's domestic politics, since Turkey was suffering political instability; clashes between the left-wing and right-wing activists, including a rising of Islamic fundamentalism using arms smuggled from Bulgaria and the Soviet Union, increased the social tension and worsened the political situation in Turkey (Dankward, 1994, p. 11).

After the military coup in Turkey in September 1980, the EU was even more concerned about the internal and external consequences of the new regime and its likely implication for European security. In fact, despite widespread human rights violations by the military regime, the EU's reaction to the military coup was not severe (Ugur, 1995, pp. 167–199). The main reasons for this soft policy stance of the EU towards the military coup in Turkey was strategic considerations; the EU and member states were more concerned about Turkey's position on NATO's southeastern flank and were anxious about not alienating Turkey in the unstable conditions of the region (Ugur, 1995, p. 171). They seemed to anticipate that strong reaction to the military regime could distance Turkey from the Europe and Western Alliance that would harm the security interest of the EU. On the basis of this, despite the military regime, some EU member states and the Commission even made some effort to reactivate the EU-Turkey Association so as to keep Turkey-EU relations alive for the sake of European security. For example, in November 1980, three months after the military coup, a delegation from the Commission paid an official visit to Turkey to discuss an emergency aid package of 75 million ECU that was granted in 1979 (*Agence Europe*, 28 November 1980, No. 3029, p. 11). Although this was not a high level visit with an economic agenda, it appeared to indicate the political willingness of the EU to find a way to reactivate its relations with Turkey. More importantly, in accordance with the agreement in 1979, the EU decided to invite Turkey for consultations within the EPC mechanism in order to calm Turkey's concern with regard to Greece's accession to the EU (*Agence Europe*, 10 December 1980, No. 3037, p. 4). Furthermore, some member states, including Germany and the UK, tried to reassure the other member states who were inclined to adopt a more critical and active stance against Turkey, in the belief that maintaining relations with Turkey would serve the security interests of the EU (Ugur, 1995, pp. 167–199).

When Turkey applied for EU membership, security considerations again played an important part in her decision. After Greece's entry to the EU, Turkish policy-makers realized that Greece's membership was affecting EU-Turkey relations, and thus harming Turkey's security interests. They believed that full membership of the EU would be the best policy course to counter the EU's favouring of Greece. Secondly, when member states of the Western European Union (the WEU) decided to reactivate the organization as part of the EU's security and defence identity after the mid 1980s,[1] Turkish policy-makers considered the implication of such a move for Turkish security interests.

In other words, the EU's effort to search for a new defence identity within the Union compelled Turkey to put the security aspect of EU-Turkey relations at the top of her foreign policy objectives. The Turkish Ambassador to London clarified this argument: 'when it was realized that the EU had been in search of a defence identity, Turkey considered that the rational policy for Turkey was to apply for full membership.'[2] As expected, Turkey applied to the WEU at the same time as she applied for EU membership. This indicated that one of the reasons behind her early application for full EU membership was related to security considerations.

Added to this, the likely effect of EU membership on domestic stability and the democratization process in the country constituted another security aspect of the Turkish decision to make an early application. On the basis of this, the importance of Turkey's domestic stability for the EU provided a useful tool for Turkey to make her membership bid more attractive to the EU. Turkish officials underlined the effect of Turkey's political stability on European security and sought to use the importance of a secular, democratic and stable Turkey for European security as a bargaining tool to support the country's bid for EU membership. For instance, the Turkish Prime Minister, Turgut Ozal, stated that:

> A democratic and politically powerful Turkey is in the interests of Europe and Western security. Therefore, the EU should promote its own security interests by accepting Turkey's application for membership (*The Guardian*, 25 June 1987).

As this shows, Turkey tended to put forward the argument that a rejection of Turkey's application for membership would be prejudicial to Turkey's effort to democratize and attach itself economically and politically to Europe and might jeopardize European security and political interests in the region. Following the application of Turkey for membership in 1987, Turkish officials, including the Prime Minister, Foreign Minister and Minister responsible for European Affairs, made an official visit to the Commission and other capitals of leading member states to gain support for Turkey's membership bid. During their visits, they used the above standard argument to persuade the Commission and the member states the importance of EU membership for the political stability of the country.

Noting Turkey's role in European security within NATO and its geographical location, Turkish policy-makers were also quick to use Turkey's role in NATO as a bargaining counter to support her bid for EU membership. Prime Minister Turgut Özal, in 1989, stated that 'Turkey had been a member of NATO and contributed generously to the common European defence in NATO and therefore, we expect some reciprocity' (*The Independent*, 28 January 1989). Furthermore, he made a direct reference to the negative prospect of the EU's rejection of Turkey's membership request on NATO, stating that 'if the EC were to refuse Turkey there would some impact on relations with NATO' (*The Independent*, 28 January 1989). However, Özal's perception of Turkey's role in European security and the linkage politics of EU membership and NATO seem to be one-sided. Firstly, as indicated above, Turkey-NATO relations were based upon the principle of reciprocity: Turkey had played an important role in the defence of the West, while the West had provided Turkey with a security guarantee with considerable military and economic assistance. Secondly, linking the politics of NATO membership and EU membership did not appear to be an entirely convincing argument since both organizations have different objectives and integration processes, although the NATO context cannot be ignored by the EU.

From a European Union perspective, the geo-strategic position of Turkey and its NATO membership seem to have been positive factors to support Turkey's EU membership bid. In fact, the strategic importance of Turkey has always been a positive point of reference in the relationship between Turkey and the EU in the context of enlargement (Redmond, 1993, p. 44). For example, a preliminary Commission paper on Turkey's application in 1987 stated that NATO membership was Turkey's 'ace' in the evaluation of Turkey's membership of the EU (European Commission, 1987). Leading members of the EU, including the UK, Germany, France and Italy, shared this Commission view. For instance, the Foreign Secretary of the UK, Geoffrey Howe, underlined the importance of Turkey for European security, stating that 'Turkey was an important NATO ally and therefore, she deserved a place in the European family' (*Financial Times*, 19 December 1987). Although the security factor seemed to be a positive point of reference in Turkey's attempt to join the EU, it cannot be sufficient for the EU, as there are a number of negative economic and political factors that militate against Turkey's membership prospects (European Commission, 1989a).

Nevertheless, by recognizing the security and strategic importance of Turkey to the EU, the EU considered that firm rejection of Turkey's 'European vocation' would harm not only the EU's security interests, but also the pro-Western and pro-European policy advocated by Turkey. Hence, the EU seemed to wish to strengthen its relations with Turkey. In other words, without casting doubt in any way on Turkey's eligibility for EU membership, the EU proposed a policy aimed at helping the country to modernize politically and economically (Bulletin of the EC, 1989, Point 2.2.37). However, it seems that the EU's policy instruments for Turkey have been inconsistent with the EU's security concern over Turkey: these instruments have not been comprehensive enough to reduce the security threats from Turkey to the EU caused by the political, economical, societal and ideological instability of Turkey, including the Kurdish issue and political Islam.

In conclusion, as seen in the above analysis, the security interdependence of the EU and Turkey was mainly responsible for establishing closer relations through the Association Agreement between the parties. Moreover, it was an important factor in both parties' efforts to normalize their relations after the end of the military regime in Turkey. Turkey had even sought to use the security assets she would represent to Europe as a bargaining chip to make her case more attractive. Nevertheless, the collapse of Communism, soon after the Turkish application for EU membership, changed the parameters of the security interdependence between the EU and Turkey. This implies that the end of the East-West ideological/military confrontation seems to have affected the character and features of Turkey as a security asset for the EU. Therefore, the next section will consider the security interdependence between the EU and Turkey and Turkey's importance as a security asset in the emerging new security and defence policy of the European Union.

The Security Interdependence between the EU and Turkey in Post-Cold War European Security

As stated above, the collapse of the Eastern bloc and Communist system has implied that the ideological and military threat from the East is no longer significant and thus has become irrelevant. As a result, the geo-strategic importance of Turkey, which she enjoyed during the Cold War, has been questioned in the EU since the major *raison d'être* for Turkey's being incorporated within the European security system seems to have declined. It is argued that Turkey has lost, to some extent, the luxury of using its strategic importance as a bargaining chip for its membership bid. As *The Economist* observed:

> For nearly four decades successive Turkish Governments have luxuriated in the assumption that, as a front line country within NATO, Turkey was indispensable to the West. It was a splendid bargaining lever in Turkey's dealing with its western friends, now, as the Soviet threat recedes, the Turks sense they are no longer as indispensable as they were (*The Economist*, 26 May 1990, p. 63).

However such an argument underestimates the new security role that Turkey can play since the Cold War. The end of the Cold War has not diminished Turkey as a security asset for the EU. It has rather only changed the parameters and features of the security interdependence between the parties. To be more specific, Turkey's new security role in the security of Europe has assumed new characteristics, which go beyond military issues to include new political, social, environmental and human related security problems for Europe, together with regional military conflicts.

This seems, if anything, to have increased the security interdependence between Turkey and the EU. This is mainly because Turkey's role has gradually been modified from a buffer state against the Communist threat to a front zone for European security within the pan-European security context. As Marc Grossman, American Ambassador to Turkey, puts it, 'Turkey's place has changed from being a wing state to a front state' (quoted in Muftuler, 1996, p. 256). Turkey have been ascribed the role and function of a stabilizing element and model for the economic, social and political developments of the countries in Central Asia and the Middle East. Being a front zone state for European security is a function of Turkey's geographic location, which touches three politically sensitive and problematic regional subsystems: the Balkans, the Caucasus and Central Asia and the Middle East. Countries in these regions have been facing a number of military conflicts.

This source of conflict has been related to the reappearance of claims by various national minorities suppressed under the old regimes, together with disputes over borders, the upsurge of nationalism and ethnic tensions. In addition, domestic and international political turmoil and the spread of religious extremism notably Islamic fundamentalism, the primitive state of democratization and the large number of regional disputes pose a major threat to the security of these regions, and thus the security of Europe. Such problems on the periphery of Europe are pervasive, and thus they would affect the overall stability and the security of Europe in many ways.

From this perspective, Turkey has become an even more important front zone country than it had been before in many ways; it has the power to exemplify a role on the periphery of Europe.

In this respect, it seems relevant to analyze the following questions through the next section:

- What are the main security issues in the regions of the Caucasus and Central Asia, the Middle East and the Balkans and how do these issues affect both Turkish and European security?
- In what ways does Turkey have a stabilizing role in these regions and why are Turkey's own security issues important for European security?

The Main Security Issues in the Regions of the Caucasus, Central Asia, the Middle East and the Balkans

Political instability and conflicts at the interstate and societal levels between and within states in these regions are new sources of conflict and thus threats to Europe. The first threat to the security of these regions is from regional military conflicts. As previous experiences have indicated, these regions are characterized as unstable with numerous unresolved problems that might further impede regional and European security. Nationalism and religious and ethnic rivalries at the interstate and societal levels between and within states in these regions still remain the biggest challenges to regional stability. Historical competitions between states, territories and minorities and their efforts to create nation states, based mainly upon ethnic identity rather than on principles of democracy, human rights and protection for minorities are factors that undermine the prospect of stability in the Balkan region, and this directly challenges European security. Jonathan Howe, the Commander in Chief of the Allied Force in NATO's southern region, has asserted that 'threats facing the NATO Alliance have shifted specifically towards South Eastern Europe' (Howe, 1991, p. 246).

This is also applicable to the countries of Central Asia and the Middle East. For instance, the civil wars in Tajikistan and Georgia, the conflict between Armenia and Azerbaijan over Nagorna-Karabakh and the Arab-Israeli dispute highlight how unstable these regions are. In addition, Kurdish nationalism, accelerated by the developments in the post-Cold War era, has emerged as an a regional issue, which poses direct threats to regional security in a different form, i.e., immigration, terrorism and collective crime. The supply of water is also likely to be a source of conflict between the states in the region. As *The Economist* put it 'the next war in the Middle East might be a fight over water' (*The Economist*, 12 May 1990, 'The Survey of Arab World' – p. 10). The use of waters from the Euphrates and the Tigris by Turkey, Iraq and Syria is liable to cause tension between the parties. The use of water is also an issue between Israel, Palestine and Syria, which is one factor intensifying the tension between the Israelis and the Arabs.

A second threat to the regional security is the prospect of rivalry between the regional powers, which might lead to the creation of new sub-regional alliances between countries in the region and regional powers. As far as the Caucasus and Central Asia are concerned, it is not only Russia which has been seeking to rebuild a sphere of influence in the region, but also Turkey and Iran, which have been engaging in competition in this respect (Gürses, 2001, p. 250). The politics of rivalry is also a source of conflict in the Middle East. There has been competition for regional power among the member states, with an effort to obtain the political and economic support of the superpowers to enhance their position. Such competition for regional dominance could easily bring the states into conflict. For instance, the chronic competition for hegemony between Iraq and Syria over Lebanon, the rivalry between Iran and Turkey in the Middle East, and between Saudi-Arabia and Egypt who have similar ambitions in the Middle East, all have implications for potential regional conflict (*The Economist*, 12 May 1990, p. 45).

The same politics of rivalry can be seen in the Balkans. The prospect of rivalry between the regional powers, which might lead to the creation of new sub-regional alliances between the states in the Balkans and outside powers, seems to be one of the main threats to regional security. It is conceivable that Russia would want to 'rebuild a sphere of influence in the region by forging a close alliance with Yugoslavia' (Bugajski, 1999, p. 2). The ethnic nationalism and anti-Western forces in Yugoslavia, discontented since the experience of the Western stance in the Yugoslav civil wars, might facilitate the forging of closer security alliances with Russia. Likewise, with the prospect of the future enlargement of NATO and the EU to the CEECs, it is conceivable that Russia would adopt a counter-balancing policy against European enlargement to strengthen its position in the region. In addition, the continuing Greek-Turkish rivalry and conflicts could generate a new source of alliances. Both countries tend to play a leading role in the region as a means of influencing the region economically and politically. Furthermore, a religious alliance could also be a threat to the security of the Balkans. Islam and orthodox Christianity are the two main religions in the region. The prospect of the disintegration of Bosnia-Herzegovina and the exclusion of Albania from a sub-regional alliance, which might be created in the Balkans, would develop a new front between the Christian Orthodox countries, Greece, Bulgaria, Serbia and Russia and a new Islamic axis, Albania, Bosnia-Herzegovina and countries in the Middle-East (Misha, 1995).

The third main threat appears with the emergence of political Islam or any form of religious authoritarianism as an ideological threat to regional security (Robertson, 1998, p. 104). The unequal distribution of national prosperity between the ruling class and the majority of citizens, corruption, sectarian divisions, economic hardship and factionalism are the main reasons for the emergence of political Islam as an alternative regime in the region. The political regime in most states in the Middle East can be characterized as repressive, unrepresentative and incompetent in character. In most cases, a very small political elite has been using the ideology to legitimize their power that is based mainly upon Arab nationalism with a religious figure. As Gorge Joffe describes it, 'the fact is that government and the apparatus of the state have became the property of a specific group within the population and the vast majority of citizens, as a result, feel alienated from the government and, indeed from the state itself' (Joffe, 1998, p. 61). This is because political Islam offers equality, prosperity and good governance, at least in theory. Since the late 1970s, there has been increased scrutiny of Islam's potential as a political force in the Middle East and Central Asia and even in some parts of the Balkans.

The Iranian Revolution in 1979, the victory of the Islamic forces in Afghanistan in 1992, the domestic turmoil and civil war between Islamic forces and the army in Algeria and the increasing popularity of Islamic doctrine in most Muslim countries, including Turkey, indicate that political Islam might emerge as an alternative regime and become a unifying factor in the region. By implication, the emergence of political Islam might pose a threat not only to regional security but also to European security on the grounds that the fundamentalist Islamic doctrine opposes not only Western values, including principles of democracy and a market economy, but also objects to closer relations with Western countries and organizations. What might be in prospect is that the rise of political Islam in the region would result in a clash between pro-Western and Islamic elements in societies. This is a particular possibility for Turkey; the pro-Islamic movement in Turkey, which has appeared to be growing, presents a major challenge to secularism and the consolidation of democracy in Turkey as well as to the Westernization of the country.

Finally, the human dimension of the security issue in the regions of the Balkans, the Middle East and Central Asia is another threat to regional stability and thus to European security. This is closely related to the authoritarian system, weak civil societies and a host of deep-seated nationalist tensions, and, in addition, to economic underdevelopment. The resurgence of nationalistic ethnic and religious disputes and the lack of institutional democracy in most countries in the Middle East, the Balkans and Central Asia have brought the issues of human rights and respect for minorities to the agenda of regional and European security. They have also generated mass flows of refugees and displaced persons. Indeed, the refugees and displaced persons have been a consequence of the violations of human and minority rights, including those related to the protection of national minorities and the creation of conditions for the promotion of ethnic, cultural, linguistic and religious identity. Economic problems in the regions of the Middle East, Balkans and Central Asia have also created the human dimension of security issues that pose a serious security threat to regional and to European security. A substantial economic gap still remains between the countries in the EU and those on the periphery of Europe in that the latter still lack technology, capital and know-how in order to sustain their development and learn to compete with the countries in the EU. This economic gap between the periphery and the core of Europe generates an economy-related security problem, entailing mass migration, terrorism, organized crime and drug smuggling. Thus, the economic dimension of security needs to be put into a broader context of new European security arrangements. This requires a framework for effective economic cooperation between the periphery and the core of Europe which might lessen the impact of the conflicts on the citizens of these countries, since economically developed societies should be less vulnerable to any kind of conflict (Taylor, 1994, p. 181).

In conclusion, these underlined regional security issues and conflicts at the interstate and social levels between and within the countries in these regions have important implications for Turkish and European security. Considering the transferable character of these issues, the security of Turkey and Europe is closely linked to the stability of the regions. To be more precise, the instability of these regions could harm both Turkey's and the EU's political, economic and security interests in many respects. For instance, due to the extent of Europe's and Turkey's dependence on oil and the other energy sources of these regions, any form of conflict in the Middle East and Central Asia would not only reduce or interrupt trade and commercial activities between the parties, but would also affect the global price of oil which would cause economic hardship to both sides. The Gulf crisis was an important case that demonstrated how vulnerable Europe and Turkey are to turmoil in the Middle East (Muftuler-Bac, 1997, p. 42). In addition, any form of regional conflict and economic hardship in these regions can bring out the human dimension of security threats to Turkey and Europe in the form of mass flows of refugees, illegal immigration, displaced persons, organized crime and smuggling. As previous experience indicates, the instability and social conflict in the Middle East and the Balkans have caused Europe to become the main destination for political refugees.[3] Given that immigrants in Europe have shown little sign of integrating with the host societies, they have become an issue in internal security of their host countries.[4] As an example, actions of racist hostility and the resurgence of xenophobia have been recorded against immigrants, thereby raising social tensions in the societies (Knowler, 1992). This all indicates that there is a mutual dependence between Turkey and Europe for their own security and thus a need for cooperation between the parties since European security is closely linked to the stability of the regions and the stability of Turkey in many respects.

Security Issues in Turkey: As a Threat to European Security

Turkey's importance for European security is also related to the fact that European security is closely connected with the social, economic and political stability of Turkey. Conflict at societal level, resulting mainly from the ideological confrontation between a secularist state and political Islam or Kurdish separatism seems to be the main threat to Turkey's internal security, together with constitutional issues, stemming from the relative weakness of her pluralist democratic constitutional tradition. The emergence of political Islam appears to pose an ideological threat to Turkish domestic security, which might cause a serious clash between pro-Western and Islamic elements in society. This presents a major challenge to secularism and the consolidation of democracy in Turkey. Political Islam in the country seems to oppose not only the notion of secularism and a Western type of regime, but also objects to closer relations with Western countries and organizations. The experience of the Islamic Refah Party highlights the increasing domestic strength of political Islam in Turkey. In the 1995 general election, it became the first party to win 22 per cent of all votes and it received 18 per cent of the votes in the 1999 general election. In addition to this, Kurdish nationalism has emerged as a security issue in Turkish politics, thereby creating a disturbing element for the domestic stability and a potential source of interstate conflict that threatens Turkey's security interests.

Closely related to this issue of political Islam and the Kurdish question, the human dimension of security has increasingly been seen as the most important security issue in Turkey. Breaches in human rights and the lack of democratic governance in the country constitute important challenges for her domestic security. The human dimension of security is also closely related to the economic underdevelopment that has led to conflicts at societal level and the spread of corruption. Poor economic performance in Turkey is considered to be an important stimulus for organized crime, drug trafficking, arms smuggling and other economy-related crimes. Basically, European security is explicitly linked to the political stability of Turkey. As previous experience has indicated, political instability and social conflict in Turkey would pose a threat to the security of Europe in the form of migrants. For example, due to a series of economic and political problems during the late 1970s as well as the military coup in 1980, the EU countries became the main destination for the Turkish citizens who were political refugees and economic migrants. More recently, in 1997, Kurdish refugees dominated the main agenda of the EU. Due to the conflict between the Turkish army and the Kurdish separatists led by the PKK terrorist organization and serious economic problems in the region, thousands of political and economic migrants, who were seeking a better life to the West, were forced to seek political asylum in the countries of the EU.[5]

After having considered the main security issues in Turkey and surrounding regions, one might argue that it would be a serious mistake to admit Turkey as a member of the EU on purely security grounds (Buzan and Diez, 1999, p. 51). To some extent it is true. The proximity of Turkey to more unstable regions and her domestic conflicts have caused some concern in the EU that enlarging the EU to include Turkey would not only bring her internal security problems into the EU, but would also lead to a direct entanglement of the EU in the security dynamic of the surrounding regions. This is, to some extent, a reason for the EU to have developed a containment policy towards Turkey, designed to maintain a closer security framework to keep Turkey a peripheral actor and insulator in the security of all regions surrounding her. However, given the complicity of its security environment and trans-boundary character of the security issues, the success of such a policy on the part of the EU is doubtful because it seems to have ignored the security implications of Turkey's exclusion from the EU's enlargement policy, not only for Turkish domestic politics, but also for the surrounding regions. This is a suitable point at which to evaluate Turkey's stabilizing role in these regions to explain why they are important for European Security.

Does Turkey Have a Stabilizing Role in the Regional Context?

As stated above, European security is closely linked to the stability of the countries at its periphery, including Turkey. By implication, Turkey's importance as a security asset for Europe has increased in the regional context. Turkey seems to have been ascribed the role and function of a stabilizing element and model for economic, social and political developments among the countries in Central Asia and the Middle East. Therefore, Turkey has become a more important front zone country than it was before in many ways as a means of exemplifying a stabilizing role in the periphery of Europe. Secondly, Turkey's importance for European security is related to the fact that European security is also closely linked to the social, economic and political stability of Turkey. The following paragraphs will explore these questions: in what ways does Turkey have a stabilizing role in these regions? And why are they important for European Security?

Turkey is an important front zone country that can exert considerable influence on the stability and security of its region. This is because Turkey has not only common linguistic, cultural, historical and political ties with the countries in these regions, in particular with independent Central Asian republics, but she has even closer relations with the Western world: she is a member of NATO, the OSCE and an associate member of the EU and the WEU. Turkey's presence in organizations of both the Western and Eastern world, such as the Islamic Conference and Economic Cooperation Organization, would make her an appropriate country to use her good offices to mediate between conflicting parties in regions of the Middle East, Central Asia and the Balkans. In fact, Turkey has made an effort to act as an agent of stability in the region; for example, she attempted to act as sole mediator to end the conflict between Armenia and Azerbaijan over Nagorno-Karabakh (Aslanlı, 2001, p. 409). Turkey was appointed a member of the OSCE peacekeeping mission to work for peace negotiations and a settlement in 1992 of the above conflict. Furthermore, in March 1993, the OSCE Council of Ministers mandated Turkey as a member of the Minsk Group along with Russia, the USA and Germany, for a negotiated settlement under the auspices of the OSCE.

Turkey's efforts to establish regional economic and political cooperation with the countries of the region highlights her importance as a stabilizing factor in the region. For example, Turkey initiated an organization for Black Sea Economic Cooperation in 1992 with the participation of 11 countries.[6] Its objective went beyond economic cooperation among the member states to include cooperation in regional security by providing a forum to settle differences and conflicts among the member states.[7] A declaration from the Black Sea Economic Cooperation stipulated that one of the main objectives of the BSEC was to turn the Black Sea into a region of peace, freedom and stability and prosperity, striving to promote friendly and good neighbourly relations.

In addition to the BSEC, Turkey has taken the initiative in engaging bilateral and multilateral agreements with the countries in Central Asia, the Balkans and the Middle East. For example, at Turkey's invitation three Caucasian states are members of the BSEC. The Economic Cooperation Organization, founded by Turkey and Pakistan in 1985, was reactivated and extended to the Turkic republics of Azerbaijan, Kazakhstan, Kyrgizstan, Turkmenistan and Uzbekistan (Nation, 1996, p. 106). Furthermore, since 1992, Summit Conferences between the leaders of Turkey and the Turkic republics have been held annually, culminating in numbers of economic, security and cultural cooperation agreements (Sezer, 1996, p. 85). Such extended relations of Turkey with these countries have seemed simultaneously to offer new possibilities for economic, social and security cooperation, as well as enhancing Turkey as a role model for the countries in the region. In this respect, the prospect of a Euro-Asian energy corridor, in particular, might provide an important ground that would increase Turkey's geo-strategic assets for Europe.[8]

Apart from this, Turkey could provide a model for the political and economic development in these countries. Turkey might act as an agent for the promotion of such values as the principle of democracy, rule of law and system of governance and a market economy in the countries of Central Asia and the Middle East. Turkey provides a valid model of a secular, democratic Muslim country, which has close relations with Western countries, including the USA. The Turkish model seems to have been accepted by most countries in the region. On a number of occasions since their independence, the leaders of Kazakhstan, Uzbekistan, Kyrgizstan, Turkmenistan and Azerbaijan have announced their intention to follow the Turkish model of development. For example, the President of Kazakhstan stated that 'we want to implement a free market economy. For this, our only model is Turkey' (*The*

Economist, 25 April 1992, p. 64). More interestingly, the President of Kyrgizstan summarized Turkey's role in the group: 'Turkey is our morning star that shows the Turkish republics the way' (*The Economist*, 25 April 1992, p. 64).

Turkey has shown a keen interest in the concept of itself as a model in the belief that, apart from the economic benefits, being a model would boost Turkey's image and enhance its ultimate objective of joining the EU. Nevertheless, Turkey has limited economic capacities with its own domestic problems; therefore, she has appealed for European and American support in helping to achieve her objective. For example, President of Turkey, Demirel, stated that 'with the support of our allies, we could take European values to Central Asia' (Milliyet, 20 December 1996). The concept of a Turkish model for the former Soviet Republics of Central Asia has also arisen in Europe and the USA. For example, during her official visit to Uzbekistan, Kyrgizstan, Turkmenistan and Kazakhstan, Mme Catherine Lalumiere, the Secretary General of the Council of Europe – an Institution presenting the core political values of Europe – declared that Turkey provided a valid model for the development of the newly independent countries in Central Asia (Mango, 1993, p. 726). Moreover, in November 1992, the Committee of the Ministers of the Council of Europe, including the President of the European Commission, Jacques Delors, acknowledged Turkey's role as a model and mediator in relations with the Central Asian Republics (Aybak, 1996). The concept of the Turkish model has been further strengthened by the USA's endorsement of Turkey's secularism, democracy and market-oriented economy as an exemplary pattern of development for the countries in Central Asia. In conclusion, adopting the Turkish model for these countries would be important for European security: firstly, it would discourage extreme nationalism and Islamic fundamentalism, which seem to be the main sources of conflict in the region. Secondly, as a member of Western security organizations, including NATO and the OCSE, Turkey's ability to use its good offices in conflicts in the region would accelerate Western efforts to stabilize the region.

To sum up, the stability of Europe is closely linked to the situation in the Middle East, Balkans and Central Asia, as well as the stability of Turkey. In this regard, Turkey's role is quite crucial in the promotion of stability, primarily because Turkey is one of the few countries in her region with long-term ties to the West and with a relatively stable system in comparison to the rest of the region. If Turkey is excluded from the emerging common security and defence policy of the EU, not only may this lead to an unstable situation in Turkey, but also to instability in the region as well; instability in Turkey may affect the region because of Turkey's pivotal regional role. In addition, Turkey has a crucial role to play in the linkage of trade, transport and energy routes from the Middle East, the Persian Gulf and Trans-Caucasian to Europe. This is a suitable point at which to evaluate the EU's security policy towards Turkey since the Cold War.

The Security and Defence Aspect of EU-Turkey Relations after the Cold War

The post-Cold War security threats to both Europe and Turkey have compelled them to rearrange the grounds on which they have built their relations in accordance with their mutual interests. Although the EU has realized the importance of Turkey as a security asset, it has shown anxieties towards the concept of bringing in Turkey as a fully integrated participant in the Common European Security and Defence Policy within the EU. The EU has rather developed a containment policy, as an alternative security and defence arrangement, for Turkey in order to anchor her as closely to Europe as possible on security grounds. However, the EU's containment policy instruments for Turkey seem to have been insufficient not only to mitigate the threats to the domestic stability of Turkey, but also to integrate Turkey within the newly emerging Common Security and Defence Policy of the EU. This implies that there have been inconsistencies not only between the EU's acknowledgment of the importance of Turkey as a security asset to the EU and the instruments of its containment policy for Turkey, but also between the EU's policy instruments towards the CEECs and that towards Turkey, despite the fact that Turkey appears to be more important to the EU than the CEECs from the security point of view. This endorses the main argument of the book that Turkey has been treated differently from the other applicant countries. To support this argument, this section will assess the security and defence aspect of the EU's containment policy after the Cold War.

Turkey's value as a security asset in the regional context has been enhanced: she has involved herself in regional cooperation to strengthen her role as an important catalyst for the economic and political stability of the regions surrounding her. Such activism of Turkey in regional politics is also related to her efforts to increase her security and defence assets as a bargaining counter to reinforce her ties with the EU, with a view to making her membership bid more attractive to the EU.

While Turkey was making an effort to enhance her security assets in the regional context in the hope of taking part in the emerging post-Cold War era of European security and defence structure, the Gulf crisis erupted in 1990. The timing of the Gulf crisis was important for Turkey in revitalizing her critical importance for the West, as her security assets in the eyes of Europe had been subject to discussion causing considerable pessimism and concern (Sayari, 1992, p. 10). Turkey viewed the Gulf War as a golden opportunity to demonstrate her loyalty to the West and thus to consolidate her important position (Gozen, 1996). Turkey's decision to get involved in the Gulf War was a politically motivated move that went beyond her immediate national security concerns. As Bruce Kuniholm puts it, 'Turkey had never been willing to commit itself wholeheartedly to the Western military endeavor without some form of quid pro quo' (Kuniholm, 1991, p. 35).

In this respect, the aims of Turkey were to redefine her role in the politics of the region as a regional power, to reinforce her image in the West and to underline the West's dependence on Turkey's strategic assets within the new European security structure. Closely related to this, Turkey anticipated that active involvement in the Gulf War would increase her bargaining power, making her membership bid more acceptable to the EU. As one observer puts it:

> The President of Turkey, Ozal, wanted a softening of the resistance in the European Community to its application for membership of the 12 nations economic bloc. Indeed, before the Gulf Crisis erupted, no foreign policy issue had been more important to Ozal than securing EC membership (Kuniholm, 1991, p. 35).

Basically, Turkey was expecting an assurance of commitment to her defence and security needs from the EU and USA that should have secured its place in the emerging new European security and defence structure. It seems that Turkey did, to some extent, achieve this objective. The Gulf War underlined Turkey's strategic importance for European security in the Middle Eastern context. The EU recognized that European security could no longer be restricted to a specific geographic area. This confirmed the increasing interdependence between Turkey and Europe in the maintenance of regional order (Aybak, 1996, p. 290). The EU acknowledged that maintaining closer relations with Turkey was necessary for its own security interests. By implication, the EU was constrained to improve its relations with Turkey, and thus it sought ways to strengthen them. For instance, the Presidency Conclusions of the European Council in Lisbon in June 1992 declared that:

> The Turkish role in the present European political situation is of the greatest importance and that there is every reason to intensify co-operation and develop relations with Turkey in line with the prospect laid down in the Association Agreement of 1964, including a political dialogue at the highest level (European Council, 1992).

A report presented by the UK in June 1992, as the successor Presidency of the EU, underlined Turkey's significant role as a regional power close to the three regions of instability. It suggested that the EU should 'have an interest in establishing relations with Turkey which would reflect and take advantage of these unique and particular factors and give consideration to Turkey in their debate on European construction' (*Agence Europe*, 24 July 1992, No. 5778, p. 5). Even the European Parliament recognized this; for instance, its resolution on Turkey in 1992 acknowledged:

> The role which Turkey has always played, and will inevitably have to play in setting problems of the Near and Middle East, the Caucasus and the Balkans, owing to its position in Europe. Turkey should remain an element of stability in a region marked by political and ethnic problems (European Parliament, 1992).

In the same way, the Committee on Foreign Affairs, Security and Defence Policy in the EP in 1994 reaffirmed Turkey's importance for European security in the regional context by stating that 'the political, economic and strategic framework in the regions of the Middle East and the Caucasus means that it is vital for Europe to set up its link with Turkey'. The report further stated, 'the fact is that its territory acts as a buffer zone between Europe, Iran, Iraq, Syria and the Caucasus'. Therefore, 'Turkey is required to play a major role at regional level and in the southeastern Mediterranean, particularly in view of the attention focused in recent years on the Middle East and its uncertain peace process and the outbreak of war' (European Parliament, 1995b).

Consequently, the EU decided to strengthen its relations with Turkey as closely as possible. At this point, it developed a containment policy for Turkey as an appropriate way to anchor Turkey to the EU. The associate membership of the WEU for Turkey and the strengthening of political dialogue within the Association Agreement constituted the main instruments for the security and defence aspects of its containment policy. An increasing security and defence interdependence between the EU and Turkey, with Turkey's growing regional security role, promoted member states of the EU to associate Turkey as fully as possible with the WEU

(Mendon and Wallace, 1994, p. 113). As a result, the EU invited Turkey to become an associate member of the WEU in 1992.

Though some specific issues arose from Turkey's associate membership of the WEU with regard to the disputes between Turkey and Greece, the EU was able to overcome the obstacles.[9] Such efforts on the EU's part to accommodate Turkey as an associate member of the WEU indicated the importance of security interdependence between the parties. Given the scope of the WEU's operational area, which does not restrict the WEU to engage in 'out of area' military operations under the 'Petersburg tasks', the EU needed Turkey's participation in WEU activities to increase the operational advantage and the scope of the WEU, due to Turkey's growing regional security role. In addition, Turkey's participation in the WEU was part of the EU's effort to the development of a strengthened European pillar, known as the European Security and Defence Identity, within NATO cooperating closely with the WEU, aimed at the creation of militarily coherent and effective forces capable of operating under the political and strategic direction of WEU (Mathiopoulos and Gyarmati, 1999, p. 65).

Eventually, decision in this area was made at NATO's 1996 ministerial meeting; it was agreed to continued development of the strengthened European pillar within NATO in cooperation with the WEU (*Atlantic News*, Berlin, 24 April 1996). It is within this context that Turkey's incorporation into the WEU was essential. Finally, the WEU Council in March 1999 declared that associate members have a right to 'participate on the same footing as full members in WEU military operation to which it has assigned its own forces'. The Cologne European Council reaffirmed this, declaring that European allies, who are not members of the EU, should take part to the fullest degree possible in participation in EU-led crisis management operations under the WEU (European Council, 1999a). This implies that Turkey can participate to an extent in the EU's security and defence structure through the associate links of the WEU, even before she has joined the EU.

However, this does not seem to have provided a sufficient formula for integrating Turkey fully with the emergence of the Common European Security and Defence Policy (the CESDP) within the EU. The post-Maastricht period of European integration has become involved in forming a political identity. On this account, the EU started to make a serious effort to create the CESDP. For instance, the Common Foreign and Security Policy was for the first time incorporated into the Maastricht Treaty as the second pillar of the EU (Treaty on European Union, Title 1, Article B). Furthermore, the WEU was incorporated into the EU 'as an integral part of the development of the EU' (Treaty on European Union, Article J 4.2). Since then, there has been substantial effort on the part of the EU to make the WEU an integral part of the defence component of the Common European Security and Defence Policy (CESDP). As an example, the Amsterdam Treaty of 1997 furthered the link between the WEU and the EU: under the Amsterdam Treaty, the EU will avail itself of the WEU, and the WEU will elaborate and implement the decisions and actions of the EU. For its part, the WEU, in the Brussels Declaration of 22 July 1997, endorsed the EU's view: firstly, the declaration stated that the WEU would 'elaborate and implement' the decisions and actions of the EU which have defence implications. Secondly, the WEU will follow the guidelines established by the European Council (Oakes, 2000, p. 31).

Most importantly, in June 1999, the Cologne European Council took a decision that made to transfer most of the functions of the WEU to the EU (European Council, 1999b). In this regard, the responsibilities of High Representative for Common Security Policy, Javier Solana, were extended to include the duties of the Secretary-General of the WEU. Even the WEU members decided to transfer the WEU Assembly into an Interim European Security and Defence Assembly (the ESDA). It appears that the EU has started to claim a larger security role by establishing the Common European Security and Defence Policy through transforming the WEU into an integral part of the EU as the defence component of the Union. By implication, the EU is gradually taking over the functions of the WEU.

The European Council at the Helsinki Summit in December 1999 took a decisive step towards the development of a new Common European Security and Defence Policy. The Helsinki European Council set out the key objectives of the CESDP to include 'develop more effective military capabilities and establish new political and military structures' in order to 'take decisions and, where NATO as a whole is not engaged, to conduct EU-led cooperation in response to the international crises' (European Council, 1999a). In order to develop European military capabilities, it was agreed that member states of the EU must be able, by 2003, to deploy within 60 days and sustain at least one-year military forces up to 60,000 persons capable of the full range of Petersburg Tasks.[10] As the NATO Secretary General, Lord Robertson, stated, 'this decision is the visible evidence that the EU is willing to go beyond new institutional mechanisms, and will also muster the military capabilities to underpin them'.[11]

The Treaty of Nice that amended the Treaty on European Union requisitioned the declared objective of the EU to strength its credibility as a security actor and to improve European defence capabilities within the framework of CFSDP. Article 17 of the Treaty stipulates that 'the progressive framing of a common defence policy which might lead to a common defence' and request to 'the member states the adoption of such decision in accordance with their respective constitutional requirements' (Article 17, Treaty of Nice).

All these developments on the part of the EU indicates the emerging political will of the EU to establish a firm wish for the CESDP to act independently, if and when necessary. Indeed, the CESDP intends to develop a military capability for the EU to conduct its own operations in the fields of peacekeeping, humanitarian relief and crisis management. This move of the EU marks that the EU has been moving beyond the rhetoric and declaratory policies to give a genuine meaning to the vision of the CESDP in close cooperation with the Atlantic Alliance.

This development within the EU has had implications for the security aspect of EU-Turkey relations. To be more precise, the current evolution of the CESDP might marginalize Turkey. The question of how Turkey might take part in the CESDP has begun to concern both the EU and Turkey. The statement of the EU's High Representative for the CFSP, Javier Solana, reflects this; as he acknowledged; 'how to get a key NATO ally like Turkey involved in the European security framework is very important' (*Financial Times*, 15 September 1997). The *Financial Times* describes it as follows: 'One of the trickiest aspects of the new European Security Defence Identity is that countries such as Turkey fear the loss of their linkage with the EU will cut them off from European defence development' (*Financial Times*, 15 September 1997).

It appeared that the EU's policy towards Turkey has been incompatible with its security objectives. The EU considered the continued relationship with Turkey within NATO and the WEU was sufficient to maintain working relationships with Turkey in the area of security and defence matters. In other words, the EU intended to maintain closer relations with Turkey through its policy of containment, designed to keep Turkey not only as a security insulator between the EU and the countries on its periphery, but also as a close associate and partner in developing relations and stabilizing the countries in the Balkans, the Middle East and the CIS region. Nevertheless, the EU finally realized that its objective to establish the CESDP requires close cooperation with Turkey for a number of reasons. Firstly, Turkey is a NATO member and active country of European security. Therefore Turkey's approval of the CESDP would make it easier for the EU to establish better patterns for cooperation between NATO and the EU, allowing the EU to use NATO assets and capabilities if required.

Secondly, Turkey's importance as a security asset for Europe in the regional context and its potential capability to act as a stabilizing influence in its region can be considered as Turkey's geographic and strategic value for EU's new Common European Security and Defence Policy. Indeed, it would be very difficult for the EU to take military action in the Middle East, the Balkans and in Eurasia, without Turkey's cooperation. The Washington Summit of NATO in 1999 and the 'new strategic concept' clearly reflected the increasing significance of 'out of area' concerns in European security. This was the case for the Balkan Civil Wars in Bosnia and Kosova. Therefore, considering Turkey's proximity to the Balkans, the Caucasus, the Middle East and the Mediterranean, which puts Turkey at the centre of a vital strategic area, the EU would face difficulties in engaging in 'out of area' peacekeeping or peace enforcement missions in its periphery, without Turkey's participation (Kirchner and Sperling, 2000, p. 36).

The third aspect of Turkey's contribution to CESDP is related to her military capability. As the recent Kosova crisis indicated the failure of the EU to deploy a European army, because it had difficulties in fielding 40,000 soldiers for peacekeeping in the Balkans. This implies that the EU probably would rely on other sources (Drozdiak, 2000). In this respect, Turkey, which has the second largest standing army in NATO (after the USA) with major conventional weapons, would be potential contributor to the military aspect of CESDP. In fact, Turkey already expressed her desire to contribute to the EU's rapid reaction force by offering brigade-size units supported by air and naval components. [12]

Arguably, the security importance of Turkey for the EU appears to be the most important appealing factor in the EU's assessment of Turkish membership. Therefore, the EU started to consider security and strategic dimensions of its policy towards Turkey. It was not a coincidence between the timing of the decision of the EU's approval of Turkish candidacy and the timing of its decision to consolidate the Common European Security and Defence Policy at the Helsinki Summit in 1999. This was probably because the EU considered that a more flexible and positive policy stance towards the Turkish prospects for membership would encourage Turkey to support the Common European Security and Defence Policy within the EU.

Although the EU's policy post-Helsinki has been more inclusive than its old policy, as it includes the Accession Partnership Document which made Turkey part of the enlargement process of the EU in the long run, the question still remains whether Turkey was convinced with the EU's approval of its candidacy, in return for full support of CEDSP. The main issue here is that the EU has been reluctant, and will continue, to grant non-EU members of the European Allies a role in decision-making of CFSDP. By implication, the question remains to be resolved in relation to the way Turkey would be incorporated into the Common European Security and its Defence Policy. Given the explicit linkage between the EU and the emerging CESDP – as the EU membership is a prior condition for the latter – and the EU's clear reluctance to admit Turkey into the EU at least for the foreseeable future, incorporating Turkey within the EU's security and defence structure seems to be controversial.

It is within this context that Turkey's approach towards the CESDP appears to be important from many aspects. First, Turkey considers that development of the CESDP within the EU could undermine the role of the non-EU NATO allies in Common European Security and Defence Policy; thus, exclusion from CESDP is not compatible with her security interests. This is the main reason why Turkey has emerged as a potential problem area for EU/NATO relations. Turkey has been a most reluctant NATO member in supporting the CESDP. Considering that Turkey is a NATO member she could oppose the use of any NATO assets in EU-led operations, which would impair the military capability of the EU to fulfil its new responsibilities under the Petersburg tasks independently from the Atlantic Alliance.

In August 2000, the Turkish Permanent Representative to the NATO issued a statement:

> There will be no automatic access by the EU to NATO assets and capabilities and that requests will have to be considered by the members of the Council of NATO including Turkey (*Atlantic News*, 17 August 2000).

Following the Feira Summit of the European Council, where the CESDP was the main agenda, Turkey declared a statement acknowledging that:

> Turkey will evaluate CESDP in the light of her national interests, while bearing in mind her responsibilities as a candidate for accession to the EU, Turkey's main objection is that the EU is trying to elaborate its relations with Turkey in the framework of CFSDP solely on the basis of crisis management overlooking the previous decisions regarding preservations of WEU *acquis* (Ministry of Foreign Affairs, Press Release, 18 July 2000).

It was also the case at the meeting between the North Atlantic Council (the NAC) and the Interim Political and Security Committee of the EU Council (the COPS), responsible for overseeing the development of a European Security and Defence Policy, Turkey took a tough stance by expressing its objection to the use of the NATO assets and capabilities by the EU (Scold, 2000, p. 3).

Despite Turkey's effort, the EU has been reluctant to grant non-EU members of the European allies real influence in the decision-making process of the CFSDP. It is within this context that the success of Turkey's incorporation into the CESDP would pose considerable difficulties which could impact on the development of CESDP. For example, as suggested above, the prospect of Turkey's veto over the use of

NATO assets by the EU would considerably undermine the success of any EU-led military operation due to the EU's dependence on the NATO assets and capabilities. Even the USA has consistently underlined the risk of Turkey's inclusion from the security arrangements of the EU under the CESDP. In fact, the USA has made efforts to convince the EU to incorporate Turkey into the CFSDP. For example, the USA ambassador to NATO, Alexander Vershbow, stated that 'European operation will have the greatest chance of success if it has the political and practical support of non-EU allies, not the least of all Turkey' (cited in Muftuler-Bac, 2000, p. 484). Recently, at the meeting of NATO Ministers in Birmingham in October of 2000, the USA Secretary of State for Defense, William Cohen, stated 'non-EU European Allies, like Turkey, should participate in decision-shaping on EU led military operation' (cited in Oakes, 2000, p. 34). The USA's support to incorporate Turkey into the CFSDP is probably part of USA security strategy, since Turkey has been not only strategically important for American security, but also she has been one of the most reliable European Allies of NATO to the USA which might allow the latter to put some influence on the CESDP matter through Turkey.

From this perspective, the main question here is that whether the EU's containment policy towards the prospect of Turkish membership would be attainable in the long run. As the above analysis suggests, although the EU-Turkey relations post-Helsinki appears to be encouraging to arrange the grounds on which they could build their security relations as regards mutual interests, the EU's policy towards the prospect of Turkey being fully incorporated into the CESDP within the EU through membership still remains doubtful. Considering that Turkey is a candidate state and thus will eventually become an EU member in the long run, an appropriate policy of the EU would be to incorporate Turkey in some way into the CESDP process. This would not only provide a formal link to facilitate the full integration of Turkey into the EU and progressive rapprochement with the EU's Common Foreign Security and Defence policy, but also it would convince Turkey to give full support for the EU's effort to establish its own security and defence policy with a military capability.

Another characteristic of the EU's security policy towards Turkey is that although the EU has given considerable concern to the defence and military aspects of security relations with Turkey, it has paid less attention to non-military security issues in Turkey. To that extent, its policy towards Turkey has even been inconsistent with its own security interests and its enlargement's security objective of reinforcing peace and stability in the European continent. In order to clarify this argument, the following section will explore the enlargement of the EU from the security perspective and compare the EU's policy towards Turkey with its policy for the CEECs in this respect.

The Security Aspect of the EU's Enlargement Policy: Turkey and the CEECs in a Comparative Perspective

Strengthening stability and prosperity in Europe has been the main motive behind the EU's enlargement policy. Considering the degree of risks and costs associated with the political and economic instability on the periphery of the EU, the EU was bound to launch an appropriate enlargement strategy for the CEECs, in order to promote stability throughout Europe. Clearly, the security motivation behind the EU's enlargement policy towards the CEECs is a closely related degree of risks and costs factors with the political and economic instability in the CEECs: the EU considered that failure to launch an enlargement policy towards the CEECs would seriously undermine the EU's own security in many ways, such as refugees and immigration, spreads of weapons, spill over of ecological disasters, organized crime, and increasing nationalism with aggressive tendencies. To that extent, the EU has offered policy instruments for the applicant countries, which included enhanced political dialogue and structured relationships, the participation of the CEECs in Community programmes and agencies and meetings between candidate states and the Union in the context of the accession process, designed to provide a support for the CEECs so as to supply their political and security needs.

As indicated in chapter 2, the EU's comprehensive accession strategy has aimed at lessening the perceived security risks of reversals in the applicant states through supporting political, social and economic stability in these countries. The primary security objective of the EU's accession strategy is to ensure political stability in the CEECs, at the minimum cost to the EU. Thus, it has focused on preventing the failure of political transformation through appropriate policy instruments for establishing political stability in the CEECs and clear accession commitment to encourage policy reforms in these countries. To that extent, this pre-accession strategy has shown the firm commitment of the EU to the CEECs accession to the EU which has forced the CEECs to make efforts not only to resolve domestic political conflict politics, such as minority and human rights issues, but also to take a constructive approach in settling their outstanding border disputes and other related issues in relations between the states in the region. In other words, the EU's clear accession credibility and strong commitment to the accession of the CEECs, on the one hand, and expectation of membership by these countries, on the other, has had a considerable effects on developments in the domestic policies of the CEECs and also on the settling of their disagreements with one another.

Moreover, the EU has not only supplied considerable financial and technical assistance for the applicant countries in stabilizing their domestic politics, but has also set up political links and institutional networks with these countries. The instruments of political dialogue and structured relationship and joint regional actions, the so-called Stability Pact for Europe, have provide an appropriate framework not only for the EU to exert its influence on the political developments and reinforce political stability in the applicant countries, but also for the applicant countries to make their foreign and security policies converge towards the EU's foreign and security policy. For example, The Essen Summit of the EU launched 'structured relationship' between the EU and the CEECs covering wide range policy areas, including the CFSP and the JHA (European Council, 1994). This has provided associates with opportunities to join the EU on common positions in international issues. The structured relationship involved regular ministerial level meetings, as well as annual meeting of the heads of state and governments. In addition, the EU has worked closely with the CEECs through the 'Stability Pact' in which the EU has focused more on the problems of the region, covering such topics as border disputes, minority rights, water rights, citizenship requirements and other vital matters. This is closely related to the EU's effort to help the CEECs meet the political criterion.

However, the EU has been inconsistent in applying these instruments for the applicant countries equally and with the same concern. Turkey has been an anomalous case in this respect. Even though the institutional structure of political dialogue in the EU's containment policy is similar to that of the institutional structure in the EU's policy towards the CEECs, the latter differs from the former in many respects. First, the political dialogue and structured relationship for the CEECs have been explicitly linked to their preparation for EU membership, because these instruments have aimed at creating lasting links of solidarity and new forms of cooperation and facilitating the integration of the states into the community of democratic nations and progressive rapprochement with the EU.[13] In fact, the political dialogue and structured relationship has established a further mechanism and set up more clear objectives in their case than the one for Turkey: as the Europe Agreements stipulate, 'political dialogue would go beyond the low politics of trade and economic co-operation and include a genuinely political dimension'.[14] Hence, it explicitly emphasizes that the political dialogue provided for in this agreement would lead to greater political convergence and to increasing convergence of position on international issues and the rapprochement of the parties on common foreign and security issues. In this respect, the EU has responded to the security issues in these countries with technical and financial assistance programmes in the form of PHARE.

However, the aspects of political dialogue and institutional cooperation in EU-Turkey relations have included neither firm accession credibility, nor clearly defined comprehensive instruments to support political stability in Turkey. The objective of political dialogue in EU-Turkey relations were designed to strengthen relations in some areas between the parties, rather then facilitating Turkey's integration into the EU. For example, the political dialogue and institutional co-operation in EU-Turkey relations did not include topics such as foreign security and defence policy. Although the political dialogue of the EU-Turkey relations foresaw the consultation between Turkey and the EU in certain CFSP working parties,[15] it did not provide an appropriate mechanism for genuine political dialogue and cooperation with the EU, owing to the lack of continuity and coordination. Though the EU realized this and proposed strengthening the institutional cooperation and political dialogue through its European Strategy for Turkey, it did not add any new element to the procedure and mechanism of the political dialogue and structured relationship (European Commission, 1998a). In fact, the European strategy for Turkey has offered cooperation only in the fields of low politics, rather than lasting links of solidarity and new forms of cooperation, similar to the CEECs. The Commission's report of 1999 with regard to Turkey admitted this and asked the Council of Ministers to find ways to initiate enhanced political dialogue with Turkey, with emphasis on progressing towards fulfilling the political criteria for accession. Building on existing European Strategy for Turkey, the Commission proposed enhancing political dialogue, with particular reference to the issue of human rights, and providing Turkey's participation of association with common positions and actions taken under the CFSP (European Commission, 1999b, p. 35). However, it should be noted that the EU's policy post-Helsinki has been more favourable in this respect.

Following the conclusions of the Helsinki European Council, political dialogue has been created between the parties. Since the Helsinki Council, Turkey has participated in all political dialogue meetings involving the EU and candidate countries at ministerial level, at political director level and European correspondent level. In addition, the Accession Partnership Document for Turkey is an important step towards enhancing political dialogue between the parties and the prospect of Turkey's participation in all community programmes and agencies including in the areas of the CFSP and the JHA. The Accession Partnership provides the enhanced political dialogue between the EU and Turkey that puts emphasis on progressing towards fulfilling the political criteria for accession with a particular reference to human rights and dialogue between Turkey and Greece (European Commission, 2000e). Nevertheless, it still remains doubtful as to whether the sprit of Helsinki process would be accomplished as smoothly as is foreseen.

Another difference between the EU's policy towards Turkey and the CEECs is that the political dialogue and structured relationship have also supported the CEECs efforts to resolve their outstanding border disputes and other related issues. The EU has used accession conditionality to put pressure on the CEECs to reach peaceful resolution of their bilateral disputes, fostering regional economic integration and sub-regional cooperation initiatives, and integration of ethnic minority groups. For example, the Stability Pact for Europe, which aims to guarantee minority rights and the inviolability of frontiers in Europe, has become part of the political dialogue and structured relationship between the EU and the CEECs. Through this, the EU has encouraged the CEECs to settle their bilateral issues by working closely with them to find ways towards the resolution of their disagreements. For the Turkish case, although the post-Helsinki character of EU-Turkey relations appears to be an encouraging step towards the rapprochement between Greece and Turkey (as approval of Turkey's candidacy by the EU has provided new imputes to the process of dialogue between Greece and Turkey), there are a number of factors preventing fruitful results for the settlement of the disputes between the parties over the Aegean Sea and Cyprus, at least for the foreseeable future.

Another characteristic of the provisions of the political dialogue and structured relationship between the EU and the CEECs is that they provide a formal link to facilitate the full integration of associate members of the CEECs into the EU and progressive rapprochement with the EU's Common Foreign and Security Policy (Lippert, 1997, p. 205). In addition, this political dialogue and structured relationship have proceeded through the pre-accession strategy of the EU that forms a more structured relationship in foreign and security matters with the CEECs. These institutional links between the EU and the CEECs have constituted an important channel not only to serve as a forum for cooperation and exchange of views between the EU members and associate members in the areas of security, defence and foreign affairs, but also to give the associate members a sense of belonging to the EU family, as well as providing a valuable insight into the workings of the EU machinery (Avery and Cameron, 1988, p. 19). Indeed, the EU's strong institutional links with the CEECs through the pre-accession strategy in several respects has already attached the CEECs to the political integration of the EU in such wide-ranging areas as foreign and security policy, domestic and legal issues, the environment, education and telecommunications. For instance, a substantial amount of technical and financial assistance in the form of PHARE has been directed to prepare the first and second round of entry to the EU with regard to border control, organized crime and money laundering, drug trafficking and migration. For instance, the EU introduced a programme with 100 million ECU to combat organized crime in the CEECs (Kirchner and Sperling, 2000, p. 34). This indicates the EU's effort to promote stability in these countries. In addition, through the 'pre-ins programme' the EU has made substantial efforts to prepare the first and second wave of applicants to apply the Schengen process, with the aim of bringing the applicants' border policies progressively into line with the Schengen *acquis* (Grabbe, 2000, pp. 519–536). This is part of the EU's efforts to extend its JHA to the applicants' eastern borders.

In the same vein, since the Essen Summit of the EU Council in 1994, the CEECs have been offered an opportunity to align themselves with activities of the CFSP (European Council, 1994). They have participated in European Council meetings with heads of state and governments of the EU members. Association Council meetings at ministerial level between the CEECs and the EU and regular joint meetings at ambassadorial level have been regularly held. They have also been connected to the Associated Correspondents' Network system, providing rapid and secure exchange of messages between the EU and associated members in the CFSP area. This can be considered as an exercise in the EU's effort to prepare these prospective entrants for the CFSP mechanism. Even the numbers of working groups in the area of the CFSP have already been established between the EU and CEECs, providing a forum to discuss a wide range of policies, from migration to transitional crime to asylum policies and police cooperation. In conclusion, the objectives of the political dialogue and structured relationship between the CEECs and the EU have been successfully achieved through the EU's pre-accession strategy.

For the Turkish case, the objective of political dialogue and structured relationship has not been implemented; in fact, political dialogue and institutional cooperation are considered areas where EU-Turkey relations have suffered from a low level of collaboration. Although the Commission and successive EU Council summits have acknowledged the need for strengthening institutional cooperation and political dialogue at the 'highest level', involving discussions and the exchange of views on many issues between the parties, the political circumstances have not allowed the pursuit of the envisaged declarations. This is because the success of political dialogue and institutional cooperation depends on the meetings of the Turkey-EU Association Council, but these have not been held regularly on political grounds. In other words, the lack of commitment on both sides, the Greek objections and the breaches of human rights in Turkey have prevented the realization of political dialogue and institutional cooperation in EU-Turkey relations. As an example, in the period between 1995 and 1999 the Association Council were able to meet only twice, as Greece blocked seven scheduled meetings. After the decision of the Luxembourg Summit in 1997 in which Turkey was not included in the list of candidate countries, Turkey suspended political dialogue with the EU. The Helsinki European Council Summit conclusions in 1999 recognized the need to initiate enhanced political dialogue and institutional cooperation with Turkey, which can be considered to be an encouraging development in that respect. In line with the Helsinki Accord, the EU has provided the option of association with common positions and actions taken under the CFSP, thus Turkey, since the Helsinki Summit, has regularly aligned her position with those of the Union and has associated herself with the Union's joint actions and common position (European Commission, 2000a, p. 67). However, Turkey has not been connected yet to the Associated Correspondents Network System, designed to provide exchange of messages between the EU and candidate countries in the CFSP.

As the above analysis suggests the instruments and the objectives of the envisaged political dialogue and institutional cooperation in the EU's containment policy for Turkey have been insufficient. Not only have they failed to reinforce political stability through minimizing the conflict at societal level and promoting European values in Turkish politics, but also they have failed to prepare Turkey to participate in the Foreign and Security Policy of the EU through helping her to align her policy towards the CFSP. Indeed, the political dialogue and institutional cooperation in EU-Turkey relations have fallen far short of the possibilities made available to the other candidates in many aspects. By implication, the EU has been less effective in influencing the development of Turkey's internal policy. This is one of the main reasons behind the Helsinki decision of the EU to revise its old containment policy of Turkey through granting Turkey a candidate status with the Accession Partnership Document. The EU's revised policy of Turkey after the Helsinki Summit have been more effective than its previous policy in terms of influencing the development of Turkish domestic policy, as well as in terms of strengthening political dialogue and structured relations between the EU and Turkey in the field of foreign policy and security. However, even the EU's revised policy post-Helsinki seems to have fallen far short of the possibilities made available to the other candidates in many ways.

Conclusions

As the analysis through this chapter has suggested, during the Cold War and afterwards, Turkey's security assets have constituted strong grounds for maintaining closer relations between Turkey and the EU. The end of the Cold War has not diminished Turkey as a security asset for the EU; it has rather only changed the parameters and features of security interdependence between the parties. This implies that Turkey's new role in European security has assumed new characteristics that goes beyond traditional military aspects of security to include political, economic, social, ideological and demographical aspects of security. By implication, in many ways, Turkey seems to be more important for the EU from the security perspective now than before.

However, it is not clear that the EU's policy towards Turkey has been compatible with her security importance, or with the security interdependence of the parties. The EU's security policy towards Turkey can be described as a containment policy, designed to maintain working relations with Turkey, rather than to integrate her gradually with the emerging of a Common European Security and Defence Policy. Predictably, the EU have considered that Turkey's security links to the EU *via* its NATO membership and associate membership of the WEU, with a strengthened political dialogue and structured relationship through the Association Agreement would be sufficient to meet its and Turkey's security concerns. However, it has become more difficult to integrate Turkey much further with the Common European Security and Defence Policy. This is because the CESDP has been an integral part of the EU, and being part of it requires membership of the EU. In this respect, the EU's clear reluctance to consider Turkish membership for the foreseeable future would make Turkey's participation in the CESDP doubtful. To that extent, although the EU appears to have revised its containment policy of Turkey after the Helsinki Summit, the EU still has not yet approached its commitment to Turkey as it has approached the CEECs.

The main proposition of this chapter is that the security aspect of the EU's containment policy seems to have been inadequate for the security needs of Turkey: while the EU has acknowledged the importance of Turkey as a security asset for the EU, its containment policy has lacked the necessary instruments to achieve the EU's promises to Turkey as a means of integrating Turkey into the new European security structure. This implies that the EU's containment policy towards Turkey has been inappropriate, not only with its security interest, but also with the security objectives of its enlargement policy. The first theme is to do with security interdependence between the EU and Turkey, because Turkey's importance for European security is not only related to her role as a stabilizing factor in the regional context, but also is related to the fact that European security is closely connected with the social, economic and political stability of Turkey. Turkey has been facing ethnic and religious extremism which poses a direct threat to European security. To that extent, the security aspect of the EU's containment policy and its instrument towards Turkey cannot be reconciled with its security interdependence and its security interests. Second, there has even been inconsistency between the security motivation of the EU's policy towards the CEECs and its policy *vis-à-vis* Turkey: the EU initiated its enlargement strategy towards the CEECs on the grounds that the security, stability, peace and prosperity of Europe can only be enhanced by fully integrating the CEECs. Hence, the EU has offered them effective policy instruments through its pre-accession strategy with clear commitment and an appropriate support by taking the security needs of these countries into account. However, the EU has shown extreme reluctance to put forward similar policy instruments for Turkey and thus has been hesitant to use the carrot of membership prospects for Turkey to encourage her to take appropriate measures to resolve her own similar security issues. This partly explains why the EU's treatment of Turkey has been insufficient and thereby has had less influence on political developments and stability in the country than its treatment of the CEECs.

However, this is not to deny that Turkey has serious security issues in its domestic politics (i.e., Kurdish issue and human rights) and in its foreign policy (disputes with Greece and Cyprus). Thus, enlarging the EU to include Turkey would not only bring her internal security problems into the EU, but would also undermine the EU's objective to establish a coherent foreign and security policy. However, given the trans-boundary character of the security issues, the cost of Turkey's exclusion from the EU's security structure would also be very high. Therefore, a policy locating Turkey's accession negotiations in the long run with a clear accession strategy instrument to support political stability in Turkey, would be a more appropriate and attainable policy for the mutual security interest of the parties.

In fact, the positive developments in the EU-Turkey relationship post-Helsinki appear to support this contention.

Notes

1 For example, at the Hague in 1987, WEU members adopted a platform on European Security Interests in which they committed themselves to build a European Union in accordance with the Single European Act and stated that 'the construction of an integrated Europe will remain incomplete as long as it does not include security and defence', quoted in Edward Mortimer (1992), 'European Security after the Cold War', *Adelphi Papers*, No. 271, p. 57.

2 Interview with Korkmaz Haktanir, Turkish Ambassador to the UK, London, 12 March 2000.

3 For example, after the Iranian Islamic revolution, thousands of Iranians fled their country for Turkey and EU member states. More recently, due to the Gulf War, thousands of Kurds were forced to seek political asylum in European countries and in Turkey. It was also the case that the conflict between Turkish army and the Kurdish separatists led by the PKK forced a number of people to seek political asylum in the EU states.

4 For example, conflicts between secularists and pro-Islamists can be noticed among the Turks, Algerians and Iranians in EU countries. Such conflicts are similar to those between the Turks and Kurds in Germany. For this, see Andrew Mango (1998), 'Turkey and European Mind, *Middle Eastern Studies*, Vol. 34, No. 2

5 For more details on the Kurdish Refuges, see the debates of the European Parliament, *Official Journal of European Communities*, No. 4–512/169. 14.1.1998.

6 These are Greece, Romania, Bulgaria, Turkey, Russia, Ukraine, Albania, Georgia, Moldova, Armenia and Azerbaijan.

7 The BEC provided a forum for the exchange of views and settling differences and conflicts among the member states. For example, the President of Georgia, Shvardnadze, raised the issue of the former Soviet Black Sea fleet, whose 300 ships were a matter of dispute between Ukraine and Russia at the Istanbul Summit. For this, see *The Independent*, 26 June 1992. In addition, the leaders of Armenia and Azerbajian discussed the Nagorna-Karabakh issue during the summit meeting in Istanbul. For this, see *The Economist,* 27 June 1992.

8 The Euro-Asian energy corridor with the existing pipeline for Iraqi oil would increase Turkey's influence in the region, as well as Turkey's strategic importance to the EU. This has been one of the main reasons behind the active support of the USA and the EU for the Turkish proposal of the Euro-Asian energy corridor. In other words, the USA and the EU's preference for the Turkish proposal over the Russian and Iranian alternatives have been politically motivated to prevent a reassertion of Russian hegemony in the region. For this, see Simon Henderson (1999), 'Caspian Energy Accords: A Job half Done' in *Policy Watch,* The Washington Institute for the Near East Policy, Washington.

9 The Brussels Treaty, Article 10, stated that disputes among the member states should be resolved either by way of judicial settlement through the compulsory jurisdiction of the International Court of Justice, or by way of reconciliation. This was incompatible to Turkey's wish to resolve its disputes with Greece through direct negotiations between the parties. Considering that the EU was determined to associate Turkey as fully as possible with the WEU, the EU found a way to disregard Article 10 in the Turkish case; it was agreed in November 1992 in the London Treaty on Turkey's accession to the WEU as an associate member that Article 10 would not apply to associate members. For this, see Aybak (1996).

10 For this, see Annex V of the Helsinki Council Presidency Conclusions, 'Presidency Progress Report to the Helsinki European Council on Strengthening of Common European Policy on Security and Defence', 10–11 December 1999, Brussels, p. 19.

11 Cited in a speech by the NATO Secretary General at the Conference, held in Istanbul, organized by TESAV, 23 November 2000.

12 For this see the Republic of Turkey Ministry of Foreign Affairs, *Press Release*, 14 February 2000.

13 For example, see Article 2, the Europe Agreement of Association between the European Communities and their members, of the one part, and the Republic of Poland, of the other part, *Official Journal of European Communities,* L348 31 December 1994.

14 See Article 2, the Europe Agreement Establishing an Association between the European Communities and their members, of the one part, and the Republic of Poland, of the other part.

15 For this, see European Commission (1995), *Resolution of the EC-Turkey Association Council on Political Dialogue*, CE –TR 130–95, 25 October 1995.

Chapter 8

Conclusions

This book has argued that the EU has treated Turkey differently compared to the other applicant countries in the present enlargement round. In this respect, before further exploring this argument, there seems to be an important question remaining: why should the EU treat all applicants 'fairly' in the enlargement process? In this respect, the question might arise as to where the borders of the EU should ultimately end. Should the EU differentiate the applicants on the basis of geographical, cultural, and historical criteria? If Turkey is being considered then what about Ukraine, Belarus, Russia and Caucasus states. It is true that Turkey is a Eurasian country in geographical terms. However, Turkey has been politically and economically aligned with Europe: she is a member of NATO, the Council of Europe and an associate member of the EU that foresaw an eventual Turkish membership. This is currently the main difference between the Association agreement of Turkey and Cooperation Agreements with Russia, Ukraine and with Caucasus states in which the EU has not extended promises for eventual membership to these countries.

Moreover, the EU should treat all applicants 'fairly' in the enlargement process because the EU has made promises of eventual membership to all the applicants, including Turkey. In addition, the EU has underlined the importance of the principle of 'equal treatment' for all candidate countries, declaring that candidate states should participate in the enlargement process 'on an equal footing'. This is because the EU has been careful not to produce a feeling for exclusion among the candidates with its economic, political and destabilization implications. Furthermore, all the applicants have similar economic politics and security motives to join the EU, in addition to being confronted with similar policy issues in achieving it. Thus, all candidates expect similar treatment from the EU.

However, a comparison of the EU's policy towards Turkey with that towards the other applicant countries as regards similar policy issues implies that the EU has been reluctant to apply to Turkey the same enlargement policy instruments and commitment to accession that it has shown towards the CEECs. While the EU has approached key issues relating to the CEECs positively with appropriate support by taking the needs of these countries into account, the EU's treatment of similar issues in the Turkish case has been incompatible with its enlargement norms. That is, similar problems (to those of Turkey) in the CEECs have attracted an entirely different response from the EU in the shape of a clear strategy for accession on the grounds that the political, economic and social reforms undertaken by these countries to meet the criteria for membership must be supported and encouraged. However, comparable issues in Turkey have attracted more rigid, critical and even negative responses from the EU.

EU membership represents the ultimate objective of Turkey's political, economic and identity aspirations and orientation (exactly as it has for the other applicants).

This makes Turkey considerably open to the EU influence, like the other applicants. Yet, the EU's policy towards Turkey has lacked the necessary instruments to help or compel Turkey to speed up its policy reforms to meet the conditions for EU membership and thus has been inappropriate for exercising influence over the developments in the political, economic and political systems of Turkey. Consequently, the EU has lost much of its potential leverage to influence the development of Turkey's internal and external policy, for example, improving the Turkish human rights situation and settling the disagreements between Greece and Turkey. Thus, the EU's role in hastening Turkey's efforts to align her political, economic and social system with the EU norms and in influencing Turkey's foreign policy choices has been less effective than in the other applicant countries.

The above arguments have been derived from the comparative analysis of a number of policy issues in EU-Turkey relations. The comparative framework for analyzing these policy issues was developed in chapter 2 and set out the norms for the enlargement policy process of the EU. These norms were based not only on the motivation and interests of the EU and the applicant countries in joining the EU but also on a characterization of the EU's enlargement instruments. For the purpose of this book, the developed analytical framework clarifies the difference between the concept of 'different treatment' in the enlargement process and the concept of 'principle of differentiation' in the accession negotiation process by taking full account of each candidate's progress in complying with the accession criteria. The term of different treatment refers to the notion of incomplete application of the EU's enlargement instruments and its norms to applicant state(s), in order to prepare them for EU membership. The concept of principle of differentiation refers to the different stage of the EU's enlargement policy and thus should not be confused with the concept of different treatment. This clarification made it possible to isolate a number of features of the EU's enlargement policy and thus the framework provided an analytical instrument not only for assessing whether Turkey has been treated differently, but also whether the EU's policy towards Turkey has itself been compatible with these norms. In addition, such clarification clarified the contention of the book which certainly does not suggests that the EU should open the accession negotiation with Turkey before she meets the criteria for accession, and thus does not imply early Turkish accession.

As is evident from the analysis of the EU's enlargement policy through chapter 2, it has used the accession carrot and its enlargement instruments to persuade, subsidize and guide the applicant countries to undertake the necessary reforms for fulfilling the Copenhagen conditions. In fact, the EU's role *vis-à-vis* the CEECs has gone beyond economic aid to include institution building and the explicit encouragement of specific political and legal reforms. Thus, the EU's policy towards the CEECs has progressed in parallel with the candidate states' preparation for membership. This made it possible to stimulate the candidates' preparatory efforts to comply with accession criteria; indeed, their aspirations to join the EU have made all the CEECs particularly vulnerable to the influence of the EU in many areas. Hence, developments and policy choices in these countries' domestic and foreign politics have been severely constrained by the EU's clear strategy for accession and firm commitment to the eastward enlargement of the EU.

However, this has not been the case for Turkey: the analysis of the development of the EU's policy towards Turkey suggests that the EU has not treated Turkey evenhandedly. This deficiency could have taken the form of incomplete application of the EU's enlargement instruments to Turkey but, in fact, the EU has preferred to pursue a different strategy for Turkey, which can best be described as a containment strategy. This seems to have been designed to delay the prospects of Turkish membership well into the foreseeable future, while keeping Turkey within the economic and political sphere of influence of the EU by strengthening the existing association framework and offering Turkey an Accession Partnership Document with vague conditions attached to it. This argument is supported in virtually every chapter of the book.

For example, it is clear from the analysis of the instruments of the EU-Turkey Association in chapter 3, that the Association has experienced considerable difficulties as a result of the incompatibility between the parties' policies and the objectives of the Agreement and their different interpretations of the road towards the ultimate objective of the Association. In other words, the instruments of the EU-Turkey Association have, to a large extent, failed to serve as a useful preparatory phase for a further agreement leading to accession; this has been due not only to Turkey's failure to put into action the necessary economic and political reforms, but also the EU's unwillingness to upgrade the EU-Turkey Association as a preliminary to full membership. In fact, the EU has rather effectively used the policy issues between Turkey and the EU, including the inadequacy of its human rights record and Greco-Turkish disputes, to legitimize its reluctant approach to reorient the instruments of the EU-Turkey Association towards membership.

However, it does not imply that these issues should not be considered major obstacles to Turkish membership; it rather suggests that the EU's 'hard line policy' approach to issues in Turkey has not been compatible with the EU's declared enlargement policy objectives. It cannot explain why similar issues in the CEECs have attracted an entirely different response on the part of the EU from those in Turkey. Moreover, these policy issues between Turkey and the EU have been less effectively pursued in the EU's efforts to strengthen the EU-Turkey Association. This seems to be a reflection of the EU's containment strategy for Turkey, with its clear preference for delaying Turkish membership in the foreseeable future, as described above.

After explicitly putting off any prospect of Turkish accession by its negative opinion on the Turkish membership application in 1989, the EU has made considerable efforts to strengthen EU-Turkish relations, including the establishment of the customs union in 1995. Nevertheless, all the instruments of EU policy towards Turkey have not really amounted to a useful preparatory phase for Turkey's accession to the EU and thus have failed to reorient the EU-Turkey Association as part of pre-accession strategy, as it has done for the CEECs. Even the EU's policy post-Helsinki appears to be limited to reorient the EU-Turkey Association towards full membership, since all the instruments available under the Accession Partnership have been designed to contribute to anchor Turkey firmly within the future architecture of Europe, rather than being oriented towards membership of the EU. Even if the Accession Partnership functions, there is no guarantee at all that accession will follow. This implies that the EU's association policy towards Turkey has been different from its association policy towards the CEECs.

In the case of the latter, the EU has explicitly linked its association policy with the CEECs to their accession to the EU. Since mid-1990, Europe Agreements have become part of pre-accession strategies, designed evidently to prepare individual associates for accession. The EU realized that the Europe Agreements were unsatisfactory and constituted an inadequate framework for relations with the CEECs and this prompted the EU to initiate a pre-accession strategy for the CEECs with considerable financial and technical aid. In addition, the EU has since made considerable efforts to update the instruments of the Europe Agreements in accordance with the need to integrate the associate members into the EU; as a result, these agreements have served as a useful preparatory phase for a further agreement leading to accession. This comparison of the two association agreements has generated the important conclusion, that while the association policy of the EU towards the CEECs has been closely linked to the latter's preparation for membership, the EU has tended to use the EU-Turkey association policy as a tool for its containment strategy to delay Turkish membership in the foreseeable future. Because the EU has been reluctant to enhance the instruments of the Ankara Agreements in accordance with the move to integrate Turkey into the EU in the context of post-Maastrich European integration.

The evidence from the analysis of chapter 4 reinforces the argument that the EU's containment strategy for Turkey has lacked the necessary instruments to prepare Turkey for EU membership. The instruments of the EU's policy to include the Association Agreement, the customs union, the European Strategy for Turkey and the Accession Partnership Document, have not been closely oriented to prepare Turkey for accession, they have been rather specifically oriented towards bringing Turkey more closely into the EU framework. Though the EU always repeats the assertion of the eligibility of Turkey for EU membership and thus recognized Turkey as a candidate at the Helsinki Summit, the instruments provided for Turkey under its containment policy have fallen short of achieving this commitment.

The above contention supported by the evidences derived from a comparative analysis of the EU's policy towards the CEECs and its policy *vis-à-vis* Turkey, with regard to preparing for the EU's single market, agricultural policy and financial and technical cooperation. This comparative analysis suggests that the EU has explicitly linked its policy towards the CEECs to their accession process, by helping them to comply with the *acquis* of the Union through the White Paper for European Single Market, Europe Agreements, instruments of pre-accession strategy and the PHARE programmes of financial and technical supports. In fact, by offering economic and political benefits and specifying requirements for membership, the EU has played a paramount role in the domestic policy choices in the CEECs and has thereby affected the speed and outcome of their reforms. However, the EU's policy instruments for Turkey have fallen well short of what is required to prepare the way for EU membership, thereby providing a possible explanation for the weaker influence exerted by the EU on political, social and economic developments in Turkey rather than in the CEECs.

As regards political issues, the EU's different approach to similar political issues in the CEECs and Turkey reinforces the main argument of the book. Turkey has clearly been treated ungenerously in that similar political problems in the CEECs seem to have attracted an entirely different response, due to the EU's claim that the democratization process and recognition of human rights must be supported and encouraged in the CEECs. To illustrate, although the EU has made it conditional that the implementation of all instruments of European Agreements and the pre-accession strategy, including financial aid, should depend upon compliance with the requirement of respect for democratic principles and human rights, this conditionality has not been applied to any country in the CEEC as strictly as it has been applied to Turkey. As indicated in chapter 5, while the EU has always underlined that the political situation in these countries presented a number of problems to do with the treatment of minority rights and the functioning of institutional democracy, it has continued to provide financial support for them with a view to facilitating their eventual membership of the EU; hence, the suspension of financial cooperation, or their exclusion from the accession strategy seems to have been considered by the EU as a policy of last resort.

Moreover, the EU's decision at the Helsinki Summit to open accession negotiations with the 'second wave' candidates supports the contention of the EU's positive response to the political issues in the CEECs. Though the Commission identified a number of political issues in the second wave candidate states, including lack of progress as regards treatment of minorities, principles of democracy and rule of law, the EU launched the process of accession negotiations with them on the grounds that negotiations progress would further encourage their efforts to comply with the Copenhagen criteria.

As far as the EU's policy towards Turkey is concerned, its approach seems not only to have been more rigid and critical, but also has lacked the necessary instruments to help the democratization process and the improvement of the human rights system in Turkey. The EU has pursued a critical and rigid human rights policy *vis-à-vis* Turkey over the issue of Turkey's membership. Indeed, the EU's human rights policy has been firm and has actually delayed Turkish membership. As a result, the EU's efforts to encourage greater respect for human rights in Turkey has been less successful than in the CEECs; it appears that the EU's greater leverage in the case of the latter is largely due to the clear prospect of EU membership, while in Turkey the EU's efforts have had less effect due to its lack of commitment to Turkey's accession to the Union.

Furthermore, as is evident from the analysis in chapter 5, there seems to have been some inconsistency within the EU's policy towards Turkey as regards human rights and other political issues. For example, the EU's approach to the political issues in Turkey has been more flexible and encouraging when it comes to implementing the EU's containment strategy. This implies that the EU's human rights policy towards Turkey has been, to a large extent, determined by its policy objectives. More specifically, the EU has taken a moderate and constructive – even an encouraging – human rights policy stance towards Turkey when it sought to improve EU-Turkey relations within the association framework. As an example, in spite of the inadequacy of Turkey's political and human rights regime, the EU has made a considerable effort to normalize the EU-Turkey relations since 1987, through the Matutes Package (1992), the customs union (1995) the European strategy for Turkey (1998) and through revising its containment policy as a means of declaring Turkey as a candidate state (1999) with some vague conditions attached to it. Conversely, however, the EU has pursued a rigid and critical human rights policy towards Turkey as a means of delaying or avoiding the prospect of Turkish membership, a policy which, in fact, seems, from this point of view, to have been wholly successful.

The above argument might be questioned on the grounds that the EU's more rigid policy approach to the political issues in Turkey should more correctly be attributed to the lack of progress on Turkey's part in making improvements in its human rights record and its political system. It is true that the lack of a political solution for the Kurdish issue, the breaches of human rights and the immaturity of political democracy in Turkey have caused a series of problems in EU-Turkey relations. Thus, Turkey's failure to put into action the necessary political reforms to fulfil the Copenhagen criteria seems to provide reasonable and legitimate grounds for the EU to delay the accession negotiation with Turkey until she meet the political criteria. However, it cannot sufficiently explain why the EU has been extremely doubtful to offer an appropriate accession strategy for Turkey in order to support her effort to comply with the Copenhagen criteria. In fact, excluding Turkey from the enlargement process of the EU is not incompatible with one of the objectives of the EU's enlargement strategy – that is, to encourage further democratization in the applicant countries. Whereas the EU has made several references to the importance of the prospect of enlargement as a political asset for consolidating and embedding principles of liberty, democracy, respect for human rights and the rule of law in the applicant countries, it has been reluctant to use it in the case of Turkey. Thus, the EU's reluctance to offer Turkey a firm membership commitment (even in the long run) with an appropriate set of enlargement instruments has differentiated its policy *vis-à-vis* Turkey from its policy towards the other applicant countries. This may explain why democratization efforts have been more successful in these candidate countries than in Turkey.

This is clearly a lost opportunity. With its 'European vocation', Turkey is probably more open to EU influence through the 'accession carrot' than most countries and, indeed, the EU has still been able to exert considerable pressure even with its more minimal containment strategy. Thus, for example, as the customs union case indicates, the EU was able through pressure and influence on the Turkish Government to cause some necessary changes to be made in the Turkish political system including such areas as the observance of human rights and the Kurdish issue. Furthermore, the EU's policy post-Helsinki provides more evidence to support the contention that Turkey has been considerably open to EU influence: since then, she has made considerable progress towards complying political criteria, although the Helsinki process has conditioned Turkey's benefit from pre-accession strategy on Turkey's progress towards fulfilling the political criteria. Therefore, a more effective policy approach than the EU's revised containment policy of Helsinki would encourage political and legal developments in Turkish domestic politics. To conclude, then, the analysis of the political aspects of EU-Turkey relations reveals considerable inconsistency on the part of the EU – not only in terms of the differentiation between Turkey and other applicant countries but also actually within its policy towards Turkey.

The treatment of the Greco-Turkish disputes in EU-Turkey relations has also been used to illustrate how the EU has effectively used a particular issue to delay the prospect of Turkish membership. Evidence derived from the analysis of the Greek factor in EU-Turkey relations throughout chapter 6 suggests that Greece has made clear her opposition to Turkish membership on account of their long-standing hostility. However, Greek policy has not amounted to an outright veto but rather has sought to link Turkish membership of the EU with the settlement of the Cyprus and of the Aegean Sea issues. Nevertheless, this strong Greek objection has provided legitimate reasons for the EU to effectively delay Turkish membership in the foreseeable future. Since Turkey officially declared its wish to be a member of the EU by applying for EU membership in 1987, the EU has not only begun to take a firm and critical policy stance *vis-à-vis* Turkey with regard to disputes between Greece and Turkey, but has also strengthened the Greek argument by making the settlement of Cyprus and of the Aegean Sea disputes pre-conditions for the consideration of Turkey's accession to the EU. It appears likely that the development of the EU policy to address Greco-Turkish disputes has been, to some extent, driven by the EU's policy objective of delaying Turkey's membership prospect.

This argument has been strengthened by the fact that the Greek factor has become less prominent in EU-Turkey relations, and has been less visible in the implementation of the EU's containment strategy for Turkey. A number of cases support this view: for example, when Greece strongly objected to the completion of the customs union on account of her political disputes with Turkey over Cyprus and the Aegean Sea, a majority of EU member states over-rode the Greek objection, which indicated that Greece alone could not determine the EU's policy *vis-à-vis* Turkey. In addition, although Greece opposed the EU's invitation to Turkey to participate in the European Conference for the same reasons, the EU once again disregarded Greek objections. Most member states believed the inclusion of Turkey to be essential in order to maintain good relations but without implying full membership in the foreseeable future. A final example occurred at the Helsinki Summit: when the EU realized that the Luxembourg decision of 1997 was not compatible with the EU's containment strategy, the EU overcame the Greek objections. It did so by persuading Greece that accepting Turkey as a candidate for EU membership who must meet political conditions was necessary not only for Greek interests but in the interests of the EU as a whole. The Helsinki Summit and Accession Partnership Document appear to support the contention that the EU has effectively delayed the prospect of Turkish membership in the foreseeable future by linking the prospects of Turkey's accession negotiations with the settlement of the Greek-Turkish disputes, including the Cyprus issue. This seems a diplomatic design of the EU to use the Greek objection to delay Turkey's membership for the foreseeable future. If the EU really wanted to offer Turkey a more satisfactory strategy (by placing Turkish accession negotiations within a more flexible and positive framework of Greek-Turkish relations from the Helsinki accords), Greek opposition would be discounted. More precisely, if other members really wanted to pursue a more satisfactory and effective strategy towards Turkey then Greek opposition would almost certainly be discounted.

However, one might argue that the EU's linkage politics only provide part of the explanation for the direction and development of EU policy. In this case, the argument would be strengthened by recognizing the EU's deep concern that unresolved political issues between the acceding states and existing member states would obstruct the Union's cohesion. From this perspective, the EU's strong objection to Turkish membership before the settlement of her disputes seems to have been reasonable and compatible with its condition that aspirant members have to resolve all their outstanding differences with their neighbours before being granted membership.

Nevertheless, the EU's approach to the Greco-Turkish disputes and its strong policy of conditionality does not seem to have been compatible with its enlargement policy objectives. As indicated in chapter 2, one of the main objectives of the EU's enlargement policy is to create political stability throughout Europe. Yet the EU's rigid condition that Turkey's disagreements with Greece should be settled before she can be included in the enlargement process seems have made the settlement of these disputes even more complicated and difficult. In this regard, it could be argued that the EU policy that offered a clear prospect for membership might have contributed rather more to reconciliation in the eastern Mediterranean, as seems to have been the case in Central/Eastern Europe. For example, the Stability Pact for Europe initiated by the EU has become part of the CEECs' preparations for fulfilling their political obligations in order to join the EU and has forced them to adopt a more cooperative and constructive attitude in perceived key areas of their domestic and foreign policies.

Differentiation in the EU's treatment of Turkey – specifically the EU's rigidity in requiring Turkey to settle her disagreements with Greece before being included in the enlargement process – once again goes hand-in-hand with a lack of commitment to Turkish accession even in the long term. On this account, it could be argued that an alternative policy of the EU, to locate Turkish accession negotiations within a more flexible and positive framework of Greek-Turkish relations and to have offered a degree of clarity and certainty about Turkish prospects for membership, might have been more effective in influencing Turkey to settle her disagreements with Greece. In fact the post-Helsinki character of the EU-Turkey relations appears to support the above contention that the accession carrot (despite some conditions attached to it regarding Cyprus and the Aegean Sea) has had some positive impact on Turkey's policy in this respect.

As indicated above, the EU has developed a containment strategy for Turkey that has the declared objective of anchoring Turkey within the EU as a stable and secular country, with a clear preference for delaying the prospects of Turkish membership in the foreseeable future. In this respect, the analysis of chapter 7 presents that the security interdependence of the parties in the new European security identity, particularly Turkey's importance as a security asset for the EU, has constituted strong grounds for the EU's containment strategy. The EU seems to be confident that Turkey can be kept within the European security and defence structure despite not being a full member of the EU, and that simply offering her associate membership of the WEU and strengthening the existing security framework will suffice.

However, this policy appears to be unattainable in the long run; it has become more difficult to integrate Turkey much further since the emerging of Common European Security and Defence Policy. This is because the CESDP has been an integral part of the EU, and being part of it requires membership of the EU. In this respect, the EU's clear reluctance to consider Turkish membership for the foreseeable future makes Turkey's participation in the CESDP doubtful. To that extent, although the EU-Turkey relations post-Helsinki appear to be encouraging as far as arranging the grounds on which they could build their security relations as regards mutual interests, the EU's policy towards the prospect of Turkey being fully incorporated into the CESDP within the EU through membership still remains doubtful. Considering that Turkey is a candidate state and thus will presumably became EU members in the long run, an appropriate policy of the EU would be to incorporate Turkey in some way into the CESDP process. This would not only provide a formal link to facilitate the full integration of Turkey into the EU and progressive rapprochement with the EU's Common Foreign Security and Defence Policy, but it would also convince Turkey to give full support for the EU's effort to establish its own security and defence policy with a military capability.

Moreover, it appears that there has been inconsistency not only between the security objectives of its enlargement policy and its containment strategy for Turkey, but also inconsistency between the EU's policy towards the CEECs and its policy *vis-à-vis* Turkey from the security point of view. As indicated in chapter 2, the EU considered the stabilization of Europe as the main objective of the next enlargement, and believed that the inclusion of the CEECs in the enlargement process would provide the necessary assets to enhance the stability and security of these countries. In the Turkish case, the perceived security challenges for the EU associated with the political, economical, societal and ideological instability of Turkey seem to have been as important as those in the other applicant countries but, nevertheless, the EU's policy instruments for Turkey have not reflected this. This implies that the revised containment strategy of the EU seems to have failed not only to satisfy Turkey but also to prevent political, economical, societal, ideological and demographical security challenges coming from Turkey and its region to the EU. Given that Turkey has been ascribed the role and function of a stabilizing element and model for the economic, social and political developments in neighbouring countries, the EU may well have undervalued Turkey as a security asset, and its containment policy may turn out to be a very high risk strategy. In other words, the EU's containment strategy for Turkey seems not to have calculated the security risks of alienating Turkey from the EU's enlargement process and, consequently, its policy for Turkey has lacked the necessary instruments to stabilize Turkey; to ensure this, the EU needs a policy which includes a clear commitment to Turkey's accession to the EU and a clear strategy for achieving it.

Basically, the analysis of the EU's policy towards Turkey throughout this book leads to two conclusions:

* The primary conclusion is that Turkey has been treated differently from other applicant countries for EU membership.
* The secondary conclusion is that the EU has been less effective than it should have been in influencing the development of Turkey's internal policy and also in influencing the settlement of the disagreements between Greece and Turkey.

The implication of these two conclusions is that the EU's containment policy (even after it was revised at the Helsinki Summit) towards Turkey has not only been different but also less effective in terms of influencing internal and external policy developments in Turkey than an alternative policy would have been. It is not sufficient to argue that Turkey is different from, and by implication a more difficult case than, other applicants: some of them started from an even lower base than Turkey but with the appropriate support from the EU through a pre-accession strategy, they are expected to join the EU eventually. In this regard, there is no good reason why Turkey could not be treated in the same way. A more effective approach than the EU's present containment policy would be for Turkey to be treated like the other applicants and for a comprehensive programme leading to Turkish accession to be put into place. This does not imply early Turkish accession. Turkey could be placed in the slow lane with some of the weaker applicants, but it would inject a degree of clarity, certainty and even-handedness into the EU's policy towards Turkey that is long overdue.

Finally, there is one outstanding question remaining: is the EU's containment policy sustainable in the long run? The most likely answer is that (possibly in a revised form) it probably could be sustained in the short to medium term. In the face of continued EU reluctance to accept Turkey as an EU member, it could continue to provide a working relationship between the parties, while avoiding the thorny issues raised by full membership. However, the viability of the EU's containment policy in the long run is more questionable; it will depend on both parties' interpretations of the post-Helsinki process and on their policy responses to the specific policy issues in their relationship. One possible scenario could be that Turkey could reform its political and economic structure sufficiently to comply with accession criteria, accompanied by a clear pre-accession strategy by the EU for Turkey to stimulate and support its reforms, as it has done for other candidate countries. Conversely, another scenario might be if one or other or both did not act in accordance with the spirit of the Helsinki process; more specifically, given that the conditionality of the post-Helsinki process is ambivalent in character, either party could take a hard-line response to the policy issues, such as the EU's accession negotiation with Cyprus and bilateral issues with Greece. In this case, EU-Turkey relations might easily fade away to rhetoric commitment, and thus the prospect of eventual Turkish membership could no longer be maintained.

However, all this does not necessarily imply that both parties could not develop an alternative policy (to either containment or EU accession); in fact, their mutual interests always require maintaining a good working relationship. Yet it is debatable as to whether the highly developed containment policy for Turkey could be the best and rational alternative framework for serving both parties' mutual interests. For Turkey, the cost of exclusion from the EU is very high and getting higher thus any alternative policy (to EU membership) would be inadequate to support the process of creating a stable and Europe-oriented Turkey. This scenario would also have adverse and destabilizing economic and political implications for the EU. To conclude, the continuation of the containment policy of the EU for Turkey in the long run depends on the two variables:

- The progress of Turkey towards meeting accession criteria (and her response to the EU's demands as regards the most contentious policy issues, such as the Cyprus problem and bilateral issues with Greece).
- The EU's response to the main policy issues in EU-Turkey relations, particularly its handling of Cypriot accession.

There is one other variable that could define the EU's policy towards Turkey: the degree of the flexibility in the European integration could radically affect the EU's options. At one extreme, a more deeply integrated EU would make Turkish membership more difficult, if not impossible, whilst at the other extreme, differentiated integration would create a 'multi-speed' and /or a 'multi-tier EU' within which Turkey might be more easily accommodated. Of course what 'membership' would actually mean then becomes uncertain. Ultimately, however, while the shape of the EU's future policy towards Turkey is obviously critical, what arguably remains even more important is that the EU's policy is clear, consistent, based on equality of treatment (with other candidates), and paves the way for eventual EU accession (even if this is heavily conditional and not expected for a very long time). In the past, it has not always been easy to identify which side was the awkward one in EU-Turkey relations.

Bibliography

I   **Official Documents**

The Additional Protocol and Financial Protocol (1972), *Official Journal of the European Communities*, L293, Brussels.

The Ankara Agreement (1964), 'Agreement Establishing an Association between the European Economic Community and Republic of Turkey', *Official Journal of the European Communities*, L217, Brussels.

The Europe Agreements (1994a), 'Establishing an Association between the European Communities and Their Member States, of the one part, and Romania of the other part', *Official Journal of the European Communities*, L357, Brussels.

The Europe Agreement (1994b),'Establishing an Association between the European Communities and their members, of the one part, and the Republic of Poland, of the other part, *Official Journal of the European Communities*, L348, Brussels.

European Commission (1976), 'The Opinion of the Commission on the Greek Application for Membership', *Bulletin of the European Communities*, Supplement, 2/1976.

European Commission (1987), *Background Report*, ISEC/B987, Brussels.

European Commission (1989a), *Commission Opinion on Turkey's Request for Accession to the Community*, SEC (89) 2290 final, Brussels.

European Commission (1989b), *The Turkish Economy: Structure and Developments*, SEC (89) 2290 final, Brussels.

European Commission (1990), *Communication to the Council on Relations with Turkey*, SEC (90) 1017 final, Brussels.

European Commission (1992), 'Europe and the Challenge of Enlargement', *Bulletin of the European Communities*, Supplement 3/7–92, Brussels.

European Commission (1993), *The Commission Opinion on the Application by the Republic of Cyprus*, COM (93) 313, Brussels.

European Commission (1994a), 'Europe Agreements Establishing an Association between the European Communities and Their Member States, of the one part, and Romania of the other part', *Official Journal of the European Communities*, L357, Brussels.

European Commission (1994b), 'The Europe Agreements and Beyond: A Strategy to Prepare the Countries of Central and Eastern Countries', COM (94) 320 final, *Bulletin of the European Union*, Supplements, 3/7 94, Brussels.

European Commission (1994c), *Minutes of the 35th Meeting of the EC-Turkey Association Council* [EC-TR 126/94 (FIN)], Brussels.

European Commission (1995a), *White Paper on Preparation of Associate Countries of Central and Eastern Europe for integration into the Internal Market of the Union*, COM (95) 0163 –C4 0166/95, Brussels.

European Commission (1995b), 'The Issue of Human Rights and Strengthening of Democracy in Turkey', *Dossier: Custom Union With Turkey*, TX/ RX NO. 4961, Brussels.

European Commission (1995c), *Resolution of the EC-Turkey Association Council on Political Dialogue*, CE-TR 130–95, Brussels.

European Commission (1995d), 'Creating New Legal Structures: How PHARE Closes the Legislative Gap with Central Europe', *Inf.-PHARE*, No. 6, Brussels.

European Commission (1995e), *The Communications from Commission on the inclusion of respect for Democratic Principles and Human Rights in Agreement between the Community and Third Countries*, COM (95) 216 final, Brussels.

European Commission (1996), *Report on the Developments in Relations with Turkey since the Entry into Force of the Customs Union*, COM (96) 491 final, Brussels.

European Commission (1997a), *Communication on the Further Development of Relations with Turkey*, COM (97) 394 final, Brussels.

European Commission (1997b),'Agenda 2000: For Stronger and Wider Union', COM (97) final, *Bulletin of the European Union*, Supplement 5/9, Brussels.

European Commission (1997c), *The Enlargement Negotiations after the Luxembourg Summit*, MEMO, European Report, European Information Services, Brussels.

European Commission (1997d), 'Commission Opinion on Slovakia's Application for Membership of the European Union', *Bulletin of the European Union*, Supplements 9/97, Brussels.

European Commission (1997e), 'Commission Opinion on Bulgaria's Application for EU Membership', *Bulletin of the European Union*, Supplement 8/97, Brussels.

European Commission (1997f), 'Commission Opinion on Romania's Application for EU Membership', *Bulletin of the European Union*, Supplement 8/97, Brussels.

European Commission (1997g), 'Commission Opinion on Latvia's Application for EU Membership', *Bulletin of European Union*, Supplement 10/97, Brussels.

European Commission (1997h), 'Commission Opinion on Estonia's Application for EU Membership', *Bulletin of European Union*, Supplement 11/97, Brussels.

European Commission (1998a), *EU-Turkey Relations: the European Strategy for Turkey*, COM (98) 208, Brussels.

European Commission (1998b), *Regular Report from the Commission on Turkey's Progress toward Accession*, COM (98) 491 final, Brussels.

European Commission (1999a), *Second Regular Report from the Commission on Turkey', Progress towards Accession*, COM (99) 491 final, Brussels.

European Commission (1999b), 'Reports on Progression towards Accession by each of the Candidate Countries', *Composite Paper*, COM (99) 712 final, Brussels.

European Commission (2000a), 'Regular Report from Commission on Turkey's Progress towards Accession', *Bulletin of European Union*, Brussels.

European Commission (2000b), 'Regular Report from Commission on Romania's Progress towards Accession', *Bulletin of European Union*, Brussels.

European Commission (2000c), 'Regular Report from Commission on Bulgaria's Progress towards Accession', *Bulletin of European Union*, Brussels.

European Commission (2000d), *The Proposal for a Council regulation on assistance to Turkey in the framework of pre-accession strategy, and in particular on the establishment of an Accession Partnership*, COM (2000) 502, Brussels.

European Commission (2000e), *Proposal for a Council decision on the principles, priorities, intermediate objectives and conditions contained in the Accession Partnership with the Republic of Turkey*, COM (2000) 714, Brussels.

European Commission (2000f), *Strengthening Preparation for Membership*, Communications from Mr Verheugen, C (2000) 3103/2, Luxembourg.

European Commission (2001), *Regular Report from Commission on Turkey's Progress towards Accession*, SEC (2001), 1756, Brussels.

European Committee for the Prevention of Torture and Inhuman or Degrading Treatment and Punishment (2000), *Report on the CPT visit to Turkey from 23 February to 3 March* CPT/ inf. 2000 17(EN).

European Council (1975), *Presidency Declaration*, Luxembourg, 24 June 1975, General Secretariat of the Council, Brussels.

European Council (1984), *Presidency Declaration*, Luxembourg, 20 March 1984, General Secretariat of the Council, Brussels.

European Council (1990), *Presidency Conclusions*, Dublin, 10–11 June, General Secretariat of the Council, Brussels.

European Council (1991), *Presidency Conclusions*, Luxembourg, 10–11 June, General Secretariat of the Council, Brussels.

European Council (1992), *Presidency Conclusions*, Lisbon, 26–27 June, General Secretariat of the Council, Brussels.

European Council (1993), *Presidency Conclusions*, Copenhagen, 10–11 December, General Secretariat of the Council, Brussels.

European Council (1994), *Presidency Conclusions*, Essen, 10–11 December, General Secretariat of the Council, Brussels.

European Council (1995), *Presidency Conclusions*, Madrid, 15–16 December, General Secretariat of the Council, Brussels.

European Council (1997), *Presidency Conclusions*, Luxembourg, 26–27 December, General Secretariat of the Council, Brussels.

European Council (1998a), *Presidency Conclusions*, Vienna, 11–12 December, General Secretariat of the Council, Brussels.

European Council (1998b), Council Regulation on Assistance to the Applicant States in the Framework of the Pre-Accession Strategy, and in particular on the Establishment of Accession Partnership', No. 622/98, *Official Journal*, L85.

European Council (1999a), *Presidency Conclusions*, Helsinki, 10–11 December, General Secretariat of the Council, Brussels.

European Council (1999b), *Presidency Conclusions*, Cologne, 3–4 June, General Secretariat of the Council, Brussels.

European Council (2000), *Presidency Conclusions*, Nice, 15–17 December, General Secretariat of the Council, Brussels.

European Parliament (1982), 'Resolution on the Death Sentences Imposed on 52 Turkish Trade Union Leaders', *Official Journal of the European Communities*, C219, Brussels.

European Parliament (1983), 'Resolution on Cyprus', *Official Journal of the European Communities* C217, Brussels.

European Parliament (1984), 'Resolution on the Continuing Violations of Human Rights in Turkey', *Official Journal of the European Communities*, Brussels.

European Parliament (1985a), 'Report of Political Affairs Committee on the Human Rights Situations in Turkey', *Working Document on Turkey*, A2–117/85, Strasbourg.

European Parliament (1985b), 'Resolution on the Human Rights Situations in Turkey', *Official Journal of the European Communities*, C 247, Brussels.

European Parliament (1986a), 'Resolution on Relations between the EC and Turkey', *Official Journal of the European Communities*, C 317, Brussels.

European Parliament (1986b), 'Resolution on the Escalation of Tension in Cyprus', *Official Journal of the European Communities*, C289, Brussels.

European Parliament (1987a), 'Resolution on Political Solution to the Armenian Questions', *Official Journal of the European Communities*, C 190, Brussels.

European Parliament (1987b), 'Resolution on the Crisis in the Aegean Sea', *Official Journal of the European Communities*, C 310, Brussels.

European Parliament (1987c), 'Resolution of the EP on a Bomb Attack in Barcelona by ETA', *Official Journal of the European Communities*, C 246, Brussels.

European Parliament (1987d), 'Resolution of the EP on Terrorist Attack by IRA in Northern Ireland', *Official Journal of the European Communities*, C345, Brussels.

European Parliament (1988), 'Resolution on the Resumption of the EEC-Turkey Association', *Official Journal of the European Communities*, C 197, Brussels.

European Parliament (1989a), 'Resolution on Economic and Trade Relations between the Community and Turkey', *Official Journal of the European Communities*, C210, Brussels.

European Parliament (1989b), 'Resolution on the Imprisonment of School Children in Turkey', *Official Journal of the European Communities*, C227, Brussels.

European Parliament (1992), 'Resolution on Turkey', *Official Journal of the European Communities*, C 337/219, Brussels.

European Parliament (1995a), *Resolution on the Draft Agreement of the Customs Union between Turkey and European Union*, DOC. PE 187.047.

European Parliament (1995b), *Report on the Proposal for a Council Decision on a Common Position by the Community in the EC-Turkey Association Council on Establishing the Final Phase of the Customs Union*, DOC PE 214.242, 29, Committee on Foreign Affairs, Security and Defense Policy, Strasbourg.

European Parliament (1995c), 'Resolution on the Need to Respects Human and Democratic Rights in the Slovak Republic', *Official Journal of the European Communities*, No. C 323/116, Brussels.

European Parliament (1996a) 'The Resolution of the European Parliament on the Political Situations in Turkey', *Official Journal of the European Communities*, Brussels.

European Parliament (1996b), 'Opinion of the Committee on Civil Liberties and Internal Affairs on the Next Enlargement of the EU towards the CEECs', Strasbourg.

European Parliament (1996c) *Debates of the European Parliament*, No. 4–477/6, 11.3.96.

European Parliament (1997), 'Resolutions on Human Rights throughout the World in 1995–96', *Official Journal of the European Communities*, C20, Brussels.

European Parliament (1999), *The Briefing on the PHARE Programme and the Enlargement of the European Union*, European Parliament Secretariat's Task Force, PE 167.944, (European Parliament website: http//www.europarl.eu.int).

EU-Turkey Association Council (1995), *Decision No 1/95 of the EC-Turkey Association Council on Implementing the Final Phase of the Customs Union*, Office for Official Publications for European Communities, Luxembourg.

EU-Turkey Association Council Annual Report (1995), *Minutes of Meeting of the 36th EU-Turkey Association Council*, [EC-TR 112/95; (FIN)], Office for Official Publications for European Communities, Luxembourg.

EU-Turkey Associations Annual Report (1994), *Minutes of the 35th Meeting of the EC-Turkey Association Council* [EC-TR 126/94 (FIN)], Office for Official Publications for European Communities, Luxembourg.

The Single European Act: A new frontier for Europe (1987) *Bulletin of European Communities*, Supplement 1/87.

Treaty of Amsterdam, Office for Official Publications for European Communities, Luxembourg.

Treaty on European Union, Office for Official Publications for European Communities, Luxembourg.

Treaty of Nice, Office for Official Publications for European Communities, Luxembourg.

II   Books and Articles

Ardy, Brian (1997), 'Agricultural, Structural Policy, the Budget and Eastern Enlargement of the European Union' in Karen Henderson (ed.), *Back to Europe: Central and Eastern Europe and the European Union*, UCL Press, London.

Arikan, Harun (1999), *The Enlargement Policy of the EU: A Gradual Integration Approach*, Working Paper, Birmingham Business School, Turkey-EU Business Research Group, No. 99, University of Birmingham.

Arikan, Harun (2002), 'A Lost Opportunity? A Critique of the EU'S Human Rights Policy Towards Turkey', *Mediterranean Politics*, Vo. 7, No. 1.

Aslanlı, Araz (2001), 'Tarihten Gunumuze Karabag Sorunu', *Avrasya Dosyası*, Cilt: 7, sayi 1, Ankara.

Avery, Graham and Cameron, Fraser (1988), *The Enlargement of the European Union*, Sheffield Academic Press, Sheffield.

Aybak, Tunc (1995), *An Analysis of the Process of Association between Turkey and the European Community in the Context of European Integration and Co-operation*, Unpublished Ph.D. Thesis, University of Hull, UK.

Aybek, Gulnur and Muftuler-Bac, M. (2000), 'Transformation in Security and Identity after the Cold War', *International Journal*, Vol.3, autumn.

Axel, Krohon (1995), 'European Security in Transition: NATO Going East; the German Factor and Security in Northern Europe and the Baltic Sea Region', *European Security*, Vol. 4, No. 4.

Bahceli, Tozun (1995), *Greek-Turkey Relations since 1955*, Westview Press, Boulder.

Barchard, David (1985), 'Turkey and the West', *The Royal Institute of International Affairs*, Chatham House Paper, No. 27, London.

Basbakanlik Insan Haklari Yuksek Kurulu – The High Co-ordination Council on Human Rights – (2000), *Kopenag Siyasi kiriterleri Isigi Altinda Turkiyenin Almasi Gereken Onlemler: Demokrasi, Hukukun Ustunlugu ve Insan Haklari Takvimi* (Measures which Turkey needs to take in the light of Political Copenhagen Criteria: Calendar for Democracy, the Rule of Law and Human Rights), Ankara.

Baysan, Tercan (1984), 'Some Economic Aspects of Turkey's Accession to the EC: Resource Shifts, Comparative Advantages and Static Gain', *Journal of Common Market Studies*, Vol. 23. No. 1.

Birand, M.A. (1978), 'Turkey and the European Community', *The World Today*.

Birand M.A. (1990), *Turkiyenin Ortak Pazar Macerasi: 1959–1990* (Turkey's Common Market Adventure), Milliyet Yayinlari, Istanbul.

Black Sea Economic Co-operation, *Declaration of the Istanbul Summit*, 5 November 1992, Istanbul.

Bohlen, C. (1997), 'At long Last, Greece and Turkey Tiptoe Toward Reconciliation', *New York Times*, 21 July 1997.

Bolukbasi Suha (1993), 'The Turco-Greek Dispute: Issues, Policies and Prospects', in Clement H. Dodd (ed.), *Turkish Foreign Policy: New Prospects*, the Eothen Press, London.

Bolukbasi Suha (1994), 'The Cyprus Dispute in the Post Cold War Era', *The Turkish Studies Associations Bulletin*, Vol. 18, No. 3.

Bolukbasi, S. (1998), 'The Cyprus Issue and the United Nations: Peaceful non-settlement between 1945–1996', *International Journal of Middle Eastern Studies*, Vol. 30, No. 3.

Borowieck, Andrew (1983), *The Mediterranean Feud*, Praeger, New York.

Boulton, Leyla (2000), 'Preparing for EU membership', *Inter Press Services*, 10 January.

Bourguignon, Rostwitha (1990), 'The history of Association Agreement between Turkey and European Community' in Evin, A. and Denton (eds), *European Community and Turkey*, Leske and Budrich, Opladen.

Brewin, Christopher (1986), 'Europe' in R.J. Vincent (ed.), '*Foreign Policy and Human Rights*, Cambridge University Press, Cambridge.

Brewin, Christopher (1996), 'Turkey and European Union, *Cambridge Review of International Affairs*, Vol. 10, No. 1, Cambridge University Press, Cambridge.

Brown, John and Mortimer (1994), 'An Outsider looking in: Turkey's hopes for closer European ties' in *The Financial Times*, 21 January 1994.

Bugge, Peter (2000), *Czech Perceptions of EU Membership: Havel vs. Klaus*, Working Paper RSC , No 2000/10, European University Institute, Florence.

Bugajski, Janusz (1999), *Balkan Security: Obstacles and Opportunities in the New Millennium*, CERS Working Paper.

Buzan, Barry (1990), *The European Security Order Recast*, Pinter Publishers, London.

Barry, B. and Diez, T. (1999), 'The European Union and Turkey', *Survival*, Vol. 41.

The Bureau of Democracy, Human Rights and Labor (1999), *Turkey: Country Report on Human Rights Practices for 1998*, USA Department of State, Washington.

Cameron, Ian (1988), 'Turkey and Article 25 of Human Rights', *International Law and Comparative Law Quarterly*, Vol. 37.

Cayhan, Esra (1997), *Turkiye-Avrupa Birligi Iliskileri ve Siyasal Partilerin Konuya Bakisi* (Turkey-EU Relations and the Positions of the Political Parties on the Subject), Boyut Maatbacilik, Istanbul.

Cendrowicz, M. (1993), 'European Community and Turkey' in C.H. Dodd (ed.), *Turkish Foreign Policy: New Prospects*, Huntingdon Eothen Press, London.

Ceyhun, Haluk (1988), 'Turkiye Avrupa Toplulugu 25 Ortak Yilinin Degerlendirilmesi' (The Assessment of 25th years in Turkey -European Community relations), *IKV Dergisi*, No. 59, Istanbul.

Charles W. and McCaski (1988), 'US-Greek Relations and the Problems of the Aegean and Cyprus', *Journal of Political and Military Sociology*, Vol. 16.

Christakis, M.G. (1993), *Greece and European Community*, Unpublished Ph.D. Thesis, University of Kent, the UK.

Christian, Peter and Muller-Graff (1997), 'Legal Framework for Relations between the European Union and Central and Eastern Europe: General Aspects' in Mark Maresceu (ed.), *Enlarging the European Union: Relations Between the European Union and Central and Eastern Europe*, Longman Publishers, London.

Constant, D. (1991), *Greek Turkish Conflict in the 1990s: Domestic and External Influences*, Macmillan Press, London.

Croft, Stuart, Redmond, J., Wyn Rees and Weber (1999), *The Enlargement of Europe*, Manchester University Press, Manchester.

Dagi, Ihsan (1993), *Human Rights in the World Politics: International Constraints and Governmental Response: the Turkish Case*, Unpublished Ph.D. Thesis, Lancaster University, Lancaster.

Dankward, A. R. (1994), 'Turkish Democracy in Historical and Comparative Perspectives' in Heper and Evin (eds), *Politics in the Third Turkish Republic*, Westview Press, Boulder.

Dinan, Desmond (1991), 'The European Political Co-operation', *The State of European Community*, Longman Press, London.

Drozdiak, William (2000), 'USA Tepid on European Defence Plan: EU leaders Dismiss War about NATO', *Washington Post*, 7 March 2000.

Duner, Bertil and Edward, D. (2000), *Too Bumpy a Road: Turkey, European Union and Human Rights*, The Swedish Institute of International Affairs, Stockholm.

Ellas J. (1990), 'The Foreign Policy of the European Parliament', *The Washington Quarterly*, Vol. 13, No. 4.

Eren Nuri (1977), 'NATO and Europe: A Deteriorating Relationship?' *The Atlantic Papers*, No. 34, The Atlantic Institute for International Relations, Paris.

Esche, Matthias (1990), 'A History of Greek-Turkish Relations' in Evin and Denton (eds.), *Turkey and European Community*, Opladen, Leske Budrich.

Evin, Ahmet (1994), 'Demilitarization and Civilianization of the Regime', in Heper and Evin (eds), *Politics in the Third Turkish Republic*, Westview Press, Boulder.

Foucher, Michel (1994), *Minorities in Central and Eastern Europe*, Council of Europe Press, Strasbourg.

Gemalmaz, M. (1991), 'Olum Cezasinin Ilgasini Amaclayan BM Uluslararasi Medeni ve Siyasal Haklar Sozlesmesinin Ikinci Secmeli Protokolu ve Turkiyede Olum Cezalari Sorunu', *Insan Haklari Yilligi*, Vol. 12, Ankara.

Gingsberg, Roy H. (1993), 'The European Community and the Mediterranean', in Juliet Lodge (ed.), *Institutions and Politics of the European Union*, Frances Pinter, London.

Gower, Jackie (1995), 'EU Enlargement to Central and Eastern Europe', *The Issues of European Integration*, University of Hull Publication, UK.

Gozen, Ramazan (1996), 'Turgut Ozal and Turkish Foreign Policy: Style and Vision', *Foreign Policy*, Vol. XX, Nos. 3–4 1996, Hacettepe University, Ankara.

Grabbe, Heather (1999), *A Partnership for Accession? Conditionality for the Central and Eastern European Applicants*, Working Paper, RSC No. 99.12, European University Institute, Florence, p. 13.

Grabbe, Heather (2000), 'The Sharp Edges of Europe: Extending Schengen Eastwards', *International Affairs*, Vol. 76, No. 3.

Grabbe, Heather and Hughes, Kirsty (1998), *Enlarging the EU Eastwards*, The Royal Institute of International Affairs, London.

Guadisart, Marc and Sinnaeve, A. (1997), 'The Role of the White Paper', in Marc Maresceau (ed.), *Enlarging the European Union: Relations Between the EU and CEECs*, Longman, London.

Gurel, Sukru S. (1993), 'Turkey and Greece: A Difficult Aegean Relationship' in Balkir and Williams (eds), *Turkey and Europe*, Pinter, London.

Gurses, Emin (2001), 'Kafkasyada Uluslararası Rekabet', *Avrasya Dosyası*, cilt: 7, sayı 1, Ankara, pp. 250–274.

Hale, William (1994), 'Turkey: A Crucial but Problematic Applicant' in J. Redmond (ed.), *The Prospective European: The New Member of European Union*, Harvester Wheatsheaf, New York.

Ham, Peter Van (1993), *The EC, Eastern Europe and European Unity: Discord, Collaboration and Integration since 1947*, Pinter, London.

Harrison, W. (1997), 'Economic Implication for Turkey of Custom Union', *European Economic Review*, Vol. 47, No. 2.

Heper, Metin (1994), 'Transition to Democracy in Turkey: Toward a New Pattern', in Heper and Evin (ed.), *Politics in the Third Turkish Republic*, Westview Press, Boulder.

Hic, Mukerrem (1995), *Turkey's Customs Union with EU: Economic and Political Perspective*, SWP, Germany.

Hodge, C. (1999), 'Turkey and the Pale light of European Democracy', *Mediterranean Politics*, Vol. 4, No. 3.

Howe, Jonathan (1991), 'NATO and Gulf Crises', *Survival*, Vol. 33(3)

Human Right Watch (2000), *Turkey: Human Rights and European Union Accession Partnership*, Washington.

Human Right Watch (2002), *World Report 2002: Turkey*, Washington.

Hyde-Price, Adrian (1991), *European Security Beyond the Cold War*, Sage Publication, London.

Ioakimidis, P. (1994), *Greece and the European Union*, European International and Social Science Research, Working Paper No. 52, University of Reading.

Joffe, Gorge (1998), 'The Relations Between West and Middle East', in Roberson (ed.), *The New Middle East and Europe*, Routledge, London.

Joseph J. (1997), *Cyprus: Ethnic Conflict and International Politics; From Interdependence to the Threshold of the European Union*, MacMillan Basingstoke, London.

Kabaalioglu, Haluk (1998), 'The Customs Union: A Final Step Before Turkey's Accession to the European Union', *Marmara Journal of European Studies*, Vol. 6, No. 1 Marmara Universitesi, Istanbul.

Kabaalioglu, Haluk (1999), 'Turkey and the European Union: Converging or Drifting Apart', *Marmara Journal of European Studies*, Vol. 7, Nos. 1–2, Marmara Universitesi, Istanbul.

Karen, Henderson (1999), 'Slovakia and the Democratic Criteria for EU Accession', in Henderson (ed.), *Back to Europe: Central and Eastern European and the European Union*, UCL Press, London.

Karluk, Ridvan (1996), *Avrupa Birligi ve Turkiye* (European Union and Turkey), IMKB, Istanbul.

Kilic, Ugur (1990), *Turkiye Avrupa Toplulugu Iliskileri: 1983–88*, (Turkey-European Communities Relationship: 1983–88), TOBB, Ankara.

Kirchner, Emil and Sperling, James (2000), 'Will Form Lead to Function? Institutional Enlargement and Creation of ESDI', *Contemporary Security Policy*, Vol. 21, No. 1.

Knowler, Donald (1992), 'Alarm over resurgence of xenophobia', *The Independent*, 24 November 1992.

Kramer, Heinz (1988), *Die Europaishe Gemeinschaft und die Turkei: Entwichlung, Probleme und Perspektiven einer Schwierigen Partnerschaft*, Baden-Baden.

Kramer, Heinz (1996), 'Turkey and the European Union: A Multi-Dimensional Relationship With Hazy Perspectives', in V. Mastny and R. C. Nation (eds), *Turkey Between East And West*, Westview Press, Boulder.

Kramer, Heinz (1997), 'The Institutional Framework of German-Turkish Relations', *The Parameters of Partnership: Germany, the USA and Turkey*, Johns Hopkins University, Washington.

Kuniholm, R.B. (1991), 'Turkey and West', *Foreign Affairs*, Vol. 72.

Kyricos, C. Markides (1977), *The Rise and Fall of the Cyprus Republic*, Yale University Press, USA.

Lasok, Dominick (1993), 'The Ankara Agreement: Principles and Interpretation', *Marmara Journal of European Studies*, Vol. 3, No. 2, Marmara Universitesi, Istanbul.

Leicester, G. (1995), *Turkey and European Union: The Case For Special Relationship*, European and International Social Science Research, Discussion Papers No. 55: University of Reading, UK.

Lippert, Barbara (1997), 'Relations with Central and Eastern European Countries: The Anchor Role of the European Union' in E. Regelsberg, W. Wessels (eds), *Foreign Policy of the European Union: From the EPC to CFSP and Beyond*, Lynne Rienner Publishers, London.

Loewndahl, H. and Loewndahl, Ebru (2000), 'Turkey's Performance in Attracting Foreign Direct Investment: Implication for EU Enlargement', *CEPS Working Document*, No. 157, CEPS, London.

Mango, Andrew (1993), 'The Turkish Model', *Middle Eastern Studies*, Vol. 29, No. 4.

Mango, Andrew (1994), *Turkey: The Challenges of New Role*, The Center for Strategic and International Studies, Washington.

Mango, Andrew (1998), 'Turkey and European Mind', *Middle Eastern Studies*, Vol. 34.

Martin, Philip L. (1991), *Unfinished Story: Turkish Labor Migration to Western Europe*, International Labour Office, Geneva.

Maurizio, Cremasco (1983), 'The Strategic Importance of Relations between Turkey and European Community', *International Spectator*, January-June 1983.

Mathiopoulos, Margarita & Gyarmati I. (1999), 'Saint Malo and Beyond: Towards European Defence', *The Washington Quarterly*, Vol. 3, autumn.

Mendon, Anthony and Wallace, William (1994), 'A European Common Defense', *Survival*, Vol. 34, No. 3.

Miles, L. and Redmond J. (1996), 'Enlarging the European Union: The Erosion of Federalism?', *Nordic Journal of International Studies: Conflict and Cooperation*, Vol. 31, No. 3, Net Publication, Copenhagen.

Ministry of Foreign Affairs, The Republic of Turkey (1998), *A Proposal of Turkey: Strategy for Developing Relations between Turkey and the European Union*, Ankara.

Misha, Glenny (1995), 'Heading for the War in the Southern Balkans', *Foreign Affairs*, Vol. 5.

Mortimer, Edward and John M. Brown (1994), 'An outsider looking in: Turkey's hopes for closer European ties', *Financial Times*, 21 January 1994.

Moschonas, Andreas (1997), *European Integration and Prospects of Modernization in Greece*, Discussion Paper of European and International Social Sciences, No. 65, University of Reading, UK.

Muftuler, Meltem (1992), *The Impact of EC on Internal Political and Economic Transformation of Turkey*, unpublished Ph.D. Thesis, Temple University, USA.

Muftuler, Meltem (1995), 'Turkish Economic Liberalization and European Integration', *Middle Eastern Studies*, Vol. 31, No. 2.

Muftuler, Meltem (1996), 'Turkey's Predicament in the post Cold-War Era', *Futures*, Vol. 28, No. 3.

Muftuler, Meltem (1997), *Turkey's Relationship with a Changing Europe*, Manchester University Press, Manchester.

Muftuler, Meltem (2000a) 'Turkey's Role in the EU's Security and Foreign Policies', *Security Dialogue*, Vol. 31.

Muftuler, Meltem (2000b), 'The Impact of European Union on Turkish Politics', *East European Quarterly*, Vol. 19, No. 2.

Michalski, Anna and Wallace, Helen (1992), *The European Community: The Challenge of Enlargement*, The Royal Institute of International Affairs, London.

Napoli, Danielle (1995), *The European Union and Human Rights*, Polity Press, London.

Nation, Cruig R. (1996), 'The Turkic and other Muslim Peoples of Central Asia, the Caucasus and the Balkans', in V.M. Mastny and Nation R. Cruig (eds), *Turkey Between West and East*, Westview Press, Boulder.

Neuwahl, A. Nanette (1999), 'The EU-Turkey Customs Union: a Balance, but No Equilibrium', *European Foreign Affairs Review*, Vol. 4.

Nugent, Neill,(2000), 'EU Enlargement and the Cyprus Problem', *Journal of Common Market Studies*, Vol. 38, No. 1.

Oakes, Mark (2000), *Common European Security and Defence Policy: A Progress Report*, Research Paper, House of Commons Library, No. 00/84, HMSO, London.

Onis, Ziya (1995), 'Turkey in the Post-Cold War Era: In Search of identity', *Middle East Journal*, Vol. 49, No. 3.

Ozal, Turgut (1991), 'Turkish Membership is delayed, but not rejected', *Turkish Review Quarterly Digest*, Vol. 2, Ankara.

Ozbudun, Ergun (1994), 'Democratization of the Constitutional and Legal Framework' in Heper and Evin (eds), *Politics in the Third Turkish Republic*, Westview Press, Boulder.

Ozbudun, Ergun (1996), 'Democratization in the Middle East, Turkey: How Far from Consolidation?', *Journal of Democracy*, Vol. 7, No. 3.

Penrose, Trevor (1981), 'Is Turkish Membership Economically Feasible' in D. Rustow and T. Penrose (eds), *The Mediterranean Challenges: Turkey and the Community*, European Research Centre, University of Sussex, Sussex.

Philip, Gordon (2000), 'Turkey and European Union after Helsinki', *The Changing Environment of Turkish Foreign Policy*, Georgetown University, Institute of Turkish Studies, Washington.

Phinnemore, David (1999), *Association: Stepping-Stone or Alternative to EU Membership*, UACES, Sheffield Academic Press, Sheffield.

Pinder, John (1991), *The European Community and Eastern Europe*, The Royal Institute of International Affairs, London.

Preston, Christopher (1997), *Enlargement and Integration in the European Union*, Routledge, London.

Pridam, G. (1991), 'The Politics of the European Community: Transitional Networks in Southern Europe' in G. Pridham (ed.), *Encouraging Democracy: International Context of Regime Transition in Southern Europe*, Leciester University Press, Leicester.

Pridham, Geoffry (1991), 'Linkage Politics Theory and Greek-Turkish Rapprochement', in Dimitry Constans (ed.), *The Greek Turkish Conflict in the 1990s: Domestic and External Influences*, Macmillan, London.

Ram, H. Melanie (1999), *Transformation Through European Integration: A Comparative Study of the Czech Republic and Romania*, Unpublished Ph.D. Thesis, George Washington University, USA.

Redmond, John (1993a), *The Next Mediterranean Enlargement: Turkey, Cyprus, Malta?* Dartmouth, Aldershot.

Redmond, John (1993b), 'The Wider Europe: Extending the Membership of the EC', in Cafruny, Alan and Rosenthal, Glenda (eds), *The State of European Community*, Vol. 2, Lynne Rienner, Boulder.

Redmond, John (1994), *The Prospective European: The New Member of European Union*, Harvester Wheatsheaf, New York.

Redmond, John (1996), 'Mediterranean Enlargement of the European Union' in P. Xuereb and R. Pace (eds), *The State of European Community*, University of Malta Press, Malta.

Roberson, B.A (1998), 'Islam and Europe' in Roberson (ed.), *The New Middle East and Europe*, Routledge, London.

Rose, Richard and Haerpfer, Christian (1995), 'Democracy and Enlarging the European Union Eastwards', *Journal of Common Market Studies*, Vol. 33, No. 3.

Saracoglu, Tevfik (1983), Avrupa Ekonomik Toplulugu (European Economic Community), IKV, Istanbul.

Saracoglu, Teyfik (1992), *Anlasmallar* (The Agreements), Akbank Yayinlari, Istanbul.

Sayari, Sabri (1992), 'Turkey: the Changing European Security Environment and the Gulf Crisis', *The Middle Eastern Journal*, Vol. 46, No. 1.

Scold, Thomas (2000), 'NATO-EU meeting on the ESDP', *NATO Notes*, the Center for European Security and Disarmament, Vol. 2, No. 3.

Sezer, Duygu Bazar (1996), 'Turkey in the New Security Environment in the Balkan and Black Sea Region', in V.M. Mastny and R.C. Nation (eds), *Turkey Between West and East*, Westview Press, Boulder.

Spencer, Clare (1993), *Turkey between Europe and Asia*, Wilton Work Paper, London.

Sunar, Ilkay (1996), 'State, Society and Democracy', in V. Mastny and R.C. Nation (eds), *Turkey: Between East and West*, Westview Press, Boulder.

Stanley, Henig (1971), *External Relations of the European Community*, Chatham House, London.

Stearns, Monteagle (1992), *Entangled Allies: USA policy towards Greece, Turkey and Cyprus*, Council on Foreign Relations Press, New York.

Taylor, Paul (1995), *The European Union in 1990s*, Oxford University Press, Oxford.

TBMM Insan Haklari Inceleme Komisyonu (2000), *Sorusturma and Kovusturma Istanbul Raporu* (Investigation and Prosecution Report for Istanbul), Ankara.

Tekeli, I. and Ilkin, S. (1993), *Turkiye ve Avrupa Toplulugu: Ulus Devletini Asma Cabasindaki Avrupaya Turkiyenin Yaklasimi* (Turkey and EC: Turkey's Approach to Europe Attempting to Transcend the Nation State), Umit Yayincilik, Ankara.

Theophanous, Andreas (2000), 'Cyprus, the European Union and the Search for a New Constitution', *Journal of Southern Europe and the Balkans*, Vol. 2, No. 2.

Togan, Subidey and Yilmaz, A. (1994), *Turkey and the European Union*, Working Paper, Bilkent University, Ankara.

Toksoz, Mina (1996), 'The Turkey-EU Customs Union', *EIU European Trends 1st Quarter*, *The Economist*, London.

Tore, Nahit (1990), 'Relations between Turkey and European Community', *European Access*, No. 3, Brussels.

Trevor, Taylor (1994), 'Security for Europe', in H. Miall (ed.), *Redefining Europe: New Patterns of Conflict and Co-operation*, Royal Institute of International Affairs, London.

Tsakaloyannis, Panos (1980), 'The EC and the Greek -Turkish Disputes', *Journal of Common Market Studies*, Vol. 11, No. 1.

Tsakaloyannis, Panos (1983), 'Greece, Old Problems and New Prospects' in Christopher Hill (ed.), *National Foreign Policies and European Political Co-operation*, Frances Pinter, London.

Ugur, Mehmet (1995), *The EU's External Policy-Making Process: The Case of the EC-Turkey Association*, Unpublished Ph.D. Thesis, LSE, London.

Ugur, Mehmet (1996), 'Customs Union as a Substitute for Turkey's Membership? An Interpretation of EU-Turkey relations', *Cambridge Review of International Affairs*, Vol. 10, No. 1.

Ugur, Mehmet (1999), *The European Union and Turkey: An Anchor/Credibility Dilemma*, Ashgate Publishing, Aldershot.

Verheugen, Gunter (2000), *Strategy Paper, Accession Partnership with Turkey and Progress Report* (European Parliament website: http: www.europarl.eu.int).

Volkan V. and Itzkowitz, Norman (1994), *Turks and Greeks: Neighbours in Conflict*, The Eothen Press, Cambridge.

Wallace, Helen and T. Ulrich (1996), 'EU Policies towards Central and Eastern Europe', in Helen Wallace and William Wallace (eds), *Policy-Making in the European Union*, Oxford University Press, Oxford.

Wallace, William (1990), *The Transformation of Western Europe*, Royal Institute of International Affairs, London.

Wilson, Andrew (1979), 'The Aegean Dispute', *Adelphi Papers*, No. 155

Wood, Pia, Christina (1999), 'Europe and Turkey: A relationship under Fire', *The Mediterranean Quarterly*, winter, No. 10.

Yeldan, E. and J. Mercenier (1997), 'Turkey's Trade Policy: Is Custom Union enough For Turkey?', *European Economic Review*, Vol. 47.

III   Periodicals

Agence Europe: Agence Internationale d' Information pour la Press (English Edition) Luxembourg-Brussels.

Annual Report of EU-Turkey Association Council, Office for Official Publications for European Communities, Luxembourg.

Atlantic News, Brussels.

Cumhuriyet (Turkish Daily), Istanbul.

Cyprus Bulletin, Press and Information Office, Nicosia.

Cyprus News, Cyprus High Commission, London.

The Economist.

Europe News Bulletin.

Eurostat (Luxembourg: Office for Official Publications for European Communities).

Financial Times.

The Guardian.

Hurriyet (Turkish Daily, Istanbul).

The Independent.

Info-Turk: Monthly Bulletin, Brussels.

International Herald Tribune.

The Macedonian Press Agency.

Milliyet (Turkish Daily), Istanbul.

Sabah (Turkish Daily), Istanbul.

IV   Press Statements

Press Statement by the Turkish Government on Turkish Accession Partnership, *Turkish Newspot*, 18 November 2000.

Press Statement of Prime Minister, Bulent Ecevit at Helsinki Summit, *Europe News Bulletin*, 11 December 1999.

Press Statement by the Turkish Prime Minister, Bulent Ecevit, on Turkey's Candidature to the EU, *Turkish Newspot*, 10 December 1999.

Press Statement by the Turkish Foreign Ministry on Greek-Turkish Relationship, *Turkish Newspot*, 22 December 1997.

Press Statement by Turkish Foreign Minister on Presidency Conclusions at the Luxembourg Summit, *Turkish Newspot*, 15 June 1997.

Press Statement by Turkish Foreign Minister on Customs Union Agreements, *Turkish Newspot*, No. 32, 7 March 1995.

Index